IOLO MORGANWG AND THE ROMANTIC TRADITION IN WALES

General Editor: Geraint H. Jenkins

Hwfa Môn and T. Gwynn Jones, Bangor, 1902

# The Literary and Historical Legacy of Iolo Morganwg 1826–1926

MARION LÖFFLER

UNIVERSITY OF WALES PRESS
CARDIFF
2007

© Marion Löffler, 2007

All rights reserved. No part of this book may be reproduced, stored in a retrieval system, or transmitted, in any form or by any means, electronic, mechanical, photocopying, recording or otherwise, without clearance from the University of Wales Press, 10 Columbus Walk, Brigantine Place, Cardiff, CF10 4UP.

*www.wales.ac.uk/press*

**British Library Cataloguing-in-Publication Data**
A catalogue record for this book is available from the British Library.

ISBN 978-0-7083-2113-3

The right of Marion Löffler to be identified as author of this work has been asserted by her in accordance with sections 77 and 79 of the Copyright, Designs and Patents Act 1988.

The publishers wish to acknowledge the financial support of the Higher Education Funding Council for Wales in the publication of this book.

Printed in Wales by Gwasg Dinefwr, Llandybïe

Noddais i' mryd yn addwyn
Er yn fâb yr awen fwyn,
Yn iâs îr ei naws eirian
Fy myd i gyd oedd y Gân;
I'mhoen fyth! am hyn o fai
Un o'm ceraint ni' m carai.

Warm from a child I lov'd the bardic muse,
My worlds of bliss all center'd in her views;
Sweet fancy revell'd in my thrilling heart;
But this warm passion for the tuneful art
Was deem'd a crime, was mark'd with bitter blame,
Till every friend a ruthless foe became.

('Welsh motto and translation by the late Edward Williams, of Glamorgan', *Cambrian Quarterly Magazine*, IV, no. 16 (1832), 487.)

Other volumes already published in the series:

*A Rattleskull Genius: The Many Faces of Iolo Morganwg*, edited by Geraint H. Jenkins (University of Wales Press, 2005).

*Bardic Circles: National, Regional and Personal Identity in the Bardic Vision of Iolo Morganwg*, by Cathryn A. Charnell-White (University of Wales Press, 2007).

*The Truth against the World: Iolo Morganwg and Romantic Forgery*, by Mary-Ann Constantine (University of Wales Press, 2007).

*The Correspondence of Iolo Morganwg*, edited by Geraint H. Jenkins, Ffion Mair Jones and David Ceri Jones (3 vols., University of Wales Press, 2007).

# Contents

| | |
|---|---|
| List of Figures | ix |
| Preface | xi |
| Acknowledgements | xiii |
| List of Abbreviations | xv |

1. Introduction — 1
2. The Mythical Iolo Morganwg — 9
3. The Public Legacy of Bardism — 41
4. The Legacy of Invention — 78
5. The Forgotten Iolo Morganwg — 116
6. The Case against Iolo Morganwg — 130

## DOCUMENTS

1. Eben Fardd and the '*Vita*' of Iolo Morganwg — 151
2. Iolo Morganwg's Chair — 152
3. Pilgrimages to Flemingston — 153
4. The Generosity of Iolo Morganwg — 156
5. The Discovery of the Samson Cross or Pillar — 157
6. Iolo Morganwg and the Bishop of St David's — 158
7. *The Rights of Man* — 159
8. 'Strike a Welshman if you dare' — 160
9. Gorsedd Beirdd Ynys Humbug — 162
10. The Grand Eisteddfod of Llangollen, 1858 — 165
11. A Monumental Sculpture in Merthyr Tydfil — 173
12. The Druids of Dresden — 174
13. Authenticating Druidism — 175
14. The Llanover Collection — 177
15. 'The Summer' — 179

| | |
|---|---|
| 16. The Bardic Line of Succession at Tir Iarll | 182 |
| 17. 'The Lark' | 184 |
| 18. In the Service of the Unitarian Faith | 185 |
| 19. Assessing Early Criticism | 185 |
| 20. Thomas Stephens and the Bardic Script | 186 |
| 21. Edward Owen and the Madogwys | 198 |
| 22. John Morris-Jones and the Gorsedd of the Bards | 200 |
| 23. John Morris-Jones as Uthr Bendragon | 206 |
| 24. The Demise of Rhys Goch ap Rhicert | 209 |
| Select Bibliography | 216 |
| Index | 229 |

# *Figures*

| | | |
|---|---|---|
| Frontispiece | Hwfa Môn and T. Gwynn Jones, Bangor, 1902 | |
| Fig. 1 | The grave of Richard Jones Owen (Glaslyn), 1909 | 19 |
| Fig. 2 | Cadair Trecefel: Iolo Morganwg's Chair | 21 |
| Fig. 3 | An eisteddfod procession at the Royal Albert Hall, London, 1909 | 65 |
| Fig. 4 | A plaque with a bardic inscription at Cynwyl Elfed | 69 |
| Fig. 5 | A Gorsedd licence granted to Griffith Griffiths (Gutyn Ebrill), Patagonia, 1881 | 73 |
| Fig. 6 | A Gorsedd assembly at the National Eisteddfod at Bangor, 1902 | 75 |
| Fig. 7 | The title-page of *Druiden-Zeitung*, 15 January 1902 | 76 |
| Fig. 8 | A postcard of Hwfa Môn, *c.*1904 | 90 |
| Fig. 9 | The successful *peithynen* at the Carmarthen National Eisteddfod, 1867 | 97 |
| Fig. 10 | The title-page of *Ceinion Llenyddiaeth Gymreig*, 1875 | 102 |
| Fig. 11 | T. C. Evans (Cadrawd) holding a *peithynen* | 112 |
| Fig. 12 | 'I'r meirwon mae Duw'r mawredd – yn addaw' | 122 |
| Fig. 13 | A column in the *Western Mail*, 11 January 1927 | 145 |

# *Preface*

This book, which is based on a diverse range of sources published in the period under study, aims to explore the *public* cultural legacy of the stonemason, antiquary, forger and poet, Edward Williams (Iolo Morganwg, 1747–1826), over the hundred years following his death. It seeks to show how the Welsh public perceived the figure of Iolo Morganwg, how the eisteddfod and the Gorsedd of the Bards of the Isle of Britain evolved into national institutions, how his historical vision influenced the writing of Welsh literary history in the nineteenth century, which aspects of his legacy were conveniently forgotten, and how the critique of his work paved the way for the development of Welsh scholarship in the twentieth century. I hope that this volume, by critically assessing the uses made of his literary and historical legacy, will contribute meaningfully to current discourses regarding Welsh culture and its place in the complex processes of nation-building in nineteenth-century Europe.

The University of Wales Centre for Advanced Welsh and Celtic Studies prides itself on being an institution in which collaboration and teamwork are paramount. As a member of the project 'Iolo Morganwg and the Romantic Tradition in Wales', I am deeply indebted to my fellow researchers, Cathryn A. Charnell-White, Ffion Mair Jones, Hywel Gethin Rhys and the project leader Mary-Ann Constantine, for their support and help. I owe a special debt of thanks to the Centre's director, Professor Geraint H. Jenkins, who, as the moving spirit behind this project and the editor of this series, has provided constant advice and guidance. I am also grateful to other colleagues at the Centre, particularly to Glenys Howells, Marian Beech Hughes, John T. Koch and Ann Parry Owen, for patiently answering all kinds of queries, and to Nia Davies for her efficient secretarial support. I also gladly record my thanks to members of the Advisory Committee of this project. The financial support of the Arts and Humanities Research Council for this project is deeply appreciated, as is the generosity of the University of Wales. The staff at the University of Wales Press have coped admirably at all stages of publication and I am especially grateful to Dafydd Jones and Nicola Roper for their cooperation.

This book has benefited greatly from the Centre's proximity to the superb collection of manuscripts, published sources and works of art kept at the National Library of Wales, but even more so from the expertise of its staff. Above all, Huw Walters deserves warm thanks for placing his unrivalled store of information about nineteenth-century Welsh publishing and culture at my disposal, and also for commenting on my work. I am also grateful to Lona

Mason for helping me to explore the visual aspects of the legacy of Iolo Morganwg. A special debt is owed to all members of the reading room staff, notably Jayne Day, Rhidian Davies and Iwan ap Dafydd, for tracking down first editions of rare books, lost numbers of early periodicals, and even documents and pamphlets which, according to the catalogues, should not have been at the National Library of Wales at all. I have also benefited from the willingness of staff at other institutions in Wales and abroad to give their advice freely. I am grateful to Christopher Harvie and Neil Evans for providing me with helpful information, and also to Diana Luft, Huw Pryce and Sara Elin Roberts for answering queries. I should also like to express my gratitude to the staff of the National History Museum at St Fagans, the National Museums and Galleries of Wales, and the Glynn Vivian Art Gallery at Swansea. Last but not least, I am grateful to my husband Peter J. Roberts for reading drafts of chapters and to our children for their patience.

May 2007                                                                                           Marion Löffler

## *Acknowledgements*

Gwynedd Archives and Museums Service: Fig. 6
Marion Löffler: Figs. 4, 12
The National Library of Wales: Frontispiece, Figs. 1, 2, 3, 5, 7, 8, 9, 11, 13
University of Wales Centre for Advanced Welsh and Celtic Studies: Fig. 10

# *Abbreviations*

| | |
|---|---|
| *Arch. Camb.* | *Archaeologia Cambrensis* |
| BL | British Library |
| BL Add. | British Library Additional Manuscripts |
| *CA* | *The Carmarthen[shire] Antiquary* |
| *DWB* | *Dictionary of Welsh Biography down to 1940* (London, 1959) |
| *HBC* | E. B. Fryde, D. E. Greenway, S. Porter and I. Roy (eds.), *Handbook of British Chronology* (3rd edn., Cambridge, 1986) |
| *HGB* | Geraint and Zonia Bowen, *Hanes Gorsedd y Beirdd* (Cyhoeddiadau Barddas, 1991) |
| *HHSC* | R. T. Jenkins and Helen M. Ramage, *The History of the Honourable Society of Cymmrodorion and of the Gwyneddigion and Cymreigyddion Societies (1751–1951)* (London, 1951) |
| *IMChY* | G. J. Williams, *Iolo Morganwg a Chywyddau'r Ychwanegiad* (Llundain, 1926) |
| *Iolo Manuscripts* | Taliesin Williams, *Iolo Manuscripts: A Selection of Ancient Welsh Manuscripts* (Liverpool, 1848) |
| *JWBS* | *Journal of the Welsh Bibliographical Society* |
| *MAW* | Owen Jones, Iolo Morganwg and William Owen Pughe (eds.), *The Myvyrian Archaiology of Wales* (3 vols., London, 1801–7) |
| NLW | National Library of Wales |
| *NLWJ* | *National Library of Wales Journal* |
| *RAEW* | Elijah Waring, *Recollections and Anecdotes of Edward Williams* (London, 1850) |
| *Rattleskull Genius* | Geraint H. Jenkins (ed.), *A Rattleskull Genius: The Many Faces of Iolo Morganwg* (Cardiff, 2005) |
| *THSC* | *Transactions of the Honourable Society of Cymmrodorion* |
| *TLlM* | G. J. Williams, *Traddodiad Llenyddol Morgannwg* (Caerdydd, 1948) |
| *WHR* | *Welsh History Review* |
| Williams: *IM* | G. J. Williams, *Iolo Morganwg – Y Gyfrol Gyntaf* (Caerdydd, 1956) |
| Williams: *PLP* | Edward Williams, *Poems, Lyric and Pastoral* (2 vols., London, 1794) |
| *ZcP* | *Zeitschrift für celtische Philologie* |

# 1
## *Introduction*

> Since the revival of learning in Europe, most nations have been emulous of bringing forward their respective stores of ancient memorials, in order to enrich the common stock; but a vast treasure is contained in the Welsh language, in manuscripts, and the oral traditions of the people, of which barely a notice has hitherto been given to the world.[1]

Thus did the *Cambrian Register* seek to direct 'the attention of History' and of the world to the cultural potential of the Welsh nation in 1796. Late eighteenth-century thinkers were popularizing the concept of the nation as a natural category for the organization of mankind, and patriots were keen to assert that Wales could aspire to such nationhood through having preserved its original language and folklore, and by priding itself on a venerable history and literature.[2] Their attitude exemplifies why the legacy of Edward Williams (Iolo Morganwg, 1747–1826) exercised such a powerful hold on the minds of Welsh people during the long nineteenth century. His biography provided the basis for the construction of a mythical figure who connected them with the eighteenth-century renaissance in Welsh learning and with an idealized pre-industrial people.[3] His invented bardic tradition, which found public ceremonial expression in the Gorsedd of the Bards of the Isle of Britain, served as a central cultural institution whose apparent antiquity appealed to a large part of the Welsh nation, while remaining, it was hoped, inoffensive to the English.[4] The counterfeit material Iolo had added to the sources of Welsh history came to the aid of Welsh scholars in their search for a core historical narrative in a century during which Romanticism and nationalism jointly created a sustained demand for a historicist view of nationhood. Part of the process of the appropriation of Iolo's legacy was the suppression of some aspects of it, notably his Unitarianism and his political radicalism, which might

---

[1] 'Preface', *Cambrian Register*, I (1796), v.
[2] Elie Kedourie, *Nationalism* (4th edn., Oxford, 1993), p. 1.
[3] On iconic figures and heroes in nineteenth-century European politics, see Chapter 2.
[4] For the high point of this tradition, see Nicola Gordon Bowe and Elizabeth Cumming, *The Arts and Crafts Movements in Dublin and Edinburgh* (Dublin, 1998), pp. 35–7, 44, 156, 163–5; Hywel Teifi Edwards, 'Pasiant Cenedlaethol Caerdydd 1909' in idem, *Codi'r Hen Wlad yn ei Hôl, 1850–1914* (Llandysul, 1989), pp. 239–83; John S. Ellis, 'The Prince and the Dragon: Welsh National Identity and the 1911 Investiture of the Prince of Wales', *WHR*, 18, no. 2 (1996), 272–94. For a comparison of Scottish and Welsh pageants between 1908 and 1911, see Elfie Rembold, *Die Festliche Nation: Geschichtsinszenierungen und Regionaler Nationalismus in Grossbritannien vor dem ersten Weltkrieg* (Berlin, 2000).

have disturbed this image of antiquity and respectability.[5] Even the comprehensive critique of Iolo's legacy after the end of the nineteenth century was part of the process of national legitimization since it allowed professional Welsh scholars to correct their historical narrative along scientific lines.[6]

Similar processes of nation-building which drew on a store of ancient shared national characteristics, most often a common history, language, literature or religion, were at work throughout Europe during the nineteenth century. Eric Hobsbawm, Terence Ranger and Benedict Anderson have shown how such traditions were invented and communities imagined, while Anthony D. Smith has examined the application of history by nineteenth-century Romantic nationalists.[7] Their assumptions are borne out by developments and events on the Continent. Some national movements, like those in Ireland and Denmark, chose to employ carefully selected and interpreted archaeological finds in staking their claim to a shared past. Early Irish nationalists constructed a Celtic 'Golden Age of Early Christian Ireland' in order to transcend sectarian and linguistic divisions.[8] Although, later in the century, Irish nationhood became identified with Catholicism and, to a degree, with the Irish language, the visual expression of this Celtic Christianity remained a powerful component of the national struggle.[9] On the other hand, Denmark sought refuge in its prehistory when it had been forced to redefine itself as a nation after the enormous reduction in its influence and national territory following the loss of Norway to Sweden in 1814 and of Schleswig-Holstein to Germany in 1868.[10] In contrast to Ireland and Denmark, Romantic nationalists in Norway and the Slavonic nationalities of the Austro-Hungarian empire chose to develop their

---

[5] For introductions to the use of history in nineteenth-century nationalism, see Eric Hobsbawm and Terence Ranger, *The Invention of Tradition* (Canto edn., Cambridge, 1992); Anthony D. Smith, *Myths and Memories of the Nations* (Oxford, 1999); Josep R. Llobera, *The God of Modernity: The Development of Nationalism in Western Europe* (Oxford, 1994). See also Chapter 4 below.

[6] Christopher Harvie, 'Anglo-Saxons into Celts: The Scottish Intellectuals 1760–1930' in Terence Brown (ed.), *Celticism* (Amsterdam, 1996), pp. 235–6; Anthony D. Smith, 'History and Modernity: Reflections on the Theory of Nationalism' in David Boswell and Jessica Evans (eds.), *Representing the Nation: A Reader* (London, 1999), p. 54. See also Chapter 6 below.

[7] Hobsbawm and Ranger (eds.), *The Invention of Tradition*; Benedict Anderson, *Imagined Communities* (revised edn., London, 1991); Smith, *Myths and Memories of the Nations*. See also *Nations and Nationalism*, X, nos. 1/2 (2004), which debated and further developed the ethno-symbolic approach suggested by Anthony D. Smith.

[8] Gabriel Cooney, 'Building the Future on the Past: Archaeology and the Construction of National Identity in Ireland' in Margarita Díaz-Andreu and Timothy Champion (eds.), *Nationalism and Archaeology in Europe* (London, 1986), pp. 146–63.

[9] Cyril Barrett and Jeanne Sheehy, 'Visual Arts and Society, 1850–1900' in W. E. Vaughan (ed.), *A New History of Ireland, VI: Ireland under the Union II, 1870–1921* (Oxford, 1996), pp. 436–74; eidem, 'Visual Arts and Society, 1900–20' in ibid., pp. 475–99; Máirtín Ó Murchú, 'Language and Society in Nineteenth-century Ireland' in Geraint H. Jenkins (ed.), *Language and Community in the Nineteenth Century* (Cardiff, 1998), pp. 355–68.

[10] Marie Louise Stig Sørensen, 'The Fall of a Nation, the Birth of a Subject: the National Use of Archaeology in Nineteenth-century Denmark' in Díaz-Andreu and Champion (eds.), *Nationalism and Archaeology in Europe*, pp. 24–48.

languages and literatures as the expressions of their national identity which most easily distinguished them from the other subjects of the larger entities in which they found themselves. Ivar Aasen, the son of a simple Norwegian peasant, 'turned antiquarianism into nationalism' by using his research on the origins of the rural dialects of his country to develop Landsmaal, a national standard Norwegian based on those dialect forms which corresponded most closely with Old Norse equivalents, thus distancing it from the more commonly used but Danish-influenced Bokmål.[11] Aasen became a national hero and Landsmaal a powerful tool in rallying Norwegian nationalist sentiments against Swedish rule.[12] In central Europe, as R. J. W. Evans has shown, there were particularly close parallels between the situation in Wales and the development of the Czech and Slovak languages and literatures as symbols of national identification.[13] In Bohemia, counterfeit literary memorials were proudly incorporated in the first histories of the country's literature and civilization. These were written by revered figures like František Palacký and Josef Dobrovský before bitter excoriation turned the former hero, the forger Václav Hanka, into a villain.[14] For all these would-be nations, their histories, languages and literatures, together with those who had cultivated them, played a powerful part in the development of their national cause, whether it was ultimately successful or not.[15]

The general reception of Iolo Morganwg's legacy thus mirrored processes which were at work in other European nations in the making. However, the form it took varied from region to region and from decade to decade. Industrial south Wales was generally more enthusiastic about it than were people in the rural heartlands of north Wales. Iolo had, after all, been a native

[11] Oddmund L. Hoel, 'The Fortunes of the Nynorsk Language in Norway', an unpublished paper delivered at the University of Wales Centre for Advanced Welsh and Celtic Studies, Aberystwyth, December 2004. See also idem, 'Language Traditionalism and the Nationalism Conflict after 1814' in Unn Røyneland (ed.), *Language Contact and Language Conflict* (Volda, 1997), pp. 297–304. Landsmaal is now known as Nynorsk.

[12] For an overview of the use of language and history in nineteenth-century Norwegian nationalism, see Knut Gjerset, *History of the Norwegian People* (New York, 1927), pp. 464–5, 489–500. For a short Marxist appraisal of this period in Norwegian history, see Miroslav Hroch, 'The integrated type in conditions of political autonomy: the Norwegians' in idem, *Social Preconditions of National Revival in Europe* (New York, 2000), pp. 33–43.

[13] R. J. W. Evans, 'Language and Society in the Nineteenth Century: Some Central-European Comparisons' in Jenkins (ed.), *Language and Community in the Nineteenth Century*, pp. 397–424. For an exposition on the parallels between Pan-Celticism and Pan-Slavism, see Marion Löffler, 'Der Pankeltismus vor dem Ersten Weltkrieg im Europäischen Kontext' in Erich Poppe (ed.), *Keltologie heute, Themen und Fragestellungen* (Münster, 2004), pp. 281–6; Paul Vyšný, *Neo-Slavism and the Czechs, 1898–1914* (Cambridge, 1977).

[14] For an examination of the literary forgeries of Václav Hanka, see R. J. W. Evans, '"The Manuscripts": The Culture and Politics of Forgery in Central Europe' in *Rattleskull Genius*, pp. 51–68. See also Robin Okey, *The Habsburg Monarchy, c.1765–1918: From Enlightenment to Eclipse* (New York, 2001), pp. 108–12, 115–19, 285.

[15] For an anthology of further European case studies which takes a *longue durée* approach, see Mikuláš Teich and Roy Porter (eds.), *The National Question in Europe in Historical Context* (Cambridge, 1993).

of the county of Glamorgan and had celebrated its cultural inheritance with great vigour. More importantly, as early as the 1830s, the fast-changing society of industrial south Wales mourned the loss of an idyllicized rural past and its oral traditions, of which Iolo was seen to be representative. Merthyr Tydfil, the home of Iolo's son Taliesin Williams (Taliesin ab Iolo) as well as that of the most persistent critic of both men, Thomas Stephens, grew from being a small market town of 7,705 inhabitants in 1801 into the largest industrial community in Wales with 46,083 inhabitants by 1851.[16] Cardiff's rise from a village of 1,870 people in 1801 to a metropolis with a population of 164,333 by 1901 was even more impressive, and reflected the massive socio-economic changes which had transformed the demographic profile of Wales.[17] 'Evanescence rather than continuity ... impermanence and instability', accompanied by periodic outbursts of violent social unrest, characterized south Wales in the mid-Victorian era.[18] It is therefore not surprising that its middle class yearned for a counterbalance. This it found not only in the Nonconformist religion but also in cultural societies, literary festivals, grand processions and bardism. In rural mid- and north Wales, where society was not changing at the pace of the industrial south, Iolo's legacy was received less enthusiastically although there too, key advocates, notably John Williams (Ab Ithel), strove to promote his cultural inheritance through the eisteddfod.

Iolo's influence was at its most powerful from the mid-nineteenth century. Greater numbers of males (and a growing number of women) began to participate in the democratic process, a development which was greatly advanced by the passing of the Reform and Redistribution Acts in 1884–5, which allowed the eventual triumph of Liberal politics and the acknowledgement that Wales was a political entity with national rights.[19] At the same time, however, the harsh living conditions endured under early industrial capitalism led to the development of radical working-class movements, notably the Chartists. Moreover, the British state was bent on centralizing its administration and imposing English-language culture on the regions and on ethnic groups under its governance. In Wales this climaxed early with the publication in 1847 of the results of the Inquiry into the State of Education in Wales, an event which the outraged Welsh middle classes termed the 'Treachery of the Blue Books'.[20]

[16] John Williams, *Digest of Welsh Historical Statistics* (2 vols., Aberystwyth, 1985), I, p. 63. For a history of Merthyr Tydfil, see Glanmor Williams (ed.), *Merthyr Politics: The Making of a Working-Class Tradition* (Cardiff, 1966); Joseph Gross, *A Brief History of Merthyr Tydfil* (Newport, 1980).
[17] Williams, *Digest of Welsh Historical Statistics*, I, p. 63. For the rise of Cardiff, see John Davies, *Cardiff and the Marquesses of Bute* (Cardiff, 1981); Neil Evans, 'The Welsh Victorian City: The Middle Class and Civic and National Consciousness in Cardiff, 1850–1914', *WHR*, 12, no. 3 (1985), 350–85.
[18] Ieuan Gwynedd Jones, *Mid-Victorian Wales: The Observers and the Observed* (Cardiff, 1992), p. 2.
[19] Matthew Cragoe, *Culture, Politics, and National Identity in Wales 1832–1886* (Oxford, 2004), pp. 1–3.
[20] For analyses of the reports, see Prys Morgan (ed.), *Brad y Llyfrau Gleision: Ysgrifau ar Hanes Cymru* (Llandysul, 1991); Gwyneth Tyson Roberts, *The Language of the Blue Books: The Perfect*

It accelerated an existing process which led to the almost complete exclusion of the Welsh language from state education by the time of the Education Act of 1870.[21] The result was that, while some groups were inspired to act on behalf of the Welsh working classes and their nation, others were left with a deep inferiority complex and a desire to re-establish Welsh respectability in the eyes of their dominant English neighbour by referring to its ancient history and tradition. This lay behind the amplification of those aspects of Iolo Morganwg's legacy which were most likely to rehabilitate the nation's respectable Christian credentials. The European revolutions of 1848 set in motion the second phase of nineteenth-century nationalism, during which its adherents sought to popularize their notions of national histories, languages and traditions with the help of the emerging mass media.[22] In Wales, the decades between 1850 and 1890 thus marked the high tide of Iolo's legacy. Soon afterwards, the strength of the Romantic movement which had sustained it began to wane, as even nationalist circles increasingly eschewed myth and romance in favour of historical narratives based on more scientific principles.

If Romantic nationalism fuelled Iolo's legacy, the communications revolution of the nineteenth century accelerated its transmission. In 1805 Iolo had written as follows to his metropolitan friends Owen Jones (Owain Myfyr) and William Owen Pughe:

> We want very much a well conducted periodical publication in the Welsh language, and London is of all others the most proper place to print and publish it. Every part of Wales has an easy and direct communication with London, but north and south Wales have no more intercourse with each other than they have with the man in the moon.[23]

Iolo's heirs developed a periodical press which aided the propagation of his cultural tenets within Wales while, at the same time, the rapidly expanding railway system at least partly mitigated his remarks on geographical impediments. During the second half of the nineteenth century, a period that has been called a golden age of Welsh publishing, a system of local, regional and national papers and periodicals emerged.[24] Never merely 'a mirror reflecting Victorian culture', the press was actively engaged in constructing a new

---

*Instrument of Empire* (Cardiff, 1998); Prys Morgan, 'From Long Knives to Blue Books' in R. R. Davies et al. (eds.), *Welsh Society and Nationhood: Historical Essays Presented to Glanmor Williams* (Cardiff, 1984), pp. 199–215.

[21] Robert Smith, 'Elementary Education and the Welsh Language 1870–1902' in Geraint H. Jenkins (ed.), *The Welsh Language and its Social Domains 1801–1911* (Cardiff, 2000), pp. 483–504.

[22] R. J. W. Evans and Hartmut Pogge von Strandmann (eds.), *The Revolutions in Europe 1848–1849: From Reform to Reaction* (Oxford, 2000); Eric Hobsbawm, *The Age of Capital, 1848–1875* (London, 1995), pp. 82–98.

[23] BL Add. 15027, ff. 79–80, Iolo Morganwg to Owen Jones (Owain Myfyr) and William Owen Pughe, 21 September 1805.

[24] Philip Henry Jones, 'Printing and Publishing in the Welsh Language 1801–1914' in Jenkins (ed.), *The Welsh Language and its Social Domains 1800–1911*, pp. 317–18.

Wales.²⁵ *Seren Gomer*, arguably the most important Welsh periodical in the first half of the nineteenth century, had linked itself to the new representatives of Welsh culture shortly after its foundation in 1819, when its editor urged:

> Dylai pob Cymro gefnogi y Cymdeithasau Cymröaidd a ffurfiwyd yn ddiweddar, a phob cyhoeddiad Seisnig tueddol i egluro rhagoroldeb y Gymraeg, gan fod tuedd ynddynt i ddwyn dynion na fedrant darllen *Seren Gomer*, i weled godidawgrwydd ein hiaith ardderchog; eithr gallwn haeru yn ganolog, nad oes na chymdeithasau na llyfrau o'r fath ynghyd, mor wasanaethgar i'w chadw yn *iaith fyw* a Chyhoeddiad Cymreig a fyddo yn cynnwys amrywiaeth o bethau buddiol i'w gwybod.²⁶

(Every Welshman should support the Welsh societies which were formed recently, and every English publication which seeks to explain the excellence of the Welsh language, because they tend to attract men who cannot read *Seren Gomer* to see the grandeur of our renowned language; but we can claim heartily, that no societies nor such books can together be more serviceable to keep her a *living language* than a Welsh Publication which will contain a variety of beneficial things to know.)

As the nineteenth century progressed, middle-class Welshmen formed a web of interconnected debating societies, and their periodicals became cultural focuses for groups of readers, advertisers, contributors and editors, notably in the south of the country.²⁷ Periodicals were eagerly awaited, and were read in the emerging public libraries and reading rooms as well as on the hearth.²⁸ According to one writer, students, miners and shopkeepers in south Wales assembled 'closely around the fire' ('yn dynn o gwmpas y tân') – once the lady of the house had gone upstairs – in order to discuss the latest issue of their favourite magazine.²⁹ Close links existed between different groups of contemporary periodicals, such as *Seren Gomer* and *Yr Ymofynydd*, the *Red Dragon* and *Bye-Gones*, and *Cymru*, *Wales* and *Y Geninen*. Periodicals were specifically founded in order to serve as platforms for different schools of thought. In 1852, for instance, the editor of *Archaeologia Cambrensis* indicated that he was no longer prepared to allow the journal to be a conduit for Iolo's bardism, which led its main proponent, John Williams (Ab Ithel), to establish his own *Cambrian Journal*.³⁰ In the 1890s Sir Owen M. Edwards founded the magazines *Cymru* and *Wales* in order to propagate his notion of *y werin* (the peasantry) to his compatriots.³¹ *Y Beirniad* was founded by Sir John Morris-Jones in 1911 in

---

²⁵ Lyn Pykett, 'Reading the Periodical Press: Text and Context' in Laurel Brake, Aled Jones, Lionel Madden (eds.), *Investigating Victorian Journalism* (Basingstoke, 1990), p. 7.
²⁶ Y Golygydd, 'Rhagymadrodd', *Seren Gomer*, II (1819), iii–iv.
²⁷ Aled Jones, 'Brecknock at the Crossroads: Journalism, History and Cultural Identity in Nineteenth-Century Wales', *Brycheiniog*, XXXV (2003), 103–4. See also idem, *Press, Politics and Society: A History of Journalism in Wales* (Cardiff, 1993), pp. 3–4.
²⁸ Phylip Jones, *Resolfen Reading Room* (Resolfen, 1996), pp. 6–7.
²⁹ Gwalch Morgannwg, 'Clefyd y Rhamantu a'r Dynwared', *Y Geninen*, XXXI, no. 2 (1913), 78.
³⁰ Ben Bowen Thomas, 'The Cambrians and the Nineteenth-Century Crisis in Welsh Studies, 1847–1870', *Arch. Camb.*, CXXVII (1978), 1–16.
³¹ For Owen M. Edwards's notion of *y werin Gymreig*, see pp. 27–8.

order to promote new standards of scholarship but also to deromanticize and modernize the Welsh nation.[32] The importance of periodical literature in Wales is indicated by the sheer number of publications, their longevity and their circulation figures. Close to 200 titles were founded in the period between 1835 and 1850, a figure which had more than doubled by 1900.[33] Many of these titles proved to be short-lived, but a substantial number of them (many of which are considered in this study) survived for decades and attracted a wide readership.[34] Periodicals and popular volumes on the history and culture of the Welsh were largely responsible for shaping the reception of Iolo Morganwg's legacy, notably following the repeal of the last stamp-duty on periodicals and newspapers in 1851. The community of editors, contributors and readers of the periodical press perpetuated many of Iolo's anecdotes and embellished them over time.[35] All aspects of the eisteddfod movement and its appended Gorsedd were advertised, promoted and reviewed. This made them national talking-points, even if their initial impact had only been regional.[36] By the end of the nineteenth century it was openly acknowledged that the success of the National Eisteddfod held at Cardiff in 1899 depended on the support of the press.[37] Most importantly, perhaps, periodical literature and popular volumes disseminated and popularized the unpublished writings of Iolo held at Llanover, and developed their ideas through discussion and debate.[38]

As the nineteenth century unfolded, Iolo's legacy benefited not only from the expanding periodical press but also the developing railway system. By the early 1850s Wales had become connected to a rapidly spreading railway network which linked the major towns and cities of England.[39] The 'South Wales Railway' reached Carmarthen in 1852, and from 1850 the 'Irish Mail' ran from London to Holyhead along the north Wales coast.[40] By 1870 these trunk lines had been joined by a large number of other main-line, cross-country routes, which bound Wales closer to England, but which also facilitated internal communication.[41] Trains took Welsh newspapers and

---

[32] John Morris-Jones, 'Annerch', *Y Beirniad*, I (1911), 1–2.
[33] Dot Jones, *Statistical Evidence Relating to the Welsh Language 1801–1911* (Cardiff, 1998), pp. 499–510.
[34] Ibid., pp. 513–16; Aled Jones, 'The Welsh Newspaper Press' in Hywel Teifi Edwards (ed.), *A Guide to Welsh Literature c.1800–1900* (Cardiff, 2000), pp. 1–23.
[35] See Chapter 2 below.
[36] See Chapter 3 below.
[37] Pascen, 'Eisteddfod Genedlaethol Caerdydd', *Y Geninen*, XVII, no. 4 (1899), 286.
[38] See Chapter 4 below.
[39] R. Emrys Jones, *Rheilffyrdd Cymru/The Railways of Wales* (Penygroes, 1979), p. 78; Hywel Gethin Rhys, 'Dyfodiad y Rheilffordd i Ganolbarth Cymru, 1845–1870' (unpublished University of Wales Ph.D. thesis, 2004), pp. 9–11.
[40] Ibid., pp. 13–16.
[41] For the positive impact of rail transport on Welsh culture, see ibid., pp. 226–9. For its negative effects, see Dot Jones, *The Coming of the Railways and Language Change in North Wales, 1850–1900* (Aberystwyth, 1995); the maps on page 3 illustrate the development of the railway network by 1914. For a brief overview, see Jack Simmons, 'Wales' in Jack Simmons and

periodicals to most parts of the country, and enabled thousands of Welsh people to attend cultural events which would otherwise have been out of their reach, among them eisteddfodau and Gorseddau, as the following report from the Llanelli Eisteddfod of 1856 indicates:

> The excitement began to manifest itself at an early hour, and the streets were filled with visitors in holiday attire. Up to ten o'clock the number continued to increase, and soon after that hour, by the arrival of excursion trains on the South Wales Railway, from east and west, and on the Llandeilo line, from the north, the multitudes were swelled to such an extent as to render the road from the station to the town almost impassable.[42]

Virtually every detailed eisteddfod report after 1870 began with similar descriptions of the 'excursion trains' which brought thousands of visitors into small towns.[43] The enormous popularity of the National Eisteddfod and the Gorsedd from the 1880s can thus partly be explained by their accessibility. The railway system made it possible for these institutions to fulfil their task of 'pulling the nation together' by providing an annual geographic and demographic focus for the nation.

Iolo Morganwg may have laid the foundations of his fame during his own lifetime, but it was the cultural patriots of Victorian and Edwardian Wales who immortalized those aspects of his legacy which embodied their longing for national respectability, ended their search for a suitable past, and provided them with highly distinct cultural institutions. Some of their creations, notably the mythical Iolo Morganwg, disappeared when their role had been fulfilled. Others, like the romantically embellished history of Wales based on Iolo's forged sources, were replaced by a modern narrative with solid academic foundations. But the Gorsedd survived and prospered as an expression of Welsh cultural nationhood. Iolo Morganwg's legacy, notably his bardo-druidism and his additional materials for the history of Welsh civilization, played a substantial role in the evolution of the Romantic tradition in Wales and beyond. Its influence on Welsh culture reverberated long into the twentieth century. When Sir Glanmor Williams came to assess the impact of Iolo Morganwg's theoretical history in 1989, he scolded Iolo for infecting Wales with the undesirable 'virus of an uncritical and over-romanticized excitement about the past', but he also acknowledged that 'he and his friend, William Owen (Pughe), and others like them injected into their own and later generations a potent stimulus to historical curiosity and delight'.[44]

---

Gordon Bridle (eds.), *The Oxford Companion to British Railway History* (Oxford, 1997), pp. 554–5.
[42] John Williams, 'Llanelli Eisteddfod', *Cambrian Journal*, III (1856), 290.
[43] 'The National Eisteddfod', *Bye-Gones*, 22 September 1886, 125.
[44] Glanmor Williams, 'Local and National History in Wales' in D. Huw Owen (ed.), *Settlement and Society in Wales* (Cardiff, 1989), p. 8.

# 2

## *The Mythical Iolo Morganwg*

'Myth is a *value*, truth has no guarantee for it',[1] wrote Roland Barthes in 1957:

> It is a kind of ideal servant; it prepares all things, brings them, lays them out, the master arrives, it silently disappears: all that is left for one to do is enjoy this beautiful object without wondering where it comes from. Or even better: it can only come from eternity.[2]

Nineteenth-century Europe witnessed a revolution in the way history was mythologized for political and social purposes by the state and the public alike. The growing force of popular politics of all persuasions was facilitated by the development of mass education and fuelled by the increase in popular periodical literature, which allowed the public to gain knowledge and circulate it. Dominant, divided and 'submerged' nations and social groups alike pressed historic figures into service as founding fathers, and as national heroes and heroines.[3] In Germany, the names of Arminius (or, rather, 'Hermann der Cherusker') and Friedrich Barbarossa were used by conservatives in their pursuit of national unity.[4] In France, Vercingetorix was elevated to the status of a national hero by lobbyists close to the state and, by dint of the force of 'popular memory and collective imagination', he was joined by Napoleon Bonaparte.[5] In Victorian Britain, history, or what passed for history, was so widely used for political and religious purposes that scholars have referred to an 'addiction to historical allusion and argument' and a 'sustained cultural fashion' which encompassed literature as well as the visual arts.[6] As a forefather of the political and religious emancipation so important in the politics of nineteenth-century Britain and as a model of masterly control of a nation's fate, Oliver Cromwell was turned 'from a villain into a hero'.[7]

---

[1] Roland Barthes, *Mythologies* (London, 1993), p. 123.
[2] Ibid., p. 151. A review of recent writings on myth can be found in George S. Williamson, *The Longing for Myth in Germany: Religion and Aesthetic Culture from Romanticism to Nietzsche* (London, 2004), pp. 5–7.
[3] For an introduction to this field, see Eric Hobsbawm and Terence Ranger (eds.), *The Invention of Tradition* (Cambridge, 1983).
[4] Williamson, *The Longing for Myth in Germany*, passim.
[5] Annie Jourdan, 'The Image of Gaul during the French Revolution: Between Charlemagne and Ossian' in Terence Brown (ed.), *Celticism* (Amsterdam, 1996), p. 203; Sudhir Hazareesingh, *The Legend of Napoleon* (London, 2005), p. 2. See also André Simon, *Vercingétorix et l'idéologie française* (Paris, 1989).
[6] Olive Anderson, 'The Political Uses of History', *Past and Present*, 36 (1967), 89, 92.
[7] Blair Worden, *Roundhead Reputations: The English Civil Wars and the Passions of Posterity*

For their part, the Welsh cultivated 'national redeemer' figures, such as Owain Glyndŵr, and Nonconformist cultural icons such as Ann Griffiths.[8] The process of mythologization entailed the publication of biographies and the circulation of well-worn anecdotes, the reissue of important statements and the republication of major works. Images and figurines of popular literary and religious figures such as Thomas Edwards (Twm o'r Nant) and Christmas Evans were published and circulated widely.[9] Texts, images and artefacts were introduced to the public by intermediaries, a role mainly undertaken by Nonconformist ministers, poets, authors and amateur scholars, who were often closely associated with the Welsh publishing world. The word was spread through sermons and Sunday schools, through societies, such as the local Cymrodorion and Literary and Scientific Institutes, as well as through popular publications and periodicals.[10] In so doing, the intermediaries kept in the public eye those aspects of a myth which served the varying political and social functions of the times. In this way, figures who, in a different age, might have disappeared from the public view very soon after their death, survived and prospered.[11] One of them was Iolo Morganwg.

Iolo became a key figure in the cultural and patriotic movements of Victorian and Edwardian Wales because his myth enabled Welsh people to celebrate their past and derive from it a much-needed sense of pride in their culture. Iolo was the connecting thread which brought 'the earliest account of Britain to the present' and thus gave the Welsh a past that stretched back beyond historical writing and even imagination.[12] The manuscripts which he had brought to the attention of the public were used to advance the view that the Welsh were not only devoted to religion but were also the people with the longest-surviving Christian tradition. In an age when scholars and others were obsessed with history and its sources, his activities as a collector, transcriber and

(London, 2002), p. 15. See also J. P. D. Dunbabin, 'Oliver Cromwell's Popular Image in Nineteenth-century England' in J. S. Bromley and E. H. Kossmann (eds.), *Britain and the Netherlands. Volume V: Some Political Mythologies* (The Hague, 1975), pp. 141–63.

[8] Elissa R. Henken, *National Redeemer: Owain Glyndŵr in Welsh Tradition* (Cardiff, 1996), pp. 19–22. See, for instance, John Hughes, *Cofiant Mrs Ann Griffiths, Dolwarfechan* (Llanfyllin, 1847), which first appeared in *Y Traethodydd* in 1846 and was reprinted in 1854. See also Morris Davies, *Cofiant Ann Griffiths gynt o Dolwar Fechan* (Dinbych, 1865), which was reprinted in 1893, 1901, 1908 and 2003.

[9] See Peter Lord, *The Visual Culture of Wales: Imaging the Nation* (Cardiff, 2000), pp. 203–7, 217; idem, 'The Popular Iconography of the Preacher' in idem, *Gwenllian: Essays on Visual Culture* (Llandysul, 1994), pp. 43–72. According to an article published in the *Western Mail*, 23 December 1926, Swansea potteries had planned to manufacture a cup and saucer depicting Iolo, but found his features to be 'far too ordinary to form a fitting centre decoration'.

[10] For instance, J. J. Williams, the first external speaker invited by the Cymrodorion Society of Aberdare in January 1909, lectured on 'Iolo Morganwg'. See Brynley F. Roberts, '"Yn Wladgarol, Iaithgarol a Chenedlgarol": Cymdeithas Cymrodorion Aberdâr' in Hywel Teifi Edwards (ed.), *Cwm Cynon* (Llandysul, 1997), p. 266.

[11] For this approach, see Aled Jones, 'Brecknock at the Crossroads – Journalism, History and Cultural Identity in Nineteenth-century Wales', *Brycheiniog*, XXXV (2003), 103–4.

[12] *Glamorgan Gazette*, 12 May 1876.

editor of manuscript material were highly valued.¹³ He was perceived to have rescued from oblivion an ancient civilization which rivalled those of Scotland and Ireland, and had thus validated contemporary Welsh culture. He represented the Welsh eighteenth-century renaissance and its achievements, among them the internationally acclaimed three volumes of *The Myvyrian Archaiology of Wales* (1801–7), which were considered milestones in the annals of Welsh patriotism and scholarship.¹⁴ Even the radical aspects of the myth of Iolo flourished, since they offered a safe point of identification for those who yearned to associate with certain aspects of the radical tradition but could not risk their reputation by pursuing real political objectives. As the cultural pressures exerted by the British state through government commissions, such as the Inquiry into the State of Education in Wales which brought forth the notorious 'Treachery of the Blue Books' in 1847, and through legislation, such as the Education Act of 1870, became fiercer, the importance of Welsh historical figures like Iolo grew exponentially.¹⁵ Discovering and celebrating patriotic scholars like Iolo Morganwg, and recounting their achievements, helped to dispel the feelings of inferiority which arose in response to political pressures emanating from England and provided cultural nourishment for Welsh patriots during the nineteenth century.

## *The origin of the myth*

It is highly ironic that someone who deceived his fellow countrymen within his own lifetime by concocting literary and historical forgeries and propagating myths and legends also became a posthumous mythical figure on the basis of material which he himself had prepared and made public. Iolo had published biographical sketches in the *Gentleman's Magazine* in 1789 and in his *Poems, Lyric and Pastoral* (1794), and had included references to his bardic persona in the preface to William Owen's *Heroic Elegies and other Pieces of Llywarç Hen* (1792).¹⁶ He had shared many colourful anecdotes of his life with his biographer Elijah Waring and numerous others. Iolo's romanticized autobiographical narratives, composed in order to attract the interest of the public and of possible friends and sponsors (like the biographies of the literary figures with whom he peopled Glamorgan), reflected British Romantic tastes but, more importantly for their later success in Wales, they also followed the patterns found in Welsh folklore and hagiography.¹⁷ Like a latter-day saint, Iolo

---

¹³ See Chapter 4 below.
¹⁴ See Chapter 4 below.
¹⁵ See p. 4.
¹⁶ J. D., 'Letter to the Editor', *Gentleman's Magazine*, LIX, no. 2 (1789), 976–7, 1035–6; Williams: *PLP*, I, pp. xiv–xvii; William Owen, *The Heroic Elegies and other Pieces of Llywarç Hen* (London, 1792), pp. v–ciii.
¹⁷ Elissa R. Henken, 'The Saint as Folk Hero: Biographical Patterning in Welsh Hagiography' in

depicted himself as being of noble lineage, his parents' relationship as unusual, and his own position in the family and the surrounding society as unique. On his father's side, he claimed descent from Oliver Cromwell, whom he referred to as 'my uncle'.[18] His mother's lineage, he once declared, could be traced to 'Cadwalader King of Wales and England and Scotland, and Ireland'.[19] The relationship between his father, a stonemason, and his mother, 'a woman of uncommon mental abilities' and the daughter of a gentleman, was one which straddled social divisions.[20] Unlike his brothers, Iolo had received no formal schooling and had acquired the foundations of his knowledge from his mother.[21] Excerpts from his extraordinary childhood, written along hagiographical lines, were reproduced in a review of Iolo's *Poems, Lyric and Pastoral* as early as 1794. These became an essential part of Elijah Waring's writings about him and were included in most of the biographical sketches about Iolo published between 1826 and 1926.[22] In his celebrated *Scenery, Antiquities, and Biography, of South Wales*, published in 1804, Benjamin Heath Malkin not only quoted Iolo on subjects ranging from English poetry to stone quarrying, architectural styles and human longevity, but also dedicated over four pages to 'a man who is capable of doing the world more service, than the world seems willing either to receive or to return . . . unrecommended by external rank in society; yet are his mental powers of a superior order'.[23] The text of his short account of Iolo's life prior to *c.*1800 resembled closely the 'anecdotes of my life' which prefaced the first volume of *Poems, Lyric and Pastoral*.[24] Although Malkin's name was not included in the list of subscribers, he had clearly read those 'highly meritorious' volumes, in addition to talking to Iolo personally

Patrick K. Ford (ed.), *Celtic Folklore and Christianity: Studies in Memory of William W. Heist* (Santa Barbara and Los Angeles, Calif., 1983), pp. 58–74. For a compelling analysis of the creation and consumption of Romantic identities, see Damian Walford Davies, *Presences that Disturb: Models of Romantic Identity in the Literature and Culture of the 1790s* (Cardiff, 2002). For the growing importance of presenting the right image, see Scott Hess, *Authoring the Self: Self-representation, Authorship, and the Print Market in British Poetry from Pope through Wordsworth* (London, 2005).

[18] *RAEW*, pp. 137–8; NLW 21284E, letter no. 1023; *RAEW*, Appendix, pp. 162–3.
[19] NLW 21400C, p. 32; Davies, *Presences that Disturb*, p. 139.
[20] Williams: *PLP*, I, pp. xv–xvi; Williams: *IM*, pp. 92–3.
[21] Williams: *PLP*, I, pp. xiv, xvi.
[22] Anon., 'Poems, Lyrical and Pastoral. By Edward Williams. Review', *Critical Review*, XI (1794), 168–75. For the first and the last reference to the passages within the period of this study, see Robert Williams, *A Biographical Sketch of some of the Most Eminent Individuals which the Principality of Wales has produced since the Reformation* (London, 1836), pp. 72–3; J. Breese Davies, 'Rhai o'n Gwyr Mawr: 1. – Iolo Morganwg', *Y Winllan*, LXXVI, no. 1 (1923), 12.
[23] Benjamin Heath Malkin, *The Scenery, Antiquities, and Biography, of South Wales* (London, 1804), p. 126. Malkin (1769–1842), a Londoner by birth, married Charlotte Williams, the daughter of the master of Cowbridge grammar school, and lived at Cowbridge from 1830. At least one letter from Iolo Morganwg to Malkin, written in 1809, is extant. It is clear from passages in Malkin's *Scenery* that he had met Iolo and had received much of his information directly from him. The influence of Malkin's volume was enhanced by the fact that it was serialized in the *Monthly Review* in 1805.
[24] Williams: *PLP*, I, p. xiv.

during his travels through Glamorgan.²⁵ Elijah Waring, in turn, took care to refer to Malkin in his first commemorative series on 'Iolo Morganwg', which appeared in the *Cambrian* between January and March 1827.²⁶ Passages from *Poems, Lyric and Pastoral*, often filtered through Malkin and Waring, would be utilized time and again in Wales and further afield. The German historian Ferdinand Walter, in his well-researched work *Das Alte Wales* (1859), added a footnote on Iolo which showed that he had been wholly taken in by Waring's description of the character of the 'simple stonemason' ('einfache Steinmetz'), 'with all its force, simplicity and naivety' ('mit Allem, was sie Kräftiges, Einfaches und Treuherziges hat').²⁷

Before the 1850s, however, the Welsh Nonconformist public did not make much use of the material provided for them to create a mythical Iolo Morganwg. A long hiatus followed the elegiac poems and Elijah Waring's first series of biographical sketches, all of which were published during the months after Iolo's death.²⁸ The prize of three guineas offered at the Cardiff eisteddfod of 1834 for the best poem to be engraved on Iolo Morganwg's gravestone elicited only a few sorry stanzas which sank without trace.²⁹ Neither the thirty pages devoted to Iolo's gift as a storyteller by the Quaker Charles Redwood in his *Vale of Glamorgan: Scenes and Tales among the Welsh*, published in 1839, nor the biographical sketch published by Daniel Evans (Daniel Ddu) in *Y Gwladgarwr* in 1841, were taken up in other periodicals or publications before the middle of the nineteenth century.³⁰ There were several reasons for this hiatus. The 1830s and 1840s were decades of great social unrest, but also of considerable cultural activity generated by the eisteddfod movement, especially in south Wales, where Iolo had exerted his greatest influence and where memories of him were strongest. Nonconformist leaders who might have publicized his achievements were otherwise occupied, serving on delegations which petitioned on behalf of workers and organizing a cultural and religious Nonconformist infrastructure for the fast-growing industrial communities. As far as public access was concerned, Iolo Morganwg's manuscripts, which were

---

[25] Malkin, *The Scenery, Antiquities, and Biography, of South Wales*, p. 126.
[26] Elijah Waring, 'Iolo Morganwg', *Cambrian*, 13 January 1827.
[27] Ferdinand Walter, *Das Alte Wales: Ein Beitrag zur Völker-, Rechts- und Kirchengeschichte* (Bonn, 1859), p. 4. See also Chapter 4 below.
[28] Daniel Evans (Daniel Ddu), 'Englynion o Barchus Goffadwriaeth am y Diweddar Enwog Fardd ac Hanesydd, Iolo Morganwg', *Seren Gomer*, X, no. 137 (1827), 52; J. Jones, 'Englynion o Goffadwriaeth am y Rhagorol Fardd ac Hanesydd, Iolo Morganwg', ibid., X, no. 138 (1827), 86; Gwilym Morganwg, 'Cywydd Coffadwriaeth am yr Enwog Brif-fardd a Hynafieithydd Iolo Morganwg', ibid., X, no. 141 (1827), 180.
[29] 'Eisteddfod Caerdyf', *Seren Gomer*, XVI, no. 219 (1833), 370–1; Iolo Fardd Glas, 'Ysgrifen-fedd y Diweddar Odidog Fardd, Iolo Morganwg', ibid., XVII, no. 231 (1834), 366.
[30] Charles Redwood, *The Vale of Glamorgan: Scenes and Tales among the Welsh* (London, 1839), pp. 230–60; Daniel Evans (Daniel Ddu), 'Bywgraffyddiaeth: Cofiant Edward Williams (Iolo Morganwg)', *Y Gwladgarwr*, IX, no. 100 (1841), 97–100; idem, 'Bywgraffyddiaeth: Cofiant Edward Williams (Iolo Morganwg)', ibid., IX, no. 101 (1841), 129–32.

said to have included extensive autobiographical writings, were kept by his son, Taliesin Williams (Taliesin ab Iolo), a schoolmaster in Merthyr Tydfil, who had announced his intention of writing his father's biography.[31] Had Taliesin written this biography, more of the historic Edward Williams might have survived, but he had unfortunately inherited his father's procrastinatory ways.[32] Although he showed a keen interest in Elijah Waring's series of articles published in the *Cambrian* in 1827 and had corrected what he considered to be errors, he never wrote a biography of his father and never encouraged others to do so.[33] As late as 1848, the year after Taliesin's death, the competition for the best essay on Iolo Morganwg advertised by the Abergavenny Cymreigyddion did not attract a single entry.[34] Iolo's manuscripts were sold to Augusta Hall, Lady Llanover, in 1853. Approved scholars made use of them at Llanover Court until 1916, when they found a permanent home at the National Library of Wales.

Thus, the myth of Iolo Morganwg came to rest on biographical details which had been in the public domain since the late eighteenth century and on the writings of the man with whom Iolo had spent many hours in his old age. In 1850 the Quaker Elijah Waring did for Iolo Morganwg what Thomas Carlyle had done five years earlier for Oliver Cromwell. By publishing his *Oliver Cromwell's Letters and Speeches*, Carlyle had produced a book 'which spoke to Victorians with extraordinary power'.[35] Similarly, the myth of Iolo Morganwg which swept through mid-Victorian Wales can justly be said to rest on Elijah Waring's *Recollections and Anecdotes of Edward Williams*, a work of homage which the author understood to be 'a debt long due to the country of my adoption, and to the memory of a man, who did honour to the name and to the literature of Wales'.[36] Waring's biography, which amplified material he had written up over twenty years earlier, saved Iolo from oblivion by reminding the public of his extraordinary life and works. Between 1850 and 1853 extracts of the biography were serialized in the *Cambrian*.[37] The fact that Waring's interpretation of Iolo's life was thus published on three separate occasions, of which two were in the most influential newspaper in south Wales at that time, helps to explain its far-reaching influence. Moreover, the timing of publication was crucial. Following the furore of the Blue Books in 1847, Welsh

[31] On Taliesin Williams, see Brynley F. Roberts, '"The Age of Restitution": Taliesin ab Iolo and the Reception of Iolo Morganwg' in *Rattleskull Genius*, pp. 461–79.
[32] William Williams, 'Iolo Morganwg [Recollections and Anecdotes of Edward Williams, the Bard of Glamorgan; or Iolo Morganwg, B. B. D. By Elijah Waring. London: Charles Gilpin. 1850]', *Y Traethodydd*, XI (1855), 42–3; Geraint H. Jenkins, *'Perish Kings and Emperors, but Let the Bard of Liberty Live'* (Aberystwyth, 2006), pp. 3–4.
[33] *Cambrian*, 10 February 1827.
[34] 'Eisteddfod y Fenni', *Seren Gomer*, XXXI, no. 398 (1848), 345.
[35] Worden, *Roundhead Reputations*, p. 263.
[36] *RAEW*, p. viii.
[37] See *Cambrian*, 27 September 1850; 1 November 1850; 29 November 1850; 10 June 1853; 1 July 1853; 8 July 1853; 15 July 1853; 26 August 1853.

Nonconformists, determined to prove that the Welsh were a perfectly respectable and loyal people, began searching for national figures of historic importance who could help them to re-establish the good name of the Welsh people.[38] The revolutions of 1848 had initiated the second phase of the European age of nationalism and had created an even greater interest in national histories and origins than had been shown in the first half of the nineteenth century.[39] Since those nations considered to lack a 'historical narrative' were in danger of losing their claim to nationhood by being absorbed by the larger 'nation states' and empires, a patriotic antiquary like Iolo Morganwg, who had helped to preserve and publicize materials for a national history and literature, was a most welcome addition to the pantheon of national heroes.[40]

Waring set the tone for his influential volume by reproducing two images of Iolo Morganwg which were created, at his request, by the caricaturist Robert Cruikshank. Both images highlighted the personal description of the Welsh bard. The first revealed an elderly, wizened bard sitting in his high-backed chair, holding a manuscript in his hand, while the second depicted a sturdy antiquary, his satchel stuffed with papers, holding a long staff in one hand and a book in the other, embarking on his tireless quest for literary remains. These iconic images were reproduced and redrawn on so many occasions that the Victorian mind readily internalized the appearance of one of the Welsh nation's most illustrious sons:

> About thirty years ago, there was often seen, on the highways and bye-ways of Glamorganshire, an elderly pedestrian, of rather low stature, wearing his long grey hair flowing over his high coat-collar, which, by constant antagonism, had pushed up his hat-brim into a quaint angle of elevation behind. His countenance was marked by a combination of quiet intelligence, and quick sensitiveness; the features angular, the lines deep, and the grey eye benevolent but highly excitable. He was clad in rustic garb; the coat blue, with goodly brass buttons, and the nether integuments good homely corduroy. He wore buckles in his shoes, and a pair of remarkably stout well-set legs, were vouchers for the great peripatetic powers he was known to possess. A pair of canvas wallets were slung over his shoulders, one depending in front, the other behind. These contained a change of linen, and a few books and papers connected with his favourite pursuits. He generally read as he walked, 'with spectacles on nose,' and a pencil in his hand, serving him to make notes as they suggested themselves. A tall staff, which he grasped at about the level of his ear, completed his travelling equipment; and he was accustomed to assign as a reason for this mode of using it, that it tended to expand the pectoral muscles, and thus, in some degree, relieve a pulmonary malady inherent in his constitution.[41]

---

[38] See, for instance, Thomas Watkins (Eiddil Ifor), 'Diwylliant y Werin Gymreig', *Seren Gomer*, XXXVII, no. 465 (1854), 245, in which he defended the Welsh against accusations of immorality by analysing census statistics.
[39] Eric Hobsbawm, *The Age of Capital 1848–1875* (London, 1995), pp. 84–8.
[40] See Chapter 4 below.
[41] *RAEW*, pp. 1–2.

Nonconformists in Wales seized on Waring's material and reworked it to convey the image of Iolo as a saint-like figure, a selfless, innocent, otherworldly instrument of God. From this was derived the character of 'old Iolo', the most scrupulous, honest and industrious collector and antiquary of the eighteenth-century renaissance, and of the 'Bard of Liberty', a proud Welsh artisan who selflessly sacrificed his personal ambitions and the comforts of his family on the altar of his high moral principles and the Welsh nation. These three aspects of Iolo Morganwg's character – the saintly sage, the renowned antiquary, and the highly-principled humanitarian – were singled out for memorization and popular celebration. They personified that which was important to the male middle classes who made up the bulk of the contributors and readers of Welsh newspapers and periodicals: religion, history and national pride.

## *The saintly sage*

The overarching mould in which the Nonconformist public cast the myth of Iolo Morganwg was that of a saintly sage. Mid-Victorian Welsh society, in which religion played a dominant role, had no difficulty in recognizing the religious cues present in the enthralling material which Waring had provided. The language used whenever a narrative touched on 'the genius of that wonderful man' was generally suffused with religious superlatives.[42] Iolo was always 'ever-famed' (*byth-glodus*) and 'immortal' (*anfarwol*).[43] He was 'innocent' (*diniwed*) and 'pure' (*pur*), 'a man of childlike innocence and guilelessness'.[44] Through his 'self-dying efforts' he had sacrificed glorious prospects on the altar of patriotism.[45] He had 'consecrated' his life to collecting the 'treasures of the nation'.[46] The first and most important of those texts which focused on this saint-like person, who was beyond the reach of mortal criticism, was a three-part biographical sketch by D. Rhys Stephen (Gwyddonwyson) – one of the superstars of the Baptist preaching circuit – which was published in *Seren Gomer* in 1851.[47] Stephen's fame and social position lent the text gravity and

[42] 'Parish Sketches of the Vale: At the Tomb of Iolo Morganwg. Flemingstone, III', *Glamorgan Gazette*, 12 May 1876.
[43] J. Davies Brychan, 'Gohebiaeth: Amddiffyniad Brychan', *Yr Ymofynydd*, III, no. 31 (1850), 70; Mathonwy, 'Gohebiaethau: Coelbren y Beirdd, a Llywelyn a'i Gi', *Y Brython*, III, no. 19 (1860), 191–2.
[44] Daniel Ddu, 'Bywgraffyddiaeth: Cofiant Edward Williams, (Iolo Morganwg)', 131; T. Marchant Williams, 'Y Beirdd a Chyhoeddi'r Eisteddfod', *Y Geninen*, X, no. 1 (1892), 25; W. Llewelyn Williams, 'Iolo Morganwg', *Welsh Outlook*, VIII, no. 9 (1921), 198.
[45] John Williams, 'Reviews: Recollections and Anecdotes of Edward Williams, the Bard of Glamorgan; or, Iolo Morganwg, B. B. D. By Elijah Waring. London: Charles Gilpin. 1850', *Cambrian Journal*, I (1854), 102; Dolenog, 'Daniel Silvan Evans', *Cymru*, LVII, no. 336 (1919), 36.
[46] Glaslyn, 'Ellis Owen, Cefn y Meusydd', *Cymru*, XXVI, no. 150 (1904), 29.
[47] The series 'Iolo Morganwg gan Dafydd ap Rhys Stephen' appeared in nos. 424, 426 and 430

importance, and this was enhanced by the fact that it appeared in a periodical of long standing which, though published by Baptists, bore the subtitle 'a medium of general knowledge' ('cyfrwng gwybodaeth gyffredinol'). The series opened with a reference to Elijah Waring's biography which expressed a sense of shame that the life of such a remarkable Welshman should not only have been written by an Englishman but also in English.[48] Uninterested in the facts of Iolo's life, Stephen focused on establishing the greatness, indeed the superiority of Iolo Morganwg, as a son of 'peace, morality, and literature' ('heddwch, moes, a llên') to be set against other favourites of popular history, such as Napoleon Bonaparte and the Duke of Wellington, who had won fame through their military pursuits.[49] Iolo was elevated because he practised the stringent moral and religious principles in which Stephen believed, but which he reckoned were neglected by the majority of his contemporaries. The anecdotes which he selected, including those regarding 'Prime Minister Pitt and Iolo's papers', the 'Bard of Liberty', 'Iolo and the *Rights of Man*', and 'Iolo's refusal of the slave money', were presented as testimony to Iolo's extraordinarily principled behaviour.[50] The conclusion drawn in the final paragraph, which may well have been meant as a warning shot to sceptics, elevated Iolo Morganwg to a pedestal which lay beyond criticism:

> Peidiwch dynesu at IOLO MORGANWG, nac at un dyn geirwir, gonest, didwyll, calonog arall. Y mae dyn o'r fath hyn yn aneddu mewn mangre rhy uchel i chwi â'ch llygaid gwyrgam, ei weled yn oleuglaer; ac yn arogli awyr rhy iachusber i'ch cylla a'ch ysgyfaint chwi ei hanadlu, heb beri arteithiau i'ch calonau – cedwch rhagddi, da chwithau, er eich mwyn eich hunain. Am dano ef, a'i fath, nid yw eich crach-feirniadaeth nac yma nac acw. Safant y gwir ddynion ar uchelfan, allan o sŵn sisial yr hystyngwr, a'r clapgi, a dirmygwr ei frawd yn ei absenoldeb.[51]

> (Do not approach IOLO MORGANWG, nor any other truthful, honest, guileless, high-spirited man. Such a man resides in a place which is too high for you and your crooked eyes, to see him in clear light; and the air he breathes is too wholesomely fragrant for your windpipe and your lungs to breathe in without causing torture to your hearts – keep away from it, I urge you, for your own sake. For him, and his kind, your petty criticism is neither here nor there. Real men stand on elevated ground, beyond the sound of the malicious whisper of the advocate, and the gossip-monger, and the scorner of his brother in his absence.)

The theme of elevation and saintliness was sustained and embellished by other prominent and mostly Nonconformist poets, writers and artists of the age. In his review of Waring's biography, the poet and Calvinistic Methodist

---

of vol. XXXIV (1851) of *Seren Gomer*. It was planned to be a series of five or six instalments, but illness intervened and D. Rhys Stephen died in 1852.
[48] Dafydd ap Rhys Stephen, 'Iolo Morganwg', *Seren Gomer*, XXXIV, no. 424 (1851), 8.
[49] Ibid., 10.
[50] Dafydd ap Rhys Stephen, 'Iolo Morganwg II', ibid., XXXIV, no. 426 (1851), 98–9.
[51] Idem, 'Iolo Morganwg III', ibid., XXXIV, no. 430 (1851), 315.

schoolmaster Ebenezer Thomas (Eben Fardd) described Waring as the writer of the '*Vita*' (*Buchedd*) of the immortal Iolo Morganwg, and composed a series of *englynion* in praise of Waring's service to the nation (Document 1).[52] In the same year, the defence which William Richard John (Mathonwy) mounted against anonymous critics played on the image of the saint:

> Felly y gadawed yr hen Iolo oleuedig yn llonydd, o herwydd un o'r cyfryw oedd, ac esgynodd yn uchel uchel, mor uchel yn wir nes cyrhaedd lle, ac enwogrwydd ym mhlith neillduolion dynolryw, gan hyn na osoded dynion eu bysedd duon ar ei fantell wen: canys nid wrth ei ddarostwng y gellir dyfod yn ogyfuwch ag ef.[53]

(So leave the enlightened old Iolo in peace, because he was one of those who rose high high, so high, if truth be told, that he achieved status and fame among the mighty of mankind, therefore men should not place their black fingers on his white mantle: because it is not by undermining him that one can attain his standing.)

The Baptist minister and poet Robert Ellis (Cynddelw) contributed to the ascent of 'Saint Iolo' through his much-admired and oft-quoted contribution to the popular volume *Cymru Fu: yn cynnwys Hanesion, Traddodiadau, yn nghyda Chwedlau a Dammegion Cymreig* (1862).[54] Like other publications edited by Isaac Foulkes (Llyfrbryf), the founder of the newspaper *Y Cymro*, it was designed to nourish pride in Welsh history and enhance patriotism by providing material on the folklore, history and literature of Wales in easily readable and entertaining form. *Cymru Fu* contained passages from the Mabinogi, Welsh folk-tales, and stories from Welsh history (some of which had been derived from the *Iolo Manuscripts*, published in 1848). It contained biographical sketches of 'Llywelyn ein Llyw Olaf' and 'Owen Glyndŵr', but no chapter on St David.[55] Instead, the reader was introduced to a saint from the days of the eighteenth-century Welsh renaissance, Iolo Morganwg:

---

[52] Eben Fardd, 'Elijah Waring', *Y Brython*, III, no. 17 (1860), 102. Eben Fardd (1802–63) became well known when he won the chair at the Powys Eisteddfod in 1824 for his ode on the destruction of Jerusalem, a poem which exerted considerable influence on the development of Welsh lyric poetry in the nineteenth century. See E. G. Millward, *Eben Fardd* (Caernarfon, 1988). The interest shown in Waring as Iolo's biographer did not wane until later in the century. See *Bye-Gones*, December 1881, 354; Owen M. Edwards, 'Afon Nedd a'i Theulu', *Cymru*, XXVIII, no. 164 (1905), 188.

[53] Mathonwy, 'Gohebiaethau: Coelbren y Beirdd, a Llywelyn a'i Gi', 191–2. The attack had been published in *Y Brython*, III, no. 18 (1860), 153. William Richard John (Mathonwy) was admitted to Myfyr Morganwg's Gorsedd in 1855 and became its swordbearer. *HGB*, pp. 179, 184, 201; Huw Walters, *Cynnwrf Canrif: Agweddau ar Ddiwylliant Gwerin* (Llandybïe, 2004), pp. 206, 214; idem, 'Beirdd a Phrydyddion Pontypridd a'r Cylch yn y Bedwaredd Ganrif ar Bymtheg: Arolwg' in Hywel Teifi Edwards (ed.), *Merthyr a Thaf* (Llandysul, 2001), p. 291.

[54] See, for instance, H. Cernyw Williams, 'Cynddelw', *Y Traethodydd*, XXX (1876), 69–4; Cynddelw, 'Iolo Morganwg', *Y Geninen*, VI (Gwyl Dewi, 1888), 74–5.

[55] Isaac Foulkes (Llyfrbryf) (ed.), *Cymru Fu yn cynwys Hanesion, Traddodiadau, yn nghyda Chwedlau a Dammegion Cymreig (oddiar lafar gwlad a gweithiau y prif awduron)* (Wrexham, 1862).

Fig. 1 The grave of Richard Jones Owen (Glaslyn), 1909. Like other devotees of Iolo, Glaslyn had the mystic sign inscribed on his gravestone.

Un o'r dynion rhyfeddaf a fagodd Cymru erioed ydoedd. Dyn isel yn y byd – dyn yn diystyru cyfoeth, ac yn hollol amddifad, mae'n debyg, o ddoethineb a chyfrwysdra y byd hwn . . . Ni bu dyn mwy caredig, dyngarol, a dirodres yn rhodio daear erioed. Nid oedd un aberth yn ormod ganddo i'w gwneuthur er lles eraill.[56]

[56] Cynddelw, 'Iolo Morganwg' in ibid., p. 331. For a reprint, see Cynddelw, 'Iolo Morganwg', *Y Geninen*, VI (Gwyl Dewi, 1888), 74–5.

(He was one of the most extraordinary men Wales has ever raised. A man of low standing in the world – a man who disregarded wealth, and was wholly bereft, so it is said, of the wisdom and cunning of this world . . . Never did a kinder, more loving and unassuming man walk the earth. There was no sacrifice which was too great for him to undertake for the well-being of others.)

The contributions of men as well known and respected as Gwyddonwyson, Eben Fardd and Cynddelw ensured that the vision of the saint-like Iolo Morganwg became firmly engrained on the memory of the Nonconformist nation. Authors, poets, preachers, folklorists and antiquarians of a romantic cast of mind, such as William Richard John (Mathonwy), the historian of Calvinistic Methodism William Williams, the Chartist Morgan Williams, Griffith 'Penar' Griffiths, Richard Jones Owen (Glaslyn), William Thomas (Gwilym Glanffrwd) and T. C. Evans (Cadrawd), as well as disciples of Iolo's bardism, such as John Williams (Ab Ithel), Evan Davies (Myfyr Morganwg) and Owen Morgan (Morien), followed suit in this chorus of praise. The lone representative of rational investigation, Thomas Stephens, was heavily outnumbered by a phalanx of patriots who leapt readily to the defence of Saint Iolo.

Saints leave relics and, in the course of time, several objects associated with Iolo Morganwg came to be treated as relics. Since it was well known that for the best part of thirty years of his life the effects of asthma had prevented Iolo from sleeping in a bed, tales of Iolo spending the night in high-backed chairs in libraries and by firesides abounded.[57] One particular chair was thought to have played a special role in his life. It was said to have been specially fashioned for him by a carpenter at the behest of Thomas Johnes, the many-sided owner of the Hafod Uchtryd estate in Cardiganshire. Iolo had spent three weeks at his famous library of books and manuscripts, which included Edward Lhuyd's Welsh manuscripts, in May 1799.[58] Iolo's transcripts, indeed, 'provide virtually the only clues to the contents of the . . . Welsh manuscripts destroyed in the Hafod fire of 1807'.[59] The sale of items following this disastrous fire became the source of an anecdote fully related in *Cymru* in 1907 (Document 2).[60] Joseph Jenkins (Amnon II), of Trecefel farm near Tregaron, a well-known Unitarian, poet and author, who had taken Iolo's volumes of poetry with him on his epic journeys through Australia and even recorded his dreams of him in

---

[57] See *RAEW*, pp. 23–4; Isaac Foulkes, 'Williams, Edward (Iolo Morganwg)' in idem (ed.), *Geirlyfr Bywgraffiadol: Enwogion Cymru: Yn Rhyfelwyr, Pregethwyr, Beirdd, Gwyddonwyr, Meddygon, Seneddwyr, &c* (Liverpool, 1870), p. 992; Morgan Williams, 'Notable Men of Wales: Iolo Morganwg (Edward Williams)', *Red Dragon: The National Magazine of Wales*, II (1882), 102.

[58] Dafydd Jenkins, *Thomas Johnes o'r Hafod* (Caerdydd, 1948), pp. 53–5.

[59] R. J. Moore-Colyer, 'Thomas Johnes of Hafod (1748–1816): Translator and Bibliophile', *WHR*, XV, no. 3 (1991), 402; idem (ed.), *A Land of Pure Delight: Selections from the Letters of Thomas Johnes of Hafod 1748–1816* (Llandysul, 1992), p. 37.

[60] E. B. Morris, 'Hafod Ychtryd', *Cymru*, XXXII, no. 190 (1907), 273; 'Manion ac Hanesion: Hen Gadair', *Yr Ymofynydd*, XXIV, no. 150 (1900), 147; Isgarn, 'Gohebiaethau: Cadair Iolo Morganwg', *Y Geninen*, XXIX, no. 4 (1911), 288.

Fig. 2 Cadair Trecefel: Iolo Morganwg's Chair. This chair-cum-table, said to have been made for Iolo Morganwg by Thomas Johnes of Hafod, was formerly kept by the family of John Jenkins (Amnon II) at Trecefel farm near Tregaron, and is now in the National Library of Wales.

his celebrated diaries, had acquired 'Iolo Morganwg's chair'.[61] In the family home, the chair-cum-desk had been set up and maintained as a shrine to the poet. An apposite piece of poetry by John Lewis of Henfynyw (Ioan Mynyw) hung above it. Following Jenkins's death in 1898, the family kept the shrine intact, and in 1956 the descendants donated the chair to the National Library of Wales, where it remains part of the collections to this day.

Likewise, Iolo's books and manuscripts were shown respect which bordered on religious worship. The Merthyr artist Joseph Edwards who, like Iolo, was the son of a stonecutter, held Iolo in such awe that, when he borrowed the *Iolo Manuscripts* from a friend, 'he retained the book for a very short time, and returned it bound in half calf, with the observation that such a book ought to be returned by a borrower in a better condition than that in which he received

---

[61] See William Evans, *Diary of a Welsh Swagman 1869–1894* (London, 1975), pp. 67, 108, and Bethan Phillips, *Rhwng Dau Fyd: Y Swagman o Geredigion* (Aberystwyth, 1998).

it'.[62] Ab Ithel, one of Iolo's most ardent supporters, considered the 'seventy-six MS volumes, which he left behind him ... standing monuments of his literary industry and patriotic zeal', and trusted that every care would be taken 'of these relics'.[63] Moreover, the very ground which Iolo had trodden was believed to be sacred. 'Flemingston, is holy ground' ('Trefflemin, daiar santaidd yw') was the opening line of a poem by Jonathan Owen Reynolds (Nathan Dyfed) on the grave of Iolo Morganwg:

> Trefflemin, daiar santaidd yw
> Lle bu gweinidog Dyn a Duw, –
> Y drigfod seml – llys didwyll
> Yr Awen – Heddwch pur a phwyll.[64]
>
> (Flemingston, is holy ground
> Where the minister of Man and God was, –
> The simple habitation – court without deceit
> The Muse – Peace pure and measured.)

When Iolo Morganwg's final resting-place in Flemingston parish church was eventually marked by a memorial plaque, it was sought out by generations of pilgrims. The plaque's words and, subsequently, photographs of it were regularly reproduced in newspapers, periodicals and books.[65] According to Morien, Iolo Morganwg's grave was visited by 'pilgrims from every clime', and he predicted that locations connected with his name would 'become as sacred as those of Shakespeare'.[66] D. Arthen Evans, the indefatigable secretary of the National Union of Welsh Societies, took Iolo's grave and Flemingston as a point of reference when he bemoaned the Anglicization of the Vale of Glamorgan.[67] Groups of patriotic Welshmen and women went on excursions to Iolo's old haunts in order to pay homage to 'a man who engraved his name very deeply on the slate of his nation's memory and heart' ('gŵr a argraffodd ei enw yn ddwfn iawn ar lech cof a chalon ei genedl').[68] Group photographs

---

[62] William Davies, 'Joseph Edwards. Sculptor. IX: – The Vord Gron', *Wales*, III, no. 21 (1896), 24. See also Chapter 4 below.

[63] Williams, 'Reviews: Recollections and Anecdotes of Edward Williams, the Bard of Glamorgan', 102–3.

[64] D. Howell, 'Adgof am Nathan Dyfed', *Y Geninen*, XIX, no. 2 (1901), 178. For another example, see Thomas Williams, 'Myfyrdod Uwch Beddrod Iolo Morganwg' in idem, *Awen y Maen Chwyf: yn cynnwys Awdlau, Cywyddau, Caniadau, ac Englynion* (Merthyr Tydfil, 1890), p. 81.

[65] Owen Morgan, 'Iolo Morganwg', *Glamorgan Gazette*, 18 May 1876; A. Macadam, 'Notes and Queries: Iolo Morganwg's Tomb', *Red Dragon*, XI (1887), 374; Enoch Jones, 'Llythyrau at y Golygydd. III: Cof-Ysgrif Iolo Morgannwg', *Cymru*, VIII, no. 45 (1895), 195; 'Iolo's Portraits', *South Wales Daily News*, 2 August 1904; Owen M. Edwards, 'Llyfrau a Llenorion [Illus. Cofadail Iolo Morganwg]', *Cymru*, XLVI, no. 275 (1914), 329.

[66] Owen Morgan, 'Iolo Morganwg', *Glamorgan Gazette*, 18 May 1876.

[67] D. Arthen Evans, 'Y Gymraeg a'r Llanw Seisnig', *Cymru*, XXXVII, no. 216 (1909), 35. For an assessment of Evans's work, see Marion Löffler, '"Eu Hiaith a Gadwant": The Work of the National Union of Welsh Societies, 1913–1941', *THSC* (1998), 124–52.

[68] T. Lovell, 'Tro i Wlad Iolo Morgannwg', *Cymru*, XL, no. 236 (1911), 155–6.

were taken at Flemingston church to commemorate such occasions and moving reports of visits were published, in which young people were urged to visit such sacred places in order to familiarize themselves with the lives and labours of national figures (Document 3).[69]

The view of Iolo as a saint-like hero – exemplified by his simple lifestyle and disregard of material wealth, his uncommon kindness towards the poor and the unfortunate, and his prophet-like gift of experiencing providential dreams and premonitions – was expressed in many of the anecdotes which circulated. Elijah Waring had set the tone with his remark that 'Edward Williams was remarkably simple and uniform, caring little for animal food, and utterly indifferent to wine ... Tea and bread and butter were his great luxuries'.[70] Cynddelw believed that Iolo's life was 'astonishingly unadorned and primitive' ('hynod o ddiaddurn a chyntefig'), Morgan Williams called him the 'most frugal of men', and Glaslyn pronounced him 'one of the simplest and most honest men in his age' ('yn un o'r dynion mwyaf syml a geirwir yn ei oes').[71] In 1890 an anonymous member of the Oxford-based Dafydd ap Gwilym Society described Iolo's deeds as being principally characterized by limitless love and empathy with all those who were suffering.[72] Iolo's legendary refusal to ride a horse or travel in a carriage was an integral part of his saintly image. Tales of Iolo leading his horse to Cardiff, carrying his heavy satchel, and setting out on foot in search of lost manuscripts in Pembrokeshire, leaving behind the horse which his son Taliesin had urged him to ride at Carmarthen, figured in many narratives. Other tales described Iolo's refusal to board carriages which had been sent for his convenience.[73] This group of anecdotes was designed to indicate Iolo Morganwg's love for God's innocent creatures, and purveyors of his myth interpreted his sympathy towards them as evidence that he had understood 'the tender and wise intentions of the Creator' ('bwriad tyner a doeth y Creawdwr'). By contrast, local people were inclined to view this as stubborn foolishness on his part (Document 3).[74]

Iolo's proverbial love of children and general kindness towards the needy figured prominently in many accounts (Document 4).[75] Griffith 'Penar'

---

[69] Ibid. See the photograph in J. Gwynfor Jones, *Y Ganrif Gyntaf: Hanes Cymrodorion Caerdydd 1885–1985* (Caerdydd, 1987), facing p. 43. See also Pererin [Henry Davies, John Evans, T. Richards], 'Ar Bererindod', *Yr Ymofynydd*, XV, no. 11 (1915), 241–4.

[70] *RAEW*, p. 22. This was noted, in a very grudging manner, by Thomas Stephens, 'Iolo Morganwg: Ei Nodweddion', *Yr Ymofynydd*, VI, no. 65 (1853), 10–11.

[71] Cynddelw, 'Iolo Morganwg', p. 332; Morgan Williams, 'Notable Men of Wales: Iolo Morganwg (Edward Williams)', 102; Glaslyn, 'Llythyrau Dafydd Ddu Eryri', *Cymru*, XXVIII, no. 166 (1905), 249.

[72] Anon., 'Dr Johnson a Iolo Morgannwg', *Cymru Fydd*, III, no. 2 (1890), 78. The reasons why this author might have chosen to remain anonymous are revealed in Chapter 6 below.

[73] Daniel Ddu, 'Cofiant Edward Williams', 132; *RAEW*, pp. 18–22; Foulkes, 'Williams, Edward (Iolo Morganwg)' in idem (ed.), *Geirlyfr Bywgraffiadol*, pp. 987–8.

[74] Glaslyn, 'Dyn ac Anifail', *Cymru*, XXI, no. 120 (1901), 6; Pererin, 'Ar Bererindod', 242–3.

[75] *Glamorgan Gazette*, 12 May 1876; Cathryn A. Charnell-White, 'Women and Gender in the Private and Social Relationships of Iolo Morganwg' in *Rattleskull Genius*, pp. 374–5.

Griffiths set the scene of his over-romanticized sketch of Iolo's life by imagining passing the walls of 'one of the simple but hallowed cemeteries of the Vale of Glamorgan, with the weary sun pushing towards the west' ('un o fynwentydd syml ond cysegredig Bro Morgannwg, a'r haul yn pwyso yn lluddedig i'r gorllewin'). Here, the boy Edward Williams had mastered the letters of the alphabet by watching his father chisel names and poems on gravestones. Years later, now a grown man with greying hair, he could be seen cutting letters on stones in the same cemetery, a 'blind Welsh girl on his lap, trying to teach her to write her name' ('geneth ddall o Gymraes rhwng ei ddeulin, ac yn ceisio ei dysgu i ysgrifennu ei henw').[76] While this story might well have been a personal way of visualizing what for him, and for others, was an important trait in the character of Iolo Morganwg, the text, conveyed by a local man, may represent a local tradition which had some basis in the truth. The letter which Iolo Morganwg wrote on behalf of Evan Evans (Ieuan Fardd), another talented but tortured poet during the eighteenth-century renaissance, was similarly used as the basis of a narrative which developed the theme of his kindness (Document 4). Another anecdote relating to Iolo's supposed tenderness towards women featured in a fragment of verse attributed to the 'old poet':

> Once, when in London, Iolo came across an exceedingly pretty girl singing most charmingly in the street. But the eccentric appearance of the old poet so frightened the poor damsel that she failed to proceed with her song. So, with a deeply reverential bow, Iolo addressed her thus –
>
> > Oh! glorious beauteous Betty, – how lavish
> > Has Love been of beauty!
> > Sing more, lass; sing merrily:
> > Don't fair maid, pray don't fear me![77]

However, the most widely circulated tale of Iolo's generosity towards others was his supposed encounter with a poor, sick pedlar in Cardiganshire, who, on a cold and stormy night, could not pay cash for his lodgings and begged the innkeeper to accept payment in kind. When the innkeeper refused, Iolo threw his last shilling on to the counter to pay for the poor man's accommodation, left the inn, and walked through the night until he reached the house of a friend, where he himself fell sick and lay there for weeks afterwards. This oft-told tale was unfailingly used to affirm the generosity and selflessness of Iolo.[78]

[76] Penar, 'Iolo Morgannwg', *Cymru*, VII, no. 40 (1894), 213.
[77] D. Delta Evans, *The Ancient Bards of Britain (sometimes called 'Druids'): Being a Critical Inquiry into Traditions concerning their History, Philosophy, Religion, Ethics, and Rites, in the Light of Science and Modern Thought* (Merthyr Tydfil, 1906), p. 54. For an earlier Welsh version of this anecdote, featuring a slightly different poem, see Golygydd, 'Parodrwydd Iolo Morgannwg', *Cymru*, XXVII, no. 150 (1904), 99.
[78] For further versions of the tale, see *RAEW*, pp. 55–8; Stephens, 'Iolo Morganwg', *Yr Ymofynydd*, V, no. 62 (1852), 223–4; William Williams, 'Iolo Morganwg', 48; Glaslyn, 'Tomos Britwn', *Cymru*, XII, no. 66 (1897), 63; A. Emrys-Jones, *The Life and Works of Edward Williams*

More mystical in character, though similarly illustrating that 'to be the agent of good to any fellow-being was felicity to himself', were the tales of his 'seeing three women in his sleep' and of 'helping a drunk from the road'. These centred around Iolo Morganwg's premonitions, which he either experienced in his sleep or while he was awake, and through which he was purportedly able to save lives.[79] The origins of these anecdotes lay with Iolo himself; he had mentioned them in conversation with Waring in order to illustrate his belief in a 'superintending Providence'.[80] William Williams and the Unitarian Thomas D. Thomas reproduced these tales in 1855 and 1857, but such tales never became as popular as other anecdotes.[81] One possible explanation is that from the 1850s onwards the belief in dreams and premonitions as expressions of divine providence was waning, and it became more fashionable to heed 'scientific' explanations provided by organizations like the Society for Psychical Research founded in 1882.[82] Since a variety of material about Iolo Morganwg was available, tales which no longer reflected the *Zeitgeist* were thus readily abandoned.

## 'Old Iolo' the antiquary

Out of the general theme of the artless, saint-like Iolo sprang narratives and anecdotes of 'old Iolo', the patriotic antiquary. Iolo's honesty and lack of guile also became his trademark as a collector and transcriber of old manuscripts since they enabled him to gain access to the private libraries of his day, wherein the nation's literary treasures lay hidden:

> Canys oddiar y farn oedd gan bobl am ei ddiniweidrwydd, rhoddid iddo dderbyniad croesawus i dai y mawrion a'r moddus, yn enwedig i'r palasau hynny lle y byddai llyfr-gelloedd ystôr-fawr, a hen lawysgrifau gynnil-gamp; ac yno y caniatteid iddo fyned ac aros y pryd a'r hyd y mynnai, a chael ymgymmysgu a chyd fywioliaethu â'r

---

*(Iolo Morganwg), The Bard of Glamorgan (Reprinted from the Manchester Quarterly)* (London, 1889), pp. 10–11; Penar, 'Iolo Morganwg', 218; Marianne Robertson Spencer, *Annals of South Glamorgan, Historical, Legendary, and Descriptive Chapters on some Leading Places of Interest* (Carmarthen, 1913), pp. 246–7.

[79] *RAEW*, pp. 69–73, 75–7.

[80] Elijah Waring, 'Iolo Morganwg', *Cambrian*, 24 February 1827; *RAEW*, pp. 71–3. As in *RAEW*, the two tales were often combined with a third, in which Iolo tricked a superstitious English employer in Kent. There was a fine line between supernatural experience in the service of God and the superstitions of ordinary people, especially if they happened to be English. There is also a related story, in which the premonition of a farmer's wife saved Iolo's life by rescuing him from a limekiln. See NLW 13128A, pp. 450–1; *Bye-Gones*, 23 May 1883, 244–5; 'Hunangofiant Robert Griffith (22)', *Y Drysorfa*, LXXXII, no. 12 (1966), 254.

[81] William Williams, 'Iolo Morganwg', 56–7; T. D. Thomas, *Byugraffiad Iolo Morganwg, B. B. D., sef Edward Williams, Diweddar Fardd ac Hynafiaethydd o Forganwg* (Caerfyrddin, 1857), pp. 120–2. The story of Iolo 'seeing three women in his sleep' and the story 'with the lime kiln' were retold in *Bye-Gones*, 8 March 1882, 27, and ibid., 23 May 1883, 244–5.

[82] William F. Williams (ed.), *Encyclopedia of Pseudo Science* (London, 2000), pp. 88–9, 275–7, 320.

teuluoedd fel pe buasai yn aelod o ohonynt ... Fel hyn y cafodd weled ymron bob cyfryw lyfr-gell yn y Dywysogaeth, a phigo y mel a'r mêr o honynt oll, ac felly ychwanegai yn ddirfawr at ei wybodaeth o hyd.[83]

(Because of the opinion people had of his innocence, he was given a hearty welcome to the houses of the great and the well-to-do, particularly to those palaces where there were extensive libraries, and old manuscripts of great refinement; and there he was permitted to go and stay as long as he wished, and to mix and live together with the families as if he belonged to them ... Thus he got to see almost every one of those libraries in the Principality, and to pick the honey and marrow of all of them, thereby continually adding greatly to his knowledge.)

His gift for premonition led him to discover monuments which less spiritual men might have ignored. Most notable of all was his astonishing account of the discovery of the 'Pillar of Samson' in the church of Llantwit Major, which he himself had published in the *Cambrian Visitor* as early as 1813.[84] This interwove Iolo's knowledge of Welsh folklore with his talent for precognition and his determination to succeed (Document 5).[85] His untiring efforts in travelling 'hundreds of miles in search of old libraries' were so widely admired in prose and verse that T. Lovell (Tudur Taf) was lost in admiration:[86]

> Iolo Morganwg
> Gŵr o naws gwir hanesydd – oedd Iolo,
> Ddilys hynafieithydd, –
> O anian gwych awenydd, –
>
> Mawr ei ddawn, – prif Gymro'i ddydd.
> Arweinydd i gyfrinion – a lechent
> Dan lwch oesau meithion:
> Ei ddêl iaith, addolai hon;
> A'i golud swynai'i galon.[87]

---

[83] Daniel Ddu, 'Cofiant Edward Williams', 130. See also Foulkes, 'Williams, Edward (Iolo Morganwg)' in idem (ed.), *Geirlyfr Bywgraffiadol*, p. 986.

[84] E. W. S., 'A sketch of the ancient History and antiquities of Lantwit Major, in the County of Glamorgan – Compiled from original documents collected by Edward Williams', *Cambrian Visitor*, Appendix 1813 (1813), pp. 508–21; Brian Davies, 'Archaeology and Ideology, or how Wales was Robbed of its Early History', *New Welsh Review*, 37 (1997), 38–51.

[85] This account was also quoted in Thomas Rees, *A Topographical and Historical Description of South Wales* (London, 1815), pp. 678–9; E. S. A., *Welsh Sketches, Chiefly Ecclesiastical, to the Close of the Twelfth Century: First Series* (London, 1853), p. 111; Thomas Nicholas, *The History and Antiquity of Glamorganshire and its Families* (London, 1874), p. 69; Abraham Morris, *Glamorgan: Being an Outline of its Geography, History, and Antiquities with Maps and Illustrations* (Newport, 1907), pp. 418–19.

[86] W. Crwys Williams, 'Y Llenor yng Nghymru', *Y Geninen*, XXXI, no. 4 (1913), 247; 'Hunangofiant Robert Griffith (22)', 254; Penar, 'Iolo Morganwg', 219.

[87] T. Lovell, 'Tro i Wlad Iolo Morgannwg', 156. For other poems in this vein, see Cymro Gwyllt, (Noah Morgan Jones), 'Nodweddiad Iolo Morganwg', *Y Brython*, IV, no. 34 (1861), 313–14; J. L. Thomas (Ieuan Ddu), *Cambria upon Two Sticks or, the Eisteddfod and the Penny Readings, to which is added Two Cantos entitled Harry Vaughan, and a Selection of Songs and Poems* (Pontypridd, 1867), p. 20. Some of the passages in *Cambria upon Two Sticks* which featured Iolo Morganwg

> (Iolo Morganwg
> A man of the quality of a real historian – was Iolo,
> A genuine antiquarian, –
> A poet of fine genius, –
>
> Great was his talent, – main Welshman of his day.
> Leader to secrets – which lurked
> Under the dust of long ages:
> His pretty language, he worshipped her;
> And her riches captivated his heart.)

In popular memory, Iolo's industriousness, undiminished by his asthma, acquired Herculean proportions. For example, travel sketches imagined how difficult it must have been for the old man to walk up a steep hill, let alone embark on long itineraries in search of manuscripts.[88] The three weeks he had spent reading and transcribing at the Hafod Uchtryd library were amplified into months, thereby providing a warrant for the tale that brought together the squire, the antiquary and the chair specially designed for him (Document 2).[89] A second tale of Iolo the antiquary and a chair similarly elevated his relationship with yet another representative of the Anglican elite, Thomas Burgess, bishop of St David's, by inventing a friendship between the two men.[90] The tale of this friendship, first told by Waring, had been resurrected by the Glamorgan antiquary John Rowland (Giraldus), Welsh librarian to Sir John Phillips of Middle Hill and sometime editor of the periodical *Yr Haul* (Document 6). His version of events was immediately disputed by the Carmarthen antiquary Alcwyn Caryni Evans who, even though he was a Unitarian and a member of the Carmarthen Literary and Scientific Institution, was disinclined to believe Waring's effusions, which had been the foundation of Rowland's account.[91] But Evans's own conclusions and the famous Southey stanza dedicated to 'Iolo, old Iolo', which he appended to his work, reveal that he himself was not entirely free from the influence of the myth of Iolo Morganwg (Document 6).[92] Others loudly sang Iolo's praises as a recorder of the past. The radical Morgan Williams, for instance, foreshadowed ideas which would be expressed

---

were reprinted several times, for instance in *Wales*, III, no. 31 (1896), 520, and *Yr Ymofynydd*, XII, no. 127 (1898), 168.

[88] E. B. Morris, 'O Bont Rhyd Fendigaid i Bont ar Fynach', *Cymru*, XXXII, no. 189 (1907), 238.

[89] For a reference to 'months' of reading, see R. Ellis, 'Cofion am Wiliam Morys, yr Hynafiaethydd Dysgedig o Gefn y Braich', *Y Brython*, II, no. 2 (1858), 26.

[90] J. Rowland (Giraldus), 'Iolo Morganwg and the Bardic Chair of Dyfed' in Arthur Mee (ed.), *Caermarthenshire Notes and Miscellany for South West Wales (Antiquarian, Topographical, And Curious). Reprinted with Additions from the Welshman* (3 vols., Llanelly, 1889–91), II, p. 33. For an analysis of Iolo's relationship with Bishop Burgess, see Geraint H. Jenkins, 'The Unitarian Firebrand, the Cambrian Society and the Eisteddfod' in *Rattleskull Genius*, pp. 269–92.

[91] *RAEW*, pp. 123–5. See also Thomas Stephens, 'Iolo Morganwg', *Yr Ymofynydd*, V, no. 64 (1852), 269–70; William Williams, 'Iolo Morganwg', 46.

[92] Alcwyn C. Evans, 'Iolo and the Bishop of St. David's' in Mee (ed.), *Caermarthenshire Notes and Miscellany for South West Wales*, III, pp. 75–6.

more clearly by a new generation of Liberals, notably Owen M. Edwards and T. E. Ellis, and which were immortalized by the poet Crwys in his poem 'Gwerin Cymru' ('The Welsh People') in 1910. Williams presented Iolo as a worthy representative of the idealized Welsh people ('y werin Gymreig'), a man not only dignified and skilled in the pursuit of his craft, but also well versed in the lore of his country:[93]

> Occasionally he worked at his trade, and was once so employed at Llandaff Cathedral when Sir Charles Morgan and a friend came in, and sauntered around reading the inscriptions, or at all events attempting, for of many they could not make anything. Coming near the mason, Iolo looked up, hearing them trying to decipher, and said, 'Would you like a guide?' 'Certainly', said Sir Charles, and so ably were the old monastic inscriptions read that Sir Charles stopped him abruptly, and exclaimed, 'What are you?' 'A mason', said Iolo. 'Yes, yes, but what is your name?' 'Well, my name is Edward Williams, but I am called Iolo Morganwg'; and simultaneously with the remark Sir Charles gripped his hand and shouted his gladness. Iolo then had won a name, and was a great favourite with many of the country gentry.[94]

Iolo's knowledge and efforts on behalf of Welsh scholarship, especially his contribution to *The Myvyrian Archaiology of Wales*, were widely celebrated. Rees Jenkin Jones (T.C.U.), Unitarian minister at Aberdare and the most prolific Unitarian preacher between 1890 and 1910, judged Iolo's achievements to be all the more astonishing given that here was a man who had never received any formal schooling and who had worked as a humble stonemason:

> Nid oedd ond dyn tlawd – saer maen wrth ei alwedigaeth – hunan-addysgedig (ni chafodd awr o ysgol eriod), gyda gwraig a thŷaid o blant, i'r rhai yr oedd dan orfod ennill cynaliaeth drwy chwys ei wyneb. Y syndod i mi, pan ystyriwyf y cwbl, yw, sut y gallodd wneuthur cymaint. Meddylier am y cannoedd o filltiroedd a deithiodd, gan fwyaf ar draed; y llyfrgelloedd yr ymwelodd â hwynt; y llu cyfrolau – tua chant – a ddarllenodd ac a gopïodd er mwyn ceisio achub ein hen lenyddiaeth rhag difancoll. Rhodder chwareu teg i'r hen Iolo, o leiaf; a thawed y grwgnachgwyr hyd oni chyflawnant yr hanner a wnaeth.[95]

> (He was only a poor man – a stonemason by vocation – self-educated (he never had an hour of schooling), with a wife and a houseful of children, for whom he was forced to earn a living by the sweat of his brow. When I consider everything, what

---

[93] For Owen M. Edwards's notion of *y werin Gymreig*, see his preface to the first volume of *Cymru* (1891). See also Peter Lord, 'Yr Etifeddiaeth – Delwedd y Werin' in Ivor Davies and Ceridwen Lloyd-Morgan (eds.), *Darganfod Celf Cymru* (Caerdydd, 1999), pp. 98–102; Hywel Teifi Edwards, 'O'r Pentre Gwyn i Llaregyb' in M. Wynn Thomas (ed.), *DiFfinio Dwy Lenyddiaeth Cymru* (Caerdydd, 1995), pp. 13–19; Christopher Harvie, 'The folk and the *gwerin*: the myth and the reality of popular culture in nineteenth-century Scotland and Wales', *Proceedings of the British Academy*, 80 (1991), 19–48.

[94] Morgan Williams, 'Notable Men of Wales: Iolo Morganwg (Edward Williams)', 99. This anecdote also provided a convenient explanation of Iolo's first acquaintance with Sir Charles Morgan, for whose son he wrote the poem 'On the Birth Day (completing his 21st year) of Chas. Morgan, Esq. son of Sir Charles Morgan, Bart. of Tredegar, April 10, 1813', which appeared in the *Cambrian* on 17 April 1813.

[95] T. C. U., 'Iolo Morganwg – Gair o Amddiffyniad iddo', *Y Geninen*, XXVI, no. 1 (1908), 72.

is astonishing to me is how he managed to do so much. Think of the hundreds of miles he travelled, mostly on foot; the libraries he visited; the host of volumes – around a hundred – he read and he copied in order to save our old literature from oblivion. Grant the old Iolo fair play, at least; and be the grumblers silent until they achieve half of what he did.)

Morgan Williams summed up the general opinion of the nation's favourite antiquary when he wrote: 'let Iolo be forgotten, and all that he accomplished disappear, and our knowledge of the literature of the past would be meagre in the extreme'.[96]

## *The humanitarian*

Although material regarding the saint-like antiquary was widely circulated, the most successful group of tales in the Victorian and Edwardian era depicted Iolo Morganwg as a humanitarian. Taking its cue from Daniel Ddu's judgement that Iolo's guiding principle was liberty, this theme ran through Victorian and Edwardian publications like a golden thread.[97] The main texts expressing this motif were the story of Iolo as the 'Bard of Liberty' who composed the 'Newgate Stanzas', the accounts of Iolo's two meetings with the prime minister, William Pitt, the tale about him and the *Rights of Man*, and the anecdotes illustrating Iolo's rejection of the slave trade.[98] The prominence of these anecdotes appears paradoxical. Although they celebrated political radicalism, they were created by, and for, the same respectable mid-Victorian clientele which so eagerly lapped up stories of the saint-like Iolo. A closer reading, however, reveals that such tales were often reproduced in a context which compromised their radicalism by sprinkling the narratives with disapproving remarks.[99] Moreover, Iolo, as the main protagonist, was often depicted as rejecting what were perceived to be unwelcome aspects of radicalism – ungodliness, social unrest and violence – thereby relieving him of any responsibility for its extremes and rendering his political credentials harmless.[100] By becoming part of the body of narrative about 'the great and good Iolo', the Bard of Liberty was thus emasculated. His feats became those of a timeless folk hero who fed the nation's pride, but did not inspire radical political action. Recounting episodes in Iolo Morganwg's life which showed him confronting English kings

[96] Morgan Williams, 'Notable Men of Wales: Edward Williams (Iolo Morganwg)', 103.
[97] Daniel Ddu, 'Cofiant Edward Williams', 130. The phrase was quoted by Anon., 'Dr Johnson a Iolo Morgannwg', 78, and Penar, 'Iolo Morganwg', 218.
[98] See 'Iolo Morganwg – Ei Ddigllonedd yn erbyn Caethfasnach (o *Seren Gomer* Rhagfyr 2, 1818)', *Yr Ymofynydd*, IV, no. 44 (1851), 79–80; Emrys-Jones, *Life and Works of Edward Williams (Iolo Morganwg)*, p. 9.
[99] See ap Rhys Stephen, 'Iolo Morganwg II', 98.
[100] Thomas Stephens, 'Iolo Morganwg', *Yr Ymofynydd*, V, no. 59 (1852), 152; William Williams, 'Iolo Morganwg', 51.

and politicians was a means of acknowledging Welsh radicalism without bearing the consequences of having to develop convincing political programmes or foment strife.

Each of the anecdotes included in this group highlighted different positive qualities in the character of radical Iolo. The circumstances which led him to sign himself 'Bard of Liberty' in a prison visitors' book and to compose the 'Newgate Stanzas', and his heroic defence of Thomas Evans (Tomos Glyn Cothi), focused on his loyalty to imprisoned friends while also providing an explanation of how poems came to be written.[101] Iolo's unswerving loyalty to his principles and his quick wit in the face of overwhelming political power were amply demonstrated in the narratives about his meetings with William Pitt during the turbulent 1790s,[102] while the hugely popular anecdote about Iolo and the *Rights of Man*, which headed the Victorian story-charts, revealed how this shrewd folk-hero triumphed over corrupt government spies by selling them a bible purporting to be the incendiary work of Tom Paine (Document 7).[103] Just as powerful was the anecdotal evidence marshalled in favour of Iolo as a campaigner against slavery.[104] According to Welsh Americans, his refusal to accept ill-gotten gains from his slave-owning brothers in Jamaica 'should be inscribed in golden letters in the Temple of History'.[105] By the time Waring's biography was reviewed in 1855, the story of Iolo's stance had been embellished to include an alleged journey he had made to Jamaica to liberate his brothers' slaves and distribute their inheritance among them.[106]

[101] Gol., 'Beirdd Dyfed: 1800–1900: Thomas Evans (Tomos Glyn Cothi)', *Cymru*, XXXIX, no. 232 (1910), 239; W. Davies, 'Dafis, Castell-Hywel', *Yr Athraw*, II, no. 4 (1867), 87; Stephens, 'Iolo Morganwg', *Yr Ymofynydd*, V, no. 59 (1852), 151–2; Thomas, *Bywgraffiad Iolo Morganwg*, pp. 28–9. See also Geraint H. Jenkins, '"A Very Horrid Affair": Sedition and Unitarianism in the Age of Revolutions' in R. R. Davies and Geraint H. Jenkins (eds.), *From Medieval to Modern Wales: Historical Essays in Honour of Kenneth O. Morgan and Ralph A. Griffiths* (Cardiff, 2004), pp. 175–96.

[102] Jenkins, 'The Bard of Liberty', pp. 183–206. For other versions of the anecdotes about Iolo and Pitt, see Thomas, *Bywgraffiad Iolo Morganwg*, pp. 26–7; Emrys-Jones, *Life and Works of Edward Williams (Iolo Morganwg)*, pp. 4–5; Robertson Spencer, *Annals of South Glamorgan*, pp. 249–50.

[103] See Daniel Ddu, 'Cofiant Edward Williams', 130–1; ap Rhys Stephen, 'Iolo Morganwg II', 98; Foulkes, 'Williams, Edward (Iolo Morganwg)' in idem (ed.), *Geirlyfr Bywgraffiadol*, p. 985; David Lloyd Isaac, *Siluriana: or Contributions towards the History of Gwent and Glamorgan* (Newport, 1859), p. 195; Emrys-Jones, *Life and Works of Edward Williams (Iolo Morganwg)*, p. 9; Owen Griffith (Giraldus), 'Enwogion Cymreig yn y chwarter cyntaf o'r ganrif hon', *Y Wawr*, XX, no. 2 (1895), 44–5; Robertson Spencer, *Annals of South Glamorgan*, p. 251; W. Rowland Jones, 'Dyngarwch a'r Beirdd Cymreig', *Y Geninen*, XXIX, no. 2 (1911), 134; D. E., 'Iolo Morganwg: The Welsh Bard of Liberty', *Welsh Gazette*, 23 December 1926.

[104] The tales are recounted in, for instance, Elijah Waring, 'Iolo Morganwg', *Cambrian*, 17 February 1827; Daniel Ddu, 'Cofiant Edward Williams', 131; *RAEW*, pp. 58–60; ap Rhys Stephen, 'Iolo Morganwg III', 314; Penar, 'Iolo Morgannwg', 217; Breese Davies, 'Rhai o'n Gwyr Mawr 1 – Iolo Morganwg', 13. See also Andrew Davies, '"Uncontaminated with Human Gore"? Iolo Morganwg, Slavery and the Jamaican Inheritance' in *Rattleskull Genius*, pp. 293–313.

[105] Y Golygydd, 'Merch Anghenus y Bardd Cymreig', *Y Cyfaill o'r Hen Wlad yn America … dan olygiad William Rowlands*, IV, no. 38 (1841), 64.

[106] William Williams, 'Iolo Morganwg', 50.

This tale held its own until the eve of the Great War, when a risible essay on 'Iolo Morganwg' in a college magazine, *The Grail*, praised him for his 'phenomenal abhorrence of slavery'.[107]

Closely associated with the group of anecdotes about the 'Bard of Liberty', which often featured some of his famous contemporaries, were accounts and references which compared him favourably with leading Englishmen of all ages, thereby boosting the brittle confidence of those Welshmen who feared that their cultural bastions were becoming increasingly embattled. Among the political figures with whom Iolo was linked, or with whom he was favourably compared, were the duke of Wellington, George III, George IV, William Pitt the Younger, Tom Paine, and every radical whose name had appeared on the subscription list of *Poems, Lyric and Pastoral*.[108] Iolo was mentioned in the same breath as authors like Shakespeare and Sir Walter Scott, and was compared with historians like Gildas and Macaulay.[109] 'Byron – Burns – Morganwg' was a line of tradition drawn up in the *Glamorgan Gazette* in May 1876. Another article embellished Waring's tale of how Tom Paine had concealed his fondness for alcohol from Iolo and, by remarking unfavourably on Samuel Johnson's hot temper, praised Iolo's moral superiority over both men.[110] The tale in which the 'Nestor' of English literature, Samuel Johnson, was confronted by the 'embryotic' antiquary Iolo in a bookshop in London was the most important in this group.[111] This famous encounter, first told by Waring in the *Cambrian* in 1827, and corrected by Taliesin, was rehearsed on many occasions.[112] By 1890 it was so well known that a young Oxford-based writer of an article entitled 'Dr Johnson and Iolo Morganwg' used it as a springboard for a four-point summary of why Iolo Morganwg deserved the blessing of his nation: he had endeared the Welsh nation to everyone he had met; he had endeavoured to convince the English of the wealth of Welsh literature; his love of liberty was undying; and he gave his life to safeguard the materials required to write the

---

[107] E. J. Lloyd, 'Iolo Morganwg', *The Grail*, VI, no. 19 (1913), 146.

[108] The list of subscribers itself became a subject of interest for James Harris, the second editor of the *Red Dragon*. See his 'The Fringe of a Welshman's Book', *Red Dragon*, VIII (1885), 582–98.

[109] Golygydd, 'Manion a Hanesion', *Yr Ymofynydd*, XI, no. 63 (1886), 262. For Sir Walter Scott, see R. O. Glaslyn, 'Pennod o Chwedlau: I. Adrodd Chwedlau', *Cymru*, XXXI, no. 183 (1906), 149. For Thomas Carlyle, see John Howells, 'Carlyle's Holidays in Wales', *Red Dragon*, V (1884), 335. For Macaulay, see James Harris, 'Notes and Queries: Iolo Morganwg and Lord Macaulay', ibid., VI (1884), 282.

[110] Ap P. A. Mon, 'Tom Paine, Iolo Morganwg, a Dr Johnson', *Y Wawr*, II, no. 1 (1877), 47–9. See also *RAEW*, p. 105.

[111] See John Bowen Jones, 'Samuel Johnson', *Y Beirniad*, XX, no. 81 (1879), 227; Ap P. A. Mon, 'Tom Paine, Iolo Morganwg, a Dr Johnson', 47–9.

[112] Taliesin insisted that Iolo had presented Samuel Johnson with three rather than two grammars. He also added that, every time the books were called for in the family, Iolo would refer to them as 'Dr Johnson's grammars'. See *Cambrian*, 10 February 1827. See also Daniel Ddu, 'Cofiant Edward Williams', 132; Thomas Stephens, 'Iolo Morganwg', *Yr Ymofynydd*, V, no. 56 (1852), 80; *Baner ac Amserau Cymru*, 18 January 1860; Isaac, *Siluriana*, p. 193; Foulkes, 'Williams, Edward (Iolo Morganwg)' in idem (ed.), *Geirlyfr Bywgraffiadol*, p. 985; Emrys-Jones, *Life and Works of Edward Williams (Iolo Morganwg)*, pp. 3–4.

history of Wales.¹¹³ Coming from a highly educated member of the younger generation, such approval was significant.

The myth of Iolo Morganwg was such an integral and well-known part of nineteenth-century Welsh culture that Iolo became a stock character within printed Welsh biographies and histories. He was inserted willy-nilly in the stories of many poets and preachers, among them Evan Evans (Ieuan Fardd), Richard Robert Jones (Dic Aberdaron), David Thomas (Dafydd Ddu Eryri), William Owen Pughe, David Davis (Dafydd Dafis) and Daniel Evans (Daniel Ddu).¹¹⁴ Likewise he became part of the history of places of local and national interest, such as Hafod Uchtryd near Aberystwyth, Hafod y Llan near Beddgelert, and Llantwit Major.¹¹⁵ Through their association with Iolo Morganwg, each of these places was invested with special importance. Iolo's name also commanded such respect that it made good sense for poets and scholars to associate themselves with him. In order to strengthen his claim to the vacant position of archdruid of the Gorsedd, Morien recounted a story of how Iolo had sought to visit his own bardic teacher Myfyr Morganwg *c.*1820 in order to initiate him in the secrets of the bardic order.¹¹⁶ The chief claim to fame of the poet John Thomas (Ioan Triddyd) was that Iolo Morganwg had held him as a baby, an improbable event since Iolo had died four years before Thomas was born.¹¹⁷ In Wales, to be able to boast a link with Iolo, however tenuous, provided status and authenticity.

Critical opinions of Iolo Morganwg appeared only rarely. Nineteenth-century Welsh society took no delight in them. The grudging, malevolent biography written by Thomas Stephens through the invitation or, rather, coercion of the editor of *Yr Ymofynydd*, which appeared between April 1852 and February 1853, was an exception to the rule.¹¹⁸ Although Stephens dutifully cited all the hagiographical sources, among them Malkin, Redwood and Waring, his own comments and style revealed his contempt for Iolo and his grave doubts regarding his mythical status. Apart from the accounts published by Waring and Thomas D. Thomas, Stephens's articles constituted the longest

---

[113] Anon., 'Dr Johnson a Iolo Morgannwg', 77–8.
[114] E. B. Morris, 'Dydd o Bererindod: Gwlad Lledrod a Ieuan Brydydd Hir', *Cymru*, XXVII, no. 158 (1904), 143; Carneddog, 'Ysgrifau Hafod y Llan', ibid., VI, no. 31 (1894), 83; Glaslyn, 'Llythyrau Dafydd Ddu Eryri', ibid., XXVIII, no. 166 (1905), 248–50; Gwilym Hughes, 'Old Eisteddfod Medals', *Young Wales*, V, no. 53 (1899), 105–7; Gol., 'Beirdd Dyfed: 1800–1900', *Cymru*, XXXIX, no. 229 (1910), 86; Anon., 'Dafis, Castell Hywel', *Y Traethodydd*, IV (1848), 204.
[115] David E. Bonner, 'Hanes Hafod Uchtryd', 156–63; Carneddog, 'Ysgrifau Hafod y Llan', *Cymru*, VI, no. 31 (1894), 83.
[116] Anon., 'Obituary: January to June. Feb. 23 – Mr Evan Davies ("Myfyr Morganwg")' in George Brierley (ed.), *Cymru Fu: Notes and Queries Relating to the Past History of Wales and the Border Counties* (2 vols., 1887–91), I, p. 212. Although the writer was anonymous, it was most probably Morien, who was seeking to strengthen his claim to be archdruid of Wales.
[117] Aneirin Talfan Davies, *Bro Morgannwg* (2 vols., Abertawe, 1976), II, p. 213. I am grateful to Huw Walters for bringing this reference to my attention.
[118] This series appeared in *Yr Ymofynydd*, V, no. 56 (1852) until ibid., VI, no. 66 (1853).

biographical sketch published before 1926. Although he went further in search of the authentic Iolo Morganwg than any of his contemporaries, his critical remarks were ignored by readers of *Yr Ymofynydd* because, as on other occasions, Stephens had gone beyond what were considered to be acceptable bounds of criticism.[119] His last paragraph indicates that he himself was aware of being out of kilter with public perceptions:

> Hyn ar air a chydwybod oedd Iolo Morganwg. Dichon fod rhai o'i bleidwyr, a ddymunasent i mi nodi ei rinweddau yn unig, i guddio ei wendidau, ac arfer dim ond canmoliaeth; ond gan mai hanesydd ydwyf ac nid bardd, nid yw gweniaith yn llafar gynnefin i mi. Dyledswydd hanesydd yw dweyd – 'y gwir, yr holl wir, a dim ond y gwir'. Felly y gwnaethum; sorred a sorro. Nid o'm dewis fy hun y cymmerais arnaf y gorchwyl. Buasai yn well gennyf ei adael ar ol, gan nad wyf yn cydfyned ac amryw o ddaliadau yr hen wr. Ond wedi cymmeryd y gwaith mewn llaw, ar daer gais Golygydd yr *Ymofynydd*, ymdrechais ei gyflawni yn gyfiawn, yn gyflawn, yn gydwybodol, ac yn ddiduedd. Pa fodd y llwyddais, barned y darllenydd.[120]

> (This on my word and conscience was Iolo Morganwg. Perhaps some of his supporters would have wished me to note his virtues only, to hide his weaknesses, and use only praise; but because I am a historian and not a poet, flattery is not a familiar voice to me. The historian's duty is to say – 'the truth, the whole truth, and only the truth'. So I did; let those who wish to be offended be offended. I did not take this task upon myself by my own personal choice. I should have preferred to let it be, since I do not agree with many of the old man's tenets. But, having taken the work in hand, on the urgent plea of the Editor of the *Ymofynydd*, I attempted to accomplish it justly, fully, conscientiously, and without bias. How far I have succeeded, the reader must judge.)

Another rare exception to the rule were two revealing letters published in a series on 'J. W. Prichard, Plasybrain' in *Y Traethodydd* in 1884.[121] On 3 May 1822 J. W. Prichard had warned Robert Roberts, Holyhead, of Iolo Morganwg:

> dyn ar ddrygau bob amser, ac yn dyfeisio rhyw gelwyddau i geisio twyllo'r byd, ac wrth hynny, nid yn unig tynu dirmyg a gwaradwydd arno ei hun, ond fe barodd lawer o ddirmyg ac anfri ar enw Mr W. O. P. Och fi! Duw a'n gwaredo rhag syrthio i rwyd y cyfryw *Anghenfil*.[122]

> (a man up to evil at all times, and devising some lies to try to deceive the world, and by this, not only bringing contempt and ignominy upon himself, but also much scorn and dishonour to the name of Mr W. O. P. Woe is me! God save us from slipping into the net of such a *Monster*.)

---

[119] For instance, an exchange of letters in the *Cambrian* between Stephens and representatives of the Abergavenny Cymreigyddion, among them Taliesin ab Iolo and Thomas Price (Carnhuanawc), 1842–3, was marred by Stephens's vitriolic personal attacks. See also Chapter 5 below.

[120] Thomas Stephens, 'Iolo Morganwg: Ei Nodweddion', *Yr Ymofynydd*, VI, no. 66 (1853), 35.

[121] Golygydd, 'Mr J. W. Prichard, Plasybrain II', *Y Traethodydd*, XXXIX (1884), 14–33.

[122] Ibid., 29. 'Mr W. O. P.' was William Owen Pughe.

Passages of this kind were so rare as to be mere drops in an ocean of admiration. Only one other token 'revealing' text was reproduced regularly – a well-known extract from a letter in which Iolo Morganwg had ridiculed William Owen Pughe – but its impact was neutralized by explanatory notes which made light of the letter. Yet, even in this form the passage provoked passionate replies in defence of Iolo and further criticism of the hapless Pughe.[123] Little stock was placed on local depictions of Iolo as 'a strange wise man', who was like 'the monk who knew a bit about natural philosophy [and] was believed to be in concert with the devil', or views of him as 'a fool' (Document 3).[124] It was far more usual for commentators to consider him as a representative of a better age:

> Most frugal of men, earnest, quaint, honest and outspoken as the day, he was a capital type of the intellectual men of his time. Very marked the contrast with the present. There was vigour, breadth, and solidity then. Greater quickness of mental power may now be met with, unquestionably; but how often is there a superficiality and a flippancy as well.[125]

## The process of transmission

The entire corpus of material regarding Iolo Morganwg, including accounts based on facts, anecdotes glorifying Iolo's deeds, and references to his name and work, exercised a powerful influence in the period between 1850 and the 1920s. Thereafter, much of the material lost its underlying function and disappeared following a brief renaissance during the celebrations of the centenary of Iolo's death.[126] The changing form of the narratives in circulation – whether they had originated in the spoken or the written word, whether they were transmitted by word of mouth or through articles in periodicals – indicates that they were not reproduced verbatim, but rather that they exhibited the careful balance of variation and conservatism which marks the development of folklore.[127] Variation occurred with regard to those aspects of an account which were not essential for maintaining the fundamental cultural meaning of the story, such as the number of participants besides Iolo, the number of objects involved or the location. Those parts of a sketch which were important to

---

[123] See, for instance, 'An Angry Bard's Letter from a copy made by the Revd J. A. Jenkins, B.A., original at Cardiff library', *Wales*, I, no. 2 (1894), 91–2; R. Ross, 'Queries: William Owen Pughe', *Bye-Gones*, 28 July 1880, 88; Chware Teg, 'Replies: William Owen Pughe', ibid., 18 August 1880, 96; N. W. S., 'Queries: William Owen Pughe', ibid., 27 April 1881, 225–6.
[124] Morgan Williams, 'Notable Men of Wales: Edward Williams (Iolo Morganwg)', 99–100.
[125] Ibid., 102.
[126] See Gethin Hywel Rhys, *'A Wayward Cymric Genius': Celebrating the Centenary of the Death of Iolo Morganwg* (Aberystwyth, 2007).
[127] Barre Toelken, *The Dynamics of Folklore* (Logan, Utah, 1996), pp. 39–40.

Welsh culture were maintained intact, through space, time and change of language, until their function changed and they took on a different form.

The process by which tales of Iolo Morganwg were transmitted and kept in the public eye may be examined by focusing on 'Strike a Welshman if you dare', an anecdote which was not part of Waring's œuvre and which can be grouped with those accounts which linked the combative Iolo with a representative of the English ruling classes. The story summed up several important aspects of Iolo's character: his pride in being a craftsman and a Welshman, his belief that all people should be treated equally, regardless of their social standing, and his swift wit and courage in the face of adversity. It also exposed the snobbery of the English upper classes and their inclination to violence. Not least, it provided an occasion to publicize four lines of poetry which acquired importance far beyond the story itself. 'Strike a Welshman if you dare' first appeared in print in *Y Traethodydd* in 1855. It was inserted by the historian of Calvinistic Methodism, William Williams, in a review of Waring's biography, between passages about Iolo's friendship with the great men of his age and descriptions of his simple, unassuming behaviour (Document 8).[128] The two versions which appeared in the *Red Dragon: A National Magazine for Wales* in the 1880s were not only subtly different from their predecessor in *Y Traethodydd* and from each other, but also in several ways more impressive. In both versions Iolo was refused entry not because the nobleman was otherwise engaged but because of his humble appearance, which made his insistence on admittance (through the front door) appear radical rather than petulant. The last line of the poem was changed from 'men of great renown' to 'a nation of renown', which expressed the national idea more clearly:

> I am glad you have given a notice and portrait of old Iolo. Perhaps the following anecdote will amuse your readers: – Iolo, when in London, was waited upon by a nobleman, who left his card, as Iolo was out, and his wish that the old Welshman would do him the honour of calling. Iolo did call, in his humble suit, and his hard rap with the stick brought a servant to the door, who eyed him in amazement. 'What do you want, fellow, by rapping like that?' 'To see Lord –', 'You should go to the back, man.' 'No, I won't.' 'What is your name?' 'That is my business. I want to see his lordship.' 'He'll horsewhip you if you don't get off.' 'No, he won't,' said Iolo. 'Tell him that a man wishes to see him.' Back went the servant, who reported that an impudent, abusive fellow was at the door, who would not give his name, but insisted on seeing his lordship, and the nobleman, a very irate worthy, seized his horsewhip and rushed to the door, crying out as he cracked his whip, 'Now fellow, you want a thrashing, do you?' 'Hold,' cried Iolo, as Lord —— came unpleasantly near. 'Hold, – Strike a Welshman if you dare,

---

[128] This version of the story was retold in Foulkes, 'Williams, Edward (Iolo Morganwg)' in idem (ed.), *Geirlyfr Bywgraffiadol*, p. 990; Penar, 'Iolo Morgannwg', 216–17.

> Ancient Britons as we are,
> We were a nation of renown
> Before a Saxon wore a crown.'

'Iolo!' exclaimed his lordship with delight, throwing his whip at the servant and holding out eagerly his hand; and forthwith the old bard was marched in, an honoured guest.[129]

The second version of the tale published in the *Red Dragon* was submitted by the young D. Rhys Phillips, the future librarian of Swansea and historian of Neath, under the pseudonym 'Beili Glas'.[130] Having heard the tale and failed to trace it in Waring's biography, he was eager to know its origins.[131] In his version the stakes were raised, since the nobleman – with whom Iolo was on first-name terms – who invited him to his home was presumed to have been George III. In the final version of this tale, which appeared in Marianne Robertson Spencer's work, *Annals of South Glamorgan* (1913), Iolo's host was believed to have been the prime minister, William Pitt himself (Document 8).[132] Since Iolo had corresponded with Pitt, and had been summoned to appear before him on two occasions, oral testimony in the Vale of Glamorgan may have been conflated with the well-known anecdotes of Iolo's meetings with Pitt to produce this new reading.[133]

Other accounts of the episode by authors from south Wales changed the characters and the circumstances in order to give it a slightly different meaning. Having reproduced the acknowledged version from *Y Traethodydd* in his Welsh biography of Iolo, Thomas D. Thomas drew the reader's attention to a different reading provided by John Shamby of Carmarthen.[134] The location had been moved to Merthyr Tydfil, though the nobleman was still an Englishman, and in order to suit the Welsh location the last line of the poem had shrewdly been changed to 'Ere a Saxon trod our ground', which extended its temporal dimension considerably.[135] A variation of this story and its territorial patriotism highlighted the claim of the Welsh to the whole of Britain and moved the time-frame even further back to the arrival of the Saxons in the British Isles. In an ad hoc reply to T. Marchant Williams's address on the merits of Welsh

---

[129] B. T., 'Draconigenae: Iolo Morganwg', *Red Dragon*, II (1882), 285.

[130] D. Rhys Phillips (Beili Glas, 1862–1952) was best known as the librarian of Swansea Library in the 1920s and 1930s, as a bibliographer, and as the author of *A History of the Neath Valley* (1925). He was an enthusiastic promoter of eisteddfodau, the Gorsedd, and the Pan-Celtic movement. See also Chapter 3 below.

[131] Beili Glas, 'Notes and Queries', *Red Dragon*, X (1886), 186.

[132] *RAEW*, pp. 82–6; Robertson Spencer, *Annals of South Glamorgan*, p. 241. The Spencer family lived close to Flemingston church, and David Spencer was said to have owned several of Iolo Morganwg's letters. See David G. Rees, 'Manion ac Hanesion: Lle Claddedigaeth Iolo Morganwg', *Yr Ymofynydd*, XVI, no. 1 (1916), 22; T. Lovell, 'Tro i Wlad Iolo Morgannwg', 156.

[133] Jenkins, 'The Bard of Liberty', pp. 195–6.

[134] Thomas, *Bywgraffiad Iolo Morganwg*, pp. 25–6, 68.

[135] Ibid., pp. 68–9.

literature at the National Eisteddfod of Wrexham in 1888, the Revd Elias Owen regaled the audience with the following account:

> His father years ago told him there was a tradition that a Welshman was very much taken up with the poetry of Shakespeare, and that he went from Wales to see the great poet, but was refused admission to the house. The Welshman said he had walked so many miles and must see the poet, and the servant took the message in. Shakespeare came out in a very great rage ... with a determination to send the impudent Welshman away from the door. But when the poet reached the door the Welshman said –
>
> > Touch a Welshman if you dare;
> > We the true-born Britons are;
> > We held our country safe and sound,
> > Before ye Saxons touched the ground.

This caused considerable mirth at the Eisteddfod, but D. Emlyn Evans gravely noted on his copy of the *Annual Report of the Eisteddfod Association* of 1888: 'This was said by Iolo Morganwg.'[136]

This theme was still fertile following the turn of the nineteenth century. Distilled versions of the tale were set in new contexts and applied to the changing political circumstances of a Wales which was by now more confidently patriotic.[137] The journalist Morien, one of the most ardent disciples of Iolo's bardism, provided the verse with a context which asserted the cultural superiority of Wales and which elevated Iolo Morganwg by reference to the scriptures:

> The scholars of England and the Continent of Europe were beginning to believe that all the ancient Britons and their language had all perished, and were buried in the same sepulchre as the Empire of the Caesars. But all of a sudden, like the ghost of another prophet Samuel, Iolo Morganwg arose, and cried:
>
> > Strike a Welshman if you dare,
> > Ancient Britons all we are;
> > We were men of great renown
> > Ere a Saxon wore a crown.
>
> England rubbed her eyes and said: 'Hark! that voice again!'[138]

Other Welsh patriots on the eve of the First World War used the antiquity of Welsh nationhood to stress the political claims of a resurgent Wales. The

---

[136] E. Vincent Evans (ed.), *The Eighth Annual Report of the National Eisteddfod Association, Together with the Transactions of the Cymmrodorion Section of the Wrexham National Eisteddfod, 1888* (Cardiff, 1889), pp. 48–9.

[137] For the concept of the 'distilled version' to describe what had traditionally been considered fragments, see Mary-Ann Constantine and Gerald Porter, *Fragments and Meaning in Traditional Song: From the Blues to the Baltic* (Oxford, 2003), p. 4.

[138] Morien, 'Iolo Morganwg', *The Cambrian: A Semi-Monthly Magazine for Welsh-Americans*, XXXI, no. 21 (1911), 9.

theologian and well-known author D. Miall Edwards's one-line version of the story, quoted in an article on nation and nationalism published in 1914, depicted Iolo's host as 'some Englishman', and Iolo himself as the heir of a long line of historic Welsh heroes:

> Credaf y safwn ni'r Cymry y prawf hwn eto. Mae i ni ein hanes yn ymestyn yn ol i'r cyn-oesoedd pell, – hanes hwy na nemor genedl yng ngorllewin y byd heddyw. Byddai gwybod mwy am yr hanes hwnnw yn faeth cryf i'r nwyd gwladgarol heddyw. Ac y mae gennym ein gwroniaid hefyd, – ein Caradog, ein Harthur, ein Llywelyn Fawr, ein Llyw Olaf, ein Glyndwr, a llawer eraill. Llawenychwn yn fawr yn y deffroad cenedlaethol presennol; ond dylid cofio mai *deffroad* ydyw hwn, nid *genedigaeth*. Cyfnod y dadeni yw, nid cyfnod y geni. Y mae i ni ein hanes. Gallwn ddweyd fel y dywedodd Iolo Morgannwg pan y bygythiodd gwr o Sais ei drin yn arw:
>
> > Touch a Welshman if you dare,
> > Ancient Britons as we are;
> > We were a nation of great renown
> > Before a Saxon wore a crown.[139]
>
> (I believe that we the Welsh will survive this trial again. We have our history which stretches far back into prehistoric ages, – a history longer than hardly any other nation in the western world possesses today. To know more about this history would be strong nourishment to the patriotic instinct today. And we have our heroes also, – our Caradog, our Arthur, our Llywelyn the Great, our Last Leader, our Glyndwr, and many more. We rejoice greatly in the present national awakening; but one should remember that this is an *awakening*, not a *birth*. It is a period of rebirth, not a period of birth. We have our history. We can say, as Iolo Morganwg said when some Englishman threatened to treat him roughly:
>
> > Touch a Welshman if you dare,
> > Ancient Britons as we are;
> > We were a nation of great renown
> > Before a Saxon wore a crown.)

In keeping with the overt political message, the verse had been subtly changed again to read 'We were a nation of great renown'. But although this eminently malleable tale was revived once more during the celebrations of the centenary of Iolo Morganwg's death, it vanished thereafter, along with most of the other anecdotes which no longer served the needs of the day.[140]

'A country's memory, not history books, decides who gains immortality' ('Cof gwlad, nid llyfrau hanes, sy'n penderfynu pwy sy'n cael anfarwoldeb'), wrote Rees Davies on the occasion of the six-hundredth anniversary of the rebellion

---

[139] David Miall Edwards, 'Cenedl a Chenedlaetholdeb II', *Y Geninen*, XXXII, no. 3 (1914), 156.
[140] D. E., 'The Welsh Bard of Liberty', *Welsh Gazette*, 23 December 1926.

of Owain Glyndŵr.¹⁴¹ The myth of Iolo Morganwg was maintained throughout the Victorian period and into Edwardian times because it fulfilled essential functions in the country's memory. It provided a link with what was considered to be a golden age which had given the nation a cultural patriot and Nonconformist folk hero. Thereafter, however, the myth lost its *raison d'être*. Even the last people who could claim to have seen the great man were disappearing, as this poignant passage reveals:

> On All Souls' Day, 1902, there was buried in the Alltblaca Chapel grounds the body of the Rev. David Lewis Evans, who, from a child to the last of his 90 years of life in this world, had been a constant worshipper there. On Sunday afternoon, the 4th of November, 1900, he had preached to a numerous congregation within its walls, taking for a text Acts iii. 19, 'Repent ye therefore, and be converted.' At the close of his sermon, and before giving the Apostolic Benediction, he requested the worshippers to sing one of *Iolo Morganwg*'s hymns, and told them he was probably the last person living who had seen and known old *Iolo* – having, as a child, seen him when a frequent visitor to his parents' house in the neighbourhood. Once he remembered being with his mother in the old Chapel at an administration of the Lord's Supper. Amongst the communicants was one, leaning on his tall staff, who received the elements standing, making reverent obeisance to them ere participating. 'See, lad,' whispered his mother as they were leaving the Chapel, 'there is the great and good *Iolo*.'¹⁴²

From 1918 onwards the political and social landscape changed. Iolo increasingly seemed a figure from the past whose name was revered only by representatives of a bygone age. The driving force behind the centenary celebrations in south Wales was the National Union of Welsh Societies, a body steeped in nineteenth-century cultural nationalism.¹⁴³ Following the centenary celebrations, the myth of Iolo Morganwg disappeared from Welsh folklore not because its factual base had been eroded by a new generation of scholars but because it had simply run its course and fulfilled its function. The Romantic age had ended and the mythological figures used to bolster claims of nationhood were being marginalized. The largely antiquarian-oriented cultural nationalism of the nineteenth century had given way to a more progressive political and language movement which concerned itself less with manuscripts and the origins of nations than with self-government and the rights of the Welsh language. To many, the demise of the mythical Iolo, created by the 'light fingers of tradition', was judged a blessing. As early as 1884, the doyen of Welsh historians, J. E. Lloyd, had maintained that one of the disadvantages of

---

¹⁴¹ R. Rees Davies, 'Owain Glyn Dŵr a'i Apêl', *Y Traethodydd*, CLV, no. 655 (2000), 207.
¹⁴² George Eyre Evans, 'Memories of Lampeter and District', *Antiquarian Notes*, III, no. 30 (1905), 129–30. David Lewis Evans (1812–1902), a well-known preacher, was the father of the antiquarian George Eyre Evans.
¹⁴³ See Rhys, '*A Wayward Cymric Genius*'. For an assessment of the different phases of nationalism, see Miroslav Hroch, *Social Preconditions of National Revival in Europe* (Cambridge, 1985).

Romanticism was that it had clouded the true virtues of great historical characters and replaced them with fakes.[144] As the myth of Iolo Morganwg waned, interest in Edward Williams, the radical and the poet, made headway. Folklore gave way to close readings of his poetry and prose, and the traditions of radicalism and pacifism which he appeared to represent.[145] Nationalists like Iorwerth C. Peate placed Edward Williams at the beginning of the anti-war tradition in Wales, and Communists like T. E. Nicholas (Niclas y Glais) and his son, Islwyn ap Nicholas, rediscovered his radical message.[146] Most of all, Iolo and his work came under the critical scrutiny of scholars like Griffith John Williams, who cared more about historical and literary accuracy than moral judgements or anecdotal evidence.[147] Thus the disappearance of the myth facilitated the emergence of a scholarly appraisal of the authentic Iolo and his ideas.

---

[144] John E. Lloyd, 'Taliesin Ben Beirdd', *Y Geninen*, II, no. 2 (1884), 148.

[145] J. Griffiths, 'Neges Gymdeithasol Iolo Morgannwg', ibid., XLI, no. 4 (1923), 202–10.

[146] Bob Owen, 'Cymru a'r Mudiad Heddwch', ibid., XLIII, no. 4 (1925), 201; Iorwerth C. Peate, *Y Traddodiad Heddwch yng Nghymru* (Dinbych, 1941), pp. 2, 6. For references to T. E. Nicholas and his son Islwyn, see Jenkins, *'Perish Kings and Emperors'*, pp. 12–14.

[147] See Chapter 6 below.

# 3
## The Public Legacy of Bardism

> Dysgeidiaeth Dderwyddol
> Ga'dd gymmaint ei chanmol,
> Nis gwn i'r hen bobl
> Ai buddiol y bu.
> Ond yn awr oes y ffeithiau
> Sy'n agor ei dorau,
> Athroniaeth a'i phwyntiau
> Ar seiliau gwell sy.[1]
>
> (Druidical learning
> Which receiv'd so much praise,
> I don't know if for the ancients
> It was of benefit.
> But now the age of facts
> Is opening its gates,
> Philosophy and its subjects
> Are on better foundations.)

As the implications of the 'Age of Progress' dawned on Welsh poets like the Dewi Mai (Dafydd Dafydd) quoted above, the future of druidism, the eisteddfod and the Gorsedd was increasingly called into question. Although the eisteddfod and the Gorsedd were publicly linked at Carmarthen in 1819, they did not develop in tandem over the following decades, and during the 1830s and 1840s both were obliged to compete with other festive expressions of local civic pride and national aspirations. The Llangollen eisteddfod of 1858, which was intended to turn them into a rallying point for Welsh culture, instead enraged the nation as a result of the pomp, nepotism and bias apparent in its proceedings. In south Wales the increasingly arcane public rituals enacted by Myfyr Morganwg in the name of the Gorsedd incurred, in equal measure, the wrath of ministers of all denominations and the scorn of satirists. The sudden dissolution of the Abergavenny Cymreigyddion Society in 1854 robbed the eisteddfod movement of institutional patronage, and the decline of periodicals such as *Seren Gomer*, *Y Brython* and the *Cambrian Journal* in the early 1860s deprived it of its most important public platforms. The eisteddfod was lampooned in *Y Punch Cymraeg* and in publications such as Ieuan Ddu's

---

[1] Dewi Mai, 'Cenedl y Cymmry a'r Hen Amseroedd', *Seren Gomer*, XLII, no. 525 (1859), 570.

satirical epic *Cambria upon Two Sticks*.² In the wake of the 'Treachery of the Blue Books', bardism was considered by 'progressives' to be an embarrassing remnant of the past rather than a worthy expression of the present, and the fate of Iolo's bardic legacy appeared to be in the balance.³ However, the years of crisis were successfully weathered and were followed by a national flowering which also had significant international ramifications. By 1921 the nation's bibliographer James 'Ifano' Jones would praise the 'years of the eisteddfod renaissance' in a European context and draw comparisons with Goethe and Wordsworth.⁴ This chapter discusses the rise of Iolo's public bardic legacy as an expression of civic pride and as part of the movement to rescue Welsh culture, examines its crisis of confidence in the middle decades of the nineteenth century, and charts its national and international success from the 1880s to the Edwardian high noon and the First World War.

## *Pontypridd 1814, Carmarthen 1819 and their aftermath*

In 1792 Iolo Morganwg staged his first two Gorsedd assemblies on Primrose Hill in London, thereby making the bardic preface that he had contributed to William Owen Pughe's *Heroic Elegies and other Pieces of Llywarç Hen* a historic reality. The public nature of the ceremonies made his ideas accessible to a wider audience, and their peculiarity attracted press coverage which ensured further publicity.⁵ On Iolo's return to his native Glamorgan in 1795, he began holding Gorsedd ceremonies there until 1799, when they were suppressed by the government.⁶ When such meetings were resumed following the Napoleonic Wars, Iolo took a crucial first step towards safeguarding their future during the nineteenth century by moving his bardic conventions from the rural Vale of Glamorgan to the developing industrial community of Pontypridd in the Rhondda valley and, concurrently, making them a public event. At least one of the two Gorsedd meetings convened at *Y Maen Chwŷf* or the Rocking-stone near Pontypridd in 1814 was preceded by a familiar

---

² 'Hois! Eisteddfod Fythgofiadwy Llangollen', *Y Punch Cymraeg*, I, no. 20 (1858), 5–6; 'Yr Arddangosfa Farddonol', ibid., II, no. 31 (1859), 4–5; Thomas (Ieuan Ddu), *Cambria upon Two Sticks or, the Eisteddfod and the Penny Readings, to which is added Two Cantos entitled Harry Vaughan, and a Selection of Songs and Poems*.

³ Griffith Edwards, 'Yr Eisteddfodau', *Y Traethodydd*, XV (1859), 137; *Baner Cymru*, 6 October 1858.

⁴ James Ifano Jones, 'Blynyddoedd Dadeni'r Eisteddfod', *Y Geninen*, XXXIX, no. 4 (1921), 220.

⁵ *Morning Chronicle*, 26 September 1792; Thomas Shankland, 'Hanes Dechreuad Gorsedd Beirdd Ynys Prydain', *Y Llenor*, III, no. 2 (1924), 94–102; *HGB*, p. 29; Cathryn A. Charnell-White, *Bardic Circles: National, Regional and Personal Identity in the Bardic Vision of Iolo Morganwg* (Cardiff, 2007).

⁶ For the Gorseddau held under Iolo's supervision in Wales between 1795 and 1799, see *HGB*, pp. 32–43; Geraint H. Jenkins, '"Dyro, Dduw dy Nawdd": Iolo Morganwg a'r Mudiad Undodaidd' in idem (ed.), *Cof Cenedl XX: Ysgrifau ar Hanes Cymru* (Llandysul, 2005), pp. 79–87.

civic preamble – a bannered procession along the high street.[7] By marching through the town, Iolo and his adherents claimed their right to recognition within the public life of this emerging urban centre alongside other social and political groups.[8] Even in their dotage, local inhabitants recalled seeing 'Iolo Morganwg and Gwilym Morganwg, a banner carried in front of them, walking at the head of a procession, over Taav Street and then over the great bridge and on to the Rocking-stone on the Common above'.[9]

A second important step toward success was taken in 1819 when Iolo succeeded in publicly linking the Gorsedd with the historically attested, if only recently revived, eisteddfod for the first time.[10] The Cambrian provincial eisteddfod, held at Carmarthen in July 1819 at the invitation of Anglican champions of the Welsh language and its culture, was partly designed to act as a cultural bulwark to stem the fast-advancing tide of religious Dissent. Instead, it was seized by Iolo – the only Dissenter invited to serve on the organizing committee – for his own purposes, much to the private dismay of Thomas Burgess, bishop of St David's.[11] Once the bishop had opened proceedings with a short and unexceptional address, Iolo rose to deliver a brilliant exposition on the historic importance of the gathering. The local press subsequently chronicled Iolo's opening speech rather than the bishop's address,[12] and particular attention was paid to the Gorsedd ceremony which closed proceedings on 10 July 1819, an event which was free and accessible to all.[13] Here, the ritual of

---

[7] The Gorsedd of 1 August 1814 was advertised in *Seren Gomer*, 9 July 1814, but there was no subsequent report. The published poems of Gwilym Morganwg, which appeared as Thomas Williams, *Awen y Maen Chwyf yn cynnwys Awdlau, Cywyddau, Caniadau ac Englynion* (Merthyr Tydfil, 1890), pp. 70–1, contain the poem 'Heddwch', which the bard recited at the Rocking-stone Gorsedd of 1 August 1814. The Gorsedd held on 1 December 1814 is referred to in a letter to the editor by Gwilym Morganwg, which appeared in *Seren Gomer*, 8 February 1814. I am grateful to Huw Walters for his advice on the early Gorseddau.

[8] Simon Gunn, *The Public Culture of the Victorian Middle Class: Ritual and Authority in the English Industrial City, 1840–1914* (Manchester, 2000), p. 182.

[9] Owen Morgan (Morien), *The History of Pontypridd and Rhondda Valleys* (Pontypridd, 1903), p. 6. For a biographical sketch of Gwilym Morganwg, see Williams, *Awen y Maen Chwyf*, pp. v–viii, and Huw Walters, 'Myfyr Morganwg and the Rocking-stone Gorsedd' in *Rattleskull Genius*, pp. 481–3.

[10] On the history of the eisteddfod, see Hywel Teifi Edwards, *The Eisteddfod* (Cardiff, 1990); Idris Foster (ed.), *Twf yr Eisteddfod* (Aberystwyth, 1968).

[11] For an analysis of the religious background, see Jenkins, 'The Unitarian Firebrand, the Cambrian Society and the Eisteddfod' in *Rattleskull Genius*, pp. 267–92. Iolo's stay at the bishop's palace and the friendship he was assumed to have established with Thomas Burgess subsequently became part of his myth. See Chapter 2 above.

[12] *Cambrian*, 17 July 1819; ibid., 24 July 1819; *Carmarthen Journal*, 16 July 1819; Caradawg, 'Hanes yr Eisteddfod a Gynhaliwyd y' Nghaerfyrddin, Yr 8fed, 9fed, a'r 10fed o Orphenhaf, 1819', *Seren Gomer*, II, no. 40 (1819), 229; Charles Ashton, 'Gorsedd Beirdd Ynys Brydain' in E. Vincent Evans (ed.), *Eisteddfod Genedlaethol y Cymry: Cofnodion a Chyfansoddiadau Buddugol Gwrecsam* (Liverpool, 1889), pp. 133–4. The last occasion on which the address was reprinted was in 'Araith Iolo yn Eisteddfod Fawr Caerfyrddin yn 1819' in T. C. Evans (Cadrawd) (ed.), *Gwaith Iolo Morganwg* (Llanuwchllyn, 1913), pp. 92–6.

[13] Caradawg, 'Hanes yr Eisteddfod', 229.

delineating the Gorsedd circle with stones, of admitting Bards, Ovates and Druids into their respective orders, and of unsheathing and sheathing a sword provided a lasting blueprint for subsequent generations.[14] Thereafter, 'Carmarthen 1819' came to be regarded as the beginning of the modern eisteddfod movement, an event duly celebrated, emulated and mythologized throughout the nineteenth century. Numerous articles and notes about the event focused on Iolo's centrality to the proceedings, notably the manner in which he had honoured the winning poet Walter Davies (Gwallter Mechain), an Anglican priest and a loyal disciple, as well as on the unexpected admittance by this promoter of Unitarianism of Bishop Thomas Burgess to the druidic order:

> Dringodd hen Fardd Morganwg, i fyny, a chlymodd ysnoden (*riband*) lâs am ei fraich ddehau, sef arwydd Bardd. Wedi hyny disgynodd Mr Edward Williams, a nesâodd at yr Esgob, gan ddywedyd wrtho ei fod wedi cael ei awdurdodi (neu ei gymhell, canys ni's gallasom ei glywed yn eithaf eglur) i wisgo ei Arglwyddiaeth âg Urdd Derwydd: Wel, eb yr Esgob, myfi a ymostyngaf i bob peth a farnoch yn gymhwys: yna rhwymodd y Bardd ysnoden wen am fraich ddehau yr Esgob. Creodd hyn ddywenydd hir a chyffredin. Dangosai hyn fod rhagfarn grefyddol wedi cael ei gadael o'r tu allan i'r gynulleidfa gan fawrion a chyffredin. Gweled *Esgob Tyddewi* yn cael ei urddo gan hen *Ymneillduwr* oedd olygfa mil mwy hyfryd gan goleddwyr cariad ac ewyllys da cyffredin, a gwrthwynebwyr rhagfarnu a phleidgarwch, na phe gwelsid Arch-esgob Caergaint, yn ei holl wisgoedd a'i rwysg prif-esgobawl, yn cyflawni'r un gorchwyl.[15]

> (The old Bard of Glamorgan climbed up and attached a blue riband to his right arm, namely the sign of the Bard. After this Mr Edward Williams descended, and approached the Bishop, telling him that he had been authorized (or urged, because I could not hear him very clearly) to dress his Lordship with the Druidic Order: Well, said the Bishop, I will bow to everything which you consider appropriate; at this point the Bard attached a white riband to the Bishop's right arm. This caused prolonged and general applause. This revealed that religious prejudice had been left outside the audience by the mighty and the common. To see the *Bishop of St David's* thus honoured by an old *Dissenter* was a sight a thousand times more beloved by the proponents of love and general goodwill, and opponents of prejudice and partisanship, than had the Archbishop of Canterbury, with all his robes and his Archiepiscopal pomp, been seen fulfilling the same task.)

'While Iolo went through the ceremony, a happy smile was on the Bishop's face' ('a thra yr elai Iolo trwy y seremoni, yr oedd gwên hapus ar wyneb yr esgob') was a subsequent, but misleading, gloss on this ritual.[16] By claiming that

---

[14] *Carmarthen Journal*, 16 July 1819; Caradawg, 'Hanes yr Eisteddfod', 233–4; Ashton, 'Gorsedd Beirdd Ynys Brydain', pp. 136–7.

[15] Caradawg, 'Hanes yr Eisteddfod', 231.

[16] 'Daniel Ddu o Geredigion', *Cymru*, III, no. 13 (1892), 79. See also Gwyneddon, 'Trem ar Eisteddfod Caerfyrddin, 1819', *Y Geninen*, I, no. 2 (1883), 112; 'Cofiant y Gwir Barch. Thomas Burgess, D.D., Diweddar Esgob Tyddewi', *Y Gwladgarwr*, VI, no. 72 (1838), 354; Ashton, 'Gorsedd Beirdd Ynys Brydain', p. 134.

Bishop Burgess was in public agreement with Iolo Morganwg it was implied that bardism reigned supreme over differences of religious creed and social authority, thus offering an ideal focus for Welsh cultural life. The historic fact that, privately, Burgess had been highly displeased by the ceremonies held at the eisteddfod and Gorsedd, and had later attempted to prevent the convening of such assemblies, was conveniently forgotten.[17] The holding of the Gorsedd also attracted the attention of writers since it appeared to signify the support of a young generation of Welsh bards for Iolo as the authentic representative of the ancient bardic tradition.[18] The nationalist periodical *Young Wales* lauded the fact that 'the *old* bard of Glamorganshire, appeared leaning on the arm of the *young* bard of Cardiganshire (Rev. D. Evans, Daniel ab Ieuan Ddu), and the contrast between youth and age, the aspirant and the proficient, rendered the circumstance peculiarly interesting'.[19] For many poets in south Wales, 'Carmarthen 1819' was also the eisteddfod which reinstated the rules of the Glamorgan classification at the expense of that which had allegedly been imposed by Dafydd ab Edmwnd at the legendary Carmarthen eisteddfod of *c*.1453.[20] After all, had not Walter Davies revealed in his winning entry 'On the definite character, and comparative advantages of the Bardic Institutions of the counties of Carmarthen and Glamorgan' ('Ar gymeriad penodol, a manteision cymharol Sefydliadau Barddonol swyddi Caerfyrddin a Morganwg') that the Glamorgan classification was superior?[21] Above all, 'Carmarthen 1819' was considered to be the heir of a long tradition which stretched back to druidic times, and the model for all future proceedings, 'the mother of poets and poetry of the present period' ('mam beirdd a barddoniaeth y prifnod presenol').[22] The history of the 'principal eisteddfodau' of Wales thus began in 1819,[23] and Iolo's

---

[17] Jenkins, 'The Unitarian Firebrand, the Cambrian Society and the Eisteddfod' in *Rattleskull Genius*, pp. 290–1. Several Gorsedd meetings were abandoned following threats made by Burgess in 1820 and 1822. See *HGB*, pp. 93, 98–9.

[18] *Carmarthen Journal*, 16 July 1819; Caradawg, 'Hanes yr Eisteddfod', 229. The scene was later described in 'Daniel Ddu o Geredigion', *Cymru*, III, no. 13 (1892), 79; 'Beirdd Dyfed 1800–1900', ibid., XXXIX, no. 229 (1910), 86; 'Ein Hathrofeydd a'n Hysgolion. VIII: Ysgol Llanbedr', ibid., VI, no. 33 (1894), 176; Gwyneddon, 'Trem ar Eisteddfod Caerfyrddin, 1819', 111. For an assessment of the life and work of Daniel Ddu, see G. J. Williams, 'Daniel Ddu o Geredigion a'i Gyfnod', *Y Llenor*, V, no. 1 (1926), 48–59.

[19] Gwilym Hughes, 'Old Eisteddfod Medals', *Young Wales*, V, no. 53 (1899), 106.

[20] For an account of the eisteddfod at Carmarthen, said to have been held in 1453, see G. J. Williams, 'Eisteddfod Caerfyrddin', *Y Llenor*, V, no. 2 (1926), 94–102.

[21] Caradawg, 'Hanes yr Eisteddfod', 231; John Acildeca, 'Eisteddfod Caerfyrddin', *Seren Gomer*, XVII, no. 221 (1834), 39–42; Watcyn Wyn, 'Y Genedl a'r Eisteddfod, Yr Eisteddfod a'r Gadair, Y Gadair a'r Bardd', *Y Geninen*, X, no. 4 (1892), 188; Ashton, 'Gorsedd Beirdd Ynys Brydain', pp. 135–6.

[22] Ashton, 'Gorsedd Beirdd Ynys Brydain', p. 132; Eben Fardd, 'Yr Eisteddfod Farddol', *Y Traethodydd*, VI (1850), 46–59.

[23] 'The Cymmrodorion Society: The History of Eisteddfodau', *Bye-Gones*, 27 May 1885, 232; Creuddynfab, 'Yr Eisteddfod: Y Pwyllgorau', *Yr Eisteddfod*, I, no. 2 (1864), 97; T. C. Edwards, 'Eisteddfodau Canrif: Rhestr o'r prif-eisteddfodau a gynhaliwyd o'r flwyddyn 1819 hyd ddiwedd y ganrif ddiweddaf', *Cymru*, XXI, no. 120 (1901), 46–50; D. M. Richards,

part in reviving the institution of the eisteddfod was magnified beyond proportion:

> Gellir olrhain y drefn bresennol o gynnal yr eisteddfod yn ol hyd eisteddfod Caerfyrddin yn y flwyddyn 1819, pan yr adgyfodwyd hi dan ymgeledd Iolo Morganwg, Idrison, a Gwallter Mechain, ar ol bod yn farw am yn agos i gant a hanner o flynyddoedd; ac y mae pob eisteddfod ar ol hono wedi dilyn gyda mwy neu lai o fanyldra y drefn a sefydlwyd yno, gan fabwysiadu ambell ddiwygiad yn awr ac yn y man ... Beth bynag a ddywedir am Iolo Morganwg a'i gyfeillion, y mae yn ffaith anwadadwy eu bod wedi gallu rhoddi symbyliad newydd i'r sefydliad hwn, a'i fod wedi 'myn'd' gyda'r genedl a'r oes, fel yn awr y teimlir nas gellir ei ddiystyru, ond fod ynddo nerth grymus er da neu er drwg, ac y dylai gwladgarwyr a dynion goreu y genedl a'r oes ymaflyd ynddo i'w ddefnyddio er lles a daioni.[24]

(The current way of holding the eisteddfod may be traced to the eisteddfod of Carmarthen in the year 1819, when it was revived under the care of Iolo Morganwg, Idrison and Gwallter Mechain, having been dead for around a hundred and fifty years; and every eisteddfod after that one has followed, in more or less detail, the order established there, adopting the occasional reform from time to time ... Whatever is said about Iolo Morganwg and his friends, it is an undeniable fact that they have been able to give this institution a new stimulus, and that it has 'gone with' the nation and the age, so that now it is felt that it cannot be ignored, but that it is a powerful force for good or bad, and that patriots and the best men of the nation and the age should seize it and use it for benefit and good.)

Historic reality in the first half of the nineteenth century, however, was more complicated. The Anglican clergy within the Cambrian Society, which had organized the eisteddfod at Carmarthen in 1819, was the moving spirit behind the provincial eisteddfodau (*eisteddfodau taleithiol*) which were held between 1819 and 1834 by the provincial Cambrian societies.[25] Iolo was present at only one other eisteddfod, that held at Brecon in 1822, but his continuing influence was reflected in the opening ceremonies performed at eisteddfodau, while the presence of his son Taliesin, as well as supporters such as Aneurin Owen, Gwilym Morganwg and Gwallter Mechain, meant that the proceedings were suitably supervised, and that assembled throngs were made familiar with bardism.[26] The organizers of the provincial eisteddfodau sought to follow the

---

'Eisteddfodau Canrif', ibid., XXI, no. 121 (1901), 90; James Ifano Jones, 'Eisteddfod Fawr Caernarfon can' Mlynedd yn ol', *Y Geninen*, XXXIX, no. 3 (1921), 154; R. T. Jenkins, 'Hanes Cymdeithas yr Eisteddfod Genedlaethol', *THSC* (1936), 140–1.

[24] J. Eiddon Jones, 'Cyfansoddiad yr Eisteddfod Genedlaethol', *Y Traethodydd*, XXXVI (1881), 407. See also Creuddynfab, 'Yr Eisteddfod: Y Pwyllgorau', 98; Gwyneddon, 'Trem ar Eisteddfod Caerfyrddin, 1819', 110.

[25] The classic account of this movement remains Bedwyr Lewis Jones, *Yr Hen Bersoniaid Llengar* (Penarth, 1963), esp. pp. 18–31. The 'provinces' or 'chairs' of Gwynedd, Dyfed, Powys and Morgannwg (including Gwent) had been devised by Iolo Morganwg.

[26] Brychan, 'Beirdd Morganwg', *Seren Gomer*, II, no. 33 (1819), 123; *Cambrian*, 18 September 1824; 'Provincial News: Eisteddvod at Denbigh', *Cambrian Quarterly Magazine*, I, no. 1 (1829), 108; 'The Eisteddvod', ibid., IV, no. 16 (1832), 538; *HGB*, pp. 48, 99–102, 114, 117–21, 124–5.

precedent set in 1819 by attaching Gorsedd assemblies to their meetings, but they often failed.[27] Gorseddau were abandoned or postponed because doubts were expressed about the antiquity of the institution, because of threats emanating from the Anglican establishment, or because the conveners lacked the necessary bardic qualifications.[28] Of fifteen eisteddfodau organized by the provincial societies between 1819 and 1835, only seven featured a Gorsedd.

The sheer number and variety of local eisteddfodau and other literary and bardic meetings convened during the two decades after Iolo's death in 1826 threatened to overwhelm his legacy. Eisteddfodau, literary meetings (*cyrddau llenyddol*) or 'festivals' (*cylchwyliau*) were held by scores of local literary societies from London to Bethesda, by friendly societies and orders such as the Druidic Order (*Urdd y Derwyddon*) and the True Ivorites (*Y Gwir Iforiaid*), and by temperance societies like the *Cymmrodorion Dirwestol* (Temperance Cymmrodorion).[29] In the Merthyr area alone nearly a dozen societies met in public houses to hold literary meetings and eisteddfodau during the 1820s and 1830s.[30] Most of those festivals did not convene Gorseddau, but were usually accompanied by processions, religious services and dinners or even grand balls.[31] Proceedings often began with a public assembly, followed by a colourful procession to church or chapel – at which a religious service might be held – or directly to the location of the literary meeting. Until the firm establishment of the form and function of the Gorsedd associated with the National Eisteddfod in the second half of the nineteenth century, most societies used the more familiar form of the procession as the preferred public face of eisteddfodau, as they did for other celebrations, such as those held on St David's day.[32] Processions and dinners were unlikely to attract accusations of pagan idolatry and proved to be effective public high points in the urban calendar for the Welsh middle classes who organized them.[33] The Powys Cymrodorion Society chose to open its provincial eisteddfod in 1824 with a procession

---

[27] Acildeca, 'Eisteddfod Caerfyrddin', 39–42; *Seren Gomer*, XVII, no. 224 (1834), 137–9; ibid., no. 225 (1834), 167–9.

[28] HGB, pp. 75, 98–9, 112, 122, 126, 127; Edward Davies, *The Mythology and Rites of the British Druids* (London, 1809), p. 33.

[29] 'Eisteddfod Llundain', *Y Gwladgarwr*, I, no. 7 (1833), 222; Gutyn Peris, 'Cymdeithas Gymreig Bethesda, Swydd Arfon', ibid., III, no. 27 (1835), 88–90; 'Eisteddfod y Bala', ibid., IV, no. 45 (1836), 250–1; 'Cymdeithas Gymreigyddol Llangynidr', ibid., VI, no. 72 (1838), 61–2; B. Evans, 'Eisteddfod Freiniol Iforaidd Aberdar', *Seren Gomer*, XL, no. 502 (1857), 329–32.

[30] This is borne out by numerous references in the periodical press. See also E. G. Millward, 'Merthyr Tudful: Tref y Brodyr Rhagorol' in Hywel Teifi Edwards (ed.), *Merthyr a Thaf* (Llandysul, 2001), pp. 19–36; Brynley F. Roberts, 'Mab ei Dad: Taliesin ab Iolo Morganwg', ibid., pp. 71–7.

[31] 'Cymdeithas Cymreigyddol Caerdydd', *Y Gwladgarwr*, V, no. 53 (1837), 137–8; 'Cymdeithas Cymreigion Abertawy', ibid., VII, no. 73 (1839), 27–8; 'Cylchwyl Cymdeithas Gymroaidd Dolgellau', ibid., VII, no. 75 (1839), 93–4; 'Eisteddfod Llantrisant', ibid., IX, no. 98 (1841), 59; 'Cymmrodorion Merthyr Tydfil', ibid., VII, no. 81 (1839), 285.

[32] For an account of St David's day celebrations which included a procession, a dinner and an eisteddfod, see 'Gwyl Ddewi Sant', *Y Gwladgarwr*, VI, no. 64 (1838), 126–8.

[33] Gunn, *The Public Culture of the Victorian Middle Class*, p. 163.

through Welshpool, 'with the bards each wearing round his arm the colour of the rank he held'.[34] The first and second of the 'literary festivals' of Taliesin ab Iolo's Cymreigyddion society opened with processions through Merthyr from their seat at the Stonemason's Arms to the parish church, where a Welsh service was held. 'It was a joy to see Nonconformist Ministers and their members unite to sing in the house and presence of Ministers of the Established Church' ('dywenydd oedd gweled Gweinidogion Ymneillduedig a'u haelodau yn uno i ganu yn nhŷ a phresennoldeb Gweinidogion yr Eglwys Sefydledig') was the delighted comment of a writer in *Seren Gomer*. From the church, members proceeded to the town court, where a new Welsh bible had been laid out as a prize. The prospect of an adjudicator sitting in the court of justice, with 'the Book of God in front of him, to reward the persistent and the talented for the fruit of their thoughts' ('Llyfr Duw o'i flaen, i wobrwyo y diwyd a'r talentog am ffrwyth eu meddyliau') was an even greater joy to behold.[35] In many ways, this colourful display was less an expression of the poetic talents of the town's bards than a celebration of the moral superiority of its law-abiding middle class.

The ten renowned eisteddfod meetings organized by the Abergavenny Cymreigyddion Society between 1834 and 1853 – the successors of the provincial eisteddfodau – likewise featured processions and religious services much more prominently than Gorsedd meetings. Only two of their eisteddfodau – the 1838 'Breton' eisteddfod and the 1840 festival – were combined with Gorseddau, but each of them opened with an impressive procession. The festive parade held in connection with the Abergavenny eisteddfod of 1838 was reported to have involved around 2,000 people. It was led by twelve harpists sitting on a monumental platform adorned with wreaths and drawn by four black horses, two Druids wearing white gowns, the society's bard, Thomas Evan Watkins (Eiddil Ifor), bearing a leek, and William Ellis Jones (Cawrdaf) and Taliesin bearing golden axes. The other society members and visitors followed in pairs, flanked by banners bearing eisteddfodic mottoes.[36] By comparison, the Gorsedd, held on the Friday morning following the eisteddfod, and at which the Breton poet and antiquary Theodore Hersart de La Villemarqué was admitted as 'Barz Nizon', was a modest, low-key affair.[37] When *Y Gwladgarwr* printed a separate, longer description of the event in a

---

[34] Dillwyn Miles, *The Secret of the Bards of the Isle of Britain* (Llandybïe, 1992), p. 85.

[35] 'Cymdeithas Cymreigyddion Cadair Morganwg', *Seren Gomer*, XIX, no. 253 (1836), 309; 'Duw a Phob Daioni: Cadair Morganwg', ibid., XXI, no. 271 (1838), 119. The procession of the third and last festival was even more extravagant and featured carriages bearing harpists. See *HGB*, p. 134.

[36] 'Cymdeithas Lëenyddol Abergafenni', *Y Gwladgarwr*, VI, no. 71 (1838), 344–9; Gwilym Mai, 'Cymreigyddion y Fenni', ibid., XXI, no. 278 (1838), 344–5. For a sketch of the order of the 1840 procession, see 'Eisteddfod Abergarwr', *Y Gwladgarwr*, VIII, no. 95 (1840), 345–9. For other processions, see Peter Lord, *Y Chwaer Dduwies: Celf, Crefft a'r Eisteddfod* (Llandysul, 1992), pp. 15–17; Miles, *The Secret of the Bards*, p. 96.

[37] Gwilym Mai, 'Cymreigyddion y Fenni', *Seren Gomer*, XXI, no. 278 (1838), 347. For La

later issue, it did so 'because it was fairly unusual, and only happens but infrequently these years' ('gan ei bod yn un led hynod, ac yn dygwydd ond yn lled anfynych yn y blynyddoedd hyn').[38]

Whenever Gorsedd meetings continued to be held during these decades, they were often unconnected, separate or relatively small-scale affairs. 'Gorsedd Idris', which was held on the peak of Cader Idris on 7 May 1824, proved to be such a small, private assembly, wholly unconnected with any eisteddfod, that it was judged hardly worthy of mention in the press.[39] The ceremony Taliesin ab Iolo planned to conduct in connection with the grand eisteddfod held at Cardiff Castle in August 1834 was postponed until 20 September in order to coincide with the autumn equinox.[40] Even Gorseddau adjoined to grand eisteddfodau, such as the Ordovician chair eisteddfod held in Liverpool in 1840, tended to be overshadowed by more spectacular public processions and dinners. While it was estimated that the procession and the opening ceremony at Liverpool were attended by 7,000 people, the Gorsedd which assembled on the final morning could muster only 'some bards and others in the court of the old hospital' ('amryw feirdd ac ereill yng nghwrt yr hen glafdy').[41] The 'copious report' from the Aberffraw Royal Eisteddfod of 1849, which contained fifty-five pages, informed its readers that it would not attempt to describe the ceremony, except to say that it was 'of Druidical origin, and therefore associated with the most remote history and the most national impressions'.[42] The concept of the Gorsedd as a central public part of *every* eisteddfod had therefore not been firmly established. Local and regional civic pride, as well as patriotism, were most clearly expressed in addresses at public assemblies and processions.

Yet the fact that processions rather than Gorseddau constituted the public face of many eisteddfodau until the 1850s did not mean that Iolo's bardic legacy was neglected. Eisteddfodau were often officially opened by public readings of Welsh and English scrolls based on the example composed by Iolo for the Carmarthen eisteddfod of 1819. In 1833 such an 'Announcement Scroll' ('Scrôl Cyhoeddi') appeared in *Y Gwladgarwr* and the *Merthyr Guardian*

---

Villemarqué's links with Iolo's legacy, see Mary-Ann Constantine, *The Truth against the World: Iolo Morganwg and Romantic Forgery* (Cardiff, 2007), esp. 'Part III: La Villemarqué'.

[38] 'Cymdeithas Lëenyddol Abergafenni', *Y Gwladgarwr*, VI, no. 72 (1838), 373–4. Of nearly four pages of the report filed on the 1840 eisteddfod two years later, only twenty-three lines were dedicated to the Gorsedd which had been held on its last morning. See ibid., VIII, no. 95 (1840), 349.

[39] *HGB*, pp. 95, 105.

[40] 'Gorsedd Pontypridd', *Seren Gomer*, XVII, no. 230 (1834), 342; *HGB*, pp. 127–8.

[41] 'Eisteddfod Gadeiriol y Gordofigion, Yn Llerpwl, a gynnaliwyd ar yr 17eg, 18fed, 19eg, a'r 20fed o Fehefin', *Y Gwladgarwr*, VIII, no. 91 (1840), 219–24; 'Eisteddfod Llynlleifiad', *Seren Gomer*, XXIII, no. 299 (1840), 248–50. See also 'Eisteddfod Llanerch-y-medd', *Y Gwladgarwr*, III, no. 31 (1835), 201; Miles, *The Secret of the Bards*, pp. 86, 88.

[42] *Aberffraw Royal Eisteddfod August 14, 15, & 16: A Copious Report of the Three Day's Proceedings, Together with the Gorsedd* (Carnarvon, 1849), p. 45.

for all to emulate.⁴³ Moreover, Gorsedd Bards took a prominent place at the head of most processions and in other public proceedings. The opening procession normally included Gorsedd Bards, Ovates and Druids, many of whom wore blue, green and white ribbons on their arms to denote their rank. Since every Gorsedd held since 1814 had swelled the ranks of their members, the processions featured an ever-growing number of well-known literary figures such as John Jones (Talhaiarn), Daniel Evans (Daniel Ddu) and Ebenezer Thomas (Eben Fardd) and socially elevated personalities such as Augusta Hall (Lady Llanover), Lord Mostyn and Sir Robert Bulkeley, who lent the institution literary and social authority. At eisteddfodau as far north as Anglesey, festive addresses bearing titles such as 'On the Privileges of the Bards of Britain' offered short histories of Welsh bardism.⁴⁴ Iolo's name was given pride of place in speeches and ceremonies, notably in the societies founded under the patronage of Taliesin and the Chair of Glamorgan ('Cadair Morganwg' or 'Cadair Tir Iarll') in south Wales.⁴⁵ Apart from maintaining Iolo's tradition by convening Gorseddau at the Rocking-stone circle, Taliesin and his followers disseminated Iolo's ideas through the literary societies affiliated to the Chair of Glamorgan, as well as through publications and orations at eisteddfodau. The literary society which Taliesin established in 1821 was named 'The Society of the Chair of Merthyr Tydfil, in the right of the Chair and the Assembly of the Lordship of Glamorgan, and Gwent and Erging and Euas, and Ystrad Yw' ('Cymdeithas Cadair Merthyr Tudfyl, ym mraint Cadair a Gorsedd Pendefigaeth Morganwg, a Gwent, ac Erging ac Euas, a Ystrad Yw').⁴⁶ Its avowed aim, and that of its branches, was to style the Chair of Merthyr 'as close as possible to genuine ancient usage'.⁴⁷ Its Gorseddau, held under the auspices of Taliesin, who had become the accepted authority on matters bardic following his father's death, maintained a direct line of tradition through the bewildering variety of literary festivals held during the first half of the nineteenth century. Moreover, he acted as first president of the Abergavenny eisteddfodau in 1834, and adjudicated there in 1835, 1838 and 1845, a privilege which did not prevent him from submitting entries to competitions – and making off with prizes!⁴⁸ He was the celebrated 'Welsh Secretary' ('Ysgrifennydd Cymraeg') of the Gwent and Dyfed Royal Eisteddfod and

---

⁴³ 'Eisteddfod Frenhinol Gwent a Dyfed', *Y Gwladgarwr*, I, no. 10 (1833), 315.
⁴⁴ Ab Ithel, 'Miscellaneous Notices: Machraeth Eisteddfod, Anglesey', *Cambrian Journal*, II (1855), 152–6. The address was given by Beaver Davies (Cuhelyn Môn).
⁴⁵ Evan Davies, 'Anerchiad a draddodwyd yn Neuadd Tref Pontyfon, ar Ail Gylchwyl Cymdeithas Cymreigyddol Cadair Morganwg', *Seren Gomer*, XXI, no. 273 (1838), 167.
⁴⁶ Roberts, 'Mab ei Dad' in Edwards (ed.), *Merthyr a Thaf*, p. 72.
⁴⁷ Ibid., p. 74; NLW 21286E, letter no. 698. For Iolo's role in the society, see, for instance, 'Cadair Merthyr Tydfil Eisteddfod Gwyl yr Alban Elfed (Medi 20, 1826)', *Seren Gomer*, IX, no. 128 (1826), 154; 'Sefydliad Cymdeithasau Cymmroaidd', ibid., XVIII, no. 232 (1835), 24–5.
⁴⁸ 'Cylchwyl Gyntaf Cymdeithas Cymmreigyddion y Fenni', Mercher 26 Tachwedd 1834, Gwesty'r Haul', ibid., XVIII, no. 232 (1835), 23–4. See also Roberts, 'Mab ei Dad' in Edwards (ed.), *Merthyr a Thaf*, pp. 77–9.

Musical Festival held at Cardiff in 1834, for which he composed and published the announcement scroll.[49] On 21 August 1834 he opened this eisteddfod in the presence of patrons like the marquess of Bute, the duchess of Kent and Princess Victoria, according to the 'traditional ritual of such occasions' ('defodau arferedig y cyfryw achlysur'), and was rewarded with the chair for his successful poem.[50] In the same year, at the pinnacle of his eisteddfodic career, he passed on the baton by admitting to the bardic order a member of his own literary society – Evan Davies (Myfyr Morganwg) – who had taken an enduring and, perhaps even deeper, interest in bardism than Taliesin himself.[51]

## Rocking-stone Gorseddau and poetic minstrelsy

Myfyr Morganwg, who was raised at Pen-coed, Glamorgan, claimed to have received no formal education. He taught himself astronomy, Welsh poetry and enough mathematics to style himself a watchmaker when he settled in Pontypridd around 1846.[52] Said to have come to the attention of Iolo at an early age, he was admitted to the Gorsedd by Taliesin at the Rocking-stone during the spring equinox assembly of 1834.[53] Under Myfyr Morganwg's leadership, the Cymreigyddion of the Chair of Glamorgan held eisteddfodau in 1837, 1838 and 1839, and resumed the tradition of convening Gorseddau at the Rocking-stone.[54] The society then fell silent until 1847 when, upon the death of Taliesin, Myfyr pronounced himself his successor as 'Archdruid of the Bards of the Isle of Britain' and renewed his interest in the Gorsedd.[55] His efforts centred on the Rocking-stone (also known as 'Y Maen Chwŷf', 'Carreg

---

[49] 'Eisteddfod Frenhinol Gwent a Dyfed', *Y Gwladgarwr*, I, no. 10 (1833), 315.

[50] 'Eisteddfodau', ibid., II, no. 13 (1834), 28; 'Eisteddfod Frenhinol Gwent a Dyfed. Y Diwrnod Cyntaf', ibid., II, no. 21 (1834), 288; 'Eisteddfod Caerdyf', *Seren Gomer*, XVI, no. 217 (1833), 310–11; 'Eisteddfod Caerdyf', ibid., XVII, no. 229 (1834), 298; R. D. (Bardd Nantglyn), 'Anerchiad i Feirdd a Chymreigyddion Merthyr Tydfil, a'r amgylchoedd, wedi Eisteddfod Caerdyf, Awst, 1834', ibid., XVIII, no. 237 (1835), 179.

[51] 'Gorsedd Pontypridd', ibid., XVI, no. 230 (1834), 342. Like Iolo, Myfyr Morganwg had a penchant for bardic names, using 'Ieuan ap Dafydd', 'Ioan Morganwg', 'Ieuan Morganwg', 'Ieuan Myfyr Uwch Celli' and, ultimately, 'Myfyr Morganwg'. See Miles, *The Secret of the Bards*, p. 71.

[52] Morgan, *History of Pontypridd and Rhondda Valleys*, pp. 82–7; Huw Walters, 'Pontypridd a'r Cylch: Gwlad Beirdd a Derwyddon' in idem, *Cynnwrf Canrif: Agweddau ar Ddiwylliant Gwerin*, pp. 237–9.

[53] See p. 49.

[54] 'Cymdeithas Cymreigyddion Cadair Morganwg', *Seren Gomer*, XIX, no. 253 (1837), 309–10; 'Duw a Phob Daioni: Cadair Morganwg', ibid., XXI, no. 271 (1838), 118–20; 'Cadair Morganwg', ibid., XXII, no. 284 (1839), 151.

[55] This new title became part of the Gorsedd of the Bards of the Isle of Britain later in the century. See Geraint Bowen, 'Archdderwydd: Y Teitl a'r Swydd', *NLWJ*, XXIV, no. 3 (1986), 358–88.

Siglo' and 'Logan Stone'), which stood on the mountainside at Pentre-bach in the parish of Eglwysilan just east of Pontypridd, the location of Iolo's first Gorseddau in post-war Wales. In June 1848 Myfyr supervised the enlargement of the site by using ideas derived from his studies of William Jones's *Asiatick Researches*.[56] The site was enhanced by enclosing it with two circles of standing stones and by adding a stone 'serpent' avenue and various other boulders in the shape of the mystic sign – *y nod cyfrin*.[57] From 1849 it became the location of his Gorsedd ritual, which was held up to four times annually over a period of twenty-five years, and which attracted admiration, criticism and satire in equal measures.[58] Although Myfyr's references to Iolo's anti-war stance were lost on the crowd, his first ceremonies were well received, if only as entertaining spectacles. Heavily advertised, they attracted large numbers of people:

> About the year 1853 he had small posters distributed throughout Pontypridd announcing that at the next Sunday nearest the Summer Solstice (June 21), a prophecy spoken by Isaiah 3,000 years ago would be fulfilled on the Pontypridd Rocking-stone. This excited great curiosity, for however Myvyr might be mistaken about religion, no one doubted his veracity and earnestness. Next Sunday, many hundreds of people were seen climbing to the Common to witness the fulfilment ... As the Sun was approaching the meridian that day a carriage containing two long white poles was seen coming towards the sanctuary of the Stone Age. There was Myvyr, and there also were several well-known local men, each like Myvyr himself, suspected of having buzzying noises in their ears ... The Archdruid now cried in a loud sonorous voice: – 'Behold! swords converted into ploughshares, and spears into pruning hooks!' The great throng seemed puzzled; some laughed, others jeered, but others clapped their hands, and cried, 'Bravo Myvyr; it is full time to fulfil that long deferred prophecy.' People returned to the town highly amused, and spread the news as to how Isaiah's credit had been saved on the Common that day.[59]

The continuation of these ceremonies, however, was jeopardized not only by the post-Blue Books paranoia of the Welsh, but also by more general mid-Victorian concerns over the appearance of its citizenry in public spaces. Myfyr's rituals offended the religious sensibilities of most of his contemporaries and annoyed others by their eccentricity (Document 9).[60] Even the editors of

---

[56] Morgan, *History of Pontypridd and Rhondda Valleys*, p. 88.
[57] Myfyr Morganwg, 'Cyhoeddiad Eisteddfod ac Agoriad Gorsedd Beirdd Ynys Prydain, ar y Maen Chwyf, o fewn Cylch Swynion Ceridwen, ar lan y Taf, Meh. 21ain, 1849', *Seren Gomer*, XXXII, no. 408 (1849), 283–6. For details of the stonework, see Roy Denning, 'Druidism at Pontypridd' in Stewart Williams (ed.), *Glamorgan Historian: Volume I* (Cowbridge, 1963), pp. 139–40 and Walters, 'Pontypridd a'r Cylch' in idem, *Cynnwrf Canrif*, p. 242.
[58] Myfyr Morganwg, 'Cyhoeddiad Eisteddfod ac Agoriad Gorsedd Beirdd Ynys Prydain'; Ysbryd Iolo Morganwg, 'Gofyniadau at Mr Evan Davies (Ieuan Myfyr), Pontypridd', ibid., XXXIV, no. 429 (1851), 270–1; 'Myfyr Meg y Sarff Dorchog', *Y Punch Cymraeg*, III, no. 81 (1864), 3; 'Congress of Bards, Pontypridd', *Cambrian Journal*, III (1856), 201–4.
[59] Morgan, *History of Pontypridd and Rhondda Valleys*, pp. 89–90. For a detailed contemporary description in English, see 'Gorsedd Beirdd Ynys Prydain', *Cambrian Journal*, IV (1857), 310–12.
[60] Callwr Cellweirus, 'Gorsedd Beirdd Ynys Humbug', *Seren Gomer*, XXXVIII, no. 479 (1855),

*Seren Gomer*, who had provided a ready platform for Iolo's ideas over a considerable period, found Myfyr's religious transgressions too outlandish to be tolerated, and used the preface to the thirty-eighth volume to distance themselves from his antics:

> Cafodd yr Athronydd, Hanesydd, Duwinydd, Dychymmygydd, Bardd, ac hyd y nod y Breuddwydydd ofergoelus, *chwarae têg*. Etto i gyd, gwerthfawrogwn, ac amddiffynwn y ffydd gyssegredig – 'y ffydd a roddwyd unwaith i'r saint' – uwchlaw pob peth. Boddlonasom i Sarff y Maen Chwyf chwarae ei champiau, cyrdeddu ei thröadau, a chonstro ei gwingiadau ger ein bron; ond pan amcanodd frathu, a rhwygo y ffydd, derbyniasom ei cholyn ar ein tarian, troisom hi o'r gampfa, i fyw neu farw, fel y myno ei hun; canys ni feiddiwn amcanu at niweidio, heb sôn am ladd, hyd y nod sarff dorchog.[61]

> (The Philosopher, Historian, Magician, Fantasist, Poet, and even the superstitious Dreamer, have all received *fair play*. Nevertheless, we appreciate, and defend the sacred faith – 'the faith which was once given to the saints' – above all else. We were willing for the Snake of the Rocking-stone to show its feats, writhe its turnings, and construe its windings before us, but when it began to bite, and tear the faith apart, we received its sting on our shield, and turned it out of our playing field, to live or die, as it wished; because we would not dare to harm, let alone speak of killing, even the coiled snake.)

'Goachul' summed up the feelings of many when he wrote in the same year that he had tired of Myfyr's eccentric performance because it was inimical to progress and encouraged blasphemy and faithlessness.[62] But in spite of their exclusion from the ranks of the respectable, Myfyr Morganwg and his circle of Pontypridd bards continued to hold Gorseddau at the Rocking-stone until 1878.[63] Given their notoriety, it is remarkable how many famous literary figures, including Robert Ellis (Cynddelw) and John Ceiriog Hughes (Ceiriog), fell under their spell, and allowed themselves to be admitted to the Gorsedd at such meetings. For over thirty years, Myfyr Morganwg thus not only engendered publicity for the institution of the Gorsedd, which might otherwise have been forgotten, but also ensured that the majority of poets active in south Wales counted themselves members of the Gorsedd in a period when the eisteddfod itself became a national institution.[64]

---

382; 'Llythyrau Cyfrinachol Rhwng William Thomas, o'r Dyffryn, a Dafydd Jones, o'r Bryn: Llythyr I', ibid., XXXIX, no. 487 (1856), 172; 'Llythyrau Cyfrinachol Rhwng William Thomas, o'r Dyffryn, a Dafydd Jones, o'r Bryn: Llythyr IV', ibid., XXXIX, no. 493 (1856), 452–6.

[61] 'Rhagymadrodd', ibid., XXXVIII (1855), iii.
[62] Goachul, 'Ieuan Myfyr a'i "Nod Cyfrin"', ibid., XXXVIII, no. 472 (1855), 29.
[63] For an analysis of the Rocking-stone Gorseddau, see Walters, 'Pontypridd a'r Cylch' in idem, *Cynnwrf Canrif*, pp. 184–274; idem, 'Myfyr Morganwg and the Rocking-stone Gorsedd' in *Rattleskull Genius*, pp. 481–500.
[64] *HGB*, pp. 178–80.

A second, less well-known, development in Iolo's bardic legacy arose in direct response to the increasing influence of Anglicization and materialism on the National Eisteddfod in north Wales in the 1860s. On 3 August 1863 William John Roberts (Gwilym Cowlyd), who had been admitted as a Bard at the National 'Reform' Eisteddfod of Denbigh in 1860, held a 'Poetic Picnic on the Shores of Geirionydd' ('Arwest Farddonol Glan Geirionydd'). Gwilym Cowlyd was a celebrated eisteddfod poet and a respected critic who corresponded with well-known literary figures, such as Ceiriog, Talhaiarn, Trebor Mai and Gwalchmai, and attracted considerable support in literary circles in north Wales.[65] At the age of twenty-three, he had won the chair at the National Eisteddfod at Conwy in 1861, but this experience and that at other eisteddfodau had left him uneasy over the lack of any settled rules for the bardic institution and the worldliness of its proceedings.[66] Between 1863 and 1904 the legendary birthplace of Taliesin became the location of an annual eisteddfod and Gorsedd which, unlike the emerging National Eisteddfod, strictly followed the bardic statute of Gruffudd ap Cynan and emphasized learning, religion and the use of the Welsh language above all else. Cowlyd used the bardic degrees described by Iolo, and the only prizes available at his Gorseddau were small silver chairs and bardic degrees. He even adhered to the tripartite division of the Gorsedd which Iolo had devised.[67] In spirit, his meetings came closer to upholding the legacy of Primrose Hill than any other bardic development in the nineteenth century. Gwilym Cowlyd, it was argued, 'did for North Wales what Iolo Morganwg had done for the South through his assertions and his imagination'.[68] His elaborate Gorsedd rules and simple ceremonies, which were a far cry from the civic pomp of urban eisteddfodau, were an inspiration to many Welsh patriots. Even more important than his festival, however, were his incessant, if at times eccentric, attacks on the Anglophone nature of the National Eisteddfod and its disregard for the sociocultural status of the native tongue.[69] Although the popularity of Cowlyd's 'Arwest' declined from the 1880s, the address given by the poet and satirist R. A. Griffith (Elphin) at the *Arwest Farddonol* which followed Cowlyd's death sharply contrasted the aims and objectives of both institutions:

> Pride went before a fall. The National Eisteddfod was a sad instance of this. Puffed with conceit and smothered with English affectations, it had almost degenerated into a big show in which the Welsh language and its literature were held of small account.

[65] G. Gerallt Davies, *Gwilym Cowlyd, 1828–1904* (Caernarfon, 1976), pp. 27, 30–1, 76–112.
[66] Until Cowlyd set up as a publisher, printer and bookseller in Llanrwst in 1862, he had worked in a variety of positions in Liverpool and its docks. He was declared bankrupt later in life, was evicted from his house in 1897, and died a poor man in 1904. See ibid., chapter 3.
[67] For an outline of the history, see *HGB*, pp. 187–95.
[68] Davies, *Gwilym Cowlyd*, p. 156.
[69] Ibid., chapter 3. See, for instance, his pamphlet *Gair Ionydd yn erbyn Cabledd Baal Sef Barddas Dragwyddol 'Iesu' yn erbyn Twyll Dderwyddiaeth, Eisteddfodaeth Fasnachol Beirdd Beli* (Llanrwst, 1896).

If this state of things continued, he for one would be inclined to call upon the little Arwest at Llyn Geirionydd to wipe out the great National Eisteddfod of Wales.[70]

The Gorseddau of Myfyr Morganwg and Gwilym Cowlyd were discontinued following their demise, but Iolo's ideas remained an integral part of the bardic legacy. By convening regular Gorseddau at which Bards, Ovates and Druids were admitted, they sustained the practice which Iolo had initiated and thus contributed to the process of turning both the eisteddfod and the Gorsedd into truly national institutions and exporting bardism to all corners of the world.

## Llangollen 1858

From the 1830s onwards the Oxford-educated Anglican priest John Williams (Ab Ithel, 1811–62) devoted considerable time to mediating Iolo Morganwg's historical and bardic vision.[71] Inspired by the *Iolo Manuscripts*, which had been published in 1848, and by the unpublished writings of Iolo Morganwg which he had consulted at Llanover Court, he began to take practical steps to popularize the eisteddfod and the Gorsedd among the rural population of north Wales. To his dismay, however, the prejudice he encountered among the rural population was even more deep-seated than the problems raised by Myfyr Morganwg's eccentricities in urban Pontypridd. When Ab Ithel began to organize his first eisteddfod at Dinas Mawddwy in 1855, most of the farmers in the area had little sympathy and enthusiasm for such 'silly old meetings' ('hen gyfarfodydd dwl') and their birchen-wreathed participants.[72] Some of them feared that divine punishment would descend on those who participated, and the fact that it rained for weeks before the Dinas Mawddwy eisteddfod in August 1855 did nothing to allay those fears; nor did the fact that 'Evan Serfel', the carpenter responsible for the pavilion which was damaged by high winds and rain, died soon afterwards 'of a broken heart'.[73] Undeterred by this setback Ab Ithel set in train a truly national event designed to unite the whole of Wales behind its bardic heritage – the 'Grand Eisteddfod' held at Llangollen on 21–24 September 1858. This landmark event was designed to:

> adhere as closely as possible to the orthodox rules and customs of bardism, which, with respect to the Gorsedd and the national congress always accompanying it, are defined and established, and the principal aim of which is the elevation of the social,

---

[70] *West Coast Pioneer*, 8 September 1905.
[71] See Chapter 4. For an overview of Ab Ithel's life and work, see Jones, *Yr Hen Bersoniaid Llengar*, pp. 42–5.
[72] John Williams, 'Miscellaneous Notices: Dinas Mawddwy Eisteddfod', *Cambrian Journal*, II (1855), 248–52.
[73] Charles Ashton, 'Eisteddfod Dinas Mawddwy, 1855', *Y Geninen*, X, no. 4 (1892), 184; J. J., 'Hen Eisteddfodau: Dinas Mawddwy, 1855', ibid., XXIV, no. 4 (1905), 265–7.

moral, and religious status of the people of Wales, the encouragement of nationality, the perpetuation of the Cymraeg, and the cultivation of Welsh literature, Welsh music, &c.[74]

Ab Ithel used the whole gamut of the Welsh press to advertise his plans and detailed programmes were published so successfully that north Wales and Liverpool were soon 'boiling with excitement', not least over the prospect of seeing the bards dressed in novel 'uniforms of blue silk'.[75] By choosing Llangollen as the location, Ab Ithel was able to maximize the advantages of cheap transport offered by the recently expanded railway links and to display 'monster placards' in railway stations.[76] He took the opportunity in the opening session to give a detailed account of the history of bardism and to enact a Gorsedd ritual which could be emulated in the future (Document 10). He gave pride of place to the *nod cyfrin* and eisteddfodic mottoes on all banners and decorations in a pavilion which held 5,000 people and which was open to the public for four days, as well as in the grand processions which were widely reported in the press.[77] Unfortunately, he also used his authority to promote the interests of his own family and friends, and to curtail those of his enemies as well as Iolo's critics. The prize for the best essay on 'Barddas' was awarded to Ab Ithel by his fellow-organizers and devotees of Iolo, Myfyr Morganwg and D. Silvan Evans (Hirlas).[78] Both of Ab Ithel's children also won prizes. His son was the only competitor for the £10 awarded for the best 'Map of Wales, *tempore* Llewelyn ap Griffith' and his twenty-year-old daughter won £10 for the 'Fullest Collection of unpublished Welsh Proverbs', which she confessed to having copied from her father's collections.[79]

The most controversial incident, however, occurred when the prize for the best essay on the Welsh Indians in America was withheld.[80] The successful

---

[74] John Williams, 'Gorsedd of the Bards of the Isle of Britain; the Royal Chair of Powys; and the Grand Eisteddfod held at Llangollen on Alban Elfed, 1858', *Cambrian Journal*, V (1858), 262. This exposition, drawn from well-meaning press reports, provided the fullest account of the event. Since it was compiled by Ab Ithel himself, critical voices were absent. See also Miles, *The Secret of the Bards*, pp. 99–100; Jones, *Yr Hen Bersoniaid Llengar*, pp. 45–8.

[75] Y Llais o'r Foel, 'Eisteddfod Llangollen', *Y Brython*, I, no. 10 (1858), 151. Advertisements included 'Miscellaneous Notices: The Llangollen Eisteddfod, 1858', *Cambrian Journal*, IV (1857), 231–3; 'Beirniaid Eisteddfod Llangollen' and 'Eisteddfod Llangollen: Alban Elfed, 1858. Hyspyslen o Weithrediadau Bob Dydd', *Y Brython*, I, no. 12 (1858), 177–83.

[76] J. Iorwerth Roberts, 'Eisteddfod Fawr Llangollen, 1858', *Transactions of the Denbighshire Historical Society*, VIII (1959), 136–46; Hywel Teifi Edwards, '"Yr Eisteddfod": 1859–68' in idem, *Gŵyl Gwalia: Yr Eisteddfod yn Oes Aur Victoria 1858–1868* (Llandysul, 1980), p. 42. The importance of transport was highlighted, for instance, by the lack of visitors from Anglesey and the north-west coast because of the absence of free trains from there, although they had been organized from elsewhere. See *Y Brython*, I, no. 14 (1858), 209.

[77] *Cambrian*, 8 October 1858; *Yr Herald Cymraeg*, 2 October 1858; *North Wales Chronicle*, 25 September 1858.

[78] Williams, 'Gorsedd of the Bards of the Isle of Britain; the Royal Chair of Powys; and the Grand Eisteddfod held at Llangollen On Alban Elfed, 1858', 276.

[79] Ibid., 299; 'Eisteddfod Fawr Llangollen', *Seren Gomer*, XLI, no. 519 (1858), 548.

[80] Gwyn A. Williams, *Madoc: The Making of a Myth* (London, 1979).

essay, written by Thomas Stephens of Merthyr, was deemed inadmissible because, having argued that the Madoc tale was a recent invention, it had neglected to address the subject.[81] To make matters worse, Stephens's protestations on the final evening were drowned when, to the fury of the audience, a brass band was ordered to play 'God Save the Queen'.[82] Although Stephens's pungent public criticisms of bardism had not endeared him to the Welsh in the past, the abominable behaviour of the organizers brought the eisteddfod into grave disrepute and left it vulnerable to vilification.[83] Llangollen was held responsible for the lack of support for the 'Reform Eisteddfod' of Denbigh of 1860, which was held without a Gorsedd because it had 'raised hatred in the thoughts of the country against the innocent old traditions and wisdoms of the pure old Welsh' ('y magwyd casineb yn meddyliau y wlad yn erbyn hen arferion diniwed a gwybodau yr hen Gymmry diledryw').[84] But the passing of time changed perspectives, and by the end of the nineteenth century Ab Ithel had redeemed himself and was considered 'the father of the eisteddfod in its present form', while the Llangollen eisteddfod was hailed as the event which 'marked a new era in the history of the institution'.[85] Whatever the immediate aftermath, which owed as much to the shadow cast over Wales by the 'Treachery of the Blue Books' as it did to Llangollen's own failings, Ab Ithel had shown how to organize all aspects of a national event on a grand scale – including advertising, transport and a pavilion – without having to rely on the sponsorship of the local gentry.[86] He had designed a robe for Gorsedd members which served as a model for the costume designed by Hubert von Herkomer in the 1890s. Above all, he had staged a national Gorsedd ceremony which was closely modelled on Iolo's writings and which included a stone circle, the ritual of unsheathing and sheathing a sword, and the declaiming of the Gorsedd prayer (Document 10).[87] He had also set in train the establishment of the

---

[81] 'Eisteddfod Fawr Llangollen', *Seren Gomer*, XLI, no. 518 (1858), 520–1. Thomas Stephens outlined the history of the competition and included quotations from the judges D. Silvan Evans, Myfyr Morganwg, the Revd T. James (Llallawg), and from Ab Ithel, in 'Eisteddfod Llangollen', *Seren Gomer*, XLI, no. 518 (1858), 539–42. For Ab Ithel's letter to the press, see 'Eisteddfod Fawr Llangollen', *Y Geninen*, XXVI, no. 4 (1908), 265–6.

[82] 'Eisteddfod Llangollen Etto', *Seren Gomer*, XLII, no. 524 (1859), 217.

[83] Robert Ellis (Cynddelw), 'Eisteddfod Fawr Llangollen', *Y Geninen*, XXVI, no. 4 (1908), 266–8. For further criticisms, see G. J. Williams, 'Eisteddfod Llangollen 1858', *Transactions of the Denbighshire Historical Society*, VII (1958), 155.

[84] 'Eisteddfod Llangollen Etto', 216. See also 'Eisteddfod Fawr Llangollen', *Seren Gomer*, XLI, no. 518 (1858), 503–4; 'Eisteddfod Fawr Llangollen', ibid., XLI, no. 519 (1858), 547; Williams, 'Eisteddfod Llangollen 1858', 158.

[85] Charles Ashton, 'Welsh Literature of the Victorian period', *Young Wales*, III (1897), 168; T. R. Roberts, *The Eisteddfod: A Short History of the Gorsedd of the Bards of the Isle of Britain and of the National Eisteddfod of Wales with Notes on the Colwyn Bay Gorsedd Circle* (Chester, 1909), p. 41. See also Rhuddenfab, 'Adgofion am Eisteddfod Fawr Llangollen', *Y Geninen*, XXV, no. 3 (1907), 204–6; Morleisfab, 'Gwyl Fawr Llangollen yn 1858', ibid., XXX, no. 2 (1912), 102; *Cof-a-Chadw am Wyl Fawr 1858. Y Prif Fuddugwyr: Eu Llun a'u Gorchest* (Lerpwl, 1908).

[86] Roberts, 'Eisteddfod Fawr Llangollen, 1858', 136–46.

[87] Ibid., 146–9.

National Eisteddfod movement by providing, in a 'Cambrian Tent' set up for the duration of his eisteddfod, a forum for discussion.[88] This Bardic Session (*Seiat y Beirdd*), which was attended by up to fifty poets, discussed Welsh orthography and forced Myfyr Morganwg to defend those of his doctrines which were 'not entirely in harmony with the Christian religion'. In its final session it voiced the need to establish a national society which would bring together the Bards, Ovates and Druids of the different chairs, provinces and Gorseddau into one society which should organize an annual national eisteddfod.[89] This was the foundation on which the National Eisteddfod and the Gorsedd of the Bards of the Isle of Britain were built: two closely linked national institutions conducted along modern lines, but also dedicated to the romantic visualization of the ancient national history.

## National reform and romance

In his preface to the fifth volume of *Y Brython*, the editor Robert Isaac Jones (Alltud Eifion) maintained that he had always endeavoured to sustain the main elements of Welsh nationality – 'the Harp, the Gorsedd, and the Language' ('y Delyn, yr Orsedd, a'r Iaith') – without which the Welsh people would become slaves to English prejudice.[90] In order to be counted among the emerging nations in mid-nineteenth-century Europe, Wales clearly required substantial national institutions of its own, but in the absence of more conventional forms it had no choice but to reform the National Eisteddfod and the Gorsedd until they fulfilled the requirements of a modern nation, thereby deflecting English criticism and the threat of cultural incorporation. In order to educate the nation, the well-known civil servant and educationist Sir Hugh Owen furnished the National Eisteddfod with a 'Science Section' and classical concerts were introduced to display its urbanity.[91] According to Lleurwg, the importance of the eisteddfod for the Welsh middle classes lay not in 'fanning

---

[88] Williams, 'Eisteddfod Llangollen 1858', 156; Roberts, 'Eisteddfod Fawr Llangollen, 1858', 150.

[89] Ab Ithel, 'Yr Orsedd a'r Eisteddfod', *Taliesin: sef Cylchgrawn Chwarterol at Wasanaeth y Cymdeithasau Llenyddol, yr Eisteddfodau, a'r Orsedd yng Nghymru*, I, no. 3 (1859), 199–200; idem, 'Diwygiad yr Eisteddfod', ibid., II, no. 7 (1860), 220; Creuddynfab, 'Yr Eisteddfod', *Yr Eisteddfod: sef Cyhoeddiad Chwarterol y Sefydliad Cenedlaethol*, I, no. 1 (1864), 2–3. See also *Y Faner*, 31 September 1858; Roberts, 'Eisteddfod Fawr Llangollen, 1858', 149–50.

[90] 'Rhag-Gyfarchiad', *Y Brython*, V (1862–3), i.

[91] This chapter considers only those aspects of the National Eisteddfod relevant to the development of the Gorsedd as the direct heir to Iolo's bardism. The most important studies on the development of the eisteddfod in the second half of the nineteenth century remain R. T. Jenkins, 'Hanes Cymdeithas yr Eisteddfod Genedlaethol', *THSC* (1936), 139–55, and Hywel Teifi Edwards, *Gŵyl Gwalia*, together with the latter's numerous articles on individual eisteddfodau, especially idem, 'The Merthyr Tydfil National Eisteddfod, 1881', *Merthyr Historian*, X (1999), 81–5. For a statistical account of the growth of the eisteddfod movement, see Jones, *Statistical Evidence Relating to the Welsh Language 1801–1911*, pp. 483–97.

the flames of patriotism',[92] but rather in the promotion of scholarship and the sciences 'in the vanguard of every present form of scholarship, academia and college learning' ('o flaen pob ffurf bresenol o ysgoloriaeth, academyddiaeth a cholegyddiaeth').[93] The Gorsedd, on the other hand, served the purpose of linking Wales with a venerable past that stretched back beyond Christianity, a rather dubious claim made by Joshua Hughes, bishop of St Asaph, in his opening address to the National Eisteddfod at Wrexham in 1876:

> A sound principle in the management of the affairs of any country [was], not to sever the present from the past. There are countries now existing that have entirely broken with the past and they are reaping the sad results of their mistake; but the ancient Cymry give you an illustration here this day of the fixedness of this principle in their minds and of their determination to act upon it as long as divine Providence may continue to bless them as a people upon this earth. What we see existed, shall I say, eighteen hundred years ago? I go still further back; it is said that bardism, as a part of the eisteddfod, actually existed 750 years before the Christian era. (Cheers.)[94]

This twofold nature of Wales's claim to nationhood explains the apparently divergent developments of the modern National Eisteddfod of Wales and Iolo's ancient Gorsedd of the Bards of the Isle of Britain, and their seemingly paradoxical marriage.[95] The steps taken at the Llangollen Eisteddfod to organize a 'National Institution' ('Sefydliad Cenedlaethol') led to the submission of four different reports to the National Eisteddfod of Denbigh in 1860. The first had been commissioned from William Williams (Creuddynfab) and Thomas Jones (Glan Alun) at Llangollen in 1858, but three further reports were submitted by John Ambrose Lloyd, the Revd William Jones (Myfyr Môn) and William Morris (Gwilym Tawe).[96] These highlighted the interest in developing a national festival, and – despite some differences – led to the foundation of a General Eisteddfod Council in August 1860 which was composed of poets and authors from north and south Wales, who chose an executive committee and decided on the subscriptions required to finance this new national institution.[97] Its most important resolution was to unite the eisteddfod by convening an annual festival alternately in the north and south, and to appoint Creuddynfab as its general secretary.[98] Without mentioning the Gorsedd, it also ruled,

---

[92] Lleurwg, 'Defnyddioldeb yr Eisteddfod: Araeth a Draddodwyd yn Eisteddfod Genedlaethol Caerfyrddin, 1863', *Y Geninen*, II, no. 1 (1884), 62.
[93] Cynfaen, 'Gweriniaeth yr Eisteddfod', ibid., II, no. 1 (1884), 39.
[94] 'The National Eisteddfod of 1876 at Wrexham', *Y Cymmrodor*, I (1877), 46; 'The Wrexham Eisteddfod: Bishop of St Asaph's Address', *Bye-Gones*, 23 August 1876, 101; *HBC*, p. 297.
[95] The power struggles between the National Eisteddfod, the Gorsedd and local committees over the National Eisteddfod movement, which added a tempestuous element to Iolo's bardic legacy, are not discussed here.
[96] Creuddynfab, 'Yr Eisteddfod', *Yr Eisteddfod: Sef Cyhoeddiad Chwarterol y Sefydliad Cenedlaethol*, I, no. 1 (1864), 2–3.
[97] *Baner ac Amserau Cymru*, 15 August 1860.
[98] Creuddynfab, 'Yr Eisteddfod', 3; idem, 'Yr Eisteddfod: Y Pwyllgorau', 100–1.

among other things, that Gorsedd ceremonies should be preserved undefiled in the form of examinations for aspiring Ovates and Bards (while Druids were to be admitted without examination by virtue of their offices as religious ministers). In his summary of the new regulations, Creuddynfab even printed the design of a certificate of admittance which was headed by Iolo's *nod cyfrin* and the mottoes of the four eisteddfod provinces, and which confirmed that the candidate in question had been admitted 'according to the Privilege and Custom of the Bards of the Isle of Britain' ('wrth Fraint a Defod Beirdd Ynys Prydain').[99]

The first series of annual national eisteddfodau held on the basis of the new regulations, which began in Aberdare in 1861, ran out of steam in 1868 because of financial difficulties and because of a north–south rivalry which prompted the emergence of northern 'counter-eisteddfodau' during those years when the National Eisteddfod was held in the south.[100] The decline of the Eisteddfod council, however, did not undermine the idea of a National Eisteddfod, but rather marked a stage in the development of the eisteddfod as a national institution which, over the following decades, was reformed more than once in order to respond to criticisms of 'perpetuating the Welsh language' from some quarters and of Anglicizing Wales from others.[101] A second series of eisteddfodau, described as 'national' by the press, were held at locations in north Wales between 1869 and 1880. In 1873 one of the nation's heroes, the poet John Ceiriog Hughes (Ceiriog), instigated the foundation of *Y Vord Gron* (The Round Table) 'to render the Eisteddvod more useful, and Gorsedd honours more honourable, and more beneficial to those who will live to love their country after us'.[102] A permanent 'National Eisteddfod Association', among whose tasks was the duty of 'upholding the authority of the Gorsedd', was established on 26 August 1880.[103] The provisional committee which was established to spell out its remit included Sir Hugh Owen, but also both the present and future archdruids, David Griffith (Clwydfardd) and Rowland Williams (Hwfa Môn), as well as members of *Y Vord Gron*, such as Ceiriog.[104] The association first met in Merthyr Tydfil on 31 August 1881, where it confirmed the arrangement of raising funds towards the eisteddfod, holding national eisteddfodau alternately in north and south Wales, publishing the transactions of each National Eisteddfod and, crucially, upholding the authority of the Gorsedd.[105] The establishment of the National Eisteddfod Association

---

[99] Idem, 'Yr Eisteddfod: Yr Urddau', *Yr Eisteddfod*, I, no. 3 (1864), 194–8.

[100] Edwards, '"Yr Eisteddfod": 1859–68' in idem, *Gŵyl Gwalia*, pp. 1–52; *HGB*, pp. 198–202. See also the cartoon on the subject 'Yspeilio'r Eisteddfod', *Y Punch Cymraeg*, no. 83 (1864), 5.

[101] Edwards, *Gŵyl Gwalia*, pp. 300–78; Miles, *The Secret of the Bards*, p. 108; Clive Betts, *A Oedd Heddwch?* (Caerdydd, 1978), pp. 38–66.

[102] Vord Gron, *The Key to the Master-Key: pro tem (Agoriad yr Arch-oriad)* (Wrexham, 1874), p. 12; Ashton, 'Gorsedd Beirdd Ynys Brydain', p. 145.

[103] The National Eisteddfod Association, *First Annual Report* (London, 1881), pp. 2–4.

[104] Ibid., p. 5. See also Edwards, 'The Merthyr Tydfil National Eisteddfod, 1881', 83–5.

[105] W. E. Davies, 'The National Eisteddfod Association' in E. Vincent Evans (ed.), *Eisteddfod*

marked both the coming of age of the eisteddfod as a major national institution and the firm inclusion of the Gorsedd within it. From 1881 the annual National Eisteddfod unfailingly opened its proceedings with a bardic Gorsedd ceremony which was described in detail in its *Transactions*.[106]

The decades between 1880 and the Great War may be viewed as the golden age of Iolo's bardic legacy. It was during these years that the National Eisteddfod became the principal institution within the national culture of Wales, that the Gorsedd moved from the margins to the centre of eisteddfod ritual, and that the influence of both institutions and their symbolism reached its peak within Wales and beyond.[107] When *Y Traethodydd* published the results of its round table discussion on the eisteddfod, Welshmen with such different views as Michael D. Jones, Thomas Edwards (Gwynedd), David Rowlands (Dewi Môn), T. Tudno Jones and Professor John Rhŷs, were united in their conviction that the National Eisteddfod and the Gorsedd were worth preserving.[108] As a 'national institution', it was hoped that the eisteddfod would unite the nation, bridge its political and social divides, and bring together 'progressives' and champions of older, more romantic, notions of Welsh nationality.[109] In the 1890s the National Eisteddfod became a 'great democratic literary festival', and even *Young Wales* judged it to be 'an ally of progressive national life'.[110] In a country obsessed with education, it was celebrated because it provided cultural sustenance for those who had few prospects of ever entering a university.[111] It was also claimed that, through its work, the eisteddfod had given rise to the university colleges, which 'on the whole, were quite respectful of their mother, although they sometimes, like all children, thought that they knew more and were wiser than their mother' ('ar y cyfan, yn bur barchus o'u mam, serch eu bod weithiau, fel pob plant, yn meddwl eu bod yn gwybod mwy ac yn ddoethach na hi').[112] Most importantly, the National Eisteddfod and the Gorsedd were still celebrated as being 'truly

---

*Genedlaethol y Cymry: Cofnodion a Chyfansoddiadau Buddugol Eisteddfod Aberdar, 1885* (Caerdydd, 1887), pp. x–xvi.

[106] Ibid., pp. lv–lviii. The *Transactions* of the National Eisteddfod at Aberdare, 1885, were the first to be published by the Association.

[107] Even in the second half of the 1870s the Gorsedd was not considered by some critics to be a necessary part of the eisteddfod. See D. Howell, 'The National Eisteddfod of 1876 at Wrexham', *Y Cymmrodor*, I (1877), 50.

[108] 'Yr Eisteddfod: Bord Gron', *Y Traethodydd*, XLV (1890), 438–55.

[109] Twr yr Eryr, 'Eisteddfod Genedlaethol Caernarfon, 1894', *Y Geninen*, XII, no. 3 (1894), 233.

[110] O. M. Edwards, 'Eisteddfod Notes', *Wales*, III, no. 28 (1896), 378; H. Elvet Lewis, 'The Development of the Eisteddfod and its Influences upon the Future of Welsh Literature', *Young Wales*, II, no. 12 (1896), 1; O. M. Edwards, 'Editor's Notes', *Wales*, III, no. 25 (1896), 235; Watcyn Wyn, 'Eisteddfodau Merthyr Tydfil yn ystod y Bedwaredd Ganrif ar Bymtheg', *Y Geninen*, XIX, no. 4 (1901), 260.

[111] Ben Davies, 'Yr Eisteddfod a'r Bwthyn', *Y Geninen*, XXXI, no. 1 (1913), 52–4.

[112] Machreth, 'Yr Eisteddfod a'r Orsedd', ibid., XXVI, no. 1 (1908), 53–4. It was at the Cymmrodorion Section of the National Eisteddfod at London in 1887 that the future of the Welsh education system and the possibility of a university charter were discussed decisively. See J. Gwynn Williams, *The University Movement in Wales* (Cardiff, 1993), pp. 115–18.

necessary for our language, our country and our nation' ('gwir angenrheidiol i'n hiaith, a'n gwlad, a'n cenedl') because they united north and south, and overcame sectarian and political fissures.[113]

Although the National Eisteddfod and the Gorsedd were sometimes exposed to harsh criticism, attacks from within Wales were mostly aimed at unwelcome developments rather than at the institutions themselves.[114] Attacks on the National Eisteddfod understandably concentrated on its Anglicized nature, its predilection for grand concerts, its neglect of native talent and traditions, and the general fairground atmosphere which sometimes accompanied it.[115] The Gorsedd was criticized for conducting 'empty ceremonies' ('seremonïau gwag'), which appeared to indicate the 'pitiful decline of this old sacred order' ('dirywiad gresynus sydd ar yr hen drefniant cysegredig hwn').[116] As part of the modern institution of the eisteddfod, it was thus reckoned to be a prime candidate for reform and renewal. As a result, a competition on the subject 'Gorsedd Beirdd Ynys Prydain' was announced for the National Eisteddfod at Wrexham 1888. The winning essay, written by the literary historian Charles Ashton, maintained that a royal charter should be granted to the institution and that it should be expected to 'purify the taste, extend the knowledge and cultivate the morals of the working classes in the Prinicpality' ('i buro chwaeth, i eangu gwybodaeth, ac i ddiwyllio moesau y dosbarth gweithiol yn y Dywysogaeth').[117] Ashton's essay became the basis of the modern Gorsedd Society, which established a constitution, appointed permanent officers, and regulated the awarding of Gorsedd degrees by examination.[118] The contribution of Myfyr Morganwg and Gwilym Cowlyd to the legacy of bardism was acknowledged by enrolling those who had already been admitted to their Gorseddau as members of the Gorsedd of the Bards of the Isle of Britain.

[113] Ben Davies, 'Yr Orsedd a'r Eisteddfod', *Y Geninen*, XVI, no. 4 (1898), 267; idem, 'Anerchiad' in E. Vincent Evans (ed.), *Eisteddfod Genedlaethol y Cymry: Cofnodion a Chyfansoddiadau Buddugol Eisteddfod Blaenau Ffestiniog, 1898* (Liverpool, 1900), p. xlix; Evan Price, 'Rhai o Hen Eisteddfodau'r Fenni', *Y Geninen*, XXXI, no. 2 (1913), 86.

[114] For the substantial academic critique of bardism as an authentic historic institution, see Chapter 6 below.

[115] Gweirydd ap Rhys, 'Eisteddfod Machraeth, Mon: Y Gwir yn Erbyn y Byd', *Seren Gomer*, XXXVIII, no. 473 (1855), 79–80; John Jones, 'Yn Eisteddfod 1891', *Y Geninen*, IX, no. 4 (1891), 266; Edward Foulkes, 'Beth am yr Eisteddfod?', ibid., V, no. 4 (1887), 271; Y Bo Lol, 'Taith Bardd i Eisteddfod y Rhyl', *Cymru*, III, no. 15 (1892), 171; Dau Gyfaill, 'Yr Eisteddfod Genedlaethol', *Y Geninen*, XIII, no. 1 (1895), 18; Gwyneth Vaughan, 'Yr Eisteddfod Genedlaethol: Awgrymiadau i'r Pwyllgorau Lleol', ibid., XVIII, no. 3 (1900), 192–4. See also Hywel Teifi Edwards, 'The Welsh Language in the Eisteddfod' in Jenkins (ed.), *The Welsh Language and its Social Domains 1801–1911*, pp. 293–316; Edwards, 'The Merthyr National Eisteddfod of 1901', *Merthyr Historian*, XIII (2001), 19–26.

[116] B. B. D., 'Gorsedd y Beirdd', *Y Geninen*, V, no. 2 (1887), 171, 174; Ioan Ddu, 'Gorsedd y Beirdd: A Oes Sail i'r Grediniaeth yn Nghylch ei Henafiaeth, Ei Hawdurdod, a Phurdeb ei Hathrawiaeth?', ibid., VI, no. 1 (1888), 46–7.

[117] Ashton, 'Gorsedd Beirdd Ynys Brydain', p. 130; Miles, *The Secret of the Bards*, p. 126.

[118] *HGB*, p. 247.

These reforms also secured for the Gorsedd an integral place within the National Eisteddfod. An address by J. Cadvan Davies on the 'Eisteddfod and the Gorsedd' instigated a reform of the Eisteddfod Association rules, adopted at the National Eisteddfod at Rhyl in 1892, which stated that 'all such Bards, Ovates, and Musicians as shall be duly qualified as Members of the Gorsedd' would also be members of the association, that both institutions would jointly decide on the location of eisteddfodau, and that part of the profits of the eisteddfod would be assigned to the Gorsedd.[119] Most importantly, however, the Gorsedd was assigned a clear function within the National Eisteddfod by being given sole responsibility for all ceremonial matters relating to it.[120] In 1898 the Gorsedd put its new role into practice by ruling that no eisteddfod of longer than a day should be held between July and September and that, apart from the honorary degrees of Druid and Ovate, only those who had passed the stringent Gorsedd examinations were entitled to call themselves members of the Gorsedd. Significantly, too, the Gorsedd urged the National Eisteddfod to give greater support than it had done in recent years to native music and musicians in the lists of subjects for competition and in its programmes, and ruled that only Welsh would be used by the Gorsedd.[121] In an age of wholesale Anglicization, this solitary 'all-Welsh rule' was a courageous step in the campaign for the official recognition of the Welsh language in the activities of the eisteddfod. The 'Rules and Constitution of the Gorsedd of Bards of the Isle of Britain', published in 1909 following a four-year process of consultation, provided the high point of the development of Iolo's bardic Gorsedd into a national institution during the long nineteenth century.[122] Although little of Iolo's radical concept of creating a debating chamber for like-minded libertarians had remained, his idea of an assembly of bards as a focus for Welsh culture had been adopted by his people.

Hand in hand with the campaign to make the Gorsedd of the Bards into a national body relevant to a modern nation and capable of withstanding English criticism came efforts to make it as expressive as possible of an ancient Celtic past. Wales was not alone in its efforts to visualize national history in this way. Nineteenth-century European culture was awash with historical novels, paintings, sculptures, operas and pageants, all of which expressed its obsession with the creation of national histories and their visualization.[123] Wales appeared to

---

[119] E. Vincent Evans (ed.), *The Twelfth Annual Report of the National Eisteddfod Association. Together with the Transactions of the Cymmrodorion Section of the Rhyl National Eisteddfod 1892* (Cardiff, 1892), pp. 6–8. See also Jenkins, 'Hanes Cymdeithas yr Eisteddfod Genedlaethol', 148–9.

[120] Dyn o'r Wlad, 'Eisteddfod 1892', *Y Geninen*, X, no. 4 (1892), 203; Miles, *The Secret of the Bards*, p. 129.

[121] E. Vincent Evans, 'Yr Orsedd' in idem (ed.), *Eisteddfod Genedlaethol y Cymry: Cofnodion a Chyfansoddiadau Buddugol Eisteddfod Blaenau Ffestiniog, 1898* (Liverpool, 1900), pp. xiv–xv.

[122] Gorsedd Beirdd Ynys Prydain, *Rheolau a Chyfansoddiad yr Orsedd* (Caernarvon, 1908). This was the final consultation draft of the constitution. NLW, Vincent Evans Papers G15. See also Miles, *The Secret of the Bards*, p. 145.

[123] See, for instance, Lord, *The Visual Culture of Wales: Imaging the Nation*, pp. 312–13; Adele M.

possess a more venerable institution than many of its neighbours, including England, but at the end of the nineteenth century the Gorsedd still lacked the external attributes which would express that antiquity.[124] The guidelines to Gorsedd ritual had been provided by Iolo Morganwg himself in his bardic writings and through the Gorseddau he had convened. The Gorsedd prayer and the colours worn by the different bardic orders had been culled from his manuscripts, and his ritual of demarcating stone circles and unsheathing and sheathing a sword had been chronicled as long ago as 1819. He had not, however, bequeathed any designs for bardic robes, nor made any attempts to equip the Gorsedd with regalia. The first steps to remedy this situation, taken by Myfyr Morganwg, William Price and, most importantly, Ab Ithel, at the Royal Eisteddfod of Llangollen in 1858, were poorly received.[125] The eccentric bardic garb and the 'druidical egg' sported by Myfyr Morganwg, the primeval fur-robe with a fox-tail hat worn by William Price, and the rainbow-coloured costume worn by Jerome Pym ap Ednyfed, a member of the local gentry, on the stage at Llangollen, proved to be irresistible grist to the mill of satirists.[126]

However, when the National Eisteddfod and the Gorsedd became truly national institutions in the 1890s, a wave of Celticism inspired Welsh and internationally renowned artists such as Thomas Henry Thomas (Arlunydd Penygarn), Sir William Goscombe John and Sir Hubert von Herkomer, Slade Professor of Art at Oxford from 1885 and Royal Academician from 1890, to equip the Gorsedd with regalia which they considered to be an integral part of a Welsh national art.[127] The 'dull and disorderly' ('swrth ac anhrefnus') Gorsedd meetings of the 1880s were judged to be in urgent need of visual reformation.[128] In 1894 Lord Bute, Lord Mostyn, Sir Watkin Williams Wynn

---

Dalsimer, *Visualizing Ireland: National Identity and the Pictorial Tradition* (Boston, Mass., 1993); Fintan Cullen, *Visual Politics: The Representation of Ireland 1750–1930* (Cork, 1997); Roy Strong, *Painting the Past: The Victorian Painter and British History* (London, 2004), pp. 162–7.

[124] Thomas Edwards, 'Yr Eisteddfod: Bord Gron: Urddas Allanol yr Orsedd', *Y Traethodydd*, XLV (1890), 445.

[125] For the extraordinary story of Dr William Price, who established cremation as a form of burial in modern Britain, see Brian Davies, 'Empire and Identity: The "Case" of Dr William Price' in David B. Smith (ed.), *A People and a Proletariat* (London, 1980), pp. 72–93. Cyril Bracegirdle, *Dr William Price: Saint or Sinner* (Llanrwst, 1997) is prefaced by several images of Price 'in druid costume'.

[126] 'Eisteddfod Llangollen Eto!', *Y Punch Cymraeg*, I, no. 2 (1858), 4. An illustration of William Price in his eccentric garb and a *Punch* cartoon based on the scene at Llangollen have been published in Walters, 'Pontypridd a'r Cylch' in idem, *Cynnwrf Canrif*, pp. 244, 247. See also Denning, 'Druidism at Pontypridd' in *Glamorgan Historian: Volume I*, facing p. 45.

[127] For a contemporary assessment of T. H. Thomas's work, see his obituary by Gwynedd, 'Arlunydd Penygarn', *Y Geninen*, XXXIV (Gwyl Dewi, 1916), 44–7. Lord, *Y Chwaer-Dduwies*, pp. 59–62; idem, *The Visual Culture of Wales: Imaging the Nation*, pp. 313–17. Hubert von Herkomer became so important for Wales that moving elegies were composed upon his death. See *Y Geninen*, XXXII, no. 2 (1914), 123.

[128] 'Araeth Llewelyn Williams oddiar y Maen Llog yng Ngwrecsam, 1912', *Y Geninen*, XXXI, no. 1 (1913), 59.

Fig. 3 A procession from the Royal Albert Hall at the Royal National Eisteddfod of Wales, London, 1909. Processions and open-air assemblies associated with the Gorsedd and the Eisteddfod were reflections of civic and national pride.

and other affluent subscribers donated funds for bardic robes to be worn at the ceremonies of the National Eisteddfod at Caernarfon, which Crown Prince Albert Edward, his wife Alexandra, and their daughters were expected to attend.[129] The robes were modelled on Ab Ithel's gown, which his daughters

[129] E. Vincent Evans, 'The Eisteddfod Record' in idem (ed.), *Eisteddfod Genedlaethol y Cymry: Cofnodion a Chyfansoddiadau Buddugol Eisteddfod Caernarfon, 1894* (Liverpool, 1896), pp. xiv, xxxiii.

had kept and readily lent to the committee, and followed Iolo's prescription in terms of their colours.[130] Black birettas and a mitre for the archdruid, adorned with the *nod cyfrin*, completed the costume.[131] Worn on the occasion of the National Eisteddfod ceremonies on 10 July 1894, they were believed to have lent Gorsedd members an 'ancient and dignified look' ('golwg hynafol, urddasol') and to have taken the audience 'back to the middle of the quiet of centuries past' ('yn ôl i ganol tawelwch y canrifoedd gynt').[132] When Hwfa Môn succeeded Clwydfardd as archdruid in 1895, he not only managed to avoid the arguments which had plagued the tenure of his predecessor but also enlivened the Gorsedd with his charismatic presence, a transformation which contributed to its national and international success between 1895 and 1905.[133] It was for him that von Herkomer designed the archdruid's crown and torque in 1895, and a second set of robes, sponsored by him, which became known as 'Herkomer's robes' ('Gwisgoedd Herkomer'), in 1896.[134] In 1896 the Gorsedd banner, designed by Arlunydd Penygarn, was carried for the first time before the Gorsedd procession at the National Eisteddfod held in Llandudno.[135] By 1897 a new grand sword, specially created by von Herkomer for the Gorsedd ceremonies, replaced the swords which had been in use since 1819.[136] In the same year, *Y Corn Hirlas* (the Hirlas Horn), presented by Lord Tredegar and designed by William Goscombe John, was first used in the opening ceremony of the National Eisteddfod at Newport.[137] The archdruid's sceptre, designed by Arlunydd Penygarn in 1910, completed the regalia.[138] In less than a decade the Gorsedd of the Bards of the Isle of Britain had been equipped with expensive historicist regalia designed by leading artists and sponsored by the affluent

---

[130] Gwynedd, 'Arlunydd Penygarn', 46.

[131] Sketches of the robes, drawn by the artist D. J. Davies, were published in the second volume of *Wales* (1894), facing p. 26. See also Lord, *The Visual Culture of Wales: Imaging the Nation*, pp. 325–6.

[132] Twr yr Eryr, 'Eisteddfod Genedlaethol Caernarfon, 1894', 235; O. M. Edwards, 'Editor's Notes', *Wales*, I, no. 4 (1894), 189.

[133] The argument arose because Morien, Myfyr Morganwg's disciple, claimed the title for himself. Craig yr Hesg, 'Eisteddfod Genedlaethol Pontypridd', *Y Geninen*, XI, no. 4 (1893), 257; Llais Uwch Adlais, 'Cipdrem ar Eisteddfod Genedlaethol Caernarfon, 1906', ibid., XXIV, no. 4 (1906), 231. See also Walters, 'Beirdd a Phrydyddion' in Edwards (ed.), *Merthyr a Thaf*, pp. 296–7; Marion Löffler, '*A Book of Mad Celts*': *John Wickens and the Celtic Congress of Caernarfon 1904* (Llandysul, 2000), p. 32; Lord, *The Visual Culture of Wales: Imaging the Nation*, p. 314.

[134] Gwynedd, 'Arlunydd Penygarn', 46. For images of the robe modelled on Hwfa Môn, and of Hwfa Môn with Gorsedd members and regalia, see Löffler, '*A Book of Mad Celts*', pp. 34–5, 70–1; Lord, *The Visual Culture of Wales: Imaging the Nation*, pp. 314, 316, 324.

[135] Gwynedd, 'Arlunydd Penygarn', 44, 46. On the occasion of the investiture of the Prince of Wales in 1911, Arlunydd Penygarn also designed a third set of robes.

[136] For an image of the sword, see Stephanie Jones, *Charles William Mansel Lewis: Painter, Patron and Promoter of Art in Wales* (Aberystwyth, 1998), p. 47.

[137] The Hirlas Horn is depicted on the cover of *HGB* and can also be seen in Lord, *The Visual Culture of Wales: Imaging the Nation*, p. 316.

[138] Gwynedd, 'Arlunydd Penygarn', 46.

landed classes.[139] By this stage the public was readier than earlier generations had been to enjoy these romantic creations as festive expressions of national identity and were less prone to criticize or satirize them. Although these invented ceremonies did not win universal approval, many were convinced that the regalia, as an expression of national art, had greatly enhanced the status of the Gorsedd as a leading national institution.[140]

## *Symbols and mottoes*

As the National Eisteddfod and the Gorsedd moved to the centre of Welsh cultural life during the course of the nineteenth century, the body of symbols and emblems which Iolo Morganwg had created or adapted during his lifetime strongly permeated Welsh visual culture and the Welsh language. Their presence was possibly the most pervasive element of Iolo's legacy. In the print culture of Victorian and Edwardian Wales the two general eisteddfod mottoes 'In the presence of the sun and the eye of light' ('Yn wyneb haul a llygad goleuni') and 'The Truth against the World' ('Y Gwir yn erbyn y Byd'), which had reached the reading public through Iolo's preface to *Heroic Elegies and other Pieces of Llywarç Hen* as early as 1792, as well as phrases like 'According to the Right and Privileges of the Bards of the Isle of Britain ('Yn ôl Braint a Defod Beirdd Ynys Prydain') and the ubiquitous three rays of the *nod cyfrin* (mystic sign) (/ | \), were rife.[141] They naturally appeared whenever and wherever eisteddfodau and Gorseddau were held. As numerous prints and photographs reveal, they were embroidered and painted on banners, woven into wreaths and garlands, engraved on eisteddfod medals, and printed on eisteddfod programmes and transactions.[142] They deeply penetrated the Welsh psyche, often insinuating themselves on to title-pages and into editorials.

Until 1830 the title-page of *Seren Gomer* showed a bardic figure, his left hand resting on a harp and his right arm outstretched towards a sun whose rays were redolent of the *nod cyfrin*. The caption surrounding the image read 'Yn Ngwyneb Haul a llygad Goleuni'. *Yr Haul*, the sounding board of the established church, from 1836 onwards bore the same motto on its title-page, but later added another of Iolo's mottoes, 'And God's Word Highest' ('A Gair Duw yn Uchaf'). At the other end of the political and cultural spectrum, similar mottoes written

---

[139] For a description of the individual parts of the regalia and their history, see Beriah Gwynfe Evans, *The Bardic Gorsedd: Its History and Symbolism* (Pontypool, 1923).

[140] Iona Williams, 'Welsh Art', *Welsh Review*, no. 1 (1906), 97. For critical voices, see Owen M. Edwards, 'Editor's Notes', *Wales*, II, no. 17 (1895), 423–4; *Baner ac Amserau Cymru*, 8 July 1896; *Y Celt Newydd*, 9 September 1904.

[141] The mottoes are explained most fully in Iolo Morganwg's unpublished essay, 'A Short Account of the Ancient British Bards', NLW 13097B, and NLW 13106B, p. 113.

[142] Iorwerth C. Peate, 'Welsh Society and Eisteddfod Medals', *THSC* (1938), 285–330. The illustrative plates reveal the widespread use of the bardic alphabet on the medals.

in the bardic alphabet adorned the title-pages of *Y Gwladgarwr* in the 1840s and the *Cambrian Journal* in the 1850s. Editors wove variations on them into the introduction of their volumes. In 1847 Samuel Evans (Gomerydd) defended the national and interdenominational stance of *Seren Gomer*:

> Nid yw y SEREN wedi bod erioed yn gwasanaethu na pherson na phlaid,– ac nid yw felly yn bresennol; eithr ei hunig amcan yw gwasanaethu *Cymro*, *Cymru*, a *Chymraeg*, heb ŵyro dim oddiwrth ei hanmhleidgarwch cynnwynol. Gwyddom fod yn annalluadwy boddhau pawb . . . ond yr ydym yn galw arnynt i gofio mai amcan SEREN GOMER yw cael allan y GWIRIONEDD, a'r 'GWIR YN ERBYN Y BYD', 'YN LLYGAD HAUL AC WYNEB GOLEUNI', yw yr hyn yr ymdrechwn ymgeisio ato bob amser.[143]

> (The Seren has never served any person or party, – and is not doing so presently; but its only object is to serve the *Welshman*, *Wales*, and *Welsh*, without deviating from its genuine non-partisanship. We know that it is impossible to please everybody . . . but we call on them to remember that the aim of SEREN GOMER is to promote the Truth, and 'THE TRUTH AGAINST THE WORLD', 'IN THE EYE OF THE SUN AND THE FACE OF LIGHT', which is what we try to aspire to every time.)

The fact that Evans had slightly rearranged the second motto – it should have read 'Yn wyneb haul a llygad goleuni' ('In the face of the sun and the eye of the light') – indicates that it was such a familiar part of his vocabulary that he did not pause to check it. In the increasingly defensive cultural climate which followed the publication of the Blue Books in 1847, bardic mottoes were also used to emphasize that eisteddfodau were held to promote the ideals of 'Religion, Law, Love, and Truth' ('Crefydd, Cyfraith, Cariad, a Gwirionedd').[144] Iolo's bardic alphabet – *Coelbren y Beirdd* (Alphabet of the Bards) – and its most primitive sign – *y nod cyfrin* – were equally ubiquitous. The membership certificate of the Abergavenny Cymreigyddion Society was adorned with a motto written in bardic script.[145] As early as 1838 Iolo's proverb 'Gorau cof cof Llyfr. Nid doeth ni ddarlleno' ('The best memory is the memory of a Book. He will not be wise who does not read') and a dedicatory text were inscribed in the bardic alphabet 'on a stone in the front wall of the village school-house' of Cynwyl Elfed in Carmarthenshire.[146] The title-page of *Y Brython* (1858–65) was headed by the *nod cyfrin* throughout its existence. The bardic alphabet appeared on volumes, gravestones and works of art, especially of those who subscribed to Iolo's ideas. William Harry (Gwilym Harri) of Garw Dyle, Penderyn, one of Iolo's contemporaries and friends, and Hugh Hughes (Tegai), the minister of Bethel chapel at Aberdare, had inscriptions in

---

[143] Samuel Evans, 'Rhagymadrodd gan y Golygydd, Caerfyrddin, Rhag. 1, 1847', *Seren Gomer*, XXX (1847), iv. See also 'Rhagdraeth', ibid., XLI (1858), iii.

[144] J. R., 'Traethawd ar Lesoldeb Cymdeithasau Llenyddol ac Eisteddfodau', *Seren Gomer*, XXXII, no. 411 (1849), 365.

[145] Lord, *Y Chwaer Dduwies*, p. 15.

[146] William Spurrell, *Carmarthen and its Neighbourhood: Notes Geographical and Historical* (Carmarthen, 1860), p. 45.

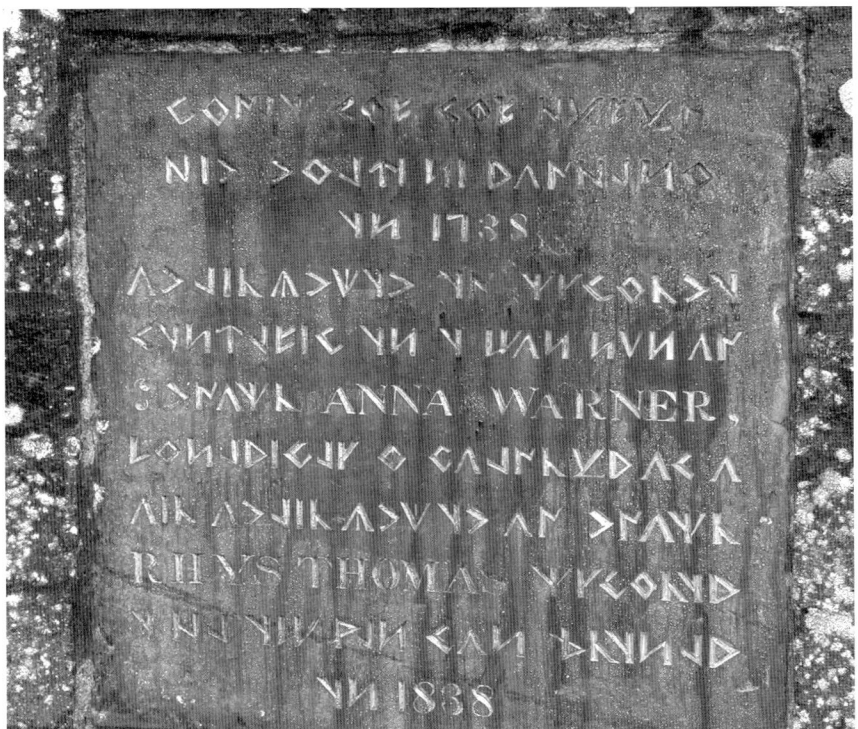

Fig. 4 A plaque with a bardic inscription at Cynwyl Elfed near Carmarthen. The proverb 'Gorau cof cof Llyfr. Nid doeth ni ddarlleno' (The best memory is the memory of a Book. He will not be wise who does not read), which Iolo had popularized, and a text thanking the benefactress Anna Warner, were inscribed 'on a stone in the front wall of the village school-house' of Cynwyl Elfed in 1838.

the bardic alphabet carved on their gravestones.[147] The Merthyr sculptor Joseph Edwards used the *nod cyfrin* on a sumptuous memorial created for Lewis Morgan in 1860, and added bardic script to some of his sculptures (Document 11).[148] The artist William Morgan Williams (Ap Caledfryn), a friend of Morien and Arlunydd Penygarn, even signed some of his prints in bardic script, and the cover of works like Gwilym Morganwg's volume of poetry *Awen y Maen Chwyf* displayed the *nod cyfrin* and the title in bardic letters.[149]

---

[147] E. B. Morris, 'Penderyn', *Cymru*, XXXIV, no. 200 (1908), 117–20; Ben Morus (Myfyr Teifi), *Enwogion Aber Dâr: Sef Byrr-nodion am rai o Gewri Ymadawedig Y Dref a'r Cylch* (Llanbedr Pont Steffan, 1910), p. 22; On William Harry, see Millward, 'Merthyr Tudful: Tref y Brodyr Rhagorol' in Edwards (ed.), *Merthyr a Thaf*, p. 14.

[148] Brynley F. Roberts, 'The Age of Restitution: Taliesin ab Iolo and the Reception of Iolo Morganwg' in *Rattleskull Genius*, p. 470.

[149] Thomas, *Awen y Maen Chwyf*, cover and title-page. Lord, *Gwenllian: Essays on Visual Culture*, p. 64.

By the 1850s Welsh culture was so heavily saturated with bardic mottoes and symbols that they became an easy target for the many critics of bardism. The presence of the *nod cyfrin* on every single banner at the Llangollen eisteddfod of 1858 provoked criticism, while 'Weakminded' ('Gwanddeall') complained about the obscurity of the so-called 'upside-down flesh-hook' displayed on the title-page of *Y Brython*.[150] The 'flesh-hook' was sometimes inverted in order to indicate that the text which it headed was of a satirical nature. It preceded bogus advertisements such as that for the 'Assembly of the Bards of the Island of Humbug' ('Gorsedd Beirdd Ynys Humbug') and 'The Reforming Eisteddfod of Denbigh' ('Eisteddfod Ddiwygiadol Dinbych'), which also coined new variations on old mottoes like 'Foolishness against the World' ('Dwli yn erbyn y Byd'), 'The Sigh against the World' ('Ochenaid yn erbyn y Byd') and 'Humbug Be Humbug!' ('Humbug Bid Humbug!') (Document 9).[151] Yet, much of the criticism and satire directed towards the *nod cyfrin* and the eisteddfodic mottoes ebbed away from the late 1870s onwards. By that stage the National Eisteddfod movement had gathered enough momentum to overshadow the more arcane ceremonies practised by the likes of Myfyr Morganwg and Gwilym Cowlyd. The crisis of the eisteddfod and the Gorsedd had passed and their symbols and mottoes once more began to assume national importance. Ceiriog's Round Table not only read the Gorsedd prayer 'in Welsh or in English' at the beginning of its meetings, but also headed its memoranda with the *nod cyfrin*.[152] The general motto 'Y Gwir yn erbyn y Byd' and the *nod cyfrin* appeared on the title-page of the annual *Transactions* published by the National Eisteddfod Association from 1885 onwards. On the iconic title-page of the influential periodical *Cymru*, a garland of *nodau cyfrin* accompanied other images emblematic of Wales, such as Harlech castle and Snowdon, from its first number in 1891 to its last in 1927. Many of Iolo's fabrications, mottoes, proverbs and catchphrases had become an integral part not only of national ceremonies within Wales but also of public and private discourse.[153] Moreover, Ioloic culture was being embraced far beyond the boundaries of Wales.

[150] *Seren Gomer*, XLI, nos. 518–19 (1858), 503–5, 519–22, 547–9; Gwanddeall, 'Gohebiaethau: Y Nod Cyfrin a'r Arwyddion', *Y Brython*, I, no. 13 (1858), 199.
[151] Callwr Cellweirus, 'Gorsedd Beirdd Ynys Humbug', 382; 'Eisteddfod Ddiwygiadol Dinbych', *Y Punch Cymraeg*, no. 30 (1859), 3; Morien, *History of Pontypridd and Rhondda Valleys*, pp. 88–9.
[152] Vord Gron, *The Key to the Master-Key*, pp. 4–5; William Davies (Mynorydd), 'Joseph Edwards. Sculptor: IX – The Vord Gron', *Wales*, III, no. 21 (1896), 26–7.
[153] See, for instance, Gwyneth Vaughan, '"Nid Da Lle Gellir Gwell": (Arawd a draddodwyd yn Ngorsedd Beirdd Ynys Prydain, yn Merthyr Tydfil, Awst 9fed, 1901)', *Y Geninen*, XIX, no. 4 (1901), 278; Christopher Williams, 'The Future of Art in Wales' in E. Vincent Evans (ed.), *The Twenty-Eighth Annual Report of the National Eisteddfod Association, Together with the Transactions of the Cymmrodorion Section of the Llangollen National Eisteddfod, 1908* (Cardiff, 1909), p. 81. For a list of common proverbs of Ioloic origin, see 'Proverbs of Bardic Origin', *Cambrian Journal*, VI (1859), 30. For photographs of eisteddfod banners bearing bardic mottoes, see 'Eisteddfod Bangor 1890', Gwynedd County Archives, Caernarfon, XS/1077/11/25, and 'The Royal

## The international impact

As the eisteddfod and the Gorsedd evolved into national institutions, they were emulated by cultural nationalists in the other Celtic countries who were eager to devise and host similar annual events in order to revivify their own cultures. In 1890 the Eisteddfod Association was successfully consulted by Scottish patriots who were bent on setting up a 'Highland eisteddfod'. As a result of these discussions the first constitution of *An Comunn Gaidhealach*, the Highland Association, 'followed closely the lines of the great Welsh Association'.[154] The *Mòd* – its annual cultural festival, first held in Oban in 1892 – was likewise based on the National Eisteddfod. The celebrated Irish writer and nationalist Douglas Hyde had shown interest in the eisteddfod idea as early as 1878, two years after joining the Society for the Preservation of Irish. *Conradh na Gaeilge*, the Gaelic League, which he co-founded in 1893 in order to 'de-anglicise Ireland', modelled its annual cultural festival, the *Oireachtas*, on the eisteddfod.[155] The Gorsedd and its archdruid Hwfa Môn were invited to preside over the second *Oireachtas*, held in Dublin in 1898.

Likewise, cultural relations between Wales and Brittany, which had been close ever since Thomas Price (Carnhuanawc) began campaigning for a translation of the Bible into the Breton language, intensified markedly.[156] This tradition had been maintained through the visits of Breton delegations to the Abergavenny eisteddfodau which were patronized by Augusta Hall (Gwenynen Gwent) of Llanover, and the presence of a Welsh delegation at the Celtic Congress of St Brieuc, held in 1867.[157] Lady Augusta Herbert of Llanover (Gwenynen Gwent yr Ail) shared her mother's enthusiasm for Celticism and, at the end of the nineteenth century, the court of Llanover once more became a second home for Breton patriots, particularly for François Jaffrennou (Taldir) and his fellow poet François Vallée (Abherve).[158] At the National Eisteddfod at Cardiff in 1899, an event which became known as the 'Pan-Celtic Eisteddfod', Brittany symbolically became part of the Welsh ritual

---

National Eisteddfod of Wales, Bangor 1902. Audience inside the Pavilion', NLW Framed Works Collection, PB3599. See also Lord, *Y Chwaer Dduwies*, pp. 33–4.

[154] NLW, D. Rhys Phillips Papers 362; Frank Thompson, *History of An Comunn Gaidhealach: The First Hundred (1891–1991)* (Inverness, 1992), pp. 11–13.

[155] Pádraig Ó Fearaíl, *The Story of Conradh na Gaeilge* (Baile Átha Cliath, 1975), p. 5; Georg Grote, *Torn between Politics and Culture: The Gaelic League 1893–1993* (Münster, 1994), pp. 22–3, 60–1.

[156] 'Monthly Register', *Cambro-Briton*, III (1821), 62–3; Carnhuanawc, 'Yr Iaith Geltaeg', *Seren Gomer*, VIII, no. 123 (1825), 361–3; Jane Williams (ed.), *The Literary Remains of the Rev. Thomas Price, Carnhuanawc, Vicar of Cwmdû, Breconshire; and Rural Dean* (2 vols., Llandovery, 1855), II, pp. 147–79; Prys Morgan, 'Thomas Price "Carnhuanawc" (1787–1848) et les Bretons', *Triade*, 1 (1995), 5–13.

[157] Marion Löffler, 'Agweddau ar yr Undeb Pan-Geltaidd, 1898–1914', *Y Traethodydd*, CLV, no. 652 (2000), 44–59.

[158] *Gwerzio Gant Abherve ha Taldir (Brezouneg ha keumraeg kenver-ouz-kenver) Er Coffadwriaeth am Eu Taith yng Nghymru* (Saint-Brieuc, 1899), pp. 14–17.

during a ceremony in which two half-swords were united.[159] In 1901 *Goursez Barzhed Gourenez Breizh-Vihan* (The Gorsedd of the Bards of Little Britain) was founded as a branch of the Welsh institution, links between which have remained strong.[160] Cornwall was the last Celtic nation to establish a cultural institution modelled on the Welsh Gorsedd. Henry Jenner, the founding father of the movement to revive the Cornish language, took heart from the encouragement of D. Rhys Phillips (Beili Glas), secretary of the newly founded Celtic Congress, at the National Eisteddfod of Neath in 1918. Through his sustained assistance and the direct involvement of the Welsh Gorsedd, the Cornish Gorsedd (*Gorseth Kernow*) was founded in August 1928.[161] The programme of the inaugural Gorsedd held at Boscawen on 21 September 1928 not only claimed that the Gorsedd of the Bards of Britain had reclaimed Cornwall 'after a lapse of at least a thousand years' but also opened its proceedings with the Gorsedd prayer recited in Cornish and ended it with the 'inter-Brythonic National Anthem' – 'Hen Wlad Fy Nhadau' – sung in Welsh, Breton and Cornish.[162]

But Iolo's pervasive legacy was not restricted to individual Celtic countries. Celtic visitors flocked to the National Eisteddfod of Llandudno in 1896, at which the Archdruid Hwfa Môn first wore the new robes and regalia designed by von Herkomer, and where many Celts were admitted as honorary members of the Gorsedd. Subsequent National Eisteddfodau became platforms for discussions over setting up a formal Pan-Celtic Association, which was duly established at Stephen's Green, Dublin, in October 1900, and which linked factions of the cultural national movements in Brittany, Cornwall, the Isle of Man, Ireland, Scotland and Wales until *c*.1913.[163] The Pan-Celtic Association emerged through the National Eisteddfod as a central Celtic meeting point,

---

[159] Gwilym Hughes, 'The Cardiff National Eisteddfod', *Young Wales*, V, no. 56 (1899), 180–7; Pascen, 'Eisteddfod Genedlaethol Caerdydd', *Y Geninen*, XVII, no. 4 (1899), 286–7.

[160] Philippe Le Stum, *Le néo-druidisme en Bretagne: Origine, naissance et développement, 1890–1914* (Rennes, 1998), pp. 41–63; Yves Le Gallo, 'La Bretagne bretonannte' in Jean Balcou, Yves Le Gallo, Louis le Gouillou (eds.), *Histoire littéraire et culturelle de la Bretagne. Tome III: L'invasion profane, de la Troisième à la Cinquième République* (3 vols., Paris, 1987), III, pp. 24–5; Miles, *The Secret of the Bards*, pp. 217–27.

[161] Amy Hale, 'Genesis of the Celto-Cornish Revival? L. C. Duncombe-Jewell and the Cowethas Kelto-Kernuak', *Cornish Studies*, 5 (1998), 100–11; Brian Coombes, '"Gathering the Fragments ...": Henry Jenner, the Old Cornwall Societies and Gorseth Kernow' in Derek R. Williams (ed.), *Henry and Katharine Jenner: A Celebration of Cornwall's Culture, Language and Identity* (London, 2004), pp. 164, 167–71.

[162] NLW, D. Rhys Phillips Papers 363, 'Programme of the Gorsedd of the Bards held at the Stone-Circle of Boscawen-Un on Friday, the 21st September, 1928, to Inaugurate a Cornish Gorsedd'.

[163] Elfyn, 'Cofnodion yr Eisteddfod' in E. Vincent Evans (ed.), *Eisteddfod Genedlaethol y Cymry: Cofnodion a Chyfansoddiadau Buddugol Eisteddfod Blaenau Ffestiniog, 1898* (Liverpool, 1900), pp. xlii–xliii, xlix; W. Pritchard, 'Adfywiad Celtiaeth', *Y Geninen*, XX, no. 2 (1902), 107–9. See also Marion Löffler, 'Der Pankeltismus vor dem Ersten Weltkrieg im Europäischen Kontext' in Erich Poppe (ed.), *Keltologie heute, Themen und Fragestellungen: Akten des 3. Deutschen Keltologensymposiums, Marburg, März 2001* (Münster, 2004), pp. 281–6.

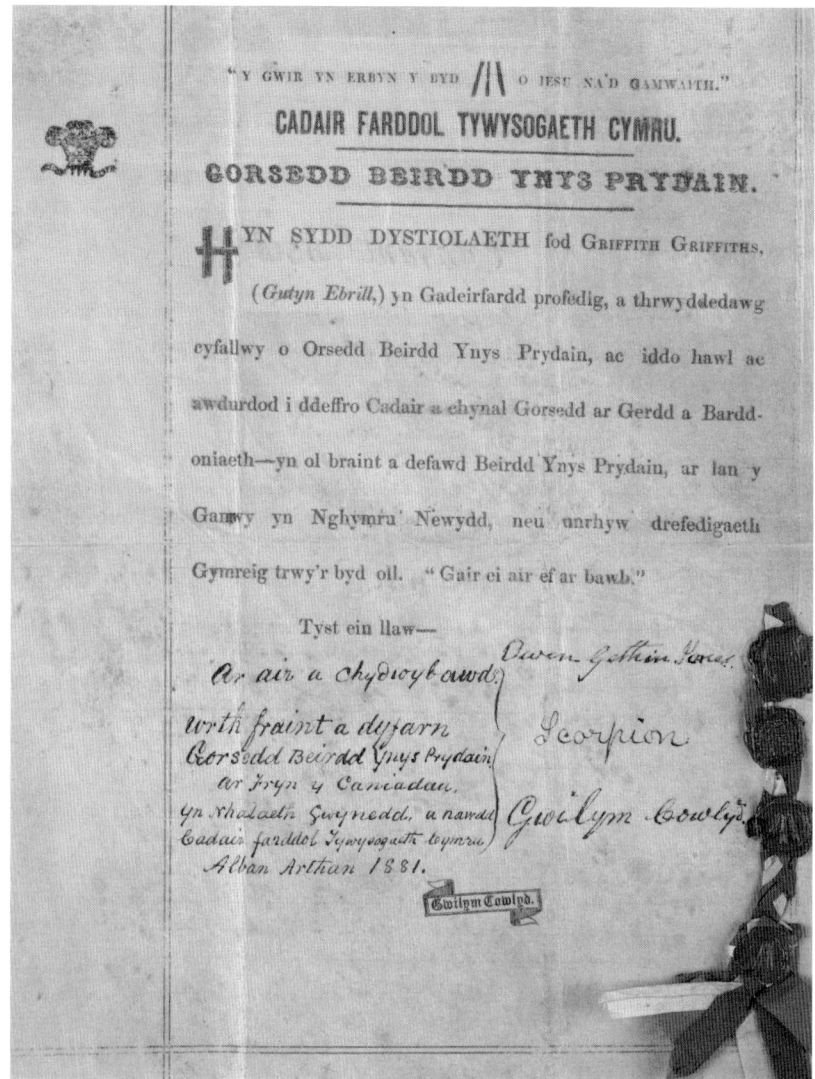

Fig. 5 A Gorsedd licence granted by William John Roberts (Gwilym Cowlyd) to Griffith Griffiths (Gutyn Ebrill), Patagonia, in 1881, which conferred the right to convene Gorseddau in 'New Wales' and in 'Welsh colonies' all over the world.

but it also adopted Iolo's bardic legacy wholeheartedly. 'Heart to Heart' ('Calon wrth Galon') became its motto, and three colourful congresses, at Dublin in 1901, Caernarfon in 1904 and Edinburgh in 1907, which brought it to the attention of the world, were opened and concluded with

Gorsedd ceremonies.[164] Even the Welsh poet T. Gwynn Jones, who had satirized the Gorsedd in 1902, was so impressed by these assemblies that the speech made by the Association's president, Lord Castletown of Upper Ossory, at the opening of the Caernarfon congress, heavily influenced his ode 'Gwlad y Bryniau', which won him the chair at the National Eisteddfod held in London in 1909.[165]

By the time Professor (later Sir) John Morris-Jones was being encouraged to launch fresh onslaughts against the Gorsedd before 'the foolish tales of the Gorsedd spread over five continents!' ('neu fe daenir chwedlau ynfyd yr Orsedd dros bum cyfandir!'), it was too late.[166] Iolo's bardic legacy had long spread to the Celtic countries and beyond. Druidism enjoyed even greater success than the National Eisteddfod and Gorsedd, though the link between Iolo's original concept and modern druidic orders and societies was often extremely tenuous. At the very least, however, the formal structure, the symbols and the regalia used by some of these societies referred to the 'Druids of the Aboriginal Britons'.[167] Some orders which maintained or sought closer contact with the Welsh institutions, however, saw themselves as the custodians of Iolo's legacy. The first American branches of the Ancient Order of Druids had been founded in 1831, but Iolo's bardism found a direct successor there in autumn 1874 when Myfyr Morganwg granted a licence to award bardic titles in his name to a certain Revd James Davies.[168] By the 1880s the American 'daughter' of Cadair Tir Iarll was issuing druidic degrees at Buffalo, New York, and publishing the periodical *The Druid*. Both attracted interest, criticism and satire in Wales.[169] In 1881 Gwilym Cowlyd granted Griffith Griffiths (Gutyn Ebrill) from Patagonia a licence to convene a 'Gorsedd of Music and Poetry – according to the rules and privileges of the Bards of the Isle of Britain, on the shore of the Camwy in New Wales, or in any Welsh colony throughout the whole world' ('Gorsedd ar Gerdd a Barddoniaeth – yn ol braint a defawd Beirdd Ynys Prydain, ar lan y Gamwy yn Nghymru Newydd, neu unrhyw drefedigaeth Gymreig trwy'r byd oll').[170]

During the same decade the German association of the United Ancient Order of Druids (Vereinigte Alte Orden der Druiden) turned to Wales to seek

---

[164] Dyfnallt, 'Cymru a'r Mudiad Celtaidd', *Y Geninen*, XL, no. 2 (1922), 77–9; Löffler, 'A Book of Mad Celts', pp. 28–32.

[165] David Jenkins, *Thomas Gwynn Jones: Cofiant* (Dinbych, 1973), pp. 147–8.

[166] *Y Celt Newydd*, 9 September 1904.

[167] Of these, the oldest was the Ancient Order of Druids, founded in London in 1718. See Ancient Order of Druids, *Introductory Book* (London, 1850), p. 4. The Loyal Order of Druids, founded in 1848, was probably the order which was most directly inspired by Iolo's ideas.

[168] 'Welsh Bards and Ovates', *Bye-Gones*, 7 October 1874, 123.

[169] James Harris, 'Druidism in Wales and America' in Brierley (ed.) *Cymru Fu*, I, p. 31; John Jones and David Davies, 'The Welsh-Druidic University', *Young Wales*, IV, no. 45 (1898), 211–13; idem, 'The Welsh-Druidic (Banchoreion) University', ibid., IV, no. 46 (1898), 238–40.

[170] NLW 18219D.

Fig. 6 A Gorsedd assembly at the National Eisteddfod of Wales at Bangor, 1902. Archdruid Hwfa Môn and Gorsedd members are flanked by Pan-Celtic delegates and visitors from Germany.

reaffiliation with the fountain of druidism.[171] In 1885 Myfyr Morganwg received an application from a group of men in Dresden for his permission, as 'Druid of the Bardic Gorsedd of Wales', to establish a Gorsedd in Germany under the auspices of the chair of Glamorgan, 'the only place in the wide world where its ancient philosophy is still taught in its pristine purity' (Document 12).[172] Through Hubert von Herkomer, the German school inspector Heinrich Fricke of Hamburg contacted the Gorsedd in 1900 in order to enquire about their 'maxims, organization, terms of membership, assemblies, rites, history, &c'.[173] In 1902 his Hamburg lodge presented an address to the National Eisteddfod of Bangor which was 'strikingly embellished ... with a watercoloured representation of an aged Druid with his harp, sword and shield, resting, beneath an oak tree'.[174] By then Fricke had not only become the German Archdruid but also a significant figure in the international druidic movement. Under his leadership the Order also sought permission to reform 'the German Order of Druids so as to make it similar to the Welsh Gorsedd, with power to confer degrees in the several departments of music, literature and art', although it is not known whether the subsequent international reform of the United Order of Druids took this into consideration.[175]

---

[171] The United Ancient Order of Druids had seceded from the Ancient Order of Druids in 1833. Its first German lodge was founded in Berlin in 1872.
[172] 'Literature, Art, and Archaeology', *Red Dragon*, VIII (1885), 498.
[173] 'Current Notes', *Bye-Gones*, 24 October 1900, 482.
[174] *North Wales Observer and Express*, 19 September 1902.
[175] *South Wales Daily News*, 7 July 1902. Shortly afterwards the International Grand Lodge of Druidism, which coordinates the Ancient Order of Druids to this day, was established on 13 July 1913.

Fig. 7 The title-page of *Druiden-Zeitung*, 15 January 1902. This issue of the newsletter of the Vereinigte Alte Orden der Druiden featured an article by the German Archdruid Heinrich Fricke on 'Keltische Literatur', in which counterfeit and genuine Welsh poetry was interpreted in druidic terms.

In 1913 the Gorsedd of the Bards of the Isle of Britain granted a licence to establish a Gorsedd of the Bards in north America and confirmed the Welshman Thomas Edwards (Cynonfardd), an extremely successful and popular Independent minister at Edwardsville, Pennsylvania, as the American archdruid. By the eve of the Great War, even America, Iolo's beacon of liberty, had embraced his bardic legacy.

During the course of the long nineteenth century, therefore, Iolo Morganwg's bardic legacy had radiated from Pontypridd to the rest of Wales, the Celtic countries and the world. The Gorsedd of the Bards of the Isle of Britain had been transformed from being a peculiar assembly of cranks and eccentrics into an expression of Welsh nationality and an inseparable part of the nation's principal cultural festival, the National Eisteddfod:

> Dyma Orsedd undeb cenedlaethol: dengys fod y genedl yn un: mae yn uno De a Gogledd, Eglwyswyr ac Ymneillduwyr, caeth a rhydd. Yma yr esgyn y llwythau fel un teulu i dderbyn barn awen 'yngwyneb haul, llygad goleuni'. Dyma uchel-lys gwladgarwch, yn ymgodi uwchlaw pleidiau cymdeithasol ac ymraniadau politi-caidd.[176]

> (This is the Assembly of national unity: it shows that the nation is one: it unites South and North, Churchmen and Nonconformists, bound and free. Here the tribes ascend as one family to receive the judgement of the muse 'in the face of the sun, the eye of the light'. This is the high-court of patriotism, rising above social parties and political divisions.)

The symbolism and vocabulary of bardism had influenced Welsh visual and literary culture to such a degree that even its critics used it unwittingly. Beyond Wales Iolo's legacy had been incorporated into national festivals in the Celtic countries which to this day bear a resemblance to, and maintain close links with, the Welsh Gorsedd. By the 1920s the historical authenticity of the Gorsedd may have been shattered, but 'druidical learning' had secured its place within world culture.

---

[176] Bethel, 'Anerchiad Bethel oddiar y Maen Llog yng Nghastell Nedd, Awst, 1918', *Y Geninen*, XXXVI, no. 2 (1919), 126.

# 4

## The Legacy of Invention

The historian Christopher Harvie has argued that the addition of fictitious sources to a corpus of authentic material and their acceptance by the public serves to create a 'theoretical history' which can buttress national movements at a certain stage in their development. In such circumstances 'members of the traditional intelligentsia, while still a minority body, create an instant past which fits into the dominant historical discourse'.[1] The reception given to Iolo Morganwg's fabricated additions to the body of Welsh authentic sources illustrates the fact that such cultural processes, which were clearly at work in other European countries, also helped to shape the interpretation of Welsh cultural and literary history in the nineteenth century.[2] Iolo's Victorian legatees were so determined to endow the Welsh nation, and within it the county of Glamorgan, with a venerable ancestry, history and literary past that they closed their minds to any doubts over the authenticity of the sources on which they relied, sometimes even against their own better judgement. Both the success and the critique of Iolo's theoretical history were part of the process through which the Welsh discovered and recorded a national historical narrative. This chapter examines the manner in which Iolo's material was disseminated and circulated, and considers its application by amateurs and professionals alike. It focuses on the use of the triads, druidism and the bardic alphabet to create an ancient past, the marshalling of a pantheon of cultural heroes headed by a romantically re-invented Dafydd ap Gwilym, and the elevation of Iolo's native Glamorgan to the historic role its nineteenth-century importance appeared to warrant.

Iolo's counterfeit material was a treasure trove for Welsh intellectuals confronted with the task of preserving and promoting Welsh-language culture in the nineteenth century. From the moment James Macpherson's Ossian epic was exposed as a forgery, thereby casting a shadow of doubt over the authenticity of the oldest Welsh poetry, they felt a pressing need to make Welsh historical source materials available.[3] As their prefaces show, the *Cambrian*

---

[1] Christopher Harvie, 'Anglo-Saxons into Celts: The Scottish Intellectuals 1760–1930' in Terence Brown (ed.), *Celticism* (Amsterdam, 1996), pp. 235–6. The second part of this hypothesis – 'then, once the native popular movement is under way, another group of intellectuals tests its maturity (and pre-empts the hegemonic power) by exposing them' – will be the theme of Chapter 6.

[2] R. J. W. Evans, '"The Manuscripts": The Culture and Politics of Forgery in Central Europe' in *Rattleskull Genius*, pp. 51–6. See also Howard Gaskill (ed.), *The Reception of Ossian in Europe* (London, 2004).

[3] G. J. Williams, 'Hanes Cyhoeddi'r "Myvyrian Archaiology"', *JWBS*, X, no. 1 (1966), 4; Mary-

*Register*, the *Cambro-Briton and General Celtic Repository* and the *Cambrian Quarterly Magazine and Celtic Repertory* were all founded for this purpose. The romantic cult of the primitive native, which influenced significant patrons of Welsh culture such as Augusta Hall (Lady Llanover) and Sir Charles Morgan, further explains the eagerness with which Iolo's material was included in reputable publications between the end of the eighteenth century and the mid-Victorian period. When Romanticism waned in the 1850s the importance of history as a foundation stone of nationhood replaced it, and the weight attached to manuscripts and ancient sources was enhanced even further. In 1859 Matthew Arnold published an essay on 'England and the Italian Question' in which he claimed (with Karl Marx) that the 'primitive static nations', such as those of the Poles, the Bretons and the Irish, which lacked a 'historical narrative', had no right to national status and were therefore justly absorbed into the emerging larger 'nation states' and empires.[4] In order to avoid such a fate, cultural patriots insisted that a Welsh historical narrative, built on extensive source material, was required. Intellectuals in south Wales experienced the additional pressure of the immense transformation being wrought by industrialization and the social unrest which accompanied it. These developments, together with the fear of cultural assimilation stoked up by the 'Treachery of the Blue Books' in 1847, stunned amateur scholars and professionals who might otherwise have applied their critical faculties more stringently to the material bequeathed by Iolo Morganwg. As a result, their resolve to compose a national, historical and cultural narrative superseded their concern for scholarly accuracy. Iolo occupied a very special place in the hearts of the Welsh and many of the battles of the present were fought through arguments based on his invented past.

## *The dissemination of Iolo's sources*

Iolo Morganwg did not publish many volumes of antiquarian writings and other material during his lifetime. His legacy rested largely on his (sometimes hidden) contributions to the publications of others and on his extensive manuscript archive. Iolo's discoveries and forgeries alike were initially invested with authority through their inclusion in works published under the imprimatur of the Cymmrodorion and Gwyneddigion societies and by their association with

---

Ann Constantine, 'Ossian in Wales and Brittany' in Gaskill (ed.), *The Reception of Ossian in Europe*, pp. 76–8. Sharon Turner's *A Vindication of the Genuineness of the Ancient British Poems of Aneurin, Taliesin, Llywarch Hen, and Merdhin* (London, 1803) was warmly endorsed throughout the nineteenth century.

[4] Daniel Williams, 'Pan-Celticism and the Limits of Post-Colonialism: W. B. Yeats, Ernest Rhys and William Sharp in the 1890s' in Tony Brown and Russell Stephens (eds.), *Nations and Relations: Writing across the British Isles* (Cardiff, 2000), pp. 1–29.

prominent London Welshmen like Owen Jones (Owain Myfyr) and William Owen Pughe.[5] Thereafter, Ioloic material, both published and unpublished, was disseminated through innumerable notes and articles in journals and magazines, popular volumes and works of reference.

*Barddoniaeth Dafydd ab Gwilym*, published by Owain Myfyr and William Owen Pughe in 1789, became the first conduit for Iolo's work. His contribution to the sketch of the poet's life, and his part in making available the sixteen poems, purportedly by Dafydd ap Gwilym, which appeared in the 'Chwanegiad' (Addendum), was so substantial that he received £10 in payment.[6] But Iolo's name as one of the editors appeared only in 1873, when a second edition of the work was published. Both editions formed the basis for studies of Dafydd ap Gwilym's poetry well into the Edwardian period.[7] A manuscript of 'Cyfrinach Beirdd Ynys Prydain' (The Secret of the Bards of the Isle of Britain) was circulated among Iolo's London acquaintants before he published an initial version of it as a bardic preface to William Owen Pughe's *Heroic Elegies and other Pieces of Llywarç Hen* in 1792.[8] Emboldened by these successes he ensured that his *Poems, Lyric and Pastoral*, published in 1794, featured many pages of triads, expositions on bardism and druidism, and translations from the work of Dafydd ap Gwilym.[9] Iolo's contributions to *The Myvyrian Archaiology of Wales*, the ground-breaking collection of Welsh sources published in three volumes between 1801 and 1807, enabled him to include extensive material of his own making, such as 'Brut Ieuan Brechfa' (The Chronicle of Ieuan Brechfa), the maxims of Catwg Ddoeth and many additional triads, alongside authentic material. A second edition, this time published in one volume in 1867, kept the material in the public domain. Between 1805 and 1807 *Y Greal* published Iolo's version of the Statute of Gruffudd ap Cynan, which upheld claims of the superiority of free-metre poetry over the twenty-four metres of Dafydd ab Edmwnd, and informed the protracted dispute over the respective merits of both metrical systems throughout the century.[10] During the first thirty years of the nineteenth century, publications like the *Cambrian Register*, the *Cambrian Quarterly* and the *Cambro-Briton* regularly published excerpts from Iolo's letters, translations of his Dafydd ap Gwilym poems and of triads he had composed himself, as well as some of his original poetry. Bardic material was also included in the preface to

---

[5] For the work of these societies, see *HHSC*, pp. 91–137.
[6] Thomas Parry, '*Barddoniaeth Dafydd ab Gwilym*, 1789', *JWBS*, VIII, no. 4 (1957), 191; Owen Jones and William Owen (eds.), *Barddoniaeth Dafydd ab Gwilym* (Llundain, 1789), pp. x, 497–530.
[7] Robert Ellis (Cynddelw) (ed.), *Barddoniaeth Dafydd ab Gwilym* (Liverpool, 1873).
[8] William Owen, *The Heroic Elegies and other Pieces of Llywarç Hen* (London, 1792), pp. v–lxxx.
[9] Williams: *PLP*, II, pp. 217–56.
[10] Iolo Morganwg, 'Rheolau Prydyddion', *Y Greal sev Cynnulliad o Orchestion ein Hynaviaid, a Llofion o amryw Van-Govion y Cyn-Oesoedd*, V (1806), 233–9; idem, 'Eisteddvodau Caerwys', ibid., VI (1806), 276–8.

Iolo's first volume of Unitarian hymns, *Salmau yr Eglwys yn yr Anialwch*, first published in 1812, and reissued in 1827 and 1857. It also bore on its title-page the *nod cyfrin* (mystic sign) which achieved such prominence later in the century.[11] Crucially, since nearly all this additional material first appeared alongside, or interspersed with, genuine sources, it readily acquired authenticity.

Although its content had been discussed since the early 1790s, Iolo's main work on bardism, *Cyfrinach Beirdd Ynys Prydain*, appeared posthumously, edited by his son Taliesin, in 1829.[12] The preface to this exposition on the intricate rules of classical Welsh poetry constituted a theoretical history of the Welsh poetic tradition, from the departure of the Romans from the British Isles to the Carmarthen eisteddfod of c.1453.[13] It was included in its entirety in the popular reference work *Geiriadur y Bardd: neu yr Odlydd Cyffredinol, at Wasanaeth y Beirdd*, published by Robert Ellis (Cynddelw) in 1874, and this ensured its continued use until the rise of the 'new poet' in the 1890s.[14] Taliesin further contributed to the dissemination of his father's work by composing the winning entry on the subject of the antiquity and authority of the bardic script, *Coelbren y Beirdd*, for the Abergavenny eisteddfod of 1838, a work which was published in 1840.[15] He failed to complete a commission from the new Welsh Manuscripts Society to select and edit his father's manuscripts but, following his death, this work was undertaken by Thomas Price (Carnhuanawc) and John Williams (Ab Ithel), and their labours served to enhance its status. When the *Iolo Manuscripts*, subtitled a *Continuation of the Myvyrian Archaiology*, finally appeared in 1848, it was hailed as a major first achievement by a society that had been founded 'for the purpose of transcribing and printing the more important of the numerous bardic and Historical Remains of Wales'.[16] In sections such as 'History', 'Ecclesiastical Antiquities', 'Fables', 'Tales' and 'Poetry', it provided a wealth of miscellaneous material which was quarried time and again during the course of the century.[17]

---

[11] See also Chapter 3 above.
[12] Edward Williams, *Cyfrinach Beirdd Ynys Prydain*, ed. Taliesin Williams (Abertawy, 1829).
[13] *Cambrian Register*, I (1796), 1–18.
[14] Robert Ellis (Cynddelw), *Geiriadur y Bardd: neu yr Odlydd Cyffredinol, at Wasanaeth y Beirdd . . . At yr hyn yr Ychwanegwyd, Cyfrinach Beirdd Ynys Prydain* (Caernarfon, 1874). For later uses, see Owen Davies, 'Geiriadurwyr a'u Geiriaduron V', *Y Geninen*, XXIX, no. 2 (1911), 124; Anon., 'Caniadau'r Gwrthryfel Mawr', *Cymru*, XXI, no. 124 (1901), 216. For the 'new poet', see Marian Beech Hughes, 'Y Bardd Newydd (The New Poet)' in John T. Koch (ed.), *Celtic Culture: A Historical Encyclopedia* (5 vols., Santa Barbara, Calif., 2006), I, p. 174.
[15] See p. 95. Taliesin Williams, *Traethawd ar Hynafiaeth ac Awdurdodaeth Coelbren y Beirdd yr Hwnn a Ennillodd Ariandlws a Gwobr Eisteddfod Y Fenni 1838* (Llanymddyfri, 1840).
[16] The aims of the Welsh Manuscripts Society were reprinted in each of the volumes it published, together with the names of its members. The *Iolo Manuscripts* were reissued in 1888, thus guaranteeing their continued influence.
[17] Taliesin Williams (ab Iolo), *Iolo Manuscripts: A Selection of Ancient Welsh Manuscripts, in Prose and Verse, from the Collection made by the Late Edward Williams, Iolo Morganwg, for the Purpose of Forming a Continuation of the Myvyrian Archaiology* (Llandovery, 1848).

Subsequently the society became one of the main disseminators of Iolo's material. Most of its publications displayed the influence of Iolo's legacy, and some volumes were entirely dependent upon it. In 1853 it published William Jenkins Rees's *Lives of the Cambro-British Saints, of the Fifth and Immediate Succeeding Centuries, from Ancient Welsh and Latin MSS., in the British Museum and Elsewhere*. It also brought out Ab Ithel's gleanings from Iolo's archive at Llanover Court: *Dosparth Edeyrn Davod Aur, or, The Ancient Welsh Grammar* (1856) and *Barddas: or, A Collection of Original Documents, Illustrative of the Theology, Wisdom, and Usages of the Bardo-Druidic System of the Isle of Britain* (1862).[18] In addition to winning the support of the Welsh Manuscripts Society, writing essays and editing manuscripts, Taliesin sustained public interest in bardo-druidism by engaging with influential writers of the time. In answer to a query from Jane Williams (Ysgafell), Carnhuanawc maintained that, having once believed druidism to be the 'mere production of the leisure hours of old Iolo Morganwg', his conversations with Taliesin had forced him to reconsider (Document 13).

Of all the works to which Iolo had contributed material, *The Myvyrian Archaiology of Wales* proved to be the most influential. It was held in the highest esteem by nineteenth-century scholars both in Wales and on the Continent and, in order to make it more accessible, parts of it were reprinted in periodicals and pamphlets.[19] Ferdinand Walter considered it the starting point for any investigation into Welsh history, describing it in 1859 as the 'main collection' (*die Hauptsammlung*).[20] When the publisher Thomas Gee began organizing a second edition in the 1860s, a tangible note of relief was sounded because such a work was reckoned to be 'indispensable for every thorough research into the nature and the worth of the old literature of our country' ('hanfodol i bob ymchwiliad trwyadl i natur a gwerth llenoriaeth henafol ein gwlad').[21] Influential politicians like the Liberal MP and national icon Tom Ellis saw it as a means of convincing 'sceptical English friends of the vitality of the Cymric language and literature',[22] and at the dawn of the twentieth century James

---

[18] William Jenkins Rees, *Lives of the Cambro-British Saints of the Fifth and Immediate Succeeding Centuries, from Ancient Welsh and Latin MSS., in the British Museum and Elsewhere* (Llandovery, 1853); J. Williams (Ab Ithel), *Dosparth Edeyrn Davod Aur, or, The Ancient Welsh Grammar* (London, 1856); idem, *Barddas: or, A Collection of Original Documents, Illustrative of the Theology, Wisdom, and Usages of the Bardo-Druidic System of the Isle of Britain*, Volume I (Llandovery, 1862). The second volume of *Barddas*, published in London, appeared posthumously in 1874. Ab Ithel also edited *Y Gododdin*, *Brut y Tywysogyon* and *Annales Cambriae* for the Society. All were embellished by him with introductions and notes which promoted Ioloic concepts and sources.

[19] O. N. Y., 'Trioedd y Cybydd', *Seren Gomer*, XI, no. 156 (1828), 261.

[20] Walter, *Das Alte Wales*, p. 4. On page 5 he quoted the *Iolo Manuscripts* as the second most important source.

[21] John Davies, 'Nodiadau Llenyddol', *Y Beirniad*, III, no. 9 (1861), 92. See also 'Adolygiadau', *Y Dysgedydd*, XLIV (1865), 58; Arthur Mee, 'Carmarthenshire Notes in the Iolo Manuscripts' in idem (ed.), *Caermarthenshire Notes (Antiquarian, Topographical, and Curious)* (2 vols., Llanelly, 1889–91), I, pp. 81–2, 87–8, 111–12.

[22] Thomas Ellis, 'Thomas Gee: A Tribute', *Young Wales*, IV, no. 46 (1898), 229.

Ifano Jones (Ifano) described the volumes as the 'Bible of history, law and literature of Wales' ('Beibl hanes, rhaith, a llên Cymru'). With great pride he quoted a review in the English *Athenæum* which had praised Iolo, 'a poor Welsh peasant', for accomplishing such a remarkable feat.[23] *The Myvyrian Archaiology of Wales* and *Cyfrinach y Beirdd* took first and second place in the 'literature' category of the fifty best books in the Welsh language which T. C. Evans (Cadrawd), an avid admirer of Iolo, published in 1888 at the behest of the journalist Arthur Mee in the 'Cymru Fu' (Old Wales) section of the *Cardiff Weekly Mail*.[24] Those who enquired about ways of building up 'basic libraries' on Wales and the Welsh were often advised to acquire volumes containing Iolo's material.[25] Works like the *Iolo Manuscripts* and *Cyfrinach y Beirdd* were regularly sought after, consulted and quoted in popular and scholarly articles.[26] Iolo's *Poems, Lyric and Pastoral* was extensively quarried for its footnotes on the history of Wales,[27] and certain parts of it, such as the 'Account of, and Extracts from The Welsh-Bardic Triads', 'Trioedd Braint a Defod', with an English translation entitled 'Institutional Triads', and 'Trioedd Barddas', were transcribed for personal use.[28] James Harris, the second editor of the *Red Dragon*, devoted a whole article to the *Poems* in which he complained about the exorbitant prices such works commanded.[29] The demand for works by Iolo remained strong well into the Edwardian period. As late as 1911 the Middlesbrough ironmaster and Welsh nationalist E. T. John was delighted to buy a first edition of the *Poems* at a bargain price of £2.[30] Iolo's published work, clearly, did not gather dust: it was transcribed, sold, resold, circulated and read by people in search of markers of nationhood.

Iolo's legacy was also made accessible to the nation by those who utilized the contents of his manuscripts and published works in order to compete at eisteddfodau, or who contributed to periodicals, newspapers, and popular and scholarly volumes. In 1853 Lady Augusta Hall of Llanover Court purchased all Iolo manuscripts in the possession of Taliesin's widow. Thereafter her home was 'ever open to all Welsh-speaking Welshmen, and to any scholar wishing to

---

[23] James Ifano Jones (Ifano), 'Llenyddiaeth Cymru Hanner Ola'r Ddeunawfed Ganrif II', *Y Geninen*, XX, no. 3 (1902), 189–94.

[24] T. C. Evans (Cadrawd), 'The Fifty Best Welsh Books' in Brierley (ed.), *Cymru Fu*, I, p. 327.

[25] Bibliophile, 'Notes and Queries', *Red Dragon*, VI (1884), 478; T. C. Evans, 'Notes and Queries: The Welsh Historical Triads', ibid., XI (1887), 281.

[26] Nicander, 'Damhegion Esop', *Y Traethodydd*, IX (1853), 217; Emrys-Jones, *Life and Works of Edward Williams (Iolo Morganwg)*, p. 15; Abraham Morris, 'Gwent: Caerlleon ar Wysg', *Cymru*, XXIII, no. 137 (1902), 267; R. E. Rowlands, 'Enwau Lleoedd Cymru', ibid., XXIX, no. 173 (1905), 283; L. M. Owen, 'Gwenynen Gwent', ibid., XXXV, no. 204 (1908), 28; J. Glyn Davies, 'Yr Eisteddfod', *Y Geninen*, XXXI, no. 2 (1913), 124.

[27] Llywarch Owain Reynolds, 'Derwyddiaeth', *Y Beirniad*, XX, no. 82 (1879), 281.

[28] NLW, Cwrtmawr 1 (C), no. 249B: 'A manuscript in the hand of David Richards (Dewi Silin) containing transcripts, from Edward Williams: *Poems, Lyric and Pastoral*, Vol. II (London, 1794), pp. 217–37.'

[29] [James Harris], 'The Fringe of a Welshman's Book', *Red Dragon*, VIII (1885), 584.

[30] NLW, E. T. John, no. 144: George Alexander, Cardiff, to E. T. John, Llanidan, 25 June 1911.

see the Iolo Manuscripts' (Document 14).[31] In the same year Ab Ithel founded the Cambrian Institute, whose *Cambrian Journal* provided Iolo's fictitious material with a public platform on a completely new scale.[32] The main aim of this periodical was to aggrandize the druidic tradition, but it also became a focal point for much more of the material which Ab Ithel transcribed from the Llanover collection.[33] Notes authored by 'Edward Williams', 'E.W.' and 'Iolo Morganwg', or simply called 'Ioloana', publicized a variety of Iolo's writings which encompassed, among other things, bardism, geology, iron-smelting, apple-growing and human longevity in Glamorgan.[34] Some issues were devoted almost entirely to such material.[35]

Following Ab Ithel's death in 1862 his role was taken over by other influential figures in Welsh public life, notably the lexicographer and professor of Welsh, D. Silvan Evans, the pioneering Welsh folklorist T. C. Evans (Cadrawd), the librarian and bibliographer D. Rhys Phillips (Beili Glas) and the journalist Owen Morgan (Morien). Throughout the second half of the nineteenth century and well into Edwardian times, they disseminated Iolo's ideas through their contributions to the periodical press as well as to scholarly and popular volumes, and by including entries in encyclopaedias. D. Silvan Evans began publishing selections of Ioloic material during his time as editor of *Y Brython* between 1858 and 1860,[36] and his dictionaries reveal how carefully he perused Iolo's material in his search for the provenance of Welsh words.[37] The by-products of such investigations appeared in periodicals such as *Y Geninen* under headings like 'Literary Remains' or 'From D. Silvan Evans's Treasure Trove'.[38] Glanffrwd Thomas and Morien favoured the *Bye-Gones* and *Cymru Fu* columns with Iolo's recipes for oatcakes, dialogues which illustrated his views on metempsychosis, and translations of counterfeit triads.[39] Cadrawd supplied *Cymru* with documents from the Llanover collection and several series on the

---

[31] Maxwell Fraser, 'Lady Llanover and her Circle', *THSC* (1969), 190.

[32] The foundation of the Cambrian Institute and its journal followed the irredeemable breakdown of relations between Ab Ithel and the Cambrian Archaeological Association. It foreshadowed the profound changes in the standards of Welsh scholarship which occurred in the second half of the nineteenth century. See Chapter 5 below.

[33] Document 14 reveals that he had 'had the MSS in his possession for some time'.

[34] See the contents of *Cambrian Journal*, V–VII (1858–60), *passim*.

[35] Ibid., V (1858), *passim*.

[36] See, for instance, 'Rhinweddau Gwahanol Ddiodyn: Hen Ddiarebion ar Fesur Dyri, gan Iolo Morganwg', *Y Brython*, III, no. 16 (1860), 60.

[37] See Anon., 'Reviews: A Dictionary of the Welsh Language ("Geiriadur Cymraeg")', *Red Dragon*, XI (1887), 356–7.

[38] D. Silvan Evans, '"Iolo Morganwg" on Transmigration' in Brierley (ed.), *Cymru Fu*, II, p. 10.

[39] Llewelyn Sion, 'Gorseddau [O hen ysgriflyfr ym meddiant y diweddar Ganghellor D. Silvan Evans]', *Y Geninen*, XXVIII, no. 4 (1910), 286; Glanffrwd Thomas, 'The Bards of Tir Iarll and the Glamorgan Gorsedd' in Brierley (ed.), *Cymru Fu*, I, pp. 175–8; idem, 'Glamorganshire Customs: The Making of Oatmeal and Oatmeal Bread' in ibid., pp. 298–9; Morien, 'Triads of the English' in ibid., II, p. 142. It should be borne in mind that material thus published reached the public twice, within the newspaper columns in which it first appeared and in the collective volumes published thereafter.

traditions of Glamorgan based on Iolo's work.[40] This small group of major legatees, as well as other amateur writers and scholars, also contributed to popular reference works of the period such as Thomas Gee's *Encyclopædia Cambrensis: Y Gwyddoniadur Cymreig* (1855–79), whose bibliographical references, listed at the end of entries such as 'bardd' (bard), popularized works based on Iolo's sources.[41] Even the ninth, tenth and eleventh editions of the *Encyclopaedia Britannica* (1875–1925) featured material by Iolo in their entries on 'Welsh literature'.[42]

A third interface between Iolo's archival material and the Welsh and international public were the popular and scholarly volumes on the history and traditions of Wales and the other Celtic countries which were published during the course of the nineteenth century. Books such as Charles Redwood's *The Vale of Glamorgan: Scenes and Tales among the Welsh*, Isaac Foulkes's *Cymru Fu yn Cynnwys Hanesion, Traddodiadau, yn nghyda Chwedlau a Dammegion Cymreig*, and David Lloyd Isaac's *Siluriana: or Contributions towards the History of Gwent and Glamorgan*, wove into their narratives selected pieces of material by Iolo. The histories of Welsh literature written by Charles Wilkins and Charles Ashton warmly praised Ioloic sources and utilized them in formulating their arguments.[43] Even those scholars who aspired to a more scientific approach fell prey to Iolo's forgeries. Although, in the preface to his history of Wales, Carnhuanawc confessed to being wary of adopting 'the claims of others, without proving them from old authorities' ('haeriadau ereill, heb eu profi trwy yr awdurdodau cysefin'), his pioneering volume still made copious reference to Iolo's additional triads and to inventions such as the mystic sign.[44] Jane Williams, whose work was celebrated as an example of the kind of scientific history which modern Wales urgently required, quoted freely from the third volume of *The Myvyrian Archaiology of Wales*, the *Iolo Manuscripts* and the *Cambrian Journal* in her description of early Wales and its cultural framework.[45] As will be shown below, Iolo's material even insinuated itself into the works of critics such as Thomas Stephens and Sir John Morris-Jones, as well as that of scholars on the Continent.

---

[40] See below pp. 112–13.
[41] 'Bardd' in *Encyclopaedia Cambrensis: Y Gwyddoniadur Cymreig. Cyfrol I* (Dinbych, 1858), pp. 525–61.
[42] William K. Sullivan, 'Celtic Literature' in *The Encyclopaedia Britannica* (9th edn., Edinburgh, 1878), V, pp. 316, 320.
[43] Charles Wilkins, *The History of the Literature of Wales from the Year 1300 to the Year 1650* (Cardiff, 1884), p. 218; Charles Ashton, *Hanes Llenyddiaeth Gymreig o 1651 O.C. hyd 1850* (Liverpool, 1893), pp. 421–4.
[44] Thomas Price (Carnhuanawc), *Hanes Cymru, a Chenedl y Cymry, o'r Cynoesoedd hyd at Farwolaeth Llewelyn ap Gruffydd* (Crughywel, 1842), pp. 9, 47–50.
[45] Jane Williams (Ysgafell), *A History of Wales, Derived from Authentic Sources* (London, 1869), pp. 5–9, 74.

## A superior civilization

Anthony D. Smith has argued that 'of particular importance among the cultural components of ethnicity are myths of ethnic origin and election, and symbols of territory and community'.[46] Writing in relation to early nineteenth-century Romantic nationalism, other authors have stressed the significance of periods in the history of nations during which literary fame, political success or cultural efflorescence had occurred, partly because the past had been used 'to subvert the present'.[47] These tendencies were at work in Wales, as in the rest of Britain, throughout the nineteenth century. Imperial circles in England pressed the Phoenicians into service as evidence that 'peace, prosperity and freedom' tended to follow in the wake of imperial expansion.[48] In Ireland scholars like George Petrie and Eugene O'Curry used ancient monuments and artefacts, such as the island's round towers and an eighth-century brooch found at Tara, to develop their vision of a Celtic Ireland based on early medieval Christian culture.[49] In Wales the fictional sources which Iolo Morganwg had added to the existing body of material boosted the popular notion of the country's ancient history and civilization as being both older than, and superior to, Anglo-Saxon and even Roman culture. Iolo was steeped in the tradition of Welsh historical writing, much of which was concerned with the origins and early history of the Welsh.[50] Not surprisingly, therefore, his heirs and legatees focused on the triads, on the Christian aspects of bardo-druidism and on the bardic alphabet as foundation stones of their narratives.

Iolo accorded the Welsh triads – three-line mnemonic devices which facilitated the oral transmission of history – high significance as a window on early Welsh culture and society. Although many of the authentic historical triads had ceased to be meaningful to all but the most well-versed in Welsh poetry, 'the oldest evidence which the Welsh possessed concerning their origins' continued to be held in considerable regard.[51] By publishing fictional triads in *Poems, Lyric and Pastoral*, and especially in the third volume of *The Myvyrian Archaiology of Wales*, alongside authentic material, Iolo took advantage of the prestige of this traditional form. Of the 126 'Triads of the Isle of Britain' (Trioedd Ynys

---

[46] Anthony D. Smith, *Myths and Memories of the Nations* (Oxford, 1999), p. 15.
[47] Josep R. Llobera, *The God of Modernity: The Development of Nationalism in Western Europe* (Oxford, 1994), p. 173; Kedourie, *Nationalism*, p. 70.
[48] Timothy Champion, 'The Appropriation of the Phoenicians in British Imperial Ideology', *Nations and Nationalism*, VII, no. 4 (2001), 452.
[49] John Hutchinson, 'Archaeology and the Irish Rediscovery of the Celtic Past', ibid., VII, no. 4 (2001), 507. For the outline of Celticism as the basis for a national revival in the arts and a depiction of the 'Tara brooch', see Henry O'Neill, *The Fine Arts and Civilisation of Ancient Ireland* (London, 1863), pp. v–vi, 52–3.
[50] Prys Morgan, 'Iolo Morganwg and Welsh Historical Traditions' in *Rattleskull Genius*, pp. 252–7.
[51] Rachel Bromwich, *'Trioedd Ynys Prydain'* in *Welsh Literature and Scholarship* (Cardiff, 1969), pp. 4, 15.

Prydain) which Iolo sent to the editors of *The Myvyrian Archaiology*, forty-two were coined by him. These gave authenticity to spurious founding fathers, such as Hu Gadarn and Dyfnwal Moelmud, made bold claims regarding the settlement of the British Isles, and fixed in the public mind the names of the first bards and teachers who had allegedly flourished long before the arrival of the Romans and the Saxons.[52] Moreover, Iolo contributed long series of triads (called 'triodd' by him) which either featured counterfeit material or were entirely fictitious, such as the triads of Llelo Llawdrwm ('Triodd Llelo Llawdrwm'), the triads of the women ('Triodd y Gwragedd'), the Welshman's triads ('Triodd y Cymro') and the Englishman's triads ('Triodd y Sais').[53] Two extensive series of the triads of Dyfnwal Moelmud ('Triodd Dyfnwal Moelmud') concluded this extended sequence.[54] During the nineteenth century these triads often superseded authentic versions and became firm favourites among the public in Wales and beyond. The *Cambro-Briton* devoted a whole section to them in 1819, and thereafter they were reprinted and translated so often that they became the basis of many accounts of Welsh history.[55] Some periodicals, notably *Seren Gomer, Y Gwladgarwr, Y Brython*, the *Cambrian Journal* and *Y Geninen*, published whole series of additional triads as source material.[56] Others paraded them to prove that early Welsh society had been more civilized than had previously been assumed:

> Drwyddynt hwy yr ydym yn dyfod yn gydnabyddus â hanesion boreuaf ein cenedl, â doethineb ein cyndadau, eu crefydd, eu moes-ddysg, eu cyfreithiau, athroniaeth, meddygyniaeth, amaethyddiaeth, barddoniaeth, cerddoriaeth, defodau, arferion, a helyntion gwladwriaethol.[57]

---

[52] Ibid., p. 18. For an annotated English translation of these triads, see eadem, 'Trioedd Ynys Prydain: The *Myvyrian* "Third Series"', *THSC* (1968), 299–338 and eadem, 'Trioedd Ynys Prydain: The *Myvyrian* "Third Series"', ibid. (1969), 127–55. See also Balbus, 'Deffrobani', *Y Brython*, III, no. 18 (1860), 138.

[53] *MAW*, III, pp. 199–282.

[54] Ibid., III, pp. 283–318. Iolo claimed to have discovered them in the 'Book of the Triads of the Bards of the Isle of Britain' ('Llyvr Triodd Beirdd Ynys Prydain').

[55] 'The Triads: No. I', *The Cambro-Briton and General Celtic Repository in Three Volumes* (1819), I, p. 7.

[56] O. N.Y., 'Trioedd y Cybydd', 262–3; 'Llyma Drioedd y Wraig Dda', ibid., XII, no. 162 (1829), 80–1; 'Trioedd Mab y Crinwas', ibid., XIV, no. 188 (1831), 147; 'Trioedd Cenedl y Cymru – Trioedd y Cymro', *Y Gwladgarwr*, IV, nos. 37, 39 (1836), 15, 66–7; 'Trioedd y Cybydd', ibid., no. 44 (1836), 210–11; 'Trioedd y Crinwas', ibid., VI, no. 67 (1838), 48; 'Trioedd Llelo Lawdrwm', ibid., VII, no. 84 (1839), 364; 'Manion ac Olion: Trioedd y Cybydd', *Y Brython*, II, no. 2 (1858), 31; 'Trioedd: Dyma Drioedd Taliesin', ibid., no. 8 (1859), 119; Ieuan Gwynfryn, 'Trioedd Ynys Prydain: Trioedd Llelo Lawdrwm o'r Coetty', ibid., IV, no. 34 (1861), 309; 'Trioedd Breintiau'r Beirdd (Allan o Lyfr Llewelyn Sion)', ibid., V, no. 41 (1863), 267; 'Moelmutian Triads: By the Late Iolo Morganwg, B.B.D.', *Cambrian Journal*, V (1858), 4–25; Iolo Morganwg, 'Gweddillion Llenyddol: Trioedd Doethineb [*O Gronfa y Parch. Ganon Silvan Evans*]', *Y Geninen*, VIII, no. 4 (1890), 294.

[57] 'Y Diarebion Cymraeg', *Y Traethodydd*, III (1847), 290.

(Through them we become familiar with the earliest histories of our nation, with the wisdom of our forefathers, their religion, their ethics, their laws, philosophy, medicine, agriculture, poetry, music, rituals, traditions, and political travails.)

Such triads helped to promote the impression that early Welsh civilization had been so advanced that the Welsh had lost more under the Romans than they had gained. The legal triads of the fictitious fifth-century king Dyfnwal Moelmud had not only informed the authentic Welsh Laws of Hywel Dda but, through Alfred the Great's Welsh adviser Asser (whom Iolo had identified as the fictitious bard Geraint Fardd Glas), had become the basis of English law.[58] Amateurs thus toured the lecturing circuit with peculiar versions of early British history based on triads which glorified early Welsh society and law. In 1860 George H. Whalley, MP for Peterborough, gave a paper at the London Mechanics' Institute in which he claimed that:

> These and other primitive laws of Britain not only rise far superior in manly sense and high principle to the laws of ancient Greece and Rome, but put to shame the enactments of nations calling themselves Christians at the present day. They contain the essence of law, religion, and chivalry.[59]

For Ab Ithel, the best-educated and most highly respected of Iolo's early legatees, the triads provided a structure for the theoretical history of Britain which he published in the *Cambrian Journal* between 1854 and his death in 1861.[60] In later decades several series of triads were quoted in Thomas Gee's *Encyclopaedia Cambrensis: Y Gwyddoniadur Cymreig* to illustrate subjects such as the belief in metempsychosis.[61] Even Oxford-educated historians of the younger generation like Owen M. Edwards quoted Ioloic triads in order, for example, to illustrate the national character of the Welsh under the Romans.[62] Up until the First World War the corpus of published triads was regularly expanded by those who were granted access to the Llanover collection.[63]

Although questions regarding the authenticity of some of the triads arose occasionally, their veracity was accepted by most writers.[64] Few scholars in Wales and England, let alone France and Germany, suspected that their view of

---

[58] Ieuan ab Gruffydd, 'Darlith ar Hanes Cynfrodorion Ynys Prydain, Eu Trafnid, Moesau, &c. Parhad', *Seren Gomer*, XVII, no. 222 (1834), 66–8.

[59] 'Ancient British History (a lecture given at the London Mechanics' Institute on 5th March) by George H. Whalley, Esq., MP of Peterborough', *Cambrian Journal*, VII (1860), 95.

[60] This series ran from Ab Ithel, 'History: The Traditional Annals of the Cymry. Chapter I. The Creation and the Deluge', *Cambrian Journal*, I (1854), 84–97, to idem, 'The Traditionary Annals of the Cymry: XXVII. The Civil Arts – Literature', ibid., VII (1861), 122–39.

[61] 'Abred' in *Encyclopaedia Cambrensis: Y Gwyddoniadur Cymreig. Cyfrol I*, pp. 28–9.

[62] Owen M. Edwards, 'Geneva: Ei Dylanwad ar Gymru', *Cymru Fydd*, I, no. 1 (1888), 29–30.

[63] D. Silvan Evans, 'Trioedd y Llafurwr', *Y Geninen*, XII, no. 3 (1894), 203–4; Cadrawd, 'Seigiau o Sir Forganwg', *Cymru*, XLII, no. 251 (1912), 326.

[64] 'The Reliability of British Records and Traditions: Paper read before the Royal Society of Literature . . . on Wednesday evening, the 25th January, by Mr R. B. Holt, a member of the council of the society' in Brierley (ed.), *Cymru Fu*, I, pp. 66–8.

early Welsh history was based on relatively recent evidence provided by a humble stonemason from the Romantic period. Since many of them were also Romantic nationalists like Iolo, his triads reflected their world view more closely than did the genuine early material, which they preferred to eschew in favour of the fictitious triads. Although Ferdinand Walter, whose monograph *Das Alte Wales* (1859) was the first study in German of the Welsh legal system (and remains the fullest to this day), established his professional credentials as a scholar by offering an admirable overview of the works hitherto published on Welsh history and literature, he was so besotted with Iolo that he quoted his triads of Dyfnwal Moelmud to illustrate what he called 'monuments of lost glory . . . in which love of the fatherland, national pride and hatred of the victor sought nourishment and a substitute' ('Denkmäler verschwundener Herrlichkeit . . . worin die Vaterlandsliebe, der nationale Stolz und der Hass gegen die Besieger Nahrung und Ersatz suchten').[65] Moreover, his detailed review of all the material, together with its value for researchers, was led by the Dyfnwal Moelmud series.[66] Although he emphasized that, being orally transmitted sources, the triads were likely to have changed through the centuries, he never suspected Iolo of having concocted them. Indeed, he believed that the fact that they had been passed down the generations made them an expression of the 'mental attitude' (*Geisteshaltung*) of the Welsh, and were thus part of their national psyche. Welshmen who studied in Germany, notably John Gruffydd Moelwyn-Hughes, upheld this tradition and, as late as 1935, the renowned Celticist Rudolf Thurneysen, in a lecture on Walter's work, dated the triads of Dyfnwal Moelmud to the later Middle Ages.[67] Later English scholars of standing also utilized the 'Moelmutian triads' as historical evidence, and referred to their inclusion in Aneurin Owen's *Ancient Laws and Institutes of Wales*, which had been published on behalf of the Welsh Manuscripts Society, as proof of their authenticity.[68] Although the Cambridge scholar Hubert Lewis suspected that they had 'evidently been much enlarged by the comments of modern expositors', they figured in his *Ancient Laws of Wales: Viewed Especially in regard to the Light They Throw upon the Origin of some English Institutions*, a work prepared for publication by the young J. E. Lloyd, and published in 1889.[69]

---

[65] Walter, *Das Alte Wales*, p. 2. See also Stefan Zimmer, 'Julius Rodenberg und Ferdinand Walter – deutsche Annäherungen an Wales im 19. Jahrhundert' in Bernhard Maier and Stefan Zimmer (eds.), *150 Jahre 'Mabinogion' – Deutsch-Walisische Kulturbeziehungen* (Tübingen, 2001), pp. 257–63.

[66] Walter, *Das Alte Wales*, p. 9.

[67] John Gruffydd Moelwyn-Hughes, *Die cymrischen Triaden, ihr Ursprung und ihr Verhältnis zu den Mabinogion* (Leipsig [sic], 1903); Zimmer, 'Julius Rodenberg und Ferdinand Walter', p. 263.

[68] Aneurin Owen, *Ancient Laws and Institutes of Wales* (2 vols., Llandovery, 1841). However, on p. ix of volume I, Owen stated that they had 'no warrant of authenticity'.

[69] Hubert Lewis, *The Ancient Laws of Wales: Viewed especially in regard to the Light They Throw upon the Origin of some English Institutions*, ed. J. E. Lloyd (London, 1889), pp. 24–5, 34–6, 105–7, 126–30, 195.

Fig. 8 A postcard depicting Rowland Williams (Hwfa Môn) who, as archdruid from 1895 until his death in 1905, appeared to many of his contemporaries to be the 'incarnation of the secrets of the early bardic circle'.

Iolo's triads provided the framework for his bardo-druidism, a belief system which was perceived by his followers to be the religion of 'a race who had attained a certain state of civilization and intellectual refinement'.[70] In English ideology the romantic image of the Druid as a peaceful priest and teacher was replaced during the first half of the nineteenth century by that of the representative of a 'failed and degenerate religion when priesthood had come between God and humanity', and of a bloodthirsty pagan hostile to early Christianity.[71] In contrast, Iolo's Welsh heirs continued to use the concept of druidism to underpin Wales's ancient Christian credentials. William Richards's *Welsh Nonconformist Memorial; or, Cambro-British Biography Containing Sketches of the Founders of the Protestant Dissenting Interest in Wales* reproduced the well-known sketch included in Aylett Sammes' *Britannia Antiqua Illustrata* (1676), which depicted a Druid accompanied by 'iconic signs associated with a revered Christian tradition of simplicity, of removal from the world and of spiritual profundity'.[72] The image was followed by a Ioloic 'Sketch of Druidism' or 'Bardism ... which has been said to comprehend all the leading principles which tend to spread liberty, peace, and happiness among mankind, and to have

---

[70] Z., 'Druidism and Darwinism', *Bye-Gones*, 7 May 1873, 165.
[71] Sam Smiles, 'The Image of the Druid in British Art, *c.*1670–1850' in Sabine Rieckhoff (ed.), *Celtes et Gaulois l'archéologie face à l'histoire: Celtes et Gaulois dans l'histoire, l'historiographie et l'idéologie moderne* (Glux-en-Glenne, 2006), pp. 118–20. See also idem, *The Image of Antiquity: Ancient Britain and the Romantic Imagination* (New Haven, Conn., 1994), pp. 88–96, 107–18. See also Champion, 'The Appropriation of the Phoenicians in British Imperial Ideology', 452.
[72] Smiles, *The Image of Antiquity*, p. 114.

been no more inimical to Christianity than the religion of Noah, Job, or Abraham'.[73] Three years later Jonathan Williams's *Druopaedia* compared the Britons and their Druids to the early Christians. Both had been victims of hostile propaganda which falsely accused them of engaging in bloody sacrifices.[74] Subsequent authors developed Iolo's claims that the Druids had rejected the principles of the Roman church on the grounds of 'purer, or at any rate less corrupt principles of Christianity than those of Rome' ('egwyddorion Cristionogaeth burach; neu beth bynnag, llai llygredig nag eiddo Rhufain').[75] Druidism was considered to be at the root of the improvements made in agriculture, mechanics, and all other arts prior to the coming of the Romans.[76] Welsh bardism, through which druidism had been passed down the generations, was claimed to be of 'divine origin' ('dwyfol darddiad'), and part of the remnants of the principles given to Adam and bequeathed to Noah, a branch of the first patriarchal religion.[77] The Christian credentials of bardo-druidism were not only celebrated by Iolo's legatees but were also reflected in weighty periodicals such as *Y Dysgedydd*, *Y Traethodydd* and *Y Beirniad*, and in the interest shown by scholars on the Continent. Adolphe Pictet, who published Iolo's writings on bardism, together with a translation, in 1856, and who bemoaned the fact that English scholarship had neglected this source, was favourably portrayed in the *Cambrian Journal*.[78] Even Jane Williams, who was venerated for working 'with historical facts . . . verified by competent authorities', drew on Ioloic sources for her accounts of druidism and bardism whenever other material was judged to be deficient.[79]

Iolo's principal heirs, however, were Ab Ithel and Evan Davies (Myfyr Morganwg), both of whom contributed prominently to the distribution, discussion and development of his bardo-druidism.[80] Ab Ithel's educational

---

[73] William Richards, *Welsh Nonconformist Memorial; or, Cambro-British Biography Containing Sketches of the Founders of the Protestant Dissenting Interest in Wales* (London, 1820), pp. 2–3.
[74] Jonathan Williams, *Druopaedia; or, A New and Interesting View of the Druidical System of Education; Elucidating the Obscurities in which the Early Parts of British History are Involved* (Leominster, 1823), p. 79.
[75] David Lloyd Isaac, 'Y Diarebion Cymraeg', *Y Traethodydd*, III (1847), 293.
[76] John Jones, *On the State of Agriculture and the Progress of Arts and Manufactures in Britain, during the Period, and under the Influence, of the Druidical System* (London, 1851), p. 3; Berwyn, 'Queries: The Lost Arts of Wales', *Bye-Gones*, 6 March 1872, 37.
[77] Salmon Llwyd, 'Llenoriaeth: Awduron Cymru. Rhif III. Llywarch Hen', *Y Brython*, I, no. 6 (1858), 83.
[78] 'Derwyddiaeth a Christionogaeth', *Y Dysgedydd*, XXXIV (1855), 102–6, 147–50, 222–5; Llywarch Owain Reynolds, 'Derwyddiaeth', *Y Beirniad*, XX, no. 82 (1879), 276–81; Adolphe Pictet, *Le mystère des bardes de l'Ile de Bretagne ou la Doctrine des bardes gallois du Moyen Age, sur Dieu, la vie future et la transmigration des ames. Texte original, Traduction et Commentaire* (Genève, 1856); Ab Ithel, 'Reviews: Le Mystère des Bardes de l'Ile de Bretagne ou la Doctrine des bardes gallois du Moyen Age . . . Adolphe Pictet', *Cambrian Journal*, IV (1857), 158–60.
[79] Charles Wilkins, 'Literary and Arts Notes', *Red Dragon*, VII (1885), 460–1; Williams, *A History of Wales*, pp. 6–9, 208, 226.
[80] On the efforts of Ab Ithel and Myfyr Morganwg to promote the Gorsedd and the eisteddfod, see Chapter 3 above.

background and social standing as an Anglican priest secured for him the national and international influence which eluded Myfyr Morganwg. As early as 1844 he had prefaced his *Ecclesiastical Antiquities of the Cymry or the Ancient British Church* with an exposition on 'Bardism' which associated Iolo's concepts firmly with the Welsh Christian tradition once more.[81] In almost every issue his *Cambrian Journal* promoted a bardo-druidism which bore Christian overtones.[82] His main contribution, however, was the publication of the first volume of *Barddas: or, A Collection of Original Documents, Illustrative of the Theology, Wisdom, and Usages of the Bardo-Druidic System of the Isle of Britain*.[83] This was the largest fully translated collection of Iolo's material and it made his views on bardo-druidism widely available to the English-speaking world for the first time. Based mainly on the triads, it began with a lengthy section on the origin and development of bardic symbolism and its alphabet. This was followed by sections on the theology of the ancient Welsh and on their wisdom. The most important part of the volume, however, was a substantial preface which outlined the history of bardism and explored its connection with the Continental druidism described by classical authors, while defending its Christian credentials against their attacks. It concluded with a sketch of its re-establishment following the departure of the Romans and its further evolution from Arthur's round table down to Edward Williams (Iolo Morganwg) himself – the last link in the chain of 'bardic succession'.[84] The second volume, published in 1874 on the basis of a manuscript found among Ab Ithel's papers, contained a detailed account of the more mundane aspects of bardism and of the Gorsedd on the basis of Iolo's bardic triads.[85] The substantial preface in the first volume of *Barddas*, which provided the basis for the entry on *bardd* (bard) in both editions of *Y Gwyddoniadur*, also publicized the various versions of the Gorsedd prayer and the bards' dress-code within the Gorsedd. Abridged translations of the work, such as Paul Ladmirault's *Abrégé du Barddas ou Livre du Bardisme*, continued to appear well into the twentieth century.[86] But Ab Ithel's *Barddas* remained the most extensive published collection of bardo-druidic material assembled from the Llanover collection. Modern Druids still venerate

---

[81] John Williams, *Ecclesiastical Antiquities of the Cymry or the Ancient Church: Its History, Doctrine, and Rites* (London, 1844), pp. 1–47.

[82] J. Williams Ab Ithel, 'General Literature: Druidism', *Cambrian Journal*, II (1855), 260–8; idem, 'Druidism: III. Bardic Reform under Prydain. IV. From Prydain to Dyfnwal Moelmud', ibid., VII, Supplemental Number (1860), 317–37; idem, 'Druidism: Chapter V. Dyfnwal Moelmud', ibid., VII (1861), 61–9.

[83] Idem, *Barddas*, I.

[84] Ibid., p. lxxvi.

[85] Idem, *Barddas: or, A Collection of Original Documents, Illustrative of the Theology, Wisdom, and Usages of the Bardo-Druidic System of the Isle of Britain, with Translation and Notes*, Volume II (London, 1874).

[86] 'Bardd' in *Encyclopaedia Cambrensis*, I, pp. 525–61; Paul Ladmirault, *Abrégé du Barddas ou Livre du Bardisme* (Paris, 1931).

it as the 'central document of the nineteenth-century Druid Revival, and a major source for Druids throughout the Western world'.[87]

Myfyr Morganwg's efforts on behalf of Iolo's bardic legacy more than equalled those of Ab Ithel, but the manner in which he developed both the public ritual of the Gorsedd and the doctrines behind it hindered the success of his labours.[88] Unlike Ab Ithel, who treated Iolo's manuscripts as Christian scriptures to be enacted and disseminated unchanged, Myfyr Morganwg took it upon himself to embellish them. The torrent of complicated interpretations of the bardo-druidic system which issued from his pen, as well as the bizarre Gorsedd ceremonies he organized, prompted his opponents to accuse him of promoting paganism. From 1855 onwards *Seren Gomer* refused to print what its editors believed to be blasphemy, and although the editor of the Unitarian periodical *Yr Ymofynydd* claimed to have great respect for Myfyr and to 'enjoy listening to him every time' ('bob amser yn hoffi gwrandaw arno'), he did not print any of his writings after the 1850s.[89] Copies of Myfyr Morganwg's lengthy works *Gogoniant Hynafol y Cymmry* and *Hynafiaeth Aruthrol y Trwn* are rare nowadays because Nonconformist ministers allegedly advised their flocks to buy copies and then burn them as the works of the devil.[90] Although a series of highly public clashes with the critic Thomas Stephens on the pages of *Seren Gomer* and *Yr Ymofynydd* offered Myfyr the opportunity to bring his ideas to a wider audience, they also provided his opponents with ample opportunity to refute his claims and subject him to ridicule.[91] Crucially, however, his critics

---

[87] John Michael Greer, Ancient Order of Druids in America, 'Advance Praise for Barddas' in J. Williams Ab Ithel (ed.), *The Barddas of Iolo Morganwg: A Collection of Original Documents, Illustrative of the Theology, Wisdom, and Usages of the Bardo-Druidic System of the Isle of Britain* (Boston, Mass., 2004), p. i.

[88] For the Gorsedd, see Chapter 3 above.

[89] 'Rhagymadrodd', *Seren Gomer*, XXXVIII (1855), iii; Myfyr Morganwg, 'Ar y Nod Cyfrin (Allan O "Seren Gomer," Chwefror, 1853)', *Yr Ymofynydd*, VI, no. 67 (1853), 72.

[90] Evan Davies, *Gogoniant Hynafol y Cymmry: sef Arddangosiad o Gyfrin-ddysg Hynaf y Byd allan o Gyfrinion Gorsedd Beirdd Cyntefigion Ynys Brydain* (Pontypridd, 1865); idem, *Hynafiaeth Aruthrol y Trwn neu Orsedd Beirdd Ynys Brydain a'i Barddas Gyfrin* (Pontypridd, 1875); Walters, 'Myfyr Morganwg and the Rocking-stone Gorsedd' in *Rattleskull Genius*, p. 495.

[91] The series in *Seren Gomer* included eight instalments, running from Bardd Cyfrin, '/|\ Stephens, Merthyr, yn Fyw; a Iolo Morganwg wedi Marw: At Olygyddion Seren Gomer', *Seren Gomer*, XXXVI, no. 449 (1853), 87–90, to idem, 'Amddiffyniad y Bardd Cyfrin i Henafiaeth y Bod Uchod ... Llythyr VIII', ibid., XXXVI, no. 470 (1854), 498–502. Parts of the series were reprinted as a reply to Thomas Stephens's writings in *Yr Ymofynydd* and duly provoked further criticism. Bardd Cyfrin, 'Ar y Nod Cyfrin', *Yr Ymofynydd*, VI, no. 67 (1853), 72–5; idem, 'Henafiaeth Mawr yr Enw a'r Nod Cyfrin: Yn erbyn ein gwrthwynebydd o Ferthyr i ddiweddaru yr arferiad o honynt gan y Beirdd Cymreig', ibid., no. 68 (1853), 93–7; idem, 'Henafiaeth Yr Enw a'r Nod Cyfrin: Yn erbyn Haeriadau Stephens o Ferthyr, i Geisio Diweddaru, a Gwatwor yr Arferiad ohonynt yn mysg Beirdd Cenedl y Cymry', ibid., no. 71 (1853), 166–9; idem, 'Ateb y Bardd Cyfrin i Ofyniad J. Jones iddo', ibid., VI, no. 74 (1853), 241–2; Myfyr Morganwg, 'Barddas', *Y Brython*, I, no. 12 (1858), 180–1; idem, 'Barddas', ibid., no. 14 (1858), 213; idem, 'Barddas', ibid., no. 15 (1858), 229. See also Walters, 'Myfyr Morganwg and the Rocking-stone Gorsedd' in *Rattleskull Genius*, pp. 493–4.

condemned his writings as 'Myfyriology' (*Myfyryddiaeth*), and chose not to mention the name of the Glamorgan stonemason who had inspired him.[92]

Following the death of Ab Ithel (1862) and Myfyr Morganwg (1888), the baton of bardo-druidism was taken up by the likes of Owen Morgan (Morien), a journalist who regularly wrote about druidism in the *Western Mail* and in periodicals such as *Cymru*, and who published a series of esoteric works on the subject in Welsh and in English.[93] Amateur scholars such as Cadrawd, the parish priest Glanffrwd and John Jones (Ioan Ddu) vigorously defended the antiquity of bardo-druidism and the Gorsedd well into the twentieth century. They derived what they believed to be irrefutable evidence from Iolo's own writings and from Ab Ithel's *Barddas*.[94] At the same time new groups from within Wales and beyond began to take possession of druidism. The Druids were pressed into service by several political activists, notably the London politician and writer 'Griffith', who used druidic tenets to defend Welsh culture against what he believed to be the vicious attacks of a prejudiced English readership, and to demand political action on matters relating to the appointment of Welsh-speaking judges and the disestablishment of the Anglican church in Wales.[95] In 1906 the Merthyr Tydfil 'Educational Publishing Company' (in whose backlist were to be found such popular titles as Owen Rhoscomyl's *Flamebearers of Welsh History*) published D. Delta Evans's *The Ancient Bards of Britain (sometimes called 'Druids'): Being a Critical Inquiry into Traditions concerning their History, Philosophy, Religion, Ethics, and Rites, in the Light of Science and Modern Thought*, a work which combined Ioloic material with modern political jargon. The bards, so it claimed, supported neither 'that baneful philosophical doctrine of Individualism' nor 'the wild theory of Socialism', but 'very wisely steered along a middle course between' them:

> and while they undoubtedly perceived that what we now call individualism, or egotism, is a mischievous disintegrating force, they nevertheless avoided everything savouring of sectarianism or mere caste. The essential elements in the whole system

[92] Thomas Stephens, 'Stephens o Ferthyr ar y Nod Cyfrin a Myfyryddiaeth', *Yr Ymofynydd*, VI, no. 75 (1853), 253–8; William Thomas (Gwilym Marles), 'Gogoniant Hynafol y Cymry [Adolygiad]', *Yr Athraw*, I, no. 11 (1866), 256–60.

[93] Morien replied to John Morris-Jones's critique of the Gorsedd in a series of articles which ran from Morien, 'Hynafiaeth Aruthrol Gorsedd Beirdd Ynys Prydain I', *Cymru*, X, no. 59 (1896), 331–3, to idem, 'Hynafiaeth Aruthrol Gorsedd Beirdd Ynys Prydain VII: Genedigaeth Gwy Ion Bach a Thaliesin, Neu yr Hu Ail', ibid., XII, no. 64 (1896), 239–42. Among his books were *Pabell Dofydd: sef Eglurhad ar Anianyddiaeth Grefyddol yr Hen Dderwyddon Cymreig* (Caerdydd, 1889) and *The Light of Britannia: The Mysteries of Ancient British Druidism Unveiled; The Original Source of Phallic Worship Revealed; The Secrets of the Court of King Arthur Revealed; the Creed of the Stone Age Revealed; the Holy Greal Discovered in Wales* (Cardiff, 1890).

[94] Glanffrwd Thomas, 'Gorsedd y Beirdd: A Oes Sail i'r Grediniaeth yn Nghylch ei Henafiaeth, Ei Hawdurdod, a Phurdeb ei Hathrawiaeth?', *Y Geninen*, VI, no. 2 (1888), 184–8; idem, 'The Bards of Tir Iarll and the Glamorgan Gorsedd' in Brierley (ed.), *Cymru Fu*, I, pp. 175–8; John Jones (Ioan Ddu), 'Gorsedd y Beirdd: A Oes Sail i'r Grediniaeth yn Nghylch ei Henafiaeth, Ei Hawdurdod, a Phurdeb ei Hathrawiaeth?', *Y Geninen*, VI, no. 1 (1888), 46–50.

[95] 'Griffith', *The Welsh Question and Druidism* (London, 1887), pp. 17–25.

of Bardism were fellowship, fraternity, and the common service of humanity, every man being a brother and 'equal in honour'.[96]

The modern science of astronomy was also enlisted in order to prove the antiquity of bardo-druidism by linking it to the erection of ancient standing stones and stone circles. In August 1908 the director of the Solar Physics Observatory, Sir Norman Lockyer, delivered a well-received lecture to the Royal Institution of South Wales in Swansea, in which he argued, on the basis of material culled from the Llanover collection and with the help of his own astronomical calculations, that the Gorsedd was 'at least forty centuries old'.[97] Such demonstrations reinforced the hold druidism exercised over the imagination of both amateur historians and creative writers.[98] The promise of an alternative world-view which purported to be ancient might not have been necessary for Welsh patriots and scholars after the First World War, but it continued to entice those who sought alternative belief-systems. In 1924, for example, an essay on *The Druids and Theosophy* written by Peter Freeman MP introduced his disciples to the basic concepts and signs of druidism, most of which were drawn from Ab Ithel's *Barddas*.[99] The Theosophical Society's president, Dr Annie Besant, contributed a preface to the work which revealed that she was utterly oblivious to advances in modern science.[100] In Continental Europe, too, Yves Berthou (Kaledvoulc'h) clung on to what he perceived to be ancient doctrines by publishing a trilingual edition of bardic triads – in Welsh, Breton and French – together with selected passages from *Barddas* in a bid to explain the main principles of druidism.[101] Even following the celebration of the centenary of Iolo's death in 1926, this arcane, but endlessly intriguing, construct continued to live on in the public mind.

The third pillar which supported the nineteenth-century belief that the early civilization of the Welsh was superior to that of its rivals was the bardic alphabet – *Coelbren y Beirdd* – which Iolo Morganwg had derived from runic writing systems by using his skills as a stonemason and his gift of imagination. Although an extended exposition on the bardic alphabet was not published until 1840, *Coelbren y Beirdd* and the *peithynen* (bardic frame) had aroused the interest of antiquaries and other scholars from the end of the eighteenth century onwards. The second volume of the *Cambrian Quarterly Magazine* published a letter from Iolo to Walter Davies (Gwallter Mechain) in which he

---

[96] Evans, *The Ancient Bards of Britain (sometimes called 'Druids'): Being a Critical Inquiry into Traditions concerning their History, Philosophy, Religion, Ethics, and Rites, in the Light of Science and Modern Thought*, pp. 40–2.
[97] Norman Lockyer, *The Antiquity of the Gorsedd: A Lecture delivered to the Royal Institution of South Wales* (Swansea, 1908), p. 13, Fig. 11, 'Plan of a Gorsedd'.
[98] Frederic Evans, *Tir Iarll: The Earl's Land* (Cardiff, 1912), p. 29.
[99] Peter Freeman, *The Druids and Theosophy* (Glasgow, 1924), *passim*.
[100] Ibid., p. 2.
[101] Yves Berthou (Kaledvoulc'h), *Sous le chêne des druides: Les Triades bardiques avec le texte original gallois; Le Mystère de la vie et du monde, d'après le Barddas; Le druidisme et la destinée de l'homme* (Paris, 1931).

described in some detail 'the ancient bardic alphabet, called Coelbren y Beirdd'. It explained the characters, and was accompanied by a small woodcut of a 'peithynen, or bardic book'.[102] In 1802 Edward Jones referred to it in his second volume of Welsh relics, *The Bardic Museum*, and by 1819 the *Cambrian Register* was using it as proof that the Britons had a system of writing which pre-dated the Romans, and referred readers to Edward 'Celtic' Davies's *Celtic Researches* and the grammar which prefaced William Owen Pughe's *Dictionary of the Welsh Language* for illustrations and explanations.[103] Eisteddfod essays on Welsh antiquities and druidism reprinted tables which explained the bardic letters and vigorously refuted accusations of forgery.[104] The gold standard on the subject, however, was set by Taliesin's prize-winning essay at the Abergavenny eisteddfod of 1838, a work which was published in 1840.[105] Following Taliesin's publication, which was believed to have removed any doubts over its provenance, the bardic alphabet appeared in a wide variety of essays on the development of writing. One of the most extraordinary was a series of essays on philology by David Lloyd Isaac (Dafydd Llwyd Isaac) in *Seren Gomer*. Although it contained surprisingly modern insights like those on the primality of sound, it bore the imprint of the bizarre theories of Aylett Sammes and insisted that *Coelbren y Beirdd* reflected authentic druidic learning and could confidently be adjudged the oldest alphabet in the world.[106] Even though some writers echoed Thomas Stephens's view that *Coelbren y Beirdd* had been devised by the poet Gwilym Tew in the fifteenth century, the overwhelming consensus was that it was authentic and as old as the runes.[107]

Writing about the bardic alphabet went hand in hand with the continued depiction and construction of *peithynau*, the wooden frames which had allegedly been used to safeguard and promote bardism. The young Carnhuanawc, a competent draughtsman whose work was reckoned good enough to be published in Theophilus Jones's *History of the County of Brecknock*, was so impressed by this device that he not only made a sketch of it but also

[102] E. W., 'On the ancient bardic alphabet, called coelbren y beirdd', *Cambrian Quarterly Magazine*, II, no. 1 (1830), 92–5.
[103] Edward Jones, *The Bardic Museum: or Primitive British Literature and Rarities* (London, 1802), p. 4; Anon., 'A Sketch of the History of the Britons continued', *Cambrian Register*, III (1819), 11; Edward Davies, *Celtic Researches* (London, 1803), p. 272; William Owen, *A Dictionary of the Welsh Language, Explained in English* (London, 1803), pp. 3–6. See also 'Welsh Language: The Bardic Letters', *The Cambro-Briton*, I (1820–1), 241–6 [faced by an illustration of 'Coelbren y Beirdd, or Bardic Alphabet']; 'Coelbren y Beirdd', *Y Gwladgarwr*, VI, no. 72 (1838), 361–4.
[104] J. Roberts, *Druidical Remains and Antiquities of the Ancient Britons, Principally in Glamorgan; Containing a General Account of the Same, in England, Wales, Scotland, France, &c.; with Notes and Illustrations on the Learning and Superstitions of the Druids – The Downfall of Druidism as a Religious System – and the Introduction of Christianity into Britain* (Swansea, 1842), pp. 34–7.
[105] Williams, *Traethawd ar Hynafiaeth ac Awdurdodaeth Coelbren y Beirdd*.
[106] Dafydd Llwyd Isaac, 'Ieitheg – Y Gymraeg I', *Seren Gomer*, XXXIV, no. 433 (1851), 443–9; idem, 'Ieitheg – Y Gymraeg III', ibid., XXXV, no. 437 (1852), 66.
[107] John Peter (Ioan Pedr), 'Hanes Ysgrifeniaeth', *Y Beirniad*, II, no. 8 (1861), 331–43; H. W. L., 'Replies: Coelbren y Beirdd', *Bye-Gones*, 8 October 1879, 307–8; R. B. Holt, 'The Reliability of British Records and Traditions' in Brierley (ed.), *Cymru Fu*, I, p. 71.

Fig. 9 The successful *peithynen* at the Carmarthen National Eisteddfod, 1867. This *peithynen* was made by David E. Williams of Llangernyw and features a *cywydd* by Lewys Glyn Cothi to Siancyn ap Tomos ap Gruffudd ap Niclas. The top and base of the frame bear the bardic mottoes 'Y gwir yn erbyn y byd' and 'Calon wrth galon'. The sides are adorned with the national symbols of leek and harp, and with the feathers of the Prince of Wales.

constructed a *peithynen* of his own.[108] John Henry Vivian, who was elected MP for Swansea in 1832, was the proud owner of one of those 'bardic books'.[109] Eisteddfodau, both great and small, popularized so-called ancient bardic traditions by organizing competitions devoted to this curious alphabet and its origins. In 1853 E. P. Meredith (Ieuan Gryg) from Monmouth won a prize for the 'Best English Translation of Taliesin ab Iolo's Essay on the Coelbren y Beirdd, with additional Remarks, Notes and a Model of the Peithynen'.[110] The prize for the best *peithynen* 'after the style of the old time' ('yn ôl dull yr hen amser'), advertised at the Llangollen eisteddfod of 1858, was awarded to E. Lloyd (Brawd Estyn).[111] The beautifully carved and inscribed bardic frame fashioned by David E. Williams of Llangernyw for the Carmarthen eisteddfod of 1867 is one of five such frames housed in the National Library of Wales.[112] As late as 1900 even Sir John Rhŷs published a description and photograph of the 'Jesus College Peithynen' which was said to have been carved and constructed by Iolo Morganwg himself.[113] The programme of the international Celtic Congress of Caernarfon in 1904 featured the photograph of a bardic frame owned by M. T. Morris of Caernarfon, which was authenticated in the accompanying text by a reference to one of Iolo's triads. Carved on the bardic frame was one of the many maxims Iolo had attributed to Catwg Ddoeth.[114] Well into the twentieth century, one of Iolo's most remarkable inventions continued to provoke interest.[115]

## *A pantheon of cultural heroes*

Iolo's theoretical history was peopled with what Rachel Bromwich has called 'culture heroes', romanticized and sometimes deified ancestors, rulers and bards, who had led the Britons to their territories, devised and upheld the rules of their ancient laws and religion, and developed their poetic arts through the millennia. These heroes were eagerly adopted by cultural patriots in Wales who, following the lead of Thomas Carlyle, embraced hero-worship and the heroic wholeheartedly, though their icons were peacekeepers and poets rather than

[108] Lord, *The Visual Culture of Wales: Imaging the Nation*, p. 251. For Carnhuanawc's *peithynen*, see NLW Roll 107.
[109] Roberts, *Druidical Remains and Antiquities of the Ancient Britons*, p. 45.
[110] 'Subjects and Prizes for the Twentieth Anniversary of the Abergavenny Cymreigyddion', *Cambrian Journal*, I (1854), 54.
[111] *Y Brython*, I, no. 15 (1858), 225.
[112] NLW Roll 108.
[113] John Rhŷs, 'The Jesus College Peithynen', *Y Cymmrodor*, XIII (1900), 164–8.
[114] *Rhaglen (Programme) Y Gynhadledd Oll-Geltaidd . . . Caernarfon, Awst 30ain – Medi 3ydd, 1904* (Caernarfon, 1904), p. 35. See also Cadrawd, 'Beirdd Margam', *Cymru*, XLVII, no. 280 (1914), 225.
[115] Freeman, *The Druids and Theosophy*, p. 13.

soldiers like Oliver Cromwell.[116] Iolo's pantheon offered the Welsh an unbroken line of succession which stretched from the earliest heroes, lawgivers and saints – Hu Gadarn, Dyfnwal Moelmud and Catwg Ddoeth – to romantic fourteenth-century poets like Rhys Goch ap Rhicert and Dafydd ap Gwilym, to the fifteenth-century national leader Owain Glyndŵr, and onwards to the seventeenth and eighteenth-century bards and scholars of the Chair of Glamorgan. By accepting his creations as theirs, Iolo's legatees inherited this continuity.[117]

Many of Iolo's heroes entered Welsh culture at the very beginning of the nineteenth century when the third volume of *The Myvyrian Archaiology of Wales* and William Owen Pughe's *Cambrian Biography* were published.[118] The latter volume in particular deeply influenced biographical writing by providing researchers with a mass of detailed information which could not be found elsewhere. A profusion of Ioloic material was used in *Y Brython*'s 'Enwogion Anghofiedig Cymru' (Wales's Forgotten Famous) and also in biographical dictionaries such as John H. Parry's *Cambrian Plutarch: Comprising Memoirs from Some of the Most Eminent Welshmen* and Robert Williams's *Enwogion Cymru: A Biographical Dictionary*.[119] Until the end of the nineteenth century volumes like *Barddas* and collections of eisteddfod poetry such as Thomas Williams's *Awen y Maen Chwyf* were prefaced with family trees and roll-calls of national heroes which began with Hu Gadarn and continued to the days of Iolo Morganwg – the last in a prestigious lineage.[120]

Triads relating to, and writings about, Hu Gadarn and Dyfnwal Moelmud personalized the widespread conviction that the Welsh could boast a superior ancient civilization. Both were mythical and shadowy figures when Iolo encountered them in his studies of medieval Welsh literature, but he transformed them into men of supreme national importance.[121] Hu Gadarn (Hu the Mighty), whose name Iolo most probably encountered in 'Cywydd y Llafurwr' by Iolo Goch, had led the 'Nation of the Cymmry to the Island of Britain ... from the Summer Country, otherwise called Deffrobani', had

---

[116] Thomas Carlyle, *On Heroes, Hero-worship and the Heroic in History* (London, 1841).

[117] Only a small selection of those whom Iolo invented or romantically enhanced can be examined here. See also *TLIM, passim*.

[118] William Owen, *The Cambrian Biography: or Historical Notices of Celebrated Men among the Ancient Britons* (London, 1803).

[119] William Rowlands (Gwilym Lleyn), 'Enwogion Anghofiedig Cymru', *Y Brython*, IV, no. 34 (1861), 281–2. The series ran until autumn 1863. John H. Parry, *The Cambrian Plutarch: Comprising Memoirs from Some of the Most Eminent Welshmen, From the Earliest Times to the Present* (London, 1834); Robert Williams, *Enwogion Cymru: A Biographical Dictionary* (Llandovery, 1852).

[120] Williams, *Barddas*, I, pp. lxxiv–lxxvi; Thomas Williams, 'Haeddedigol Goffadwriaeth am Hynafiaid y Cymry a ymdrechasant y'mhlaid Rhyddid eu Gwlad' in Taliesin Williams (ed.), *Awen y Maen Chwyf*, pp. 2–10.

[121] On the provenance of both figures, see Bromwich, 'Trioedd Ynys Prydain', *THSC* (1968), 322–4. For an assessment of the historic sources for Hu Gadarn, see also A. C. Rejhon, 'Hu Gadarn: Folklore and Fabrication' in Patrick K. Ford (ed.), *Celtic Folklore and Christianity: Studies in Memory of William W. Heist* (Santa Barbara, Calif., 1983), pp. 201–12.

established their social customs, and initiated the oral tradition in poetry as a means of recording history.[122] Dyfnwal Moelmud, whom Iolo had plucked from a paragraph in Geoffrey of Monmouth's *Historia Regum Britanniae*, was extolled as the nation's first lawgiver, to whom were attributed two series of 284 legal triads.[123] Their inclusion in William Owen Pughe's *Cambrian Biography* meant that thereafter they formed an essential part of many speeches delivered at eisteddfodau and essays on the origin and early history of the Welsh nation published in pamphlets and periodicals in Wales and England.[124] Popular writers on religious matters, such as the Englishman Ernest Silvanus Appleyard, showed their familiarity with, and trust in, Ioloic material by referring to Hu Gadarn as 'the great leader, hero, lawgiver; and, earthly honours exhausted, representative deity of the Cymry', and to Dyfnwal Moelmud as 'one of the earliest names of which we have any authentic information'.[125] Even a scholar like Carnhuanawc eulogized Dyfnwal Moelmud and his legacy at eisteddfodau, though he was rather more cautious in his own scholarly writings.[126] Doubts expressed over the apparent lack of historical evidence for Dyfnwal's laws (apart from Iolo's triads and his writings on the Druids) were refuted by noting that the Saxons had 'made bonfires and massacres of their books, their religious houses and their literature' ('coelcerthi a galanas o'u llyfrau, eu crefydd-dai, a'u llenyddiaeth').[127] In this blaze of uncritical public enthusiasm, there was little room for the fainthearted or the sceptic. Writing critically of Dyfnwal Moelmud in 1854, Thomas Stephens wearily observed that his conclusions 'were so very much at variance with those generally adopted'.[128] Not unexpectedly, his iconoclastic approach won him few friends,[129] and Ab Ithel strove to counter Stephens's animadversions in a long article designed to authenticate the nation's primary legislator.[130] Others, too,

---

[122] Bromwich, 'Trioedd Ynys Prydain', *THSC* (1968), 303, 323; eadem, 'Trioedd Ynys Prydain', ibid. (1969), 129–30, 139, 140.

[123] *MAW*, III, pp. 283–318; Bromwich, 'Trioedd Ynys Prydain', *THSC* (1968), 306, 316; eadem, 'Trioedd Ynys Prydain', ibid. (1969), 130–1.

[124] Owen, *The Cambrian Biography*, pp. 94–5, 178–80; Jones, *On the State of Agriculture and the Progress of Arts in Britain*, p. 12; Roberts, *Druidical Remains and Antiquities of the Ancient Britons*, pp. 61, 67–8; R. Powys, 'Goresgyniad y Cymry gan y Saeson', *Seren Gomer*, XXVIX, no. 373 (1846), 299–301; Moeddyn, 'Barn Iolo Morganwg am Hu Gadarn', *Y Brython*, V, no. 39 (1862), 43.

[125] Ernest Silvanus Appleyard, *Welsh Sketches, Chiefly Ecclesiastical, to the Close of the Twelfth Century. First Series* (3rd edn., London, 1853), pp. 3, 57. Between 1830 and the 1850s three editions of Appleyard's *Welsh Sketches* were published.

[126] 'Speech delivered by the Rev. Thomas Price at the Caermarthen Eisteddfod, Thursday, September 25th, 1823' in Jane Williams (ed.), *The Literary Remains of the Rev. Thomas Price, Carnhuanawc*, I, pp. 113–17.

[127] Thomas Watkins (Eiddil Ifor), 'Traethawd ar Ddylanwad Barddoniaeth, Lliwio, Cerfio, a'r Celfau Teg, ar Gymeriad y Cymry', *Seren Gomer*, XXXII, no. 406 (1849), 203.

[128] Thomas Stephens, 'Studies in British Biography: No. I. Dyfnwal Moelmud', *Cambrian Journal*, I (1854), 161.

[129] Golygydd, 'Postscript', ibid., II (1855), 59.

[130] J. Williams Ab Ithel, 'The Traditional Annals of the Cymry: VIII. Dyfnwal Moelmud', ibid. (1855), 163–72.

rallied in his support. The entry on Dyfnwal Moelmud in Williams's *Enwogion Cymru* harboured no doubts at all about his existence or the authenticity of his laws, and not until the founding of the University of Wales in 1893 were such questionable figures placed under a more critical spotlight.[131]

As the nineteenth century wore on, Hu Gadarn assumed considerable importance for the interpretation of the early Welsh as a civilized and peace-loving nation. The author of the *Druopaedia* credited him not only with leading the Welsh from Deffrobani to the British Isles but also with inventing the practice of agricultural drainage and with stabilizing the rules of druidism. Indeed, he viewed him as 'the only potentate that ever attempted to establish the dominion of perpetual peace upon earth'.[132] Hu Gadarn was identified as a Persian god by some writers and likened to Neptune by others, but the general view was that he was either Noah or was in some way associated with the deluge.[133] The image of Hu Gadarn stepping out of a coracle on to the British shore with a plough in his hand was judged important enough to become the frontispiece of the third volume of the *Cambrian Register* in 1819. It also adorned the title-page of the four-part luxury edition of *Ceinion Llenyddiaeth Gymreig* in 1875.[134] As late as 1890 the antiquary Hugh Owen (Huwco Môn) summed up the commonly held view that 'Noah is the person which is depicted in the name Hu, and the patriarch was one of the main gods of the druids' ('Noah yw y person a ddarlunir gan yr enw Hu, a bod y patriarch yn un o dduwiau penaf y derwyddon').[135] Even when the story of Noah had been superseded by more scientific explanations, some amateur scholars, among them Cadrawd's son Frederic Evans, refused to abandon their hero and took refuge in pseudo-philology:

> The traditional leader of the Celts of Britain was Hu Gadarn, who is always represented as carrying a plough, the emblem of the Aryan stock. The name 'Aryan' comes from the same root as the Celtic 'aradr', a plough, and these people were so called because they were great cultivators of the land.[136]

The third most enthusiastically received link in the line of Welsh cultural descent was the fifth-century sage Catwg Ddoeth, in whom Iolo had fused the Latin writer Cato, the fifth-century St Cadog of Llancarfan, and, possibly, a wise man known as Catwn.[137] To Catwg Ddoeth were attributed over ninety

---

[131] Williams, *Enwogion Cymru*, pp. 127–8.
[132] Williams, *Druopaedia*, pp. 6–7, 15.
[133] Ibid., p. 10; Roberts, *Druidical Remains and Antiquities of the Ancient Britons*, p. 68; Williams, *Enwogion Cymru*, pp. 223–4.
[134] William Owen Pughe, 'Memorials of Hu Gadarn', *Cambrian Register*, III (1819), 162–6; Owen Jones, *Ceinion Llenyddiaeth Gymreig* (2 vols., 4 parts; Llundain, 1875), I, title-page.
[135] Hugh Owen (Huwco Môn), *Yr Henafiaethydd: Henafiaethau Cemmaes, Llanfechell, Llanbabo, Cemlyn, Llanfairynghornwy, Tregele, Carreglefn, &c.; yn nghyd a Hanes Sefydliad Derwyddiaeth yn Mon* (Amlwch, 1890), p. 87.
[136] Evans, *Tir Iarll: The Earl's Land*, pp. 26–7, illustration 3.
[137] This point was made by Diana Luft in 'Encountering Iolo: The Case of Cato', an unpublished

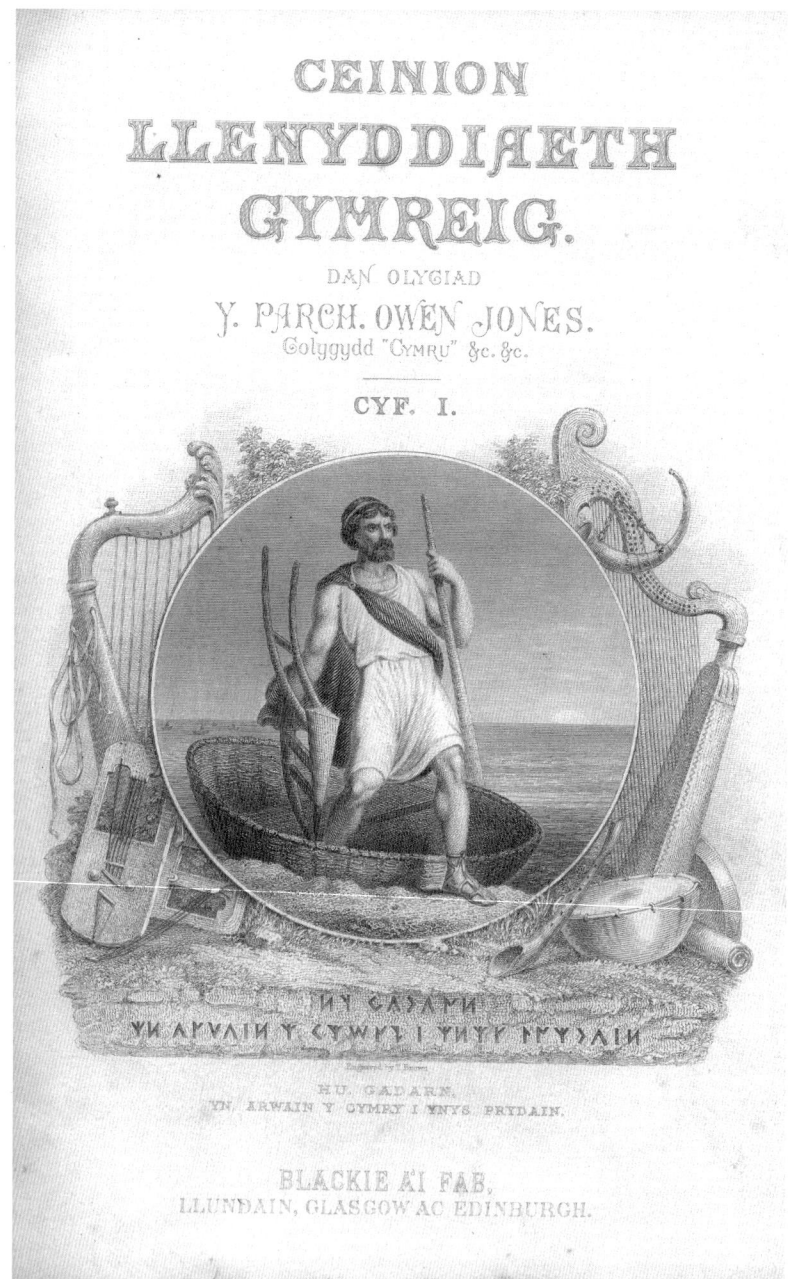

Fig. 10 The title-page of *Ceinion Llenyddiaeth Gymreig*, 1875, with 'Hu Gadarn leading the Welsh to Britain', after Abraham Raimbach, 1801. Raimbach's engraving of Iolo's creation, Hu Gadarn, adorned Cymmrodorion medals as well as the title-pages of periodicals and books.

pages of aphorisms which Iolo had published in *The Myvyrian Archaiology of Wales*.[138] Owen's *Cambrian Biography* and Rees's *Lives of the Cambro-British Saints* confirmed the identification of Catwg Ddoeth with St Cadog of Llancarfan, thereby authenticating Iolo's body of aphorisms.[139] Catwg Ddoeth's wisdom became extremely popular in nineteenth-century Wales and was frequently reproduced in Welsh, or in English translation, in periodicals such as *Y Gwladgarwr*, *Y Brython*, *Cymru Fydd* and *Bye-Gones*, and in volumes such as Abraham Morris's *Glamorgan: Being an Outline of its Geography, History, and Antiquities*.[140] Samples of the 'exhaustless inspiration and fertile genius of the immortal Sage' were regularly appended to works on druidism and the history of Glamorgan.[141] La Villemarqué made 'Saint Kadoc' one of the main subjects of his *La légende celtique et la poésie des cloîtres en Irlande, en Cambrie et en Bretagne* and included a selection of his 'Sentences, Proverbes et Aphorisme' culled from *The Myvyrian Archaiology of Wales* and the *Iolo Manuscripts*.[142] Although Henri Gaidoz expressed mild doubts over their authority, he nevertheless published a translation of sections of the 'Wisdom of Catwg Ddoeth' in his *Revue Celtique* in 1878.[143] As late as 1912 D. Rhys Phillips (Beili Glas) could not resist including, accompanied by a cautionary note, references to St Cadoc from the *Iolo Manuscripts* in his *Romantic History of the Monastic Libraries of Wales*.[144] In the eyes of the Welsh, Catwg was important because he:

> would have been a glory to any Church, an honour to any system. He combined all the characteristics of the Celtic Saint – royal descent, questionable birth, exercise of supernatural power – with all the qualities of the Latins. His piety was unbounded, his charity never failed. More of his teaching has come down to us than of any other Welsh Saint, and his principles are so democratic that it is difficult to believe any monastic scribe would have ever invented them.[145]

---

paper delivered at the University of Wales Centre for Advanced Welsh and Celtic Studies, Aberystwyth, July 2002.

[138] *MAW*, III, pp. 5–99.

[139] Owen, *Cambrian Biography*, p. 46; Rees, *Lives of the Cambro-British Saints*, p. 309. See also Williams, *The Ecclesiastical Antiquities of the Cymry*, pp. 130–5.

[140] 'Catwg Ddoeth', *Y Gwladgarwr*, VI, no. 68 (1838), 77–8; 'Nidlau Odledigion' and 'Deuparthau Catwg Ddoeth', ibid., VII, no. 84 (1839), 364–5; 'Tremynion Catwg Doeth', ibid., VIII, no. 85 (1840), 20; 'Taliesin a Chattwg (O Lyfr Sion Phylip o Treëos)', *Y Brython*, V, no. 40 (1863), 232; Alafon, 'Enyd gyda Chattwg Ddoeth', *Cymru Fydd*, II, no. 3 (1889), 122–31; 'The Wisdom of Catwg', *Bye-Gones*, 6 March 1872, 90; T. C. U., 'Notes and Queries: Catwg the Wise', *Red Dragon*, X (1886), 95; Morris, *Glamorgan: Being an Outline of its Geography*, pp. 421–3.

[141] Evans, *The Ancient Bards of Britain*, pp. 180–91; Freeman, *The Druids and Theosophy*, p. 16; Spencer, *Annals of South Glamorgan, Historical, Legendary, and Descriptive Chapters on some Leading Places of Interest*, p. 83.

[142] Hersart de La Villemarqué, *La légende celtique et la poésie des cloîtres en Irlande, en Cambrie et en Bretagne* (Paris, 1864), pp. 126–227, 303–10.

[143] Henri Gaidoz, 'Extraits des dictons du sage Cadoc, traduits du gallois par M. W. G. Jones', *Revue Celtique*, III (1876), 419–42.

[144] D. Rhys Phillips, *The Romantic History of the Monastic Libraries of Wales from the Fifth to the Sixteenth Centuries* (Swansea, 1912), p. 8.

[145] J. W. Willis-Bund, 'Welsh Saints', *THSC* (1895), 53.

In addition to these early representatives of Welsh civilization, Iolo Morganwg offered to the Welsh an unbroken line of bardic descent which began with the nation's putative first poets, the primary bards Alawn, Plennydd and Gwron, and the ninth-century poet, translator and government adviser, Geraint Fardd Glas. He romantically embellished familiar literary figures such as Taliesin, Aneirin and Llywarch Hen by endowing them with picturesque biographies and adding to the corpus of their work.[146] His most important link in the chain, however, was Dafydd ap Gwilym, who had revivified Welsh poetry with new forms and subjects which, so Iolo claimed, had prepared the ground for the style of the later poets of the Chair of Glamorgan. In order to strengthen his argument Iolo invented a predecessor for Dafydd – the nature poet Rhys Goch ap Rhicert, enhanced Dafydd's own biography, and added sixteen poems which filled what he perceived to be gaps in his œuvre.

In the opinion of Iolo's nineteenth-century legatees, the twenty poems of Rhys Goch ap Rhicert which Iolo claimed to have transcribed from 'John Bradford's Book' ('Llyfr John Bradford'), had paved the way for Dafydd ap Gwilym's poetic achievement.[147] Rhys Goch ap Rhicert's style also authenticated the verse Iolo himself had added to Dafydd's corpus.[148] Even Thomas Stephens, although he disproved Iolo's dating of Rhys Goch ap Rhicert's work and suggested a *floruit* around 1350, connected him with Dafydd ap Gwilym in the way intended by Iolo:

> Rhys Goch and Davydd ab Gwilym display such exuberance of fancy, elegance of taste, and fertility of invention, as a perusal of the works of their predecessors would not have led us to anticipate. These qualities, characteristics alike of both these bards, connect Rhys Goch with the age of the Cambrian Petrarch, 'the nightingale of Dyved'; but the absence of Cynghanedd from the poems of the former, while it pervades those of the latter, compels us to place Rhys ab Rhicert in the first half of the fourteenth century.[149]

Both Gweirydd ap Rhys, in his *Hanes y Brytaniaid a'r Cymry*, and Charles Wilkins, in his *History of the Literature of Wales from the Year 1300 to the Year*

---

[146] See, for instance, Ab Ithel, 'The Traditional Annals of the Cymry: Chapter V. The Three Primary Bards', *Cambrian Journal*, I (1854), 231–8; Robert Ellis (Cynddelw), 'Bywyd a Nodweddiad Llywarch Hen', *Y Beirniad*, VI, no. 24 (1865), 269–94; Thomas Stephens, 'Caniadau Llywarch Hen', ibid., VII, no. 26 (1865), 117–37; John Peter (Ioan Pedr), 'Y Cynfeirdd', ibid., XII, no. 46 (1870), 128–47; idem, 'Y Cynfeirdd II', ibid., XIII, no. 49 (1871), 48–60.

[147] *Iolo Manuscripts*, pp. 228–50, 645–51.

[148] 'Barddoniaeth Gymreig: Hanesyddol a Beirniadol (Traethawd Arobryn Eisteddfod Gadeiriol Meirion, a gynaliwyd yn Nolgellau, Calan, 1888)', *Y Geninen*, VI, no. 4 (1888), 236–43; W. Lewis-Jones, 'The Celt and the Poetry of Nature', *THSC* (1893), 66; Iolo Morganwg, 'Rhys Llwyd ap Rhys ap Rhisiart', *Y Geninen*, XXVII, no. 3 (1909), 214–15.

[149] Thomas Stephens, *The Literature of the Kymry, being a Critical Essay on the History of the Language and Literature of Wales during the Twelfth and Two Succeeding Centuries* (Llandovery, 1849), pp. 476–7.

*1650*, endorsed Stephens's assessment.[150] Even Sir John Morris-Jones believed that Rhys Goch ap Rhicert 'wrote a number of sweetly musical love-songs', thereby ushering in a new period in the literature of Wales.[151] As late as 1910 W. J. Gruffydd graced the pages of the eleventh edition of the *Encyclopaedia Britannica* with the judgement that Rhys Goch ap Rhicert had one advantage over his more illustrious contemporary: 'The musical lilt and the delicate workmanship of his poems, with their recurring refrain, give him a unique position among his contemporaries as the first purely lyrical poet.'[152]

Dafydd ap Gwilym's authentic canon of work – which at that time was assumed to comprise 246 poems – verified both the poetry of Rhys Goch ap Rhicert and Iolo's own additions to the life and works of Dafydd. The short biographical sketch which had preceded *Barddoniaeth Dafydd ab Gwilym* in 1789 was informed by Iolo's own interpretation, and further florid detail was inserted in the *Iolo Manuscripts*, published in 1848.[153] Both sketches became the basis for most biographical writings about the poet until the early twentieth century. The version of 1789 was reproduced twice, in the volume of *Translations into English Verse from the Poems of Davyth ap Gwilym, a Welsh Bard of the Fourteenth Century*, published in 1834 by Arthur James Johnes (Maelog), and in the second edition of *Barddoniaeth Dafydd ab Gwilym*, published in 1873.[154] The second edition of the *Iolo Manuscripts*, published in 1888, ensured that the biographical material it contained also continued to be widely accessible. Although all those who wrote about Dafydd ap Gwilym from the last quarter of the nineteenth century onwards – a time when interest in the poet enjoyed a marked revival – confessed that their knowledge of the poet's life was scanty and was based on uncertain traditions, they nevertheless either used or mentioned the stories narrated in the *Iolo Manuscripts*.[155] In 1914 Evelyn Anna Lewes's exceptionally handsome volume *Life and Poems of Davydd ab Gwilym* claimed that it was 'impossible to write a really accurate biography of this poet, the existing information furnished by old writers being meagre and often

---

[150] Gweirydd ap Rhys, *Hanes y Brytaniaid a'r Cymry* (2 vols., Llundain, 1874), II, pp. 206–10; Wilkins, *The History of the Literature of Wales from the Year 1300 to the Year 1650*, pp. 27–9.

[151] J. Morris Jones, 'A Brief History of Wales: Language and Literature' in Anon. (ed.), *Cymru a'i Phobl* (Utica, NY, 1894), p. 61.

[152] W. J. G., 'Celt: Celtic Literature iv. Welsh Literature' in *Encyclopaedia Britannica* (11th edn., New York, 1910), V, p. 645.

[153] *Iolo Manuscripts*, pp. 92–4, 484–90.

[154] Arthur James Johnes (Maelog), *Translations into English Verse from the Poems of Davyth ap Gwilym, a Welsh Bard of the Fourteenth Century* (London, 1834), pp. vii–xli; Cynddelw, *Barddoniaeth Dafydd ab Gwilym*, pp. iii–xxix.

[155] Gweirydd ap Rhys, *Hanes y Brytaniaid a'r Cymry*, II, p. 355; John Jones (Ioan Ddu), 'Dafydd ap Gwilym I', *Y Geninen*, II, no. 3 (1884), 226; D. Stanley Jones, 'Dyffryn Teifi', ibid., XVII, no. 1 (1899), 8–10. Ioan Ddu's failure to narrate the details of Dafydd's birth prompted a corrective response. See 'Hywel', 'Gohebiaethau: Dafydd ap Gwilym', ibid., II, no. 4 (1884), 317–18; W. Eilir Evans, 'Chaucer and Dafydd ap Gwilym', *Young Wales*, VI, no. 72 (1900), 268–71.

based on supposition rather than facts'.[156] Nevertheless, she dutifully recorded 'the information given in the Iolo Manuscripts' because it was 'nearer the mark'.[157]

The sixteen poems which Iolo had added to Dafydd's œuvre in 1789 likewise enjoyed success among audiences and scholars in Wales and on the Continent. Of the thirteen poems attributed to Dafydd ap Gwilym which were published (in translation and often only in part) in the *Cambrian Register* and in the *Cambrian Quarterly Magazine* before 1830, nine derived from Iolo's 'Addendum'.[158] Among them were the 'Invocation to the Summer' ('Mawl i'r Haf – Cwyn o'i Golli') and 'The Bard's Last Song' ('Y Cywydd Diweddaf a Gant y Bardd').[159] Maelog's volume of translations, published in 1834, included six of Iolo's counterfeit poems. They had been selected 'in preference to genuine poems, which look back on lost bliss with much more complex feeling and imagination than the Romantic nostalgia of Iolo Morganwg's compositions'.[160] Nine of Iolo's additional poems, among them favourites like 'Y Breuddwyd' (The Dream), 'I Forfudd – Y Bardd Mewn Henaint yn Dwyn i Gof Fal y Bu Gynt' (To Morfudd – The Bard in Old Age Recalling How It Used to Be), 'I Yrru yr Haf i Annerch Morganwg' (To Send the Summer to Greet Glamorgan), and 'Y Cywydd Diweddaf a Gant y Bardd' (The Bard's Last Song), were included in Owen M. Edwards's popular edition of Dafydd's poetry in 1901.[161] The overwhelming favourite, 'To Send the Summer to Greet Glamorgan', also found its way into popular anthologies, from *Ceinion Awen y Cymmry* in 1831 to *Cywyddau Cymru* in 1908.[162]

More significantly, some of Iolo's poems were singled out and quoted as quintessential works which best illustrated Dafydd's talent and style. Both 'The Summer' – the title chosen by him for 'To Send the Summer to Greet Glamorgan' – and 'The Bard's Last Song' illustrated the biographical sketch

---

[156] Evelyn Ann Lewes, *Life and Poems of Davydd ab Gwilym* (London, 1914), pp. 10–11.

[157] Ibid., p. 101. R. Geraint Gruffydd, *Dafydd ap Gwilym* (Caernarfon, 1987). For a summary in English of his life, see idem, 'Dafydd ap Gwilym: An Outline Biography' in Cyril J. Byrne, Margaret Harry, Pàdraig Ó Siadhail (eds.), *Celtic Languages and Celtic Peoples: Proceedings of the Second North American Congress of Celtic Studies* (Halifax, NS, 1992), pp. 425–42.

[158] 'Poems translated from the Welsh of Dafydd ab Gwilym', *Cambrian Register*, III (1819), 436–68; 'Selections from Dafydd ap Gwylym', *Cambrian Quarterly Magazine*, I, no. 1 (1829), 14–15; ibid., no. 2 (1829), 166–7, 214; ibid., no. 3 (1829), 331; ibid., no. 4 (1829), 415. On the subject of Dafydd ap Gwilym and translation, see Dafydd Johnston, 'Early Translations of Dafydd ap Gwilym' in Alyce von Rothkirch and Daniel Williams (eds.), *Beyond the Difference: Welsh Literature in Comparative Contexts* (Cardiff, 2004), pp. 158–72.

[159] *Cambrian Register*, III (1819), 459–62, 467–8; 'Introduction', *Cambrian Quarterly Magazine*, I, no. 1 (1829), 7.

[160] Johnston, 'Early Translations of Dafydd ap Gwilym', pp. 166–7.

[161] Owen M. Edwards (ed.), *Gwaith Dafydd ab Gwilym* (Llanuwchllyn, 1901), pp. 31, 37, 50, 52, 75–6, 97–8, 99–104.

[162] Thomas Ll. Jones (ed.), *Ceinion Awen y Cymmry* (Dinbych, 1831), pp. 39–41; Arthur Hughes (ed.), *Cywyddau Cymru* (Bangor, 1908), pp. 21–4. However, among the fifty poems by Dafydd ap Gwilym included in *Ceinion Llenyddiaeth Gymreig* (2 vols. in 4 parts, London, 1875), I, pp. 29–32, 58–70, none were from the 'Addendum'.

included in Maelog's volume of translations in 1834. The same passage appeared in the entry on Dafydd ap Gwilym in Parry's *Cambrian Plutarch* in the same year.[163] In addition, Maelog framed 'The Summer' with a long textual passage extolling the 'fine poem' (Document 15).[164] Both poems were also pressed into service by Gweirydd ap Rhys and Evelyn Anna Lewes in portraying both the character and poetic gifts of Dafydd ap Gwilym.[165]

Until the eve of the First World War, Welsh and international scholars who examined the poetry of Dafydd ap Gwilym regularly included Iolo's counterfeit *cywyddau* in their accounts. John Jones (Ioan Ddu) selected quotations from 'Y Cywydd Diweddaf' (The Bard's Last Song), 'Mawl i Forfudd' (Praise to Morfudd), 'Mawl i'r Clos' (Praise to the Grove) and 'I Forfudd Mewn Henaint' (To Morfudd in Old Age) to illustrate his series of articles in *Y Geninen*.[166] Sir Edward Anwyl succumbed to the attraction of Iolo's poems in his essays on the linguistic standards of Dafydd ap Gwilym in the same periodical nearly twenty years later by quoting lines from six of the poems in the 'Addendum' to prove his case.[167] Even after the paradigmatic change in Welsh scholarship had made authors more wary of the authenticity of some of Dafydd's work, Iolo's poems were sometimes still preferred to authentic material. J. Machreth Rees doubted whether Dafydd could have composed both the (authentic) elegy to Ifor Hael and Nest, and (Iolo's) 'The Bard's Last Song', since there was 'a note in the *cywydd* which the author of the elegy was never able to strike' ('nodyn yn y cywydd na fedrodd awdwr yr awdl erioed ei gyffwrdd').[168] Ludwig Christian Stern's masterly long treatise on Dafydd ap Gwilym persistently called the *Iolo Manuscripts* and *Cyfrinach y Beirdd* unreliable (*unzuverlässig*), but they were nevertheless quoted as sources for his work.[169] Although he doubted whether Dafydd had written a single poem of the 'Addendum', Stern included all of them in a list of his poems at the end of the article. To warn the reader, each poem in the 'Addendum' was followed by a question mark, but so were thirty-three poems within the main part of the list.[170] The mixture of forged and genuine material in the 1789 and 1873 editions of Dafydd ap Gwilym's poetry

---

[163] Parry, *The Cambrian Plutarch*, pp. 220–1; Johnes (Maelog), *Translations into English Verse from the Poems of Davyth ap Gwilym*, pp. xxviii–xxix.

[164] Ibid., pp. 96–100.

[165] Gweirydd ap Rhys, *Hanes y Brytaniaid a'r Cymry*, p. 357; Lewes, *Life and Poems of Davydd ab Gwilym*, pp. 71–4, 97, 110. 'The Poet Sends the Summer to Greet Glamorgan' was also quoted in an anonymous article, 'Art VI: The Poems of Dafydd ab Gwilim', *Westminster Review*, new series, LXXXVIII (1873), 391–3.

[166] John Jones (Ioan Ddu), 'Dafydd ap Gwilym II', *Y Geninen*, II, no. 4 (1886), 298; idem, 'Dafydd ap Gwilym III', *Y Geninen*, IV, no. 3 (1886), 180–1.

[167] Edward Anwyl, 'Safonau Dafydd ab Gwilym I', *Y Geninen*, XXV, no. 1 (1907), 17–18; idem, 'Safonau Dafydd ab Gwilym II', ibid., no. 2 (1907), 130–1. He used lines from poems number ii, iii, vi, vii, xiii and xiv of the 'Addendum' to illustrate his account.

[168] J. Machreth Rees, 'Dafydd ap Gwilym a'i Gyfnod', *THSC* (1907), 34.

[169] Ludwig Christian Stern, 'Davydd ab Gwilym, ein walisischer Minnesänger', *ZcP*, VII (1910), pp. 8, 11, 12, 14.

[170] Ibid., pp. 2, 258–65.

served to authenticate the former and cast a shadow of doubt over the latter group of poems. Until reliable details of the life and times of Dafydd ap Gwilym had been ascertained, a reliable edition of his poetry published, and the mythical Rhys Goch ap Rhicert laid to rest, both poets were perceived as representatives of the bardic tradition of Glamorgan. The scholarly community had yet to comprehend the full extent of Iolo's complex mosaic of forgery.

## *The pre-eminence of Glamorgan*

During his lifetime Iolo Morganwg strove not only to establish the pre-eminence of Wales over England but also to promote the importance of his native south Wales, especially the county of Glamorgan.[171] Much of his fictitious material was deliberately designed to transform the county into the 'Athens of Wales', a centre of civilization swarming with historical luminaries and cultural heroes.[172] He maintained that most of the manuscripts he purported to have discovered had been written south of the river Dyfi, and had been safeguarded by poets and scholars in libraries in south Wales.[173] He attributed the many hundreds of aphorisms and fables he contributed to *The Myvyrian Archaiology of Wales* to St Cadog of Llancarfan in Glamorgan. Both Rhys Goch ap Rhicert and the embellished version of Dafydd ap Gwilym were intimately connected with a Glamorgan whose gentry sponsored eisteddfodau and Gorseddau long after the men of the north had lost interest in the bardic tradition. The geographical signals emanating from Iolo's additional material were eagerly received and deployed by cultural entrepreneurs in south Wales who sought to preserve and depict historical continuity in a bid to counteract the unplanned and rapid change which the industrializing communities of south Wales experienced throughout the nineteenth century. Iolo's claims for the bardic tradition of south Wales also helped to provide a respectable and safe haven from the baneful effects of the English language and its culture. The folklore which Iolo had collected, the observations he had made, and the traditions he had fabricated all found a home in nineteenth-century and early twentieth-century works on the history and folklore of Glamorgan – from Benjamin Heath Malkin in 1804 to David Lloyd Isaac in 1859 and to Marianne Robertson Spencer in 1913. An astonishing range of material connected with the county, including diverse subjects such as architecture, religion, Owain Glyndŵr, apple-growing, human longevity and the tradition of whitewashing houses, were passed down from essay to essay, and repeated in many volumes of local and national history.

[171] Cathryn Charnell-White, *Barbarism and Bardism: North Wales versus South Wales in the Bardic Vision of Iolo Morganwg* (Aberystwyth, 2004).
[172] William Thomas (Gwilym Glanffrwd), 'Gwlad, Pobl, Iaith, a Deifion Morganwg', *Y Geninen*, II, no. 1 (1884), 26.
[173] *TLIM*, pp. 144–318.

In 1815 Thomas Rees published Iolo's account of the 'jurisdiction of Cadair Morganwg' – the bardic Chair of Glamorgan – in his *Topographical and Historical Description of South Wales* because 'every thing relating to the history and antiquities of the principality coming from his pen is deserving of attention'.[174] In the same volume he related Iolo's account of the discovery of the Samson Cross at Llantwit Major, a story which contained a considerable element of truth, but alongside it he also repeated Malkin's report of Iolo's fabricated tale of the introduction of the earliest 'Grecian architecture' in Britain at Beaupre castle.[175] David Lloyd Isaac took care to preface his volume *Siluriana* by noting that his source material did not correspond to Iolo's school of invention but rather aimed to provide facts in place of 'clairvoyance'.[176] However, following a pattern which others repeated, he succumbed to the lure of material which was so easily accessible in the *Iolo Manuscripts* and elsewhere. The second half of his volume was made up almost entirely of narratives based on Ioloic sources, and of verbatim repetitions of passages like 'The Roll of Glamorgan Kings from the Iolo Manuscripts' and 'Iron Making in Glamorgan'.[177] As late as 1907 Abraham Morris's history of Glamorgan singled out the *Iolo Manuscripts* as 'one of the valuable works' to which he was 'under a special obligation'.[178] He followed the pattern of his predecessors by clearly marking some material, such as the tale of Arthur's cave, as 'legendary', but also by treating forged documents about the history of Glamorgan, such as the account of the sixth-century king Morgan Mwynfawr, as authentic.[179] By repeating Iolo's account of the discovery of the Samson Cross and the building of the gateway porch at Beaupre castle, he very nearly marked the hundredth anniversary of their creation.[180] In Wales's most rapidly modernizing county, local patriotism and nostalgia continued to take precedence over scholarship well into the twentieth century.

Iolo's shorter notes on the characteristics and especially the wonders of Glamorgan were ideally suited for reproduction in essays and notes. Owain Glyndŵr, like Dafydd ap Gwilym, was bound more closely to the county of Glamorgan through several tales which narrated his visit in disguise to the castle of his enemy Sir Laurence Berkerolle, and his later life as 'Sion

---

[174] Thomas Rees, *A Topographical and Historical Description of South Wales* (London, 1815), pp. 539–42.

[175] Ibid., pp. 677–9, 672–3. See also Document 5. Malkin, *The Scenery, Antiquities, and Biography, of South Wales*, pp. 119–22. The full story also appeared as E. W., 'Traditional Anecdotes of Bewper (Beaupre) Porch and Chapel (From Richard and William Roberts of Bridgend)', *Cambrian Journal*, V (1858), 138–40. See also Richard Suggett, 'Iolo Morganwg: Stonecutter, Builder and Antiquary' in *Rattleskull Genius*, pp. 216, 222–3.

[176] Isaac, *Siluriana: or Contributions towards the History of Gwent and Glamorgan*, p. 2.

[177] Ibid., pp. 233, 318–21.

[178] Morris, *Glamorgan: Being an Outline of its Geography . . .*, p. iv.

[179] Ibid., pp. 239, 245–7.

[180] Ibid., pp. 368, 418–19. The story of the gateway porch of Beaupre was also retold by Spencer, *Annals of South Glamorgan*, pp. 160–2.

Goodfellow' in a cave in the uplands of the county.[181] Favourite tales, both old and new, were likewise claimed for Glamorgan with the aid of Iolo's emendations. When a reference to the story explaining the place name of Beddgelert in north Wales appeared in *Y Brython*, a proud native of south Wales retaliated in kind by submitting a similar tale, related in the Silurian dialect, allegedly derived from 'Iolo's manuscripts' ('ysgriflyfrau Iolo').[182] In a subsequent article its source was traced to Catwg Ddoeth's 'Dameg y Gwr a Laddwys ei Filgi' ('The Fable of the Man who Killed his Greyhound') in the *Iolo Manuscripts*, from which it was reprinted once more.[183] A short essay by Iolo on 'Iron Making in Glamorgan' found favour with many writers and publishers, not least because it gave the industrial development of Glamorgan a venerable ancestry.[184] But most of the selected material associated Glamorgan with an idyllic rural past, which appealed to the rising interest in pre-industrial folklore. The history of apple-growing and of whitewashing peasant houses in Glamorgan was frequently discussed in periodicals, newspaper columns and popular volumes.[185] In keeping with Iolo's claim, the salubrious character of the latter tradition was cited as the principal reason for the longevity of the county's inhabitants.[186] Iolo's notes on the improbably long lives of individuals like the milkmaids Ann Richman and 'Christian of Porthkerry', and the soldier Ivan Yorath, enabled the patriotic historians of south Wales to associate Glamorgan with the period of the civil wars and even with the Wars of the Roses, long before the onset of industrialization.[187]

Through the bardic tradition of Glamorgan, however, the literary history of the county could be traced back even further to the time of King Arthur. Contrary to received wisdom, Iolo believed that his native shire had been the cradle of Welsh culture, and that its poets were far superior to those of the north. His opinion was readily echoed by his legatees in south Wales:

> The Bards, or Cambro-Hybernian minstrels, of North Wales, by their slanderous and seditious songs, and impromptu rhymes, made themselves obnoxious to their English

---

[181] Morris, *Glamorgan: Being an Outline of its Geography . . .*, pp. 307, 313–14; D. Silvan Evans, 'Traddodiad am Owain Glyndwr', *Y Geninen*, XI, no. 1 ( 1893), 72; Spencer, *Annals of South Glamorgan*, pp. 156–7.

[182] Meilyr o Went, 'Gohebiaethau (At Olygydd y Brython): Y Gwr a Laddwys ei Filgi', *Y Brython*, II, no. 6 (1859), 90.

[183] 'Plwyf Bedd Gelert', *Y Brython*, IV, no. 30 (1861), 133.

[184] Iolo Morganwg, 'Iron Making in Glamorgan', *Cambrian Journal*, V (1858), 110–13; L'Allegro, 'Notes: Iron Making in Glamorganshire' in Brierley (ed.), *Cymru Fu*, I, pp. 389–90.

[185] Anon., 'Welsh Names of Apples', *Cambrian Journal*, V (1858), 45–51; Ap Adda, 'Welsh Character Sketches: The Welsh Farmer', *Red Dragon*, V (1884), 180–4.

[186] NLW 13115B, pp. 11, 114–15; Williams: *PLP*, II, p. 58; Malkin, *The Scenery, Antiquities, and Biography, of South Wales*, pp. 625–33.

[187] NLW 13152A, p. 453; Edward Williams, 'Extracts from the Parish Register of Lanmaes, in the County of Glamorgan', *Gentleman's Magazine*, LXIII (1793), 106; Isaac, *Siluriana or Contributions towards the History of Gwent and Glamorgan*, pp. 122–3; Spencer, *Annals of South Glamorgan*, pp. 201–3; Giraldus, 'The Last Battle in Glamorgan', *Red Dragon*, III (1883), 151–3. This article provoked a lively discussion over the uses of 'traditionary material'.

sovereign; and, in consequence, Edward the First is represented to have treated them with great severity: but historians have not reflected that these minstrels were instigators of civil warfare, and cowards, who never assisted in the contest ... The true system of Bardism existed only in South Wales, and more particularly in Glamorganshire.[188]

Such conceit appealed strongly to Iolo's band of admirers, and passages describing milestones in the development of this 'true bardism' were copied from his manuscripts and publications throughout the nineteenth century. The chapter which Dafydd Morganwg devoted to the literary history of Glamorgan in *Hanes Morganwg* in 1874 was almost wholly derived from works by Iolo ranging from the teachings of Catwg Ddoeth to *Cyfrinach y Beirdd*, which he described as 'the best by far in the language on the Rules of Welsh Poetry' ('y goraf yn yr iaith o ddigon ar Reolau Barddoniaeth Gymreig').[189] Thanks to Iolo, Dafydd ap Gwilym, hailed by some as the greatest poet Europe had ever produced, was widely presumed to have been a native of Glamorgan. According to Dafydd Morganwg, he had been 'president of the Gorsedd of Morganwg in 1360' ('llywydd Gorsedd Morganwg yn 1360').[190] The poetry which Iolo had composed under Dafydd ap Gwilym's name served to reinforce the image of uncivilized north Wales and 'the sweet pastoral county of Glamorgan with all its blessings'.[191] Maelog continued this tradition by eulogizing not only Iolo's poem 'To Send the Summer to Greet Glamorgan' but also the county itself in his explanatory text (Document 15).[192] Ifor Hael's genuine contribution to the literary history of Wales was enhanced by a purported 'renaissance eisteddfod' ('eisteddfod y dadeni') which Iolo claimed he had conducted at his court at Gwernyclepa in 1328. It was there that a chair had been awarded for a *cywydd* for the first time in the literary history of Wales. The prize went to Dafydd ap Gwilym, who thus became chief bard of the county and acquired the byname Dafydd Morganwg.[193]

At the heart of the bardic tradition was 'Cadair Tir Iarll' (The Chair of Tir Iarll) and its historian Cadrawd, who became the principal legatee of Iolo's additional material on the bardic history of the region. Contemporaries often described him as a second Iolo, his mind devoted to antiquities, and his pockets stuffed with manuscripts.[194] His *Folklore of Glamorgan*, his *History of Llangynwyd Parish* and his edition of religious poetry, *Hen Gwndidau, Carolau, a Chywyddau,*

---

[188] John Jones, *The History of Wales, Descriptive of the Government, Wars, Manners, Laws, Druids, Bards, Pedigrees, and Language of the Ancient Britons and Modern Welsh, and of the Remaining Antiquities of the Principality* (London, 1824), pp. 223–4, 231.
[189] Dafydd Morganwg, *Hanes Morganwg* (Aberdar, 1874), pp. 166, 174.
[190] Ibid., pp. 175–6.
[191] 'Introduction', *Cambrian Quarterly Magazine*, I (1829), 7.
[192] Johnes (Maelog), *Translations into English Verse from the Poems of Davyth ap Gwilym*, pp. 96–100.
[193] Isaac, *Siluriana or Contributions towards the History of Gwent and Glamorgan*, pp. 50–1.
[194] W. Glasnant Jones, 'Cadrawd: Ffilm o Adgofion', *Y Geninen*, XXXVII (Gwyl Dewi, 1919), 31.

Fig. 11 T. C. Evans (Cadrawd), holding a *peithynen*, shrewdly utilized the new medium of photography in publicizing Iolo's legacy.

were heavily informed by Iolo's writings.[195] He contributed articles and folklore to periodicals and newspapers such as *Cyfaill yr Aelwyd*, the *South Wales Daily News* and the *Cardiff Times*. Between the 1890s and the 1910s he published illustrated series of documents and articles in *Cymru*, which brought new material into the public domain and the county's bardic tradition into sharp focus.[196] His friend Owen M. Edwards entrusted him with the selection of material for a popular volume of Iolo's writings, which proved to be his final work.[197] Moreover, books such as *Hopkiniaid Morganwg* by his disciple L. J. Hopkin-James (Hopcyn) and *Tir Iarll: The Earl's Land* by his son Frederic Evans – a work which embodies the final and fullest bardic history of Tir Iarll – were inspired by him.[198]

Cadrawd and his disciples were able to draw on the Llanover collection and on a wide range of published material by Iolo. All of this counterfeit material provided the basis of a history of Tir Iarll which stretched from the period of Arthur's Chair of Taliesin to its last 'main teacher' ('prif athraw'), Iolo Morganwg himself (Document 16).[199] The Chair's alleged achievements reflected major milestones in the literary history of Wales. The 'Chair of Tir Iarll' was 'a very ancient one, being the direct development of the Institute of the Round Table as established by King Arthur'.[200] It was also the last to hold an eisteddfod according to the 'old rules'. Sir Charles Bassett had allegedly assembled the bards at Beaupre Castle in 1681, only a hundred years or so prior to the revival of the institution in north Wales. At this Gorsedd the bardic rules of the Chair of Glamorgan were confirmed as the 'fullest illustration of Bardism', which was eventually published in 1829 when *Cyfrinach y Beirdd* appeared.[201] The traditional metre of the *triban* (triplet) – with authentic and

---

[195] T. C. Evans, 'The Folklore of Glamorgan' in E. Vincent Evans (ed.), *Eisteddfod Genedlaethol y Cymry: Cofnodion a Chyfansoddiadau Buddugol Eisteddfod Aberdar, 1885* (Caerdydd, 1887), pp. 184–235; T. C. Evans, *History of Llangynwyd Parish* (Llanelly, 1887); T. C. Evans and L. J. Hopkin-James, *Hen Gwndidau, Carolau, a Chywyddau: being Sermons in Song in the Gwentian Dialect by Forty-Two Bards of Tir Iarll of the Tudor Period* (Bangor, 1910).

[196] See, for instance, the series 'Llên Gwerin Morgannwg', which was published from *Cymru*, V, no. 24 (1893), 5–8, to ibid., no. 28 (1893), 201–4. The series 'Seigiau Morgannwg: Detholion Dyddorol o Lawysgrifau Angyhoeddedig Iolo Morgannwg yn Llanofer', ran from ibid., XLII, no. 248 (1912), 157–8, to ibid., no. 253 (1912), 79–80.

[197] T. C. Evans (Cadrawd), *Gwaith Iolo Morganwg: Y Rhan Fwyaf wedi ei Godi o Lawysgrifau Iolo yn Llanofer* (Llanuwchllyn, 1913).

[198] Lemuel James 'Hopcyn', *Hopkiniaid Morganwg: Being a Genealogical Biography of the Hopkin Family of Glamorgan with the Works of Hopkin Thomas Philip and Lewis Hopkin* (Bangor, 1909); Frederic Evans, 'The Bardic Chair' in idem, *Tir Iarll: The Earl's Land*, pp. 65–84.

[199] T. C. Evans (Cadrawd) (ed.), 'Seigiau Morganwg V: Tir Iarll', *Cymru*, XLII, no. 249 (1912), 225; idem, 'Tir Iarll', *Cymru*, XLVI, no. 270 (1914), 19.

[200] Evans, *Tir Iarll: The Earl's Land*, p. 65. Cadrawd quoted verbatim the original passage from the *Iolo Manuscripts*, and a further elaboration from *Barddas*. Evans, *History of Llangynwyd Parish*, pp. 68–75; *Iolo Manuscripts*, pp. 211–13, 625–8.

[201] Cadrawd, *History of Llangynwyd Parish*, p. 75; idem, 'Tir Iarll: Eisteddfod y Pil', *Cymru*, XLVI, no. 273 (1914), 225–6. See also Owen, *Heroic Elegies and other Pieces of Llywarç Hen*, p. lxii; Malkin, *The Scenery, Antiquities, and Biography, of South Wales*, p. 124; Rees, *A Topographical and Historical Description of South Wales*, p. 673.

additional examples – fitted neatly into this theoretical history of Glamorgan's literature since 'it had been from a remote period one of the recognised metres of the Bardic Chair of Glamorgan', but had been rejected by the Chairs of Gwynedd, Powys and Dyfed until 1819, when the Carmarthen Eisteddfod restored it to its rightful place.[202] Many of the traditional *tribannau* of the county were attributed to Wil Hopcyn, a minor poet of whom not much was known at the beginning of the nineteenth century. But his distant relative Iolo turned him into one of the most romantic figures of Welsh literature by fathering upon him the song 'Bugeila'r Gwenith Gwyn' ('Watching the Blooming Wheat'), which described a tragic love affair between him and Ann Thomas (the Maid of Cefn Ydfa).[203] Wil Hopcyn, however, was only one member of the 'Hopkiniaid of South Wales' whose genealogies and works were largely drawn from 'Sion Bradford's Tradition' preserved in Iolo's manuscripts at Llanover.[204] In 1909 L. J. Hopkin-James devoted nearly 400 pages to an account of *Hopkiniaid Morganwg*, a volume in which Ioloic material was tightly interwoven with genuine sources. The work neatly narrated the development of the folk-poetry of Glamorgan down to the eighteenth century and thus brought a tradition which had allegedly begun with Arthur into modern times. On the eve of the First World War, Cadrawd's son closed the chapter on the bardic tradition of Tir Iarll by praising the genius of Iolo Morganwg:

> the last, but far from the least, of the members of the Chair of Tir Iarll . . . He is one of the greatest of Welsh historians, especially regarding bardic history and folklore, and so is a person of whom Tir Iarll may well be proud, for it is to the Chair of Tir Iarll we owe the production of this genius. Truly, his life and works form a fitting conclusion to the progress of such an ancient and notable institution as the Chair of Tir Iarll, which had thus existed for nearly seven hundred years as the centre of culture and learning in Glamorgan.[205]

'The strength of a scholar lies in his resolve' ('Nerth ysgolâig, ei vwriad') was one of the many maxims which Iolo Morganwg attributed to the fifth-century Glamorgan sage and saint Catwg Ddoeth.[206] It applied equally to Iolo's

---

[202] T. C. Evans, 'Ploughing with Oxen in Glamorgan II', *Red Dragon*, III (1883), 431. See also idem, 'Tir Iarll: Prydyddion Tir Iarll', *Cymru*, XLVI, no. 275 (1914), 305–10; Ab Ithel, 'Mesurau Cerdd Dafawd Cyffredin', *Y Brython*, III, no. 21 (1860), 314. On the place of the *triban* in the folklore of Glamorgan, see Allan James, *Diwylliant Gwerin Morgannwg* (Llandysul, 2002), pp. 23–48.

[203] Cadrawd, *History of Llangynwyd Parish*, pp. 109–13. A full version of the tale, including the reference to Wil Hopcyn and Iolo as relatives, as well as the poem itself, appears in ibid., pp. 89–108, 113–14. For an acccount of how Iolo enhanced this figure and attributed the poems to him, see *TLIM*, pp. 251–9.

[204] 'Hopcyn', *Hopkiniaid Morganwg*, pp. ix, 1.

[205] Evans, *Tir Iarll: The Earl's Land*, pp. 81–3. Page 82 contains a portrait of Iolo.

[206] 'Tremynion Catwg Ddoeth 14' in *MAW*, III, p. 12. It appeared, for instance, in 'Gwaith Catwg Doeth', *Y Brython*, IV, no. 30 (1861), 150.

nineteenth-century legatees, who were determined to employ the materials he had bequeathed to them in the service of their small nation and its historical narrative. Since their scholarship was mostly acquired during their leisure hours, all of them can be described as amateurs. Some of them, like Ab Ithel, Myfyr Morganwg and Morien, were so devoted to bardo-druidism that they viewed the material as sacred and beyond critical investigation. Others treated the material uncritically because they trusted the respectable authors who had used it previously and acknowledged the prestige of the publications in which it had appeared. Many, too, relished Iolo's legacy because it offered them the means of defending the Welsh language and culture against the derisive comments of scholars and writers, many of whom were English.

Those amateurs who produced the first volumes of Welsh history which still retain some academic value, notably Carnhuanawc, Thomas Stephens, Jane Williams and Charles Wilkins, were rather more reluctant to use Iolo's legacy. However, whenever their resolve weakened, necessity intervened. Carnhuanawc used Iolo's sources in elucidating some periods in his *Hanes Cymru* since they were the only ones in the public domain. Thomas Stephens faced a similar dilemma. He was highly suspicious of Iolo's additional triads, but felt compelled to engage with the material because it had been included in *The Myvyrian Archaiology of Wales*. Even the first professional academics, among them Edward Anwyl, W. J. Gruffydd and Sir John Morris-Jones, were blinded by some of Iolo's spurious material because it appeared alongside genuine sources in the published editions available to them, and different parts of his wide œuvre authenticated each other. By this stage, however, Iolo's legacy was living on borrowed time. The desire to manufacture and sustain myths as foundation stones of history was weakening as Wales began to establish its own tangible national institutions. Professional Welsh scholars began to base history, philology and literary criticism on scientific principles, and their critique of Iolo would eventually entail the wholesale condemnation of his work.

# 5

## *The Forgotten Iolo Morganwg*

In 1882 Morgan Williams, once an ardent supporter of Chartism but now an old man living on his memories, wrote as follows:

> As we drift away from some prominent landmark, we lose many features that were conspicuous when it was near us. So with Iolo. The world has lost sight of his quaintness, his politics, his religion, and the predominating characteristic which distinguished him – that of an antiquary – is the only one that has survived.[1]

Williams was at least partly right. Iolo's 'quaintness' was celebrated in dozens of biographical sketches of the kind he himself had just composed, but calls for a reliable biography which would reveal the authentic Iolo Morganwg were rare, and demands for locating and collating 'the correspondence with which he favoured his friends' remained unheeded.[2] Iolo's bardo-druidism lived on in the Gorsedd of the Bards and in druidic organizations and writings throughout the world, and his invented historical sources were eagerly embraced by patriotic Welsh scholars. But his contributions to Welsh poetry, and his religious and political radicalism, were not acknowledged on anything approaching the same scale. They were either forgotten or discarded by a nation which had no political use for them, and were only rediscovered by the generation of scholars which set out to destroy the mythical Iolo Morganwg and expose the falsity of his claims for the history of Wales. The imagined Welsh nation of the nineteenth century had no place for Iolo the poet, the Unitarian and the political radical. Iolo himself – the unrivalled manipulator of evidence and subverter of genres – might well have savoured the irony.

## *The poetry of Iolo Morganwg*

Iolo's principal posthumous influence in the thriving sphere of Welsh poetry was evident in the 'battle of the metres' ('brwydr y mesurau'). Throughout much of his adult life he had vigorously promoted the spurious, but liberating, Glamorgan classification rather than the stultifying twenty-four metres system codified by Dafydd ab Edmwnd in the celebrated Carmarthen Eisteddfod, c.1453.[3] Iolo's *Cyfrinach Beirdd Ynys Prydain*, published three years after his

---

[1] Morgan Williams, 'Notable Men of Wales: Iolo Morganwg (Edward Williams)', 103.
[2] D. J., 'Queries: Iolo Morganwg', *Bye-Gones*, 20 February 1884, 33–4.
[3] See Hywel Teifi Edwards, 'The Eisteddfod Poet: An Embattled Figure' in idem (ed.), *A Guide to Welsh Literature c.1800–1900* (Cardiff, 2000), pp. 31–2.

death, proved to be a key influence in undermining the traditional strict metres and in fostering the new vogue for composing epic free-metre poems known as *pryddestau*. As E. G. Millward has shown, the futile pursuit of the Welsh epic poem thus became a major feature of the eisteddfod tradition in the Victorian age.[4] It found promising allies in John Blackwell (Alun), Thomas Lloyd Jones (Gwenffrwd), Evan Evans (Ieuan Glan Geirionydd) and Ebenezer Thomas (Eben Fardd), whose work brought new energy to the poetic tradition.[5] In that sense, and that sense only, Welsh poets, through the poetic classification of the bards of Glamorgan, still lived beneath the shadow of Iolo.

By contrast, no school of poetry followed in the footsteps of the man who has been called 'one of his nation's ablest poets'.[6] Those who penned biographical sketches of Iolo Morganwg simply refused to engage with his poetical works, choosing instead to concentrate on the myth, as if the bardic persona which Iolo had so cleverly constructed had swallowed up his poetry instead of promoting it.[7] Some biographers, notably the Calvinist Methodist writer William Williams, pleaded incompetence, a defect which prevented them from making judgements on 'sacred' matters pertaining to bards.[8] Others at least served notice of such omissions, but the majority quietly ignored this subject.[9] Iolo was conspicuous by his absence from a list, published in 1841, which ranked Welsh poets on the basis of points awarded under the categories inspiration, knowledge, thoughts and opinion.[10] By the time this debate regarding the relative merits of Welsh poetry had reached *Y Traethodydd* in 1851, he was placed fifteenth out of twenty-nine candidates, though William Williams (Caledfryn) expressed the generally held view that Iolo's gifts as an antiquarian far surpassed his poetic talent:

> Iolo Morganwg ydoedd ddysgedig, ac yn un mawr ei wybodaeth mewn hynafiaeth. Nid yw ei brydyddiaeth o radd uchel, ond y mae yn lled loew. Yr oedd Iolo yn ieithwr da, ac yn gynghaneddwr gwell na'r cyffredin o feirdd y Deheubarth.[11]

---

[4] E. G. Millward, *Yr Arwrgerdd Gymraeg: Ei Thwf a'i Thranc* (Caerdydd, 1998).
[5] The first three poets have been assessed by Huw Meirion Edwards in 'The Lyric Poets' in Edwards (ed.), *A Guide to Welsh Literature c. 1800–1900*, pp. 97–125. For Eben Fardd, see p. 18 in this volume.
[6] Ceri W. Lewis, 'Iolo Morganwg and Strict Metre Poetry' in *Rattleskull Genius*, p. 75.
[7] On the emerging cult of the individual in romantic Wales, see Prys Morgan, 'A Private Space: Autobiography and Individuality in Eighteenth- and Early Nineteenth-Century Wales' in Davies and Jenkins (eds.), *From Medieval to Modern Wales*, pp. 160–74. For the construction of poetic personas, see Davies, *Presences that Disturb*, and for their marketing, see Scott Hess, *Authoring the Self: Self-Representation, Authorship, and the Print Market in British Poetry from Pope through Wordsworth* (New York, 2005).
[8] William Williams, 'Iolo Morganwg [Recollections and Anecdotes of Edward Williams, the Bard of Glamorgan; or Iolo Morganwg, B. B. D. By Elijah Waring. London: Charles Gilpin. 1850]', *Y Traethodydd*, XI (1855), 44.
[9] Anon., 'Dr Johnson a Iolo Morgannwg', *Cymru Fydd*, III, no. 2 (1890), 78.
[10] J. W. Thomas (Arfonwyson), 'Y Beirdd Cymreig', *Seren Gomer*, XXIV, no. 314 (1841), 334.
[11] Caledfryn, 'Beirdd Cymru', *Y Traethodydd*, VII (1851), 387; Edwards, 'Beirdd Cymru', ibid., 215–18; Tegid, Tegai, Caledfryn et al., 'Beirdd Cymru', ibid., 377–91. Ebenezer Thomas (Eben

(Iolo Morganwg was learned, and one with great antiquarian knowledge. His poetry is not of high rank, but it is quite polished. Iolo was a good grammarian, and a better maker of *cynghanedd* than the average poet from the southern parts.)

No lectures on Iolo Morganwg the poet were given in local Cymrodorion societies or Literary and Scientific Institutes. Indeed, in a paper on 'Some Minor Welsh Poets of the Georgian Era' given before the Honourable Society of Cymmrodorion on 23 January 1888, Iolo was not even mentioned, even though most of his contemporaries were included.[12] Nor was his name raised in the discussion which followed.[13] In 1902 James Ifano Jones (Ifano) remarked in an essay on late eighteenth-century Welsh literature that any of the poets of that period could have expressed Iolo Morganwg's line, 'Fy myd i gyd oedd y gân' ('But this warm passion for the tuneful art' [Iolo's translation]), better than him.[14] One obvious explanation for the neglect of Iolo as a poet is the fact that the mid-Victorian age hankered after a more contemporary hero, someone who epitomized the 'spirit of the times'. This 'spirit' was found in the nostalgic poetry of the likes of John Ceiriog Hughes (Ceiriog), who, as Owen M. Edwards put it, enabled Wales to recognize 'her own voice'.[15] In men like him the Welsh discovered a representation of the *gwerin* as they wished it to be. Another explanation for the lack of reception afforded to Iolo's poetry was the plain fact that most of it was not in the public domain. Although he had showed some of his early compositions to his friends, he had never gone to the trouble of publishing them.[16] His best Welsh verse was understood by nineteenth-century scholars to have been composed by the poets to whom he had attributed it, notably Rhys Goch ap Rhicert, Dafydd ap Gwilym and Wil Hopcyn. No published collection of Iolo's Welsh poetry appeared until 1913, when T. C. Evans (Cadrawd) edited the small volume *Gwaith Iolo Morganwg*, but even in this work poetry constituted less than half of the material, the remainder being devoted to bardic lore.[17] The two volumes of English poetry which Iolo had published in 1794, his famous *Poems, Lyric and Pastoral*, never went to a second edition even though he had begun to plan this enterprise before the first edition had come off the press.[18] When James Harris, one of

Fardd) ranked Iolo seventh out of seven, while William Rhys (Gwilym Hiraethog) ranked him fifteenth out of twenty-one.

[12] Richard Williams, 'Some Minor Welsh Poets of the Georgian Era (1714–1830)', *Y Cymmrodor*, X (1889), 46–66.
[13] Richard Williams, 'Some Poets of the Georgian Era', *Bye-Gones*, 30 January 1888, 30–1.
[14] James Ifano Jones, 'Llenyddiaeth Cymru Hanner Ola'r Ddeunawfed Ganrif II', *Y Geninen*, XX, no. 3 (1902), 189. 'Fy myd i gyd . . .' is the fourth line of the Welsh poem chosen by Iolo for the title-page of the first volume of *Poems, Lyric and Pastoral*. For the poem and Iolo's own translation of it, see p. v.
[15] Edwards, *The Eisteddfod*, p. 32.
[16] Lewis, 'Iolo Morganwg and Strict Metre Poetry' in *Rattleskull Genius*, p. 80.
[17] Evans (Cadrawd), *Gwaith Iolo Morganwg*. In addition to the Welsh texts, one English poem, the 'Newgate Stanzas', appeared on pp. 44–5 of this volume.
[18] See, for instance, NLW 21285, Letter no. 822, Iolo Morganwg to Margaret Williams, 30 October 1793.

the editors of the *Red Dragon*, acquired a copy of the work, he devoted an entire article to what he called its 'fringe' – the list of subscribers and the arcane knowledge found in its notes – rather than its poetry.[19] *Poems, Lyric and Pastoral* served as a source of bardic and historical material rather than as a valuable anthology of early Anglo-Welsh poetry.[20] The reprinting of the poem 'Solitude' in 1905, which was judged to be the 'best piece' in the first volume, was a very rare occurrence.[21] Daniel Evans (Daniel Ddu) noted this trend as early as 1841 when he commented that Iolo's anthology was valued by the Welshman simply for the 'observational notes which are connected with the poems, full of explanations on the stories and traditions of the Welsh' ('y nodiadau sylwadol y rhai sy'n gysylltiedig â'r caneuon, yn llawn o egluriadau ar hanesion a thraddodiadau y Cymry').[22]

Even though the poetry attributed to Iolo Morganwg before the First World War was not rated highly enough to be culled from the available manuscripts and to be published in anthologies or celebrated in public lectures, nevertheless fragments of his work did surface in diverse publications. These were often reproduced to illustrate anecdotes about Iolo Morganwg the antiquary and the radical. 'Er Moliant i Dduw am y Cyfryw Ymweliad Gogoneddus' ('In Praise of God for the Said Glorious Visitation'), a poem which Iolo had composed when he heard of the wrecking of slave ships during a storm in 1804, and which had been published in *Seren Gomer* in 1818, accompanied descriptions of his legendary hatred of the slave trade.[23] The poem 'Breiniau Dyn' ('Rights of Man'), which Iolo had recited at Gorseddau in Glamorgan in 1798, complemented the popular tale about Iolo and the *Rights of Man*.[24] The popularity of orally transmitted versions of Iolo's work is hard to estimate, but there is at least one recorded example which shows that by the end of the nineteenth century a ballad singer like Ned Ashton routinely declaimed a fragment or 'distilled version' of 'Breiniau Dyn' as part of his repertoire.[25] Much of the English verse

---

[19] Editor [James Harris], 'The Fringe of a Welshman's Book', *Red Dragon*, VIII (1885), 582–98. He added an interesting footnote regarding the 'Napoleon of booksellers', Bernard Quaritch (1819–90), whose bulk-buying drove up the prices of Welsh publications.

[20] John Rowland (Giraldus), 'The Last Battle in Glamorgan', *Red Dragon*, III (1883), 151–3.

[21] Glaslyn, 'Unigrwydd', *Cymru*, XXIX, no. 168 (1905), 8. 'Solitude' appeared in Williams: *PLP*, I, p. 142. Another rare reprint occurs in Charles Wilkins, 'Men Whom I have Known: John Thomas (Ieuan Ddu)' in Brierley (ed.), *Cymru Fu*, I, p. 100.

[22] Daniel Evans (Daniel Ddu), 'Bywgraffyddiaeth: Cofiant Edward Williams, (Iolo Morganwg)', *Y Gwladgarwr*, IX, no. 100 (1841), 98.

[23] Iolo Morganwg, 'Barddoniaeth: Rhoed llynges gadarn ar y môr', *Seren Gomer*, 2 Rhagfyr 1818, 368.

[24] W. Rowland Jones, 'Dyngarwch a'r Beirdd Cymreig', *Y Geninen*, XXIX, no. 2 (1911), 134; James Ifano Jones, 'Llenyddiaeth Cymru Hanner Ola'r Ddeunawfed Ganrif I', ibid., XX, no. 1 (1902), 31. For an authoritative text of the poem and notes on its origins, see E. G. Millward (ed.), *Blodeugerdd Barddas o Gerddi Rhydd y Ddeunawfed Ganrif* (Llandybïe, 1991), pp. 242–5, 331.

[25] Golygydd, 'Baledau a Baledwyr', *Cymru*, XXVII, no. 159 (1904), 166. For a new approach to assessing what had traditionally been considered 'fragments', see p. 37.

attributed to Iolo in the stories about him was risible, but some of the lines presented in such contexts, like the poem to a solicitor whom Iolo felt had wronged him, and which was used to illustrate an essay on the Welsh tradition of burying suicides and excommunicated people at crossroads, showed his wry humour.[26]

If Iolo was remembered as a Welsh-language poet at all, it was as a master of the craft of the *englyn*. His concise definition of the *englyn* vis-à-vis the English 'epigram' was cited, and his opinion on the common faults of the *englyn* was appreciated by poets of the standing of John Jones (Talhaiarn).[27] Towards the end of the nineteenth century Iolo's *englynion* found their way into several publications, notably the pages of *Y Geninen* and *Cymru*. Here, they often constituted parts of series of poems assembled for the benefit of the next generation of poets.[28] William Rowlands reckoned that Iolo's four lines to the lark figured among the best *englynion unodl union* ever composed (Document 17).[29]

Most of Iolo's published Welsh poems, however, appeared in several series promoted by his small band of legatees, notably D. Silvan Evans and Cadrawd. Published under headings like 'Yr Awen Golledig' ('The Lost Muse') and 'Gweddillion Llenyddol' ('Literary Remains'), they were perceived as belonging to the past rather than the present.[30] A small group of *englynion* in praise of God, drawn from Iolo's two volumes of hymns, *Salmau yr Eglwys yn yr Anialwch*, left a lasting legacy by being engraved on Welsh gravestones and memorials. In particular, two poems were singled out as being appropriate to adorn the graves of members of the established church, of Calvinistic Methodism and of the Unitarian faith.[31] In Cardiganshire alone, recent research has revealed that the *englyn* 'I'r meirwon mae Duw'r mawredd – yn addaw' ('To the dead the God of the mighty – promises') occurs on seventeen occasions, while 'Un a fo'n iawn ei fywyd – a gedwir' ('One who was right-

---

[26] Robert Ellis (Cynddelw), 'Gweddillion Llenyddol: Ofergoelion yr Hen Gymry', *Y Geninen*, V, no. 4 (1887), 280.

[27] Morris Davies, 'Dosbarth ar Bennillion neu Englynion', *Y Traethodydd*, XXII (1867), 431–2; John Jones (Talhaiarn), 'Gweddillion Llenyddol: Beiau Cerdd Dafod', *Y Geninen*, XXVII, no. 1 (1910), 72; Iolo Morganwg, 'Gweddillion Llenyddol: Cerdd Arwest', ibid., XXX, no. 4 (1912), 279.

[28] See, for instance, 'Blodau'r Gynghanedd', *Cymru*, XLIX, no. 290 (1915), 147; 'Blodau'r Gynghanedd', ibid., LI, no. 300 (1916), 53; Asaph, 'Diarhebion y Cymry III', ibid., LXX, no. 418 (1926), 135.

[29] William Rowlands, 'Cadwen o Englynion', *Y Traethodydd*, XXII (1867), 119. For an explanation of the characteristics of this kind of *englyn*, see John Morris-Jones, *Cerdd Dafod, sef Celfyddyd Barddoniaeth Gymraeg* (Caerdydd, 1980), pp. 321–4.

[30] D. G. G., 'Yr Awen Golledig', *Y Traethodydd*, LXIII (1908), 127; 'Gweddillion Llenyddol', *Y Geninen*, XIII, no. 2 (1895), 159; Iolo Morganwg, 'Myn Aur, Fy Mab [O Gronfa y Proffeswr D. Silvan Evans, B.D.]', ibid., V, no. 1 (1887), 71; 'Gofid [O Lawysgrifau anghyhoeddedig Iolo Morganwg]', ibid., VII, no. 3 (1889), 199.

[31] 'Gweddillion Llenyddol', ibid., XIII, no. 2 (1895), 159; *Cymru*, XVIII, no. 102 (1900), 40; ibid., XXXIV, no. 203 (1908), 272.

eous in his life – is saved') was engraved on thirty-six stones.[32] The sculptor Joseph Edwards used the former *englyn*, together with a *pietà* and the mystic sign, on the elaborate relief-memorial which he created for Lewis Morgan in 1860 (Document 11). But, despite these scattered references to Iolo's Welsh poetry, it was not until 1919, when Griffith John Williams began to publish the first fruits of his meticulous research into the manuscripts of Iolo Morganwg, that the *cywyddau* of 'Iorwerth Gwilym', the romantic nature poet, were rediscovered and rehabilitated.[33] Several generations would pass before a selection of Iolo's attractive free-metre poems entered the public domain.[34]

## Iolo the Unitarian

The swift and substantial growth of leading Nonconformist denominations – Calvinistic Methodists, Independents and Baptists – was one of the most striking features of nineteenth-century Wales. The power of the established church was severely shaken. The 1851 Religious Census revealed all too clearly that Nonconformists had won the allegiance of around three-quarters of the worshippers of Wales. During these years of spiritual renewal the leading denominations attracted worshippers in large numbers, built massive chapels to house them, and produced charismatic revivalists like Christmas Evans and John Elias who had little love for the muscular intellectualism of Rational Dissent.[35] Unitarians were ill-equipped to compete effectively against the bigger Nonconformist battalions. In terms of numbers and influence, the latter outstripped the Unitarian churches in both rural areas and within the industrial population. By 1851, the total complement of Unitarian worshippers in south Wales was only 2,777 (and perhaps considerably less).[36] The bulk of them were to be found in the notorious 'Black Spot' (Y Smotyn Du) and in urban pockets in south Wales, and only in these circles was Iolo likely to be remembered and respected.

Iolo's hymns and religious poems were allotted a place of honour within the Unitarian tradition. Of approximately 3,000 hymns he was said to have

---

[32] E. L. James and M. A. James, 'Edward Williams (Iolo Morganwg), 1747–1826: Englynion o'i Waith ar Feddau yng Ngheredigion (unpublished manuscript)', pp. 1–2. In *Salmau yr Eglwys yn yr Anialwch*, 'I'r meirwon' followed hymn no. 158 of volume II, and 'Un a fo'n iawn' followed hymn no. 195 of volume I.

[33] G. J. Williams, 'Cywyddau Cynnar Iolo Morganwg', *Y Beirniad*, VIII, no. 2 (1919), 75–91; idem, 'Rhys Goch ap Rhicert', ibid., VIII, no. 4 (1920), 211–26, 260. See also *IMChY*.

[34] Patrick J. Donovan (ed.), *Cerddi Rhydd Iolo Morganwg* (Caerdydd, 1980).

[35] D. Densil Morgan, *Christmas Evans a'r Ymneilltuaeth Newydd* (Llandysul, 1991); R. Tudur Jones, *John Elias: Pregethwr a Phendefig* (Bridgend, 1975).

[36] Ieuan Gwynedd Jones and David Williams (eds.), *The Religious Census of 1851: A Calendar of the Returns relating to Wales. Volume 1. South Wales* (Cardiff, 1976), Appendix B. Since these figures include those who worshipped in the morning, afternoon and evening on census day, the total number of members was actually a good deal smaller.

Fig. 12 'I'r meirwon mae Duw'r mawredd – yn addaw', Llannarth cemetery. Several *englynion* by Iolo were used on gravestones in Unitarian burial grounds in south-west Wales.

written, 204 were published in the first volume of *Salmau yr Eglwys yn yr Anialwch* in 1812, and a further 211 in the second volume, which appeared in 1834.[37] Twenty-two hymns were added to this corpus as an appendix to Iolo's

---

[37] Edward Williams, *Salmau yr Eglwys yn yr Anialwch: Cyfrol 1* (Merthyr Tydfil, 1812); idem, *Salmau yr Eglwys yn yr Anialwch: Cyfrol II* (Merthyr Tydfil, 1834). For an introductory overview

translation of the second edition of J. P. Estlin's catechism in 1814.[38] The first volume ran to a second edition in 1827 and, when demands for a new and less expensive edition became too clamorous to resist, both volumes were reissued as one in 1857.[39] Prominent Unitarians like Thomas Hughes of Neuaddfawr helped to popularize Iolo's work by buying copies in bulk in order to distribute them among members of the denomination. A promotional campaign was organized by *Yr Ymofynydd*, which also reprinted seventeen of Iolo's hymns between 1848 and 1898.[40] The hymn-book published by John Bowen Jones in 1877 included 208 of Iolo's hymns.[41] Nearly half of the 379 hymns contained in the Unitarian hymn-book *Emynau o Fawl a Gweddi* (1878) were composed by Iolo, as were 137 of the approximately 500 hymns published in *Perlau Moliant* (1896).[42] Iolo's hymns were sung during protest meetings (especially during the 1868 election) and appeared on the hymn-sheets of local and regional associations.[43] The religious *englynion* which Iolo printed between the hymns of *Salmau yr Eglwys yn yr Anialwch* were used by preachers of the standing of Rees Jenkin Jones in their sermons and publications, and were valuable tools in the quest for political and social justice.[44] Iolo's hymns and poems became such an integral part of a Unitarian upbringing that three of the questions in the catechism used for the instruction of more advanced pupils invited them either to learn some of his verses by heart or to interpret them (Document 18).[45]

The Unitarian denomination, which remained numerically small and beleaguered even within the Welsh Nonconformist community, was proud to celebrate that which one of its founder fathers had bequeathed to it. In fulsome

of Iolo's published and unpublished hymns, see W. Rhys Nicholas, 'Iolo Morganwg a'i Emynau', *Bwletin Cymdeithas Emynau Cymru*, I, no. 2 (1969), 14–25.

[38] R. Jenkin Jones, 'Iolo Morganwg fel Emynwr', *Yr Ymofynydd*, XXIV, no. 145 (1900), 13; *Holiadur, neu addysgiadau cyffredin, hawl ac atteb, yn athrawiaethau a Dyledswyddau Crefydd* (Merthyr Tydfil, 1814).

[39] Edward Williams, *Salmau yr Eglwys yn yr Anialwch: Cyfrol Un* (Merthyr Tydfil, 1827); John Jones (Eiddil Glan Cynnon), 'Salmau Iolo', *Yr Ymofynydd*, V, no. 76 (1853), 283–4; Edward Williams, *Salmau yr Eglwys yn yr Anialwch: Yn Ddwy Gyfrol* (3rd edn., Aberystwyth, 1857).

[40] Thomas Thomas, 'Salmau Iolo – Anrheg T. Hughes, Ysw. i'r Ymofynydd', *Yr Ymofynydd*, V, no. 54 (1863), 143.

[41] John Bowen Jones, *Hen Emynau* (Merthyr Tydfil, 1877), and later editions in 1883 and 1912.

[42] Rees Jenkin Jones, *Emynau o Fawl a Gweddi* (Aberdar, 1878; 2nd edn., 1883); *Perlau Moliant sef, casgliad o emynau, tonau, a Salm-donau, at wasanaeth eglwysi Undodaidd Cymru* (Merthyr Tydfil, 1896).

[43] Aubrey J. Martin, *Hanes Llwynrhydowen* (Llandysul, 1977), pp. 72, 77–8. For a reprint of a hymn on a local sheet, see 'St Catherine' in *Emynau a Gweddiau Urdd Benywod Undodaidd Ceredigion* (Llandysul, n.d.), p. 5.

[44] See, for instance, Rees Jenkin Jones, *'Wele Fi, Anfon Fi': Pregeth a Draddodwyd yn Nghyfarfod Chwarterol Undodiaid Deheubarth Cymru yn Llandyssul, Dydd Mercher, Ion. 3, 1894* (Aberdar, 1894), p. 8; idem, *'Y Gwyliedydd: Beth am y Nos?' Anerchiad i'r Cyhoedd, 1896* (2nd edn., Llandysul, 1903), p. 18; idem, *Yr Atheist: Ymgom ag ef* (Llandysul, 1908), p. 11.

[45] Y Gymdeithas Undodaidd Gymreig, Adran yr Ysgol Sul, *Holwyddoreg ar Elfenau Crefydd: Safon II* (Treforis and Clydach, n.d. ante 1911), pp. 3, 6, 8. See also Williams, *Salmau yr Eglwys yn yr Anialwch: Yn Ddwy Gyfrol*, I, pp. 24–5.

terms its representatives maintained that Iolo's psalms and hymns evinced such 'deep philosophical insight and a sublime spiritual strain' that for 'power and polish combined, none of the old Welsh hymn writers' could compare with him.[46] Unlike William Williams Pantycelyn, who had sought to sway the congregation through blind emotion, Iolo had appealed to the rational mind and had focused on the need for social justice.[47] Yet, as even stout defenders of Iolo's work, such as Rees Jenkin Jones, minister of Hen Dŷ Cwrdd Aberdare from 1864 until 1909, readily admitted, Iolo's hymns were rarely sung outside Unitarian churches.[48] The tide of evangelicalism which swept through Wales during the Victorian age was better attuned to the perceived spiritual needs of the day than the more hard-headed religion embraced by Unitarians. By the beginning of the twentieth century, even some Unitarians were divided on this issue.[49] In response to criticisms levelled against the worshippers at Cribyn in Cardiganshire who had neglected to sing Iolo's work, J. Islan Jones regretted his failure to leaven his hymns with greater feeling:

> gresyn na fuasai wedi ymfoddloni ar gyfansoddi hanner cymaint, a threulio mwy o amser i'w coethi a'u melusu, pan o dan ysbrydoliaeth ac eneiniad y wir awen ... Mae'n dra sicr nad oes digon o *deimlad* yn emynau Iolo i foddio'r Cymro cyffredin.[50]

> (it is a pity that he did not content himself with composing half as many, and spending more time in honing and sweetening them, when he was under the inspiration and influence of the true muse ... It is pretty certain that there is not enough *feeling* in Iolo's hymns to please the common Welshman.)

Outside Unitarian circles, Iolo's hymns were either deliberately ignored or discounted. William Alonzo Griffiths, a nineteenth-century authority on Welsh hymns, believed that Iolo's hymns were bereft of the quality which held people's affections in their celebration of God.[51] In his article on 'Welsh Hymnology', W. Glanffrwd Thomas insisted that, in comparison with his neighbouring hymn-writer, 'Iolo was the greater man of the two, but Thomas Williams the greater hymnologist.'[52] Despite Iolo's expressed aim that his work

---

[46] A. Emrys-Jones, *The Life and Works of Edward Williams (Iolo Morganwg), The Bard of Glamorgan (Reprinted from the Manchester Quarterly)* (London, 1889), p. 16. See also T. C. U., 'Notes and Queries: Welsh MSS (xi–278)', *Red Dragon*, XI (1887), 376.
[47] John Gwili Jenkins, 'Y Ddau Ofuned', *Y Geninen*, XXIV, no. 1 (1906), 112.
[48] T. C. U., 'Prydydd y Coed', *Cymru*, XII, no. 71 (1897), 294; idem, 'Cynddelw ar Iolo fel Emynwr', *Yr Ymofynydd*, XVI, no. 45 (1891), 213–14.
[49] See, for instance, B. C. D., 'Manion ac Hanesion: Salmau Iolo', ibid., XI, no. 2 (1911), 48; Talywaenydd, 'Cymeriad Iolo Morganwg', ibid., XIV, no. 9 (1914), 90–1.
[50] J. Islan Jones, 'Emynau Iolo Morganwg', ibid., VI, no. 9 (1906), 209–10. For a further defence, see B. C. D., 'Manion ac Hanesion: Salmau Iolo', 48.
[51] William Alonzo Griffiths, 'Emynwyr Cymreig y Ganrif Hon', *Y Beirniad*, XX, no. 82 (1879), 316–17; idem, *Hanes Emynwyr Cymru* (Caernarfon, 1893), p. 256.
[52] W. Glanffrwd Thomas, 'Welsh Hymnology', *Y Cymmrodor*, VI (1883), 53–87; idem, 'Welsh Hymnology', *Bye-Gones*, 16 May 1883, 241–2. For another critical opinion, see James Ifano Jones (Ifano), 'Llenyddiaeth Cymru Hanner Ola'r Ddeunawfed Ganrif II', *Y Geninen*, XX, no. 3 (1902), 193.

was addressed to all Christians, his hymns were excluded from the hymn-books of Independents, Baptists and Calvinistic Methodists.[53] Only the Wesleyan Methodists availed themselves of some of his work.[54] Among the 2,615 hymns contained in Thomas Gee's massive volume *Emynau y Cysegr*, there were none that were suspected to be of Unitarian origin.[55] Gee, the Calvinistic Methodist and influential publisher, who was remembered by later generations as a radical campaigner on behalf of Liberalism, was an avowed enemy of anti-Trinitarianism.[56] So, too, were leaders of the Nonconformist mainstream. The sole exception was Owen M. Edwards, who chose to publish seven of Iolo's hymns between 1902 and 1916, among them his favourite 'Boreu Teg o Haf' ('A Fine Summer Morning'), which featured three times.[57] Even though the Welsh were believed to be 'emphatically a nation of Nonconformists' by the 1880s, the Unitarians, the second smallest of the 'minor sects', were still regarded with suspicion or hostility.[58] It is highly ironic that Iolo's denomination pointed to the inclusion of two of his hymns in *Emyniadur yr Eglwys yng Nghymru* (1898), a hymn-book for use in the established church which Iolo had rejected, in order to confirm his success outside their own ranks.[59] Recounting how these hymns came to be included in this hymn-book also provided them with an opportunity to reiterate their judgement that 'in a literary sense, Iolo Morganwg is our best hymnologist, and in the same sense, Pantycelyn is the worst' ('mewn golygiad llenyddol, Iolo Morganwg yw ein hemynwr goreu; ac yn yr un golygiad Pantycelyn yw y gwaelaf').[60]

In contrast to the reception given to his hymns, Iolo's leading role in establishing Unitarianism in Wales remained hidden, even though he was counted among the icons of the denomination. The fact that Elijah Waring had raised doubts regarding Iolo's religious affiliations in his *Recollections and Anecdotes of*

---

[53] Jenkin Jones, 'Iolo Morganwg fel Emynwr', 13; Williams, *Salmau yr Eglwys yn yr Anialwch*, I, p. iii.

[54] Thomas Davies (Tegwyn), 'Hanes Llyfr Emynau y Wesleyaid Cymreig II', *Cymru*, XVI, no. 95 (1899), 323.

[55] Thomas Gee, *Emynau y Cysegr* (Dinbych, 1885).

[56] T. Gwynn Jones, *Cofiant Thomas Gee* (Dinbych, 1913); Ieuan Wyn Jones, *Y Llinyn Arian: Agweddau o Fywyd a Chyfnod Thomas Gee* (Dinbych, 1998); Philip Henry Jones, 'Saernïo'r Gofeb: T. Gwynn Jones a *Chofiant Thomas Gee*', *Y Traethodydd*, CXLVII, no. 625 (1992), 183–210.

[57] 'Y Gwir Gristion', *Cymru*, XXXII, no. 186 (1907), 20; 'Duw'n Fugail', ibid., XXXII, no. 191 (1907), 328; 'Teyrnas Nef yn Neshau', ibid., XLIX, no. 289 (1915), 75; 'Golwg ar Deyrnas Dduw', ibid., LI, no. 302 (1916), 146; 'Boreu Teg o Haf', ibid., XXIII, no. 132 (1902), 16; 'Boreu Teg o Haf', ibid., XXXII, no. 191 (1907), 300; 'Boreu Teg o Haf', ibid., XLIX, no. 288 (1915), 55. 'Boreu Teg o Haf' is no. 89 in the first volume of *Salmau yr Eglwys yn yr Anialwch*.

[58] Thomas Rees, *History of Protestant Nonconformity in Wales* (2nd edn., London, 1883), p. 452.

[59] Jenkin Jones, 'Iolo Morganwg fel Emynwr', 14–15; *Emyniadur yr Eglwys yng Nghymru* (Bangor, 1898), pp. 20, 22, 72. These are 'Cân Ser y Wawr yn Ber y Sydd' from Williams, *Salmau yr Eglwys yn yr Anialwch*, I, hymn no. 65, p. 72, and 'Ser y Bore'n Dyrfa Lân', previously unpublished, and 'At Rai'n Bugeilo Praidd Liw Nos', which Iolo had translated from the original by Nahum Tate.

[60] D. Silvan Evans, 'Manion ac Hanesion: Iolo Morganwg a Phantycelyn', *Yr Ymofynydd*, VI, no. 5 (1906), 120.

*Edward Williams* was resented and contested by Unitarians. A series of *englynion* praising the 'One God' was immediately offered in his defence, and his hymns were quoted as evidence of his religious convictions.[61] It is entirely possible that Waring's publication also prompted Iolo's fellow Unitarian, Thomas Stephens, to compose a fitting biography for this key member of the denomination. Stephens's work was eagerly anticipated and the audience was primed with selections of Iolo's poetry and hymns.[62] However, apart from one paragraph which described his alleged visit to the incarcerated Unitarian minister Thomas Evans (Tomos Glyn Cothi) at Carmarthen, Stephens's series, presented in twelve instalments and encompassing over fifty pages, did not cite a single document or describe a single act devoted to Iolo's role in the founding of Unitarianism in Wales.[63] Likewise, Rees Jenkin Jones's lengthy article on the evolution of Unitarianism in Wales was prefaced by one of Iolo's hymns, but did not mention his name in connection with the early history of the denomination.[64] Thus, Iolo's highly significant role in the formation of the South Wales Unitarian Society in 1802, which included the formulation and translation of its rules, remained unknown until 1927, when *Yr Ymofynydd* published discoveries from the Iolo Morganwg papers at the National Library of Wales which proved beyond doubt that he was, indeed, one of the principal founders of the movement.[65]

## *Iolo's political legacy*

The flame of Iolo's political radicalism proved to be even more difficult to sustain in the Victorian and Edwardian years. Neither his son Taliesin nor any of the scholars who were later granted access to the Iolo papers at Llanover showed any interest in his radical writings or any desire to publish them. As a result, Iolo's political legacy remained hidden and no political movement or party was founded in his honour or to disseminate his radical ideas. For most of the period under review it was the 'self-dying efforts which he made for the preservation of the ancient lore of Wales' which commanded respect and admiration rather than 'the strange and unattractive character of his religious

---

[61] H. Davies, 'Barddoniaeth: Iolo Morganwg', *Yr Ymofynydd*, IV, no. 41 (1851), 23.
[62] 'Iolo Morganwg – Dernyn o'i Brydydd-Waith', ibid., IV, no. 43 (1851), 49–50.
[63] For the series, see ibid., V, no. 56 (1852), 77–82, to ibid., VI, no. 66 (1853), 29–35; Thomas Stephens, 'Iolo Morganwg: Ei Nodweddion', ibid., VI, no. 65 (1853), 12–13. See also Geraint H. Jenkins, '"A Very Horrid Affair": Sedition and Unitarianism in the Age of Revolutions' in Davies and Jenkins (eds.), *From Medieval to Modern Wales*, pp. 175–96.
[64] Rees Jenkin Jones, 'Dechreuad a Chynnydd Undodiaeth yn Nghymru', *Y Geninen*, XXIII, no. 3 (1905), 176–83.
[65] Anon., 'Iolo Morganwg: Yr Undodwr a'r Emynydd', *Yr Ymofynydd*, XXVII, no. 3 (1927), 67–9. See also Jenkins, 'The Unitarian Firebrand, the Cambrian Society and the Eisteddfod' in *Rattleskull Genius*, pp. 279–80.

and political opinions'.[66] By the 1820s the Gorsedd of the Bards, which he had envisaged as a Jacobin circle dedicated to the promotion of liberty, equality and brotherhood, had been appropriated by the gentry and the affluent and conservatively minded middling sorts.[67] Throughout the century the likes of Taliesin, Evan Davies (Myfyr Morganwg), John Williams (Ab Ithel) and Owen Morgan (Morien) concentrated on developing the more arcane aspects of the Gorsedd, which set Bards and Druids apart from the rest of society, rather than promoting the social radicalism that Iolo had cherished.

The radical political movements of the first half of the nineteenth century, notably Chartism, used forms of physical protest of which Iolo Morganwg, an individualist who shied from the mob and who loathed violence or force of arms, would have disapproved. They addressed working-class issues for which Iolo, the artisan-liberal, did not provide a direct line of tradition, even though the banner which Hugh Williams designed for the Chartists in Wales was in white, green and blue – the colours of Iolo's Gorsedd – and bore the word 'Cyfiawnder' ('Justice'), a word which figured prominently in his writings. Only general connections, rather than points of contact in teaching and tradition, between Iolo's radicalism and the radical politics of the 1830s and 1840s, are discernible.[68] There were personal links through activists like Dr William Price, who worshipped nature and claimed the title of archdruid, but who also led the Pontypridd section of the Chartist movement. Iolo's son Taliesin not only founded Cymmrodorion societies and convened Gorseddau, but also petitioned on behalf of Dic Penderyn following the Merthyr Rising of 1831. Morgan Williams, the son of a prominent Unitarian, who recalled Iolo's visits to his childhood home, became editor of the Chartist paper, *Udgorn Cymru*.[69] In south Wales, especially in the Aberdare and Merthyr Tydfil area, cultural and radical political leadership and Unitarianism overlapped, but few invoked Iolo's name as a begetter of political reform.[70] The only reference to his ideas in *Udgorn Cymru* was the pseudonym 'Dyfnwal Moel-Mud' adopted by one of its contributors.[71] At a time when the main subjects of debate were the Poor Law, Chartist Conventions in London and high taxation, anecdotes about the political influence of a Glamorgan stonemason excited little attention.

---

[66] Williams, 'Reviews: Recollections and Anecdotes of Edward Williams, the Bard of Glamorgan', 102. See also Griffiths, *Hanes Emynwyr Cymru*, p. 255.
[67] See Chapter 2 above and also Jenkins, '"Dyro Dduw dy Nawdd": Iolo Morganwg a'r Mudiad Undodaidd' in idem (ed.), *Cof Cenedl XX*, pp. 79, 82–3.
[68] Gwyn A. Williams, *Gweriniaeth y Silwriaid / The Silurian Republic* (Casnewydd, 1988), pp. 16, 19.
[69] Islwyn ap Nicholas, *A Welsh Heretic: Dr William Price, Llantrisant* (Llandybïe, 1970), pp. 15–16; Gwyn A. Williams, *The Merthyr Rising* (Cardiff, 1978), pp. 48, 85. See also Chapter 2 above.
[70] For an appraisal of some of these connections, see, for instance, D. Ben Rees, 'Capeli Cwm Cynon a'r Diwylliant Cymraeg' in Edwards (ed.), *Cwm Cynon*, esp. pp. 77–81; Roberts, 'Mab ei Dad' in Edwards (ed.), *Merthyr a Thaf*, pp. 57–92.
[71] Dyfnwal Moel-Mud, 'Dyled y Llywodraeth', *Udgorn Cymru*, 21 May 1842, 3.

Although Welsh Liberalism in the second half of the nineteenth century fondly remembered Iolo, usually in the form of entertaining anecdotes, it did not seek recourse to his political writings. While the myth of Iolo Morganwg prospered in Victorian Wales, his political legacy sank into oblivion and Wales settled into its proud image as '*gwlad y menig gwynion*, respectable, religious, petty bourgeois in style and aspiration'.[72] Not until the very end of the Victorian era were Iolo's ideas noticed by the Liberal middle classes, and even then they played in the wings of the radical tradition, rather than taking centre stage. Examples of Iolo's stance in favour of the ideals of the French Revolution predominantly took the form of apocryphal anecdotes published in biographical sketches of Iolo Morganwg.[73] His songs to the 'Cowbridge Volunteers' and to the King of England ('God Save the King') puzzled late Victorians and Edwardians alike and compromised his credentials as a truly radical figure.[74] Although Iolo had correctly and publicly identified Anglicization and the absence of official support for the Welsh language among the major ills arising from the Acts of Union of 1536–43, he was rarely praised as a champion of the Welsh-language movement.[75] Although E. Ben Morus (Myfyr Teifi) called on the Labour party to include men such as Josiah Thomas Jones, William Williams (Carw Coch) and Iolo Morganwg 'on the roll call of its early soldiers' ('ar gofres ei milwyr cynnar'), in the heated atmosphere of the early years of the twentieth century Iolo was seldom pressed into service as a political activist whose deeds were worthy of commemoration.[76] Living political icons – Henry Richard, 'the Apostle of Peace', William Abraham, the miner's leader, Tom Ellis, the son of a tenant farmer, and David Lloyd George, the cottage-bred solicitor – were much more likely to be fêted as exemplars of the Welsh *gwerin*.

The continued publication of stories about the mythical Iolo Morganwg persistently blurred the persona of the authentic historical figure. Even the comprehensive critique of Iolo's work which began in the 1910s focused on his personal characteristics and antiquarian achievements rather than on his religion or politics. 'What kind of a man was Iolo?' ('Pa fath ddyn ydoedd Iolo?'), asked W. Llewelyn Williams in 1921, before stoutly defending him

---

[72] Ieuan Gwynedd Jones, *Explorations and Explanations: Essays in the Social History of Victorian Wales* (Llandysul, 1981), p. 270.

[73] Ifano, 'Llenyddiaeth Cymru Hanner Ola'r Ddeunawfed Ganrif I', 27–31; W. Ambrose Bebb, 'Yr Ymherodraeth Brydeinig ym Marddoniaeth Cymru', *Y Geninen*, XLII, no. 1 (1924), 34. See also Chapter 1 above.

[74] Edward Williams (Iolo Morganwg), 'Gweddillion Llenyddol: A Song Written for the Cowbridge Volunteers', *Y Geninen*, VII, no. 3 (1889), 197–9; 'God Save the King by Iolo Morganwg', *Bye-Gones*, 25 June 1902, 383.

[75] *MAW*, I, p. x; Charles Davies, '"Eu Hiaith a Gadwant"', *Y Geninen*, XVII, no. 4 (1899), 219.

[76] Ben Morus, 'William Williams (Carw Coch)', *Cymru*, XL, no. 234 (1911), 59. See also idem, *Enwogion Aber Dâr: Sef Byrr-nodion am rai o Gewri Ymadawedig Y Dref a'r Cylch* (Llanbedr Pont Stephan, 1910), p. 39.

against the accusation of forgery.[77] Not until 1923 did John Griffiths attempt to reappraise Iolo's espousal of liberty and the spirit of the French Revolution, but even he relied heavily on hoary tales about Iolo, and on the oft-rehearsed radical poems, 'Breiniau Dyn' (Rights of Man), 'Gorymbil am Heddwch' (Plea for Peace), 'Er Moliant i Dduw am y Cyfryw Ymweliad Gogoneddus' (Praise of God for the Said Glorious Visitation) and the 'Newgate Stanzas'.[78] A lonely, but refreshing, cry of dissent was sounded in 1926, when J. J. Evans, in an issue of *Yr Ymofynydd* published in the year of the centenary of Iolo's death, examined his place in the context of the revolutionary movements of his time. Evans revealed the radical ideas which had underpinned his first Gorsedd and the radical subjects which had been set in the eisteddfodau of the Gwyneddigion Society. He also linked the Madogwys legend with the quest for democracy, and confirmed that Iolo's writings and publications had remained strongly tinted with radical beliefs until his death in 1826.[79] But Evans was an exception to the rule. For more than a century Iolo's political legacy had remained almost wholly buried under those aspects of his legendary life and work which the Welsh people had found more palatable. It is one of the ironies of Welsh history that the political writings of the self-styled 'Bard of Liberty' did not become a necessary reference point during the century in which political radicalism found its voice.

In creating a sanitized myth of a saintly figure, a patriotic antiquary and a folk hero, Victorian Wales chose to neglect other aspects of the life and works of Iolo Morganwg. It developed Iolo's Gorsedd into a national institution which, side by side with the eisteddfod, took its place at the cultural heart of the Welsh nation, but dispensed with the radical concepts which had informed it. Many Welsh and international scholars closely examined Iolo's papers in search of evidence for the bardo-druidism which was believed to illuminate the early history of Wales, but they published none of its radical political or religious content. Even the critique of Iolo's counterfeit source material concentrated on those parts of his archive which had already been favoured by his legatees. The legacy of Iolo Morganwg as an accomplished poet, a founding father of Unitarianism and a champion of the ideals of the American and the French revolutions did not begin to emerge until the 1920s.

---

[77] 'Euog, a'u Rhydd', *Yr Ymofynydd*, XXI, no. 11 (1921), 171; W. Rhys Watkin, 'Beirdd Llangyfelach II', *Y Geninen*, XXXVII, no. 2 (1919), 80.
[78] Griffiths, 'Neges Gymdeithasol Iolo Morgannwg', *Y Geninen*, XLI, no. 4 (1923), 202–10. A second article, which sought to place Iolo in the context of his time, was by William Edwards, 'Iolo Morganwg ac Oes Rhamant', *Yr Ymofynnydd*, XXVII, no. 3 (1927), 45–51.
[79] J. J. Evans, 'Iolo Morganwg a'r Chwyldro Ffrengig', ibid., XXVII, no. 3 (1927), 57–8, 60. Geraint H. Jenkins is currently preparing a study of the political and religious radicalism of Iolo Morganwg.

# 6

# The Case against Iolo Morganwg

In 1892 T. Marchant Williams, the controversial founder and editor of *The Nationalist*, described Iolo Morganwg, whom he held in the highest esteem, as the 'arch-fantasist of his age' ('arch-ddychymmygwr ei oes').[1] Williams, whose acerbic wit meant that he was widely known as the 'Acid Drop', was riding the wave of criticism which by that stage had begun to threaten Iolo's legacy. The growing condemnation of Iolo's 'school of magic and make-believe' ('ysgol hud a lledrith') was a sign of changing attitudes towards the past. This European trend was part of the professionalization of scholarship in fields such as philology and history in Wales, and was also indicative of the changing character of nationalism.[2] In 1877 the Welsh had proudly celebrated the appointment of John Rhŷs as the first Professor of Celtic Philology at Oxford, and within Wales, too, significant progress was made as university colleges began to appoint lecturers and professors in Welsh history and in Welsh language and literature, among them J. E. Lloyd and John Morris-Jones, men who would become giants in their respective fields. Such scholars set their face against myth and fantasy, and nurtured the likes of Ifor Williams and Griffith John Williams, promising young researchers who would lay the foundations on which twentieth and twenty-first century scholarship was built. Their approach was in keeping with the European drive for a scientific 'self-correction' of national histories and of invented traditions.[3] In the eyes of many of these 'new scholars' in Wales, Iolo Morganwg's legacy had poisoned the sources of Welsh scholarship for too long.[4]

Suspicions regarding some of the material which Iolo had introduced into Welsh literature and history had arisen from the moment it entered the public domain, and to that extent the more rigorous scholars of the late Victorian age were simply rounding off a development which had begun in the early nineteenth century at a time when the resources and scientific tools available to antiquaries and critics were as yet strictly limited. This chapter charts the rise

---

[1] T. Marchant Williams, 'Y Beirdd a Chyhoeddi'r Eisteddfod', *Y Geninen*, X, no. 1 (1892), 25–7.
[2] Mathonwy, 'Gohebiaethau: Coelbren y Beirdd, a Llywelyn a'i Gi', *Y Brython*, III, no. 19 (1860), 192. On the professionalization of historical writing in Britain, see Robert Harrison, Aled Jones, Peter Lambert, 'The Institutionalisation and Organisation of History' in Peter Lambert and Phillipp Schofield (eds.), *Making History: An Introduction to the History and Practices of a Discipline* (London, 2004), pp. 14–20.
[3] Anthony D. Smith, 'History and Modernity: Reflections on the Theory of Nationalism' in David Boswell and Jessica Evans (eds.), *Representing the Nation: A Reader* (London, 1999), p. 54.
[4] John Morris-Jones, 'Rhagymadrodd' in *IMChY*, p. viii.

of this early criticism, focuses on Thomas Stephens as the first serious critic of Iolo's counterfeit material, and outlines the changes in paradigm which, from the 1850s onwards, marked the beginning of the end of Iolo's cultural influence, and which, amid considerable controversy, led the first professional academics in Wales to undermine his reputation.

## *The rise of criticism*

Although Iolo Morganwg's source material for the history of Wales and its civilization was generally well received in the nineteenth century, doubts were aired from the very beginning over some passages and especially the triads which dealt with the early history of Britain. Even before the public reception of Iolo's legacy began in earnest, William Williams (Gwilym Peris) and David Thomas (Dafydd Ddu Eryri) were unconvinced of the veracity of his writings and feared that they might undermine well-established interpretations of the past.[5] However, their mistrust was fuelled more by personal tensions between the critics from north Wales and Iolo than by the formers' command of the sources. But there were other experienced scholars like Theophilus Jones and Walter Davies (Gwallter Mechain) who harboured grave misgivings about the authenticity of Iolo's work.[6] Edward 'Celtic' Davies, another of Iolo's contemporaries, and a writer who considered himself an authority on druidism, bravely went so far as to use the term 'forgery' in connection with Iolo's additional material.[7] In a paragraph relating to the Chair of Glamorgan, he remarked that 'a slight enquiry into the credentials of the society itself, will discover some marks of gross misrepresentation, if not of absolute forgery'.[8] With unusual percipience he linked the notions expressed in Iolo's bardic preface to the *Heroic Elegies and other Pieces of Llywarç Hen* with 'the late anarchy in France', that is, the French Revolution, which had clearly influenced the mind of the Glamorgan bard.[9] But even Davies was taken in by most of Iolo's work, including the bardic alphabet, which he reproduced in *Celtic Researches on the Origin, Traditions & Language of the Ancient Britons* because it lent 'powerful support' to his own theories regarding druidism.[10] Since his best-known works, *Celtic Researches* and *The Mythology and Rites of the British Druids*, were themselves viewed as curiosities by later antiquaries, Davies's astute

---

[5] Ibid., p. viii; Morgan, 'Iolo Morganwg and Welsh Historical Traditions' in *Rattleskull Genius*, p. 252.
[6] See Moira Dearnley, '"Mad Ned" and the "Smatter-Dasher": Iolo Morganwg and Edward "Celtic" Davies' in *Rattleskull Genius*, pp. 426, 434, 436.
[7] Davies's relationship with Iolo Morganwg is discussed in detail in ibid., 425–42.
[8] Edward Davies, *The Mythology and Rites of the British Druids* (London, 1809), p. 33.
[9] Ibid., p. 59.
[10] Edward Davies, *Celtic Researches on the Origin, Traditions & Language, of the Ancient Britons* (London, 1804), facing p. 272; Dearnley, '"Mad Ned" and the "Smatter-Dasher": Iolo Morganwg and Edward "Celtic" Davies' in *Rattleskull Genius*, p. 429.

remarks regarding the authenticity of Iolo's material were robbed of their effect. Some reviewers buried their heads in the sand. Although the anonymous author of the 'Sketch of the History of the Britons' in the *Cambrian Register* criticized Iolo, William Owen Pughe and Edward 'Celtic' Davies indiscriminately, he nevertheless concluded that 'their labours, in general, are certainly very valuable, and have greatly contributed to increase the knowledge of British antiquities' (Document 19).[11]

Other authors voiced disparaging opinions about some of Iolo's material or his system of bardism, even though they were aware of the implications of their criticism for the well-being of the nation. For instance, having promised in the preface to his *History of Wales* 'to reject idle tradition, and to sacrifice even his national pride to the cause of truth', the London Welshman John Jones proceeded to ridicule and cast aside Iolo's Moelmutian triads:

> A great British lawyer, of the name of Dyfnwal Moelmud, is reported, among the illiterate, to have written on the Welsh laws; and weak men have published his triads, as specimens of his great wisdom, and incomparable rules of justice. Dyfnwal Moelmud denotes a profound Welshman, bald and dumb. The term Wallia, and the triadic mode of writing, were creatures of the seventh or eighth century; and the triads attributed to Dyfnwal consist of low and wretched adages, not reconcilable, in any instance, to either logic or jurisprudence. With this rejection the Chapter on Laws contains passages from the Anglo-Saxon laws relating to Welshmen; a summary of the laws of Howel; and abstracts of the English statutes, down to the last enactment inclusive.[12]

Jones stood by his promise and based his section on the Welsh laws exclusively on the authentic tradition of Hywel Dda, but even he was bamboozled into believing that the account of the Gorsedd of the Bards, which he had read in *Poems, Lyric and Pastoral*, was 'worthy of high consideration'.[13] David Lloyd Isaac also prefaced his volume *Siluriana* by noting that he did not belong to Iolo's 'School of Vertigo' ('Ysgol y Bendro') but, unlike John Jones, this native of Cardiganshire duly succumbed to Iolo's lure in the course of his book.[14]

The most sustained early critique of Iolo's triadic and bardo-druidic material during the 1830s came from Algernon Herbert. A Fellow of Merton College, Oxford, and a well-regarded antiquary, Herbert published *Britannia after the Romans; Being an attempt to Illustrate the Religious and Political Revolutions of that Province in the Fifth and Succeeding Centuries* in 1836, and *An Essay on the Neodruidic Heresy in Britannia* in 1838.[15] Whereas the former severely censured

---

[11] Anon., 'A Sketch of the History of the Britons continued', *Cambrian Register*, III (1819), 9.
[12] John Jones, *The History of Wales, Descriptive of the Government, Wars, Manners, Laws, Druids, Bards, Pedigrees, and Language of the Ancient Britons and Modern Welsh* (London, 1824), p. vii.
[13] Ibid., p. 190.
[14] Isaac, *Siluriana: or Contributions towards the History of Gwent and Glamorgan*, p. 2. See also Chapter 4 above.
[15] Algernon Herbert, *Britannia after the Romans; Being an Attempt to Illustrate the Religious and Political Revolutions of that Province in the Fifth and Succeeding Centuries* (London, 1836); idem, *An Essay on the Neodruidic Heresy in Britannia. Part the First* (London, 1838).

William Owen Pughe's lexicographical work, the latter was written because the 'crudest speculations of Celtic antiquities' had found their way 'into more than one of those amiable and useful little volumes, that are composed for the improvement of children'.[16] Herbert denounced the Moelmutian triads as the 'pretend laws of Pseudo-Dyvnwal (the forgery of a fiction)', an obvious fake 'palmed upon the moderns for the same book which Gildas translated'. He was convinced that the whole system was 'a modern Welsh device'.[17] Well versed in the classics, he sought to disprove various facets of Iolo's bardo-druidism, such as the claim that the Druids had believed in metempsychosis and that they had been peacekeepers among the nations.[18] His judgement of the bardic preface to the *Heroic Elegies and other Pieces of Llywarç Hen* was that 'its author either fabricated matter of which the institutional volume does not contain a word ... or else that book is itself a palpable and unskilful fabrication'.[19] Other claims made by Iolo betrayed 'the inadequacy of his researches and, at the same time, the nullity of the uninterrupted Bardic tradition which he imagined that he in conjunction with Mr Evan of Aberdar had received from the ages of antiquity'.[20] His final appraisal reiterated Edward Davies's remarks that the 'doctrines of equality and of the community of property' inherent in 'this spurious bardism' betrayed its recent origins during the years of the French Revolution.[21]

Herbert's criticism was taken more seriously than Davies's remarks, and must have informed the judgement of some Welsh historians, even though his volumes were not easily available. When Jane Williams (Ysgafell) asked Thomas Price (Carnhuanawc) for advice on the matter of druidism, the latter recommended both volumes and offered to forward them to her (Document 13).[22] Like some of her colleagues, notably William Owen Pughe's son Aneurin Owen and Carnhuanawc himself, she found herself torn between her attraction to the Ioloic material and doubts about its veracity. Owen accepted Ioloic material for his publications, but in a letter to Taliesin Williams (Taliesin ab Iolo) concerning the pedigrees of the saints, he confessed to having misgivings over the authenticity of some passages which, 'for the credit of our annals', he wanted to clarify.[23] Both Carnhuanawc and Owen expressed their suspicions over the authenticity of Iolo's version of the 'Chronicle of the Princes' ('Brut y Tywysogyon') which, masquerading as the 'Chronicle of Aberpergwm' ('Brut Aberpergwm'), had been printed in the third volume of *The Myvyrian*

---

[16] Ibid., p. i.
[17] Ibid., pp. 7, 35.
[18] Ibid., pp. 19–20, 66–70.
[19] Ibid., p. 52.
[20] Ibid., p. 20.
[21] Ibid., pp. 51–2.
[22] For an account of Jane Williams and her acquaintance with Carnhuanawc, see Maxwell Fraser, 'Jane Williams ((Ysgafell) 1806–1885)', *Brycheiniog*, VII (1961), 95–114.
[23] NLW 21274E, Letter no. 397, Aneurin Owen to Taliesin Williams, 29 November 1829.

*Archaiology of Wales*, but Carnhuanawc still quoted widely from it in his history of Wales.[24] As late as the 1870s Thomas Nicholas, whose *History and Antiquity of Glamorganshire and its Families* repeatedly noted how Iolo's counterfeit material jarred with the genuine sources, acknowledged that 'as to the position of Iolo Morganwg generally, we can say in passing that a critic of philological and historical competency to deal with it has yet to appear'.[25] Most of the antiquaries and scholars who were active in the first half of the nineteenth century did not possess either the educational background or the knowledge of Welsh history and literature which might have enabled them to embark on a thorough reappraisal of his work. Like 'Meirionwyson', they found the triads a disorderly mixture of fact and fable which needed to be treated with considerable care until such time someone came forward to 'list them according to the time of their composition, and to date them as closely as possible; and to draw clear history from the uncertainty of the fictional stories' ('a'u rhesu yn ol amser eu hysgrifeniad, a'u dyddio mor agos ag y gellir; a thynu hanes eglur allan o ansicrwydd y chwedlau ffugiol').[26]

The first scholar to address this thorny problem was Thomas Stephens, a book-loving chemist from Merthyr who served as secretary of the town library for twenty-five years. He not only shared Iolo's Unitarianism but also attended the same chapel as his son Taliesin.[27] From 1836, when Thomas Stephens first arrived in Merthyr as a chemist's apprentice, until his untimely death in 1875, he conducted a sustained scholarly assault on those, including Iolo, who had romanticized and embellished the history of Wales by forging material. His Unitarian background, which secured for him a good classical education at the boarding school of the Unitarian John Davies at Neath, also compelled him to follow the path of reason and to seek the truth.[28] His education and voracious reading enabled him to examine Iolo's counterfeit material more closely than any of his contemporaries and to reappraise its scholarly value.[29] Stephens contributed winning entries to eisteddfodau from 1840 onwards, but acquired national fame at the Abergavenny eisteddfod of 1848, at which he won the prize for the best essay on the 'Literature of Wales during the twelfth and succeeding centuries'. His volume *Literature of the Kymry* (1849) was based on this essay. It was the only piece of work to appear in his lifetime and it made

---

[24] Thomas Stephens, 'The Book of Aberpergwm', *Arch. Camb.*, 3rd series, IV, no. 13 (1858), 79–80.

[25] Thomas Nicholas, *The History and Antiquity of Glamorganshire and its Families* (London, 1874), p. 25. See ibid., p. 32, for an example of his acute powers of observation.

[26] Meirionwyson, 'Haniad y Cymry', *Seren Gomer*, XXXI, no. 399 (1848), 369.

[27] Margaret S. Taylor, 'Thomas Stephens of Merthyr (1821–1875)', *Merthyr Historian*, II (1978), 137–8. Joseph Edwards, a keen follower of Iolo's ideas, created the sculptures of both Thomas Stephens and Taliesin ab Iolo.

[28] Morgan D. Jones, 'Thomas Stephens o Ferthyr Tudful', *Barddas*, no. 163 (1990), 20; Taylor, 'Thomas Stephens of Merthyr (1821–1875)', 135–6.

[29] Thomas Stephens, 'Studies in British Biography: No. I. Dyvnwal Moelmud', *Cambrian Journal*, I (1854), 160–72.

him a figure of seminal importance in Europe. It was translated into German in 1864 and a second edition followed in 1876.[30] As we have seen, his harsh treatment at the Llangollen eisteddfod of 1858 had caused a national outcry and made him a legendary figure, even though the publication of the volume based on his rejected essay, *Madoc: An Essay on the Discovery of America by Madoc ap Owen Gwynedd in the Twelfth Century*, was delayed until 1893.[31] Stephens's importance as a harbinger of change, however, was based on the success of his 'History of Trial by Jury' which had been submitted to the Abergavenny eisteddfod in 1853. His researches for this treatise had persuaded him to subject the early sources of British legal history to critical scrutiny on Rankean lines, and to call for the application of those principles to the writing of Welsh history:

> One of the necessities of our time, one of the imperative duties of Cambrian writers, is to institute a rigid examination of the sources of our national history, and to submit our records to the test of an honest and searching, yet kindly criticism. Until this be done, it will be vain to look for any history of Wales worthy of lasting approbation.[32]

Stephens contributed hundreds of pages of scholarly and polemical articles, notes and letters to *Seren Gomer*, *Yr Ymofynydd*, the *Cambrian Journal*, *Y Brython*, *Archaeologia Cambrensis*, *Y Traethodydd*, *Y Beirniad* and the *Cambrian*. Although he tailored his prose to suit each individual publication, he did not compromise his scholarly standards. His research focused almost entirely on Iolo's prose works: the Moelmutian triads, whose authenticity he disproved in a series of articles in the *Cambrian Journal* in 1855;[33] the 'Chronicle of Aberpergwm', which he subjected to a thorough textual analysis in 1858;[34] the Glamorgan tradition of bardism, which he so bitterly excoriated in *Seren Gomer* in 1855–6 that it invoked the wrath of Myfyr Morganwg in *Yr Ymofynydd*;[35] the 'Triads of the Isle of Britain', whose third series he censured in *Y Beirniad* in 1863–4;[36] and *Coelbren y Beirdd*, which he traced back to the sixteenth century in a

---

[30] Albert Schulz (San Marte) (ed.), *Geschichte der wälschen Literatur vom XII. bis zum XIV. Jahrhundert: Gekrönte Preisschrift von Thomas Stephens aus dem Englischen übersetzt und durch Beigabe altwälscher Dichtungen in deutscher Übersetzung ergänzt* (Halle, 1864).

[31] See Chapter 3 above. Thomas Stephens, *Madoc: An Essay on the Discovery of America by Madoc ap Owen Gwynedd in the Twelfth Century* (London, 1893).

[32] Stephens, 'The Book of Aberpergwm', 77–96.

[33] Thomas Stephens, 'Studies in British Biography: No. I. Dyvnwal Moelmud', 160–72; idem, 'Studies in British Biography. No. II: The Laws of Dyvnwal Moelmud', *Cambrian Journal*, II (1855), 33–59. Owing to the vicious attacks in response to his articles, he published his findings thereafter in the rival publication, *Archaeologia Cambrensis*.

[34] Stephens, 'The Book of Aberpergwm', 77–96.

[35] Thomas Stephens, 'Athrawiaeth y Nod Cyfrin: Llythyr I', *Seren Gomer*, XXXVIII, no. 482 (1855), 501–2; idem, 'Nodiadau ar y Nod Cyfrin a Myfyryddiaeth: Llythyr II', ibid., XXXIX, no. 485 (1856), 52–5; idem, 'Sylwadau ar y Nod Cyfrin a Myfyryddiaeth: Llythyr IV', ibid., no. 487 (1856), 49–52. For Myfyr Morganwg's replies, see Chapter 4.

[36] Thomas Stephens, 'Trioedd Ynys Prydain', *Y Beirniad*, IV, no. 16 (1863), 378–92; idem, 'Trioedd Ynys Prydain', ibid., V, no. 17 (1863), 58–65; idem, 'Trioedd Ynys Prydain', ibid., V, no. 18 (1863), 137–44; idem, 'Trioedd Ynys Prydain', ibid., V, no. 19 (1863), 214–20; idem,

lengthy contribution published in *Archaeologia Cambrensis* (Document 20).[37] In shorter notes and in published eisteddfod adjudications he exposed the myths of the 'Treachery of the Long Knives' ('Brad y Cyllyll Hirion') and of Ysgolan the bookburner, and traced the origin of legendary figures such as Hu Gadarn to French medieval literature.[38] Substantial eisteddfod essays on more general themes, notably 'The Civilizing Condition of the Welsh' ('Sefyllfa Wareiddiol y Cymry'), comprehensively reassessed the early history of Wales.[39]

But even though Stephens believed that 'old Iolo could deceive as well as anyone else' ('medrai yr hen Iolo dwyllo cystal a neb'), he preferred to attribute all forgeries and inventions to an anonymous group of poets from the fourteenth to the sixteenth century in south Wales.[40] To launch a public assault on the mythical Iolo, who, as Stephens acknowledged, had by then become 'half a saint' ('hanner sant'), was unthinkable.[41] It is possible that his sympathy for an early member of his own embattled Unitarian church, a small denomination whose rightful place within the Christian community was contested by other Nonconformists, prompted him to refrain from directly accusing Iolo of forgery.[42] His acerbic writing and sometimes venomous onslaughts on leading figures in the eisteddfod establishment, notably Carnhuanawc, Taliesin ab Iolo and other organizers and adjudicators at the Abergavenny eisteddfodau, had gained him the respect, but not the affection of his contemporaries, and he might have been wary of alienating them entirely.[43] As it was, his animadversions were deplored by champions of 'traditionary evidence' as late as 1885, when James Harris complained that if Stephens had:

> allowed a little of it to grow in his dreary potato plot; had he been a little less vigorous with his hoe, trodden a little more carefully with those awkward hobnailed boots of his between the ridges, we might have had the occasional patches of colour to lighten up the miserable waste he has made of the glorious field of Celtic fancy.[44]

'Trioedd Ynys Prydain', ibid., V, no. 20 (1864), 292–305; idem, 'Trioedd Ynys Prydain', ibid., VI, no. 22 (1864), 126–44; idem, 'Trioedd Ynys Prydain', ibid., VI, no. 24 (1865), 295–308.

[37] Thomas Stephens, 'An Essay on the Bardic Alphabet called "Coelbren y Beirdd"', *Arch. Camb.*, 4th series, III, no. 11 (1872), 181–210.

[38] Thomas Stephens, 'Eisteddfod Iforawl Merthyr, 1855: Y Feirniadaeth', *Seren Gomer*, XXXVIII, no. 482 (1855), 497–500; idem, 'Hu Gadarn: At Olygydd y Brython', *Y Brython*, V, no. 41 (1863), 337–8.

[39] Thomas Stephens, 'Sefyllfa Wareiddiol y Cymry: Y Traethawd Gwobrwyedig yn Eisteddfod Cymrodorion Dirwestol Merthyr Tydfil, Nadolig, 1856', *Y Traethodydd*, XIII (1857), 230–40; idem, 'Sefyllfa Wareiddiol y Cymry II: Y Cyfnod Cristionogol', ibid., 297–323.

[40] Edeyrn Dafod Plwm, 'Coelbren y Beirdd: At Olygydd y Brython', *Y Brython*, III, no. 18 (1860), 138; Thomas Stephens, 'Nodiadau ar y Nod Cyfrin a Myfyryddiaeth: Llythyr II', *Seren Gomer*, XXXIX, no. 485 (1856), 52–5.

[41] Morris-Jones, 'Rhagymadrodd' in *IMChY*, p. xi. See also Chapter 2 above.

[42] See Chapter 5.

[43] See, for instance, *Cambrian*, 5 November 1842; ibid., 12 November 1842, and esp. ibid., 28 January 1843, as well as Taliesin ab Iolo's reply in ibid., 4 February 1843. I owe these references to Gethin Hywel Rhys.

[44] James Harris, 'The Massacre of the Welsh Bards: An Examination of a Passage in Stephens' *Literature of the Kymry*', *Red Dragon*, VII (1885), 537.

However, a year later, Stephens's position as a forerunner of the new movement in Welsh scholarship was gratefully acknowledged by Edward Owen:

> One of the greatest debts which Welsh scholarship owes to the memory of Thomas Stephens, of Merthyr, is due to his steadfast opposition through much evil report to the wild speculations and monstrous assumptions of the Morganwg school, and to his firm purpose of proving all things and holding to those alone which he believed to be true.[45]

Stephens had pioneered a new and different approach to historical research in Wales, but the controversy over what kind of history would best serve the Welsh nation in the modern era had only just begun.

## *A change in paradigm*[46]

It would be foolish to pretend that the Welsh eagerly embraced new scholarly standards during the late Victorian age. Old habits of thought and writing died hard.[47] Amateur antiquaries and patriots remained deeply attached to romance and myth – much of which was inspired by the *Iolo Manuscripts* and *The Myvyrian Archaiology of Wales* – as a basic component of their work because it was reassuring to believe that Wales possessed a history which stretched back to the ancient Christian civilization. They revered patriotic authors like Theophilus Evans, William Owen Pughe and Iolo Morganwg, and deferred to the traditional evidence, folklore and myth contained in their work. For historians like David Lloyd Isaac and Marianne Robertson Spencer, and for antiquaries such as T. C. Evans (Cadrawd), John Rowland (Giraldus) and John Howells, popular tradition 'thundered down the corridors of time' to link a Wales in turmoil and change (nowhere more so than in south Wales) with calmer, less troubled times.[48] But change was under way. Caught in the process of transition were historians such as Charles Wilkins, who refused to believe that the history of Madoc was based on false evidence, even though his own research spoke to the contrary.[49] Yet, when he regretted the death of the historian Jane Williams, it was because he believed that her *History of Wales* was 'the only work of its kind conceived on true historical principles, dealing as it does in a very lucid and clear style with historical facts, the usual "traditions" and hearsay bardic tales, unless verified by competent authorities, finding no place

---

[45] Edward Owen, 'The Story of Prince Madoc's Discovery of America II', ibid., IX (1886), 182.
[46] For a definition of Thomas Kuhn's notion of the paradigm and its application to historiography, see Lambert and Schofield, 'Introduction' in idem (eds.), *Making History*, pp. 2–3.
[47] For an overview of the process of change, see Neil Evans, 'Finding a New Story: The Search for a Usable Past in Wales, 1869–1930', *THSC*, new series, 10 (2004), 144–62.
[48] Charles Wilkins, 'Notable Men of Wales: Richard Mason and the Literature of his Time', *Red Dragon*, III (1883), 291.
[49] Edward Owen, 'The Story of Prince Madoc's Discovery of America III', ibid., IX (1886), 352.

therein'.⁵⁰ Others, notably John Peter (Ioan Pedr), in a valuable essay on Welsh manuscripts, condemned both Welsh schools as the 'credulous tribe' ('y tylwyth hygoelus') and the 'suspicious tribe' ('y tylwyth amheus'). He believed that the only reputable way of conducting modern research was to follow the 'scientific tribe' ('y tylwyth gwyddorol'), which, apart from Edward Lhuyd, had never boasted any representatives in Wales, but which was now being practised to splendid effect in Germany.⁵¹

As increasing numbers of amateurs began to embrace the new paradigm, they were keen to discard what they considered embarrassing baggage in order to gain access to authentic source material which could form the basis of a new national history. During the second half of the nineteenth century, as Neil Evans has pointed out, 'myth was no longer enough. Footnotes and a critical approach to sources were also necessary.'⁵² Establishing the authenticity of sources was superseding the importance of maintaining a patriotic stance.⁵³ From the 1860s onwards contributors to periodicals like *Yr Athraw* and *Y Traethodydd* began to doubt whether 'fake-historical' bardism 'possessed sufficient foundations to counterbalance the evidence of the main authors' ('yn meddu ar seiliau digonol i wrthbwyso tystiolaethau y prif awduron').⁵⁴ Thomas Stephens's work ensured that the value of the triads as a basis of scholarly investigation was increasingly questioned, even though their importance from a patriotic point of view continued to be recognized.⁵⁵ Iolo's claim that the early British church was 'strongly tinctured with Druidism' was deemed to be 'too gross and manifest a fable to obtain any credence'. It filled the 'modern antiquary with alarm' and provoked 'an uneasy smile of contempt'.⁵⁶ The wider availability and study of manuscripts made researchers aware that the 'shadows of Iolo' ('cysgodion Iolo') lay over many of them, and even led to doubts regarding the authenticity of *The Myvyrian Archaiology of Wales*, a work which had been unassailable for the best part of a century.⁵⁷ The highly revered collection of Iolo's writings was now mocked as 'that remarkable collection of fact

---

⁵⁰ Charles Wilkins, 'Literary and Arts Notes', ibid., VII (1885), 460–1.
⁵¹ John Peter (Ioan Pedr), 'Yr Hen Lawysgrifau', *Y Beirniad*, X, no. 40 (1869), 367–8.
⁵² Evans, 'Finding a New Story: The Search for a Usable Past in Wales, 1869–1930', 145.
⁵³ William Roberts (Nefydd), 'Crefydd yr Oesoedd Tywyll; neu Henafiaethau Cenedl y Cymry', *Seren Gomer*, XXXV, no. 447 (1852), 559.
⁵⁴ William Thomas (Gwilym Marles), 'Gogoniant Hynafol y Cymry [Adolygiad]', *Yr Athraw*, I, no. 11 (1866), 257; Griffith Edwards, 'Derwyddiaeth', *Y Traethodydd*, XVI (1860), 429.
⁵⁵ John Lloyd Jones, 'Cenedlyddiaeth y Cymry', *Y Beirniad*, II, no. 6 (1860), 113; Hugh Hughes (Huw Tegai), 'Dylanwad Eisteddfodau Cymru ar ei Llenyddiaeth', ibid., II, no. 7 (1861), 247–8.
⁵⁶ E. J. Newell, 'Celtic Saints and Celtic Symbols: V. The Struggle with Paganism' in Brierley (ed.), *Cymru Fu*, I, pp. 381–2.
⁵⁷ O. Gaianydd Williams, 'Yr Ysgrif-lyfrau a Ysgrifenwyd ac a Gasglwyd gan y Morisiaid III', *Y Traethodydd*, LXIII (1908), 7–25, esp. 24; idem, 'Yr Ysgrif-lyfrau a Ysgrifenwyd ac a Gasglwyd gan y Morisiaid IV', ibid., LXIII (1908), 96–105; E. Vincent Evans, 'Isaac Foulkes (Llyfrbryf)', *Y Geninen*, XXIII, no. 1 (1905), 33.

and fiction anomalously called the *Iolo Manuscripts*.[58] Even some of Iolo's champions expressed doubts over the authenticity of some of the stages of the romantic life of Dafydd ap Gwilym. Daniel Silvan Evans wondered whether Dafydd's biography had been designed 'by the men of Glamorgan, with the aim of making him one of their compatriots' ('gan wyr Morganwg, gyda'r amcan o'i wneuthur ef yn un o'u cydwladwyr hwynt'). If it was a work of fiction, he concluded presciently, it was indeed 'an ingenious work' ('yn waith athrylith').[59]

The stage was thus set for Edward Owen, a civil servant who spent sixty years of his leisure time researching in the British Museum and who published the fruits of his labours in the *Catalogue of the MSS Relating to Wales in the British Museum* (1900–22).[60] In 1908 he was appointed the first secretary of the Royal Commission for Ancient and Historical Monuments of Wales, and became editor of its publications. As early as 1886 he had written a series of articles which not only reiterated Thomas Stephens's views about the myth of the settlement of America by Prince Madoc but also contextualized the evolution of the story and pointed the finger at Iolo Morganwg (Document 21):

> As Geoffrey had been able by the fascinating form of his legends to lay the clearest intellects of the Middle Ages under his spell, so was Iolo Morganwg through the sheer force of his individuality able to impose his views upon men of much greater learning than himself. Endowed with indefatigable energy, burning with a patriotism that was ever at the white heat of enthusiasm, and possessed with the idea that whatever redounded to the glory of Cambria must be accepted and supported with implicit faith and unswerving devotion, no wonder he exercised such power over his contemporaries as to warp their judgments and take captive their common sense.[61]

The time was therefore ripe for the first Welsh academics to take up the case against Iolo Morganwg. The change in paradigm which had already affected the views of sceptical amateurs was hastened by the professionalization of Welsh scholarship. Government support began to facilitate the rediscovery and publication of widely dispersed manuscripts and enable the first salaried scholars in Wales to develop rigorous methods of appraising such material. The first two generations of professional Welsh scholars, notably Sir John Rhŷs, Dr John Gwenogvryn Evans, Sir John Morris-Jones, Sir Ifor Williams and Professor Griffith John Williams, provided a comprehensive critique of Iolo's material to which amateur scholars could not aspire. Thanks to Thomas Stephens's pioneering efforts, they first turned their attention to Iolo's texts on bardo-druidism and the Chair of Glamorgan, his triads, and the Gorsedd of the Bards of the Isle of Britain.

---

[58] Elphin, 'Welsh Legend', *Arch. Camb.*, 4th series, III, no. 12 (1872), 359.
[59] Edward Foulkes, 'Dafydd ab Gwilym', *Y Geninen*, XIV (Gwyl Dewi, 1896), 12–13.
[60] Edward Owen, *Catalogue of the MSS. Relating to Wales in the British Museum* (2 vols., 4 pts., London, 1900–22).
[61] Idem, 'The Story of Prince Madoc's Discovery of America II', 181–2.

Iolo's most mordant critic was Sir John Morris-Jones. He had had the good fortune to receive an excellent classical education at the famous Friars Grammar School at Bangor, at Christ College, Brecon, and at Jesus College, Oxford.[62] Apart from his epoch-making scholarly work on philology, his most public contribution to the Iolo controversy was a series of five iconoclastic articles in *Cymru*, in which he dissected the Gorsedd with a scientific precision heavily laced with patriotic and personal indignation.[63] Morris-Jones showed his disdain for the Welsh bards of his day, warning them that he refused to heed the empty claims made about the Gorsedd because of 'the fraud and the deceit upon which its claims are based' ('y ffug a'r twyll y seilir ei honiadau arnynt').[64] He demonstrated how previous generations had suppressed the modest research which had come close to discovering the provenance of the Gorsedd. Quoting from personal correspondence with authors like Charles Ashton, who had been so ashamed of the eisteddfod essay he had written on the subject in 1888 that he now wished it had never been written and published he called his opponents' work 'uncritical rot and dross' ('truth ac ansothach anfeirniadol').[65] Morris-Jones's articles were based on two simple fact-based observations: that every manuscript which mentioned the Gorsedd had been written in Glamorgan after the middle of the sixteenth century, and that none of the many Welsh manuscripts, which had by then been transcribed and partially published by the Oxford-trained and government-appointed palaeographer J. Gwenogvryn Evans, made any reference to the institution.[66] He argued that the institution had been devised by 'some three or four of the bards of Glamorgan' ('rhyw dri neu bedwar o feirdd o Forgannwg') in the fifteenth century and had ultimately been passed down to Iolo Morganwg.[67] The final essay in the series charted the rise of the institution from 1451 until the 1830s and detailed the way in which it had been attached to the genuine eisteddfod by Iolo and his legatees. It culminated in an exhortation to bring to an end this 'foolish play' ('chware ffôl'), and to abandon the institution of the Gorsedd because it was 'futile and its degrees worthless' ('ddifudd a'i graddau'n ddiwerth') (Document 22).[68]

Although Morris-Jones's devastating critique reiterated the claims of Thomas Stephens, no one before his day had condemned the Gorsedd in such an outspoken manner and no one had advocated the demise of this colourful

---

[62] For a short biography of John Morris-Jones, see Allan James, *John Morris-Jones* (Cardiff, 1987).
[63] For an annotated bibliography of John Morris-Jones's work, see Huw Walters, *John Morris-Jones 1864–1929: Llyfryddiaeth Anodiadol* (Aberystwyth, 1986).
[64] John Morris Jones, 'Gorsedd Beirdd Ynys Prydain', *Cymru*, X, no. 54 (1896), 21.
[65] Ibid., 23.
[66] Ibid.
[67] John Morris Jones, 'Gorsedd Beirdd Ynys Prydain II', *Cymru*, X, no. 55 (1896), 134–6; idem, 'Gorsedd Beirdd Ynys Prydain III', ibid., X, no. 56 (1896), 153–61; idem, 'Gorsedd Beirdd Ynys Prydain IV', ibid., X, no. 57 (1896), 197.
[68] Idem, 'Gorsedd Beirdd Ynys Prydain VI', ibid., X, no. 59 (1896), 298–9.

and much-loved institution. Morris-Jones's words struck the nation 'like a bolt from the blue, and spread dismay among a believing people' who did not welcome the 'uprooting of early beliefs'.[69] It provoked Morien to publish an immediate rejoinder in which he once more associated the writings of Iolo and Edward 'Celtic' Davies with Hinduism, Buddhism and other religious creeds.[70] But Morris-Jones's criticism reached a wider circle than Iolo's faithful legatees because it challenged the status of the poet in Welsh society. T. Gwynn Jones noted the commotion which the presence of Morris-Jones caused when he appeared at the National Eisteddfod of Llandudno in 1896, a month after the last instalment in his series had been published. Leading the now splendidly garbed druidic procession, Archdruid Hwfa Môn 'gesticulated in John Morris-Jones's direction and mumbled in a somewhat agitated fashion. Having been restrained by one of his fellow-bards the archdruid finally led the procession on its way'.[71] The archdruid's tetchy reaction provided a very public expression of the tide of disapproval which had swept over Wales. English-language summaries of Morris-Jones's articles, published in Owen M. Edwards's *Wales* and in the *Western Mail*, 'caused much searching of hearts' in the country, but also widespread anger.[72] Morris-Jones might have been considered the principal academic cock o' the walk in the ivory towers of Bangor, but the Gorsedd was an illustrious event with a strong 'flavour of antiquity' about it.[73] Satirists seized the opportunity to depict him as a patriotic blood-red dragon ('Uthr Ben Dragon') from 'the Druids' Island' ('Ynys y Derwyddon') who had rampaged through Wales, massacring bards and fraudsters (Document 23).[74] Once the tumult had subsided, wiser counsel prevailed. Since the Gorsedd had become an expression of the 'Republic of Letters' in Wales, it was judged better to improve rather than abolish it. Owen M. Edwards used his position as editor of *Wales* to confirm the cardinal importance of the institution to the sociocultural life of modern Wales:

> Professor Jones will probably succeed in proving that nothing connected with the Gorsedd can be traced back to a date earlier than Tudor times. It is to be hoped that, henceforth, the ignorant generalising concerning hoary antiquity and impossible druids will cease. The Gorsedd, divested of the humbug which is too often associated with it, might serve a good purpose. It might be used to show to the thousands

---

[69] [Gwenogvryn], 'Jottings: Professor John Morris Jones, M.A. (Not related within the ninth degree) by John Jones-Jones, Esq., J.P., of Jones Hall', *Wales*, III, no. 27 (1896), 322.

[70] The series written by John Morris Jones ran from *Cymru*, X, no. 54 (1896) to ibid., no. 59 (1896). Morien's replies appeared from ibid., X, no. 59 (1896) to ibid., XI, no. 64 (1896). The fact that the editor gave both sides the opportunity to defend their respective positions indicates the strength of the old school.

[71] James, *John Morris-Jones*, p. 21.

[72] Editor, 'Queries and Replies', *Wales*, III, no. 22 (1896), 93.

[73] H. Elvet Lewis, 'The Development of the Eisteddfod and its Influences upon the Future of Welsh Literature: Postscript', *Young Wales*, II, no. 14 (1896), 29.

[74] Elphin, 'Enwogion Cymru V: Y Gwladgarwyr', *Y Geninen*, XIV, no. 2 (1896), 119–20.

that frequent the Eisteddfod how Literature and Music and Art are honoured in our Republic of Letters in an Eisteddfod that is the creation of a literary peasantry.[75]

But John Morris-Jones refused to capitulate. By 1911 he had not only come closer to exposing the Gorsedd fraud but had also founded a journal which provided his new school of scholarship with a valuable platform. The first issue of the aptly named *Y Beirniad* (The Critic) opened with a reassessment of his work on the Gorsedd in which he had the satisfaction of claiming that it had been invented either by Iolo Morganwg himself or by one of his mentors.[76] The identity of the perpetrator, he admitted, could not be ascertained 'without searching the original writings' ('chwilio'r ysgrifau gwreiddiol'), which were still kept at Llanover.[77] He sternly repeated his warning that unless the Gorsedd rejected the fabrications on which it had been built, no well-educated Welshman 'with respect for his country and respect for himself' ('sy'n parchu ei wlad ac yn ei barchu ei hun') would attend it.[78] By this stage, of course, Morris-Jones was an eisteddfod adjudicator of long standing, a man who loved the limelight and who had cooperated with the Gorsedd on several occasions. To Iolo's admirers, therefore, his exhortation smacked of hypocrisy. T. Marchant Williams denounced him as the 'greatest charlatan of all', and condemned the 'breath-taking fury' and 'cheap scorn' with which he had libelled those who had made the National Eisteddfod of Wales a colourful and well-attended pageant.[79] He derided Morris-Jones's second onslaught as

> nothing but academic conceit. The Professor seeks to discredit the officials of the Gorsedd by saddling them with pretensions which they never so much as entertained. The gravamen of his charge against Clwydfardd and Hwfa Môn and their contemporaries is that they believed all this nonsense and knew no better; against Dyfed and his colleagues that they pretended to believe it although the 'Athro' has proved to be an imposture. The former were fools, the latter are cheats and rascals. He has not produced a particle of evidence in support of his sweeping charge. He is accuser, judge, and jury all in one and dispenses with such trifles as proofs, taking for his model the methods of the Spanish Inquisition. Why should the Gorsedd be held responsible for the harebrained theories and rhapsodies of the author of *Mona Antiqua*? He was not an Eisteddfodwr. The Gorsedd of our day is an eminently prac-

---

[75] O. M. Edwards, 'Editor's Notes', *Wales*, III, no. 25 (1896), 235. See also Charles Ashton, 'Gorsedd Beirdd Ynys Brydain' in Evans (ed.), *Eisteddfod Genedlaethol y Cymry: Cofnodion a Chyfansoddiadau Buddugol Gwrecsam*, pp. 138–40; Watcyn Wyn, 'Y Genedl a'r Eisteddfod, Yr Eisteddfod a'r Gadair, Y Gadair a'r Bardd', *Y Geninen*, X, no. 4 (1892), 186–90; Ben Davies, 'Yr Orsedd a'r Eisteddfod', ibid., XVI, no. 4 (1898), 267–8; Cynfaen, 'Gweriniaeth yr Eisteddfod', ibid., II, no. 1 (1884), 38–9.

[76] John Morris Jones, 'Derwyddiaeth Gorsedd y Beirdd', *Y Beirniad*, I, no. 1 (1911), 66–71. The journal survived until 1920, when it fittingly ended with an article by G. J. Williams in which he exposed Rhys Goch ap Rhicert as a figment of Iolo's imagination.

[77] Ibid., 71.

[78] Ibid.

[79] T. Marchant Williams, 'The Conspiracy against the Gorsedd', *The Nationalist*, IV, no. 36 (1911), 34, 36–7.

tical institution, and its claims to our respect are based on its solid service to popular culture ... No pedantry or sophistry will blind us as to the frantic ambition of the academical gang to capture this unique national institution. They would like to walk into the labours of the men whom they bespatter with their venom. They see a grand instrument of culture in the hands of simple bards without University degrees and would wrestle it from them by sheer impudence and violence ... But he may rest assured that not all the invective, nor all the misrepresentations or machinations of the 'New School', will ever alienate the affections of the Welsh people from the Gorsedd.[80]

For the 'simple, plebeian Welshman' ('Cymro syml, gwerinol'), the provenance of the National Eisteddfod and the Gorsedd had long ceased to matter. Its future role and well-being were much more important.[81]

In scholarly circles, however, more critical judgements of Iolo's legacy were winning ground. In 1911 J. Glyn Davies, a colleague of the internationally renowned Celtic scholar Kuno Meyer at the University of Liverpool, excluded from his *Welsh Metrics* all poems published in the 'Addendum' to *Barddoniaeth Dafydd ab Gwilym* in 1789, and called three of them 'palpable forgeries'.[82] Shortly afterwards, John Morris-Jones's student Ifor Williams began to prepare the first authoritative edition of medieval Welsh poetry – *Cywyddau Dafydd ap Gwilym a'i Gyfoeswyr*. Unlike the amateurs of the nineteenth century, Williams was assisted by six undergraduates, as well as by colleagues from London and Dublin, who transcribed and compared different versions of the poems.[83] His preface set out the stringent lines along which all research would proceed in future years. The team collected every available manuscript copy of a poem, compared each version, and chose the best reading for publication. Material discovered in recent copies was either excluded or at least marked as dubious.[84] Williams rejected the biographical sketches of Dafydd which had become part of the 'nation's creed' ('credo'r genedl') because their detail and inconsistencies betrayed them as recent romances.[85] In a separate section on the authenticity of the poems ('dilysrwydd y cywyddau') he revealed that, among the fifteen poems in the 'Addendum', there were twelve 'of which no one knew until Iolo Morganwg!' ('na wyddai neb am danynt hyd Iolo Morganwg!'), a fact which deepened his suspicions and prompted him to wonder 'whether the man from Glamorgan was either credulous or malevolent' ('prun ai ehud ynteu dichellddrwg oedd y gŵr o Forgannwg').[86]

---

[80] Ibid., 35–7.
[81] Evan Price, 'Rhai o Hen Eisteddfodau'r Fenni', *Y Geninen*, XXXI, no. 2 (1913), 85–8; T. Marchant Williams, 'The Conspiracy against the Gorsedd', 34.
[82] J. Glyn Davies, *Welsh Metrics* (Cardiff, 1911), p. 7.
[83] Ifor Williams a Thomas Roberts, *Cywyddau Dafydd ap Gwilym a'i Gyfoeswyr wedi eu Golygu o'r Llawysgrifau gyda Rhagymadrodd, Nodiadau a Geirfa* (Bangor, 1914), p. v.
[84] Ibid., p. 4.
[85] Ibid., pp. xi–xiii.
[86] Ibid., pp. lxxxiii–lxxxiv.

It was at this stage that Griffith John Williams, a young Cardiganshire-born postgraduate research student began a study which would transform the scholarly and public image of Iolo Morganwg. By 1916 the Llanover collection had reached the National Library of Wales and he immediately began to peruse its contents for his researches into the literary tradition of Glamorgan. He found himself, in the words of John Morris-Jones, 'as if in the workshop of a minter of counterfeit money, where one could see his moulds and the tools of his craft, with examples of his experiments and his improvements on various of his products' ('megis yng ngweithdy bathwr arian drwg, lle gellid gweld ei foldiau ac offerynnau ei grefft, ynghydag esiamplau o'i arbrofion a'i wellianau mewn amryw o'i gynhyrchion').[87] He soon discovered the unpublished nature and love poems which the young Iolo had composed under the bardic name 'Iorwerth Gwilym'. These had not been published by Iolo himself, nor had they been of much interest to his legatees following his death. Although they had been forgotten, in Williams's view they far surpassed the mechanical compositions of many of Iolo's contemporaries.[88] More importantly, a comparison of their characteristics with the many other drafts of poems in Iolo's papers provided the 'key to explaining the secret' ('allwedd i esbonio'r dirgelwch') of the 'Addendum':[89]

> Y mae'r ffeithiau uchod – y cyfnewid a fu ar y cywyddau, y llinellau a dynnwyd trwyddynt, y cwpledi a wasgwyd i mewn rhwng llinellau, y dernynnach anorffen a geir yma a thraw ar hyd y llawysgrifau – yn arwain yn naturiol at yr unig esboniad y medrwn ei roddi arnynt, sef mai Iolo Morganwg ei hun a gyfansoddodd y cywyddau, ac a'u priodolodd, wedi hynny, i Ddafydd ap Gwilym.[90]

> (The above facts – the changes made in the *cywyddau*, the lines which were drawn through them, the couplets which were squeezed in between lines, the unfinished scraps which are found here and there throughout the manuscripts – lead naturally to the only explanation we can offer, namely that it was Iolo Morganwg himself who composed the *cywyddau*, and who attributed them, afterwards, to Dafydd ap Gwilym.)

Standing on the shoulders of his professional predecessors, conscious of the privilege of having unlimited access to the Iolo papers at the National Library of Wales and, most importantly, willing to subject an iconic figure to rigorous critical scrutiny, Williams proved that Iolo himself had written twelve of the poems of the 'Addendum' to *Barddoniaeth Dafydd ab Gwilym* and had substantially altered the others; that Rhys Goch ap Rhicert, to whom twenty poems were attributed, was a piece of fiction (Document 24); and that Iolo had invented the Gorsedd of the Bards of the Isle of Britain.[91] What began as a

---

[87] Morris-Jones, 'Rhagymadrodd' in *IMChY*, p. xiv.
[88] See Chapter 4.
[89] Griffith J. Williams, 'Cywyddau Cynnar Iolo Morganwg', *Y Beirniad*, VIII, no. 2 (1919), 75–91.
[90] Idem, 'Cywyddau'r Ychwanegiad at Waith Dafydd ap Gwilym', ibid., VIII, no. 3 (1919), 162.
[91] Idem, 'Rhys Goch ap Rhiccert', ibid., VIII, no. 4 (1920), 211–60; *IMChY*, passim; *TLIM*, passim.

# MODERN BARDS ON IOLO.

## DENOUNCED AS MAN AND WRITER.

## LOVE OF GLAMORGAN

## "HATRED & JEALOUSY OF NORTH WALES."

"Iolo Morganwg a Chywyddau'r Ychwanegiad," gan G. J. Williams, M.A. Gyda rhagymadrodd gan Syr John Morris-Jones, M.A., LL.D., D.Litt. Cyhoeddedig gan Gymdeithas yr Eisteddfod Genedlaethol, 64, Chancery-lane, London. Pp. xviii., 271.

### FIRST NOTICE.

Following close upon the celebration of the centenary of Iolo Morganwg's death, the appearance of this new volume, characterised as it is by relentlessness of scholarship, is of unusual significance.

Sir J. Morris-Jones.

The author, Mr. G. J. Williams, who is now a lecturer in Welsh at the University College, Cardiff, won in 1921 a prize of £40 at the National Eisteddfod for a thesis on the relation between Iolo Morganwg and the poems (known as "Cywyddau'r Ychwanegiad") attributed to Dafydd ap Gwilym. He was also awarded the M.A. degree of the University of Wales for a similar thesis. It is an enlargement and amplification of those theses that we have now before us. It is a formidable volume, distinguished by its thoroughness, its meticulous care, even over tiny detail.

Fig. 13 *Western Mail*, 11 January 1927. G. J. Williams's pioneering study, *Iolo Morganwg a Chywyddau'r Ychwanegiad* (1926), was published during the centenary of Iolo's death.

prize-winning eisteddfod essay turned out to be a lifetime's work. The masterful volume *Iolo Morganwg a Chywyddau'r Ychwanegiad* (1926) provided detailed proof of Iolo's poetic forgeries.[92] Published, ironically, in the year of the centenary of Iolo's death, it was prefaced by the intemperate words of the scourge of Iolo, Sir John Morris-Jones:

> Fe ddyfeisiodd bob math ar chwedlau di-sail am hanes Cymru o'r oesoedd cyn-Crist hyd ei oes ei hun; fe sgrifennodd gyfresi o drioedd ffug-hynafol a lluosogrwydd o ffug-gofnodion o bob math am fucheddau saint, a beirdd, ac eisteddfodau, a phob cyfryw beth; ac fe gopïodd rannau helaeth o'r hen lenyddiaeth, gan newid a llygru'r cwbl, a gwthio i mewn frawddegau a pharagraffau o'i waith ei hun er mwyn iddynt gyfateb i'w honiadau ef a'u cadarnhau. Yr ydym yn araf yn ymysgwyd o'i faglau; ond wedi cael yn rhydd o un twyll, byddwn yn aml yn ein cael ein hunain yn rhwym mewn un arall. Ac y mae lle i ofni y bydd ein llên a'n hanes am oes neu ddwy eto cyn byddant lân o ôl ei ddwylo halog ef.[93]

> (He devised all kinds of unfounded tales about the history of Wales from the pre-Christian ages to his own age; he wrote a series of pseudo-archaic triads and a multitude of counterfeit notes of all kinds about the lives of saints, and poets, and eisteddfodau, and every such thing; and he copied large parts of the old literature, changing and corrupting all of it, and inserting sentences and paragraphs of his own work in order that they corresponded with his own assertions and confirmed them. Slowly we are shaking off his snares; but having freed ourselves of one fraud, we often find ourselves caught in another one. And there is room to fear that our literature and our history will do so for an age or two again, until they will be cleansed of the stain of his soiled hands.)

## *The critics criticized*

The assault on the theories, methods and sources which were perceived to have outlived their usefulness, and on the writers who had used them, provoked a vigorous response from the last generation of Romantic writers. Seized by a deep sense of anger, they once more rallied to Iolo's defence. Amateur writers and professional scholars who threatened to abolish this school of romance and myth found themselves in the line of fire even up to the centenary of Iolo's death in 1926. They were often perceived as traitors to their country because they sought to rob the nation of its distinctive traditions and dispossess it of one of its iconic figures. The first amateur historians who publicly queried the authenticity of Iolo's material, among them Thomas Nicholas, were accused of un-Welsh behaviour and of being frauds themselves.[94] In contrast, Daniel

---

[92] Griffith J. Williams, *Iolo Morganwg a Chywyddau'r Ychwanegiad* (London, 1926).
[93] Morris-Jones, 'Rhagymadrodd' in *IMChY*, p. xvi.
[94] D. J., 'Queries: The "Books" of Wales', *Bye-Gones*, 6 February 1884, 25.

Silvan Evans, who defended Iolo against English accusations 'that the *Iolo MSS* were in great part the forgeries of the old Glamorganshire bard and antiquary himself', was widely eulogized.[95] Following the publication of Thomas Stephens's articles on Dyfnwal Moelmud in the *Cambrian Journal*, he was publicly vilified.[96] As late as the 1880s champions of the old school still expressed their incredulity that Stephens, 'himself a Welshman', could display such a 'deadly hatred of popular tradition' in his *Literature of the Kymry*.[97] Charles Wilkins, who fondly remembered Ab Ithel, especially the 'fertility of his imagination and the strength of his belief', had misgivings about Stephens's work because it meant that 'some of the most cherished traditions of Wales have been scattered to the winds ... enough to have roused old Iolo from his grave'.[98] Those who doubted the antiquity of creations like *Coelbren y Beirdd*, and who intimated that Iolo had devised the alphabet himself or had been deceived by early-modern forgers, were accused of high treason. Having denied the authenticity of the mystic sign, D. Tudor Evans was called upon to resign his post as secretary of the Cambrian Society.[99] Sir John Rhŷs's volume *Celtic Britain*, the first major work by a Welsh academic to conform to the new professional standards, was attacked by Welsh commentators and reviewers alike. Charles Wilkins warned darkly that

> Iolo and Ab Ithel are long since dead, Myfyr Morganwg is too old to take up the cudgels, but there are younger spirits left upon whom the mantles of the departed worthies have fallen, and against these – we do not mean the mantles – let Professor Rhŷs keep a sharp look-out.[100]

'Brython', who dedicated an extended essay to reviewing the book, considered this a matter of national importance, and Rhŷs's conclusion that the Britons had no letters before the coming of the Romans was judged to be not only erroneous but also highly disloyal:

> After assuring us that no tribe north of the Trinovantes 'had a coinage of their own when Cæsar landed in this country', he adds, 'nor does it appear that any British tribe whatever had then begun *to have its coins lettered*' (*Celtic Britain*, p. 20). These are very important statements; for they evidently imply that our author – our Professor of Celtic in the University of Oxford! – is of opinion that, differently from all surrounding nations, the *Cymry* had no letters before Cæsar's time, after which they adopted the Roman characters. Really, this point, historically and otherwise viewed, is of the greatest national consequence, and therefore requires to be closely investigated, especially as Professor Rhŷs condescends to favour us with no proof of the

---

[95] Charles Wilkins, 'Literary and Art Notes of the Month', *Red Dragon*, V (1884), 282–5.
[96] Golygydd, 'Postscript', *Cambrian Journal*, II (1855), 59.
[97] Harris, 'The Massacre of the Welsh Bards: An Examination of a Passage in Stephens' *Literature of the Kymry*', 537.
[98] Wilkins, 'Notable Men of Wales: Richard Mason and the Literature of his Time', 290–1.
[99] Iorwerth, 'Notes and Queries: Y Nod Cyfrin', *Red Dragon*, VII (1885), 283.
[100] Charles Wilkins, 'Marginal Notes on Library Books', ibid., III (1883), 461.

correctness of his allegation ... He knows, or should know, that, contrary to his aspersions, a certain alphabet, materially differing from that of Rome or Greece, has been exhibited as having been in use by the Cymry from time immemorial; that that profound antiquary 'Iolo Morganwg', in conjunction with Dr Owen Pughe and others of our principal literary men, at the end of the last and the beginning of the present century, exhibited numerous specimens of such an alphabet, so as to cause a warm and prolonged controversy between the literati of Wales; that at the Royal Eisteddfod held in Cardiff Castle in 1838 [sic], a prize was won by Taliesin ab Iolo for a Welsh essay on the given subject of the 'Authenticity and Antiquity' of this alphabet, abounding with irrefragable proofs of its genuineness, which essay was afterwards published, and that at the grand Eisteddfod held at Abergavenny in 1853 a prize was won by 'Ieuan Gryg' of Monmouth, for the best English translation of this essay. These and many other facts the Professor should have been conversant with before he insinuated that we had no letters till the Romans taught us.[101]

Such writers were determined never to allow the ghost of Iolo Morganwg to be exorcised. Even those who agreed that bardo-druidism, and its heroes, triads and bardic script, were unlikely to have been as old as Iolo and his legatees had claimed, clung to the theory that they must have been late medieval forgeries since Iolo was too truthful and honest to have committed fraud.[102] They simply could not bring themselves to concede that 'one of the most honest and conscientious men who ever grasped a writing pen' ('un o'r dynion gonestaf a chydwybodolaf a ymaflodd mewn ysgrif-bin erioed') could have deceived his contemporaries so shamelessly.[103] Credulous he might have been, but the accusation that he was a 'premeditated forger' ('yn dwyllwr bwriadol') was hotly contested.[104] As late as 1911 those whom T. Marchant Williams dubbed 'plodding, piffling pedants' – among them W. J. Gruffydd and Sir John Morris-Jones – were castigated for 'slandering one of the most upright, truthful and honest Welshmen that ever trod the earth'.[105] Even after the appearance of G. J. Williams's first essays in 1919 some writers were convinced that exonerating evidence would shortly appear which would silence Iolo's traducers forever.[106] When this line of defence could no longer be sustained, his actions were excused by reference to his patriotic zeal which, as in the case of Macpherson before and La Villemarqué after him, had led him astray.[107] The condemnation of Iolo Morganwg was seen as emblematic of the contemptuous attitude which Welsh academics showed towards Welsh history, the

---

[101] Brython, 'Readings in Rhys's "Celtic Britain" I', ibid., X (1886), 57; idem, 'Readings in Rhys's "Celtic Britain" IV', ibid., 142–3.
[102] Owen M. Edwards, 'At Ohebwyr', *Cymru*, LVIII, no. 345 (1920), 136.
[103] David Watkin Jones (Dafydd Morganwg), 'Y Beirdd a Chyhoeddi'r Eisteddfod', *Y Geninen*, X, no. 2 (1892), 58
[104] Lewis Davies Jones (Llew Tegid), 'Ein Llenyddiaeth: Taith Frysiog Trwy'r Canrifoedd', ibid., XVI, no. 2 (1898), 86–8.
[105] T. Marchant Williams, 'Our Point of View', *The Nationalist*, IV, no. 36 (1911), 3–4.
[106] W. Rhys Watkin, 'Beirdd Llangyfelach II', *Y Geninen*, XXXVII, no. 2 (1919), 80.
[107] W. Llewelyn Williams, 'Iolo Morganwg', *Welsh Outlook*, VIII, no. 9 (1921), 198

Welsh language and its literature, and the folk traditions of the people of Wales. In an address at the National Eisteddfod of Wales at Caernarfon in 1921, W. Llewelyn Williams urged the new pedants to preserve the identity of the Welsh people:

> Dywedaf yn groew fod Cymru mewn perygl o golli rhai o'i phethau goreu drwy'r ysgolorion newydd. Gogoniant llen Cymru yw mai llen gwerin ydyw. Pobl '*without the pedantry of court and school*' yw ei phrif awduron. Cana'r bardd yn Gymraeg fel gwna'r eos yn y llwyn, am fod ei galon ar dân a Duw wedi rhoddi llais iddo i draethu ei feddwl. Beth os yw ei orgraff yn wallus? Beth os yw ei weithiau yn troseddu yn erbyn gofynion gorfannwl gramadeg? Mae enaid Cymro yn ei gân, ei hysbryd yn ei galon, ei hathrylith a'i hawen ar ei dafod. Dyna wreiddyn y mater; a neges yr Eisteddfod heddyw i'r ysgolorion ddylai fod – 'Na ddiffoddwch yr ysbryd.'[108]

> (I say plainly that Wales is in danger of losing some of its finest things through the new scholars. The splendour of the literature of Wales is that it is a folk literature. Its main authors are people *without the pedantry of court and school*. The Welsh poet sings like the nightingale in the bush because his heart is on fire and God has given him a voice to express his mind. What if his orthography is faulty? What if his works transgress against the over-detailed demands of grammar? The Welshman's soul is in his song, its spirit in his heart, its genius and its muse on his tongue. That is the root of the matter; and the message of the Eisteddfod today to the scholars should be – 'Don't extinguish the spirit.')

The sustained campaign to cleanse the Welsh nation of Iolo Morganwg and his tainted legacy provoked such robust and unexpected reactions that it achieved only partial success. The Gorsedd of the Bards of the Isle of Britain had become an integral part of the National Eisteddfod and was thus able to survive the furious assaults of Sir John Morris-Jones. Its historical authenticity had ceased to take precedence over its contemporary role of uniting a nation divided by geography as well as by religious and political affiliations. Deploring the savage outbursts of pedants, the Welsh *gwerin* rallied in support of one of their most cherished annual events. Professional scholars were more successful in academic circles. Here, Iolo's invented history of Wales and his counterfeit literary material were replaced with scholarly accounts based on the examination and interpretation of authentic sources. Yet, Iolo's creations were more than mere counterfeit sources; they were emblematic of a lost world and therefore so attractive that even some professional scholars regretted their departure. It grieved Griffith John Williams, who devoted his life to exposing Iolo's forgeries but whose admiration for Iolo grew with each passing year, to have to lay to rest in the pedigree books Rhys Goch ap Rhicert 'from where he had

---

[108] 'Anerchiad Llewelyn Williams oddiar y Maen Llog yng Nghaernarfon', *Y Geninen*, XXXIX, no. 4 (1921), 215.

been resurrected by Iolo, over a hundred years ago, to play his role in the literary history of Glamorgan, as Iolo wished that history to be' ('o'r lle y cyfodwyd ef gan Iolo, dros gan mlynedd yn ol, i chware ei ran yn hanes llenyddol Morgannwg fel y mynnai Iolo i'r hanes hwnnw fod').[109] Like many other men and women of his generation, Williams realized that, with the passing of figures like Iolo Morganwg, Rhys Goch ap Rhicert and Dyfnwal Moelmud, Wales's Romantic era, the true age of its *gwerin*, had come to an end. The modern Wales which emerged from the crucible of the First World War had lost its Edwardian optimism and now faced the unimaginable hardships of the inter-war years without recourse to a glorious past.

---

[109] Williams, 'Rhys Goch ap Rhiccert', 226.

# *Documents*

In order to retain the historical character of the documents, editorial changes in orthography and grammar have been kept to a minimum. Some extensive footnotes in the original, which would have been inappropriate in the context of this book, have been deleted.

### *1. Eben Fardd and the 'Vita' of Iolo Morganwg*

*Following the death of Elijah Waring, Iolo's first biographer, in 1857, the poet Ebenezer Thomas (Eben Fardd) eulogized him in a series of* englynion. *In a short introduction he warmly thanked Waring for writing the 'vita' (*buchedd*) of one of the nation's most industrious and patriotic authors, for his success in capturing the main characteristics of his subject and for giving a balanced assessment of him, thereby displaying his own Christian principles of gentleness and fairness. The* englynion *celebrate Waring for reminding the nation of Iolo's achievements, and Iolo himself for glorifying 'old Wales'.*

Eben Vardd, 'Elijah Waring', Y Brython, *III, no. 17 (Mawrth 1860), 102.*

. . . yr wyf finnau, os caniatâ y BRYTHON, am ddefnyddio tudalen o'i eiddo i greirio cofnod byr a serchog am y gŵr da a enwir uchod, sef ysgrifenydd *Buchedd* yr anfarwol IOLO MORGANWG; llyfr, ym mha un y dengys yr awdwr ei fod yn caru ein cenedl ni, ac yn dwyn mawr serch at goffadwriaeth un o'n llenyddion mwyaf llafurus a gwladgarol. Wrth ysgrifenu 'Buchedd IOLO,' amlygodd Mr Waring ei fod yn feddiannol, i fesur helaeth, ar deithi anhebgor Bucheddegwr; yn gynnwysedig mewn craffder yn narluniad cywir y nodweddiad, mewn dangosiad ffyddlawn, rhydd, a diduedd, o reddfau ac arferion ei wrthddrych, mewn barn a chwaeth coethedig yng ngradd ac ansawdd ei adroddion, ac mewn ysbryd tymmerus, boneddigaidd, a Christionogol, wrth ymdrin â pherson a chymmeriad tra anghyffredin, ac anhawdd ei drin yn deg, a'i brisio yn briodol, yn ei goffadwriaeth hanesol yn gystal ag yn ei anianawd a'i reddfau personol . . . Y mae fy rhagymadrodd wedi myned yn rhy hir; yr Englynion canlynol oedd yn fy ngolwg i'w cynnyg i'r BRYTHON, er coffadwriaeth am y teilwng ELIJAH WARING; a dyma nhw, os cânt ymddangos.

        Waring a aeth i orwedd, – fel ereill,
          I falurion llygredd;
        Ni ŵyr boen yn nhir y bedd,
        Gan henaint, nac anhunedd.

Carodd, anwylodd hen Walia, – a'i dysg,
  A'i dawn, tra fu yma;
  Hawddgared oedd, y gŵr da,
  Hyd derfyn pwynt ei yrfa!

Athrylith f' *Ewythr* Iolo – a'i nawdiau,
  A nododd yn gryno;
  Clasurol fu'n clws eirio
  Hanes syn ei einioes o.

Mae 'Bywyd Iolo,' 'm mhob dalen – yn llawn
  O'r llynol nodd trylen;
  Gwiw y mawrhäes Gymru hen,
  Ei dyhewyd a'i hawen.

Ond Waring fwyn, awdurol, – y casglydd;
  Aeth i'r cysgle marwol;
  Collodd Cymru ei gu gol,
  A'i holl nodded llenyddol.

Cymru yn ei *du* sy'n d'od – ar gyfer
  Ei geufedd, aml ddiwrnod;
  Ger ei fedd, hi garai fod,
  Yn serchus, hynaws warchod.

Gorphwysed, huned mewn hedd – oni ddêl
  Ban ddolef tangnefedd,
  A ddwg ar newydd agwedd
  Ei natur yn bur o'r bedd.

## 2. *Iolo Morganwg's Chair*

*This account describes how Thomas Johnes, the celebrated squire of Hafod Uchtryd in Cardiganshire, supposedly commissioned a chair-cum-table for Iolo, whose bouts of respiratory disorders did not permit him to lie down to sleep. Following the fire which destroyed the library at Hafod, this 'relic' (*crair*) was said to have been bought by someone from Pontrhydfendigaid who then sold it to the poet Joseph Jenkins (Amnon II) of Trecefel farm, near Tregaron. On the wall above the chair, the family hung an* englyn *composed by Ioan Mynyw which warned visitors that only accredited bards and certainly no fools should sit on it. The chair, which is shown on page 21, is now part of the collections of the National Library of Wales.*

E. B. Morris, 'Hafod Ychtryd', *Cymru*, XXXII, no. 190 (1907), 273.

... eithr y mae un crair teilwng o sylw ar gael o'r Hafod yng nghadw yn Nhrecefel, Tregaron, sef cadair Iolo Morgannwg. Fel y traethwyd eisioes, treuliasai y bardd, a'r cerddwr mwyaf welodd Cymru, fisoedd lawer yma ar ei grwydriadau ymchwiliadol hyd blasdai ac amgueddfeydd anhysbys y Dywysogaeth. Fel y gwyddis, blinid ef ymron hyd ei oes gan ddiffyg anadl, ac anaml y medrai orffwys mewn gwely … Am y rheswm hwn, mae'n debyg, y gwnaeth y Milwriad Johnes y gadair ddyddorol a rhyfedd hon i Iolo. Nid cadair yn unig ydyw; eithr y mae iddi fwrdd hylaw a chysurus tuag at ysgrifennu, yr hwn a orffwys ar y cefn pan y gwneir yn eisteddle. Pwrcaswyd hi gan ŵr o Bont Rhyd Fendigaid; yntau drachefn a'i gwerthodd i Mr Joseph Jenkins (*Amnon II*), bardd, llenor, a sylwedydd diledryw, a chyda'i weddw a'i ferch yn Nhrecefel y gwelir hi'n awr. Uwchben y gadair, mewn ffram, gwelir a ganlyn yn llawysgrif dlos Ioan Mynyw, –

'Englyn rhybudd i'w osod uwchben Cadair Iolo Morgannwg, yn Nhrecefel, Tref Caron, Ceredigion, –

> Na ro'er ffol yng nghadair Iolo, – enwog,
>     Heb bur anian ynddo;
>     Ond bardd hardd gwedi'i urddo
> A goder idd ei gadair o.'

## 3. Pilgrimages to Flemingston

*The two texts below describe different pilgrimages to Flemingston church, where Iolo was buried. In the first, Tudur Lovell, a member of the Cardiff Cymrodorion Society, notes that it has become a tradition for his society to visit locations connected with the nation's heroes. He then describes a 'pilgrimage' (pererindod) to Iolo's grave, the memorial plaque to Iolo and his son Taliesin in Flemingston church, and some facts connected with Iolo's life. He recounts parts of the speeches delivered by the society's president Sir T. Marchant Williams, and by Evan Owen, David Beynon and J. Austin Jenkins, each of whom focused on Iolo's genius, his importance for the preservation of Welsh historical remains, the deep affection felt for him and his standing as a self-educated man. Lovell was convinced that visits to 'sacred' places of national significance were critically important means of introducing young people to some of the principal figures in the literary history of the nation.*

Tudur Lovell, 'Tro i Wlad Iolo Morgannwg', *Cymru*, XL, no. 236 (1911), 155–6.

Y mae wedi tyfu yn arferiad bellach gan Gymrodorion Caerdydd i dalu ymweliad â mangre gysegredig bedd, neu le genedigol, neu weithiau bob un o'r ddau, rhai o anfarwolion ein gwlad a'n cenedl. Y llynedd ymwelwyd â gwlad Islwyn, yr hwn a adawodd enw a berarogla byth ar ddalenau barddas a llên Cymru. Ar nawn Sadwrn, Gorffennaf 16, y flwyddyn ddiweddaf, aeth nifer liosog o Gymry pybyr ar bererindod at fan fechan bedd un arall o enwogion ein gwlad, gŵr a argraffodd ei enw yn ddwfn iawn ar lech cof a chalon ei genedl.

...Yna cychwynwyd trwy y fro brydferth tua phentref Trefflemyn, yr hwn nad yw ond lle bychan iawn, ac a wneir i fyny o ychydig dai annedd, ffermdy y Spencers, yr eglwys a'r rheithordy. Yma y bu Iolo Morgannwg byw ran helaeth iawn o'i oes, mewn ty nad oes heddyw unrhyw olion o'i weddillion. Mae yr eglwys mewn cadwraeth ragorol, ac yn dyddio tua'r unfed ganrif ar bymtheg. Casglwyd ynghyd gan y rheithor, y Parch. R. Morris, lawer o gofnodion dyddorol, y rhai gedwir ganddo yn ofalus. Cychwyna gyda'r cofnodion cyntaf sydd ar gael yn y flwyddyn 1575, a chynhwysa y cronicl hanesion dyddorol a ddigwyddant yn rhediad yr oesau dilynol gyda'r gofal a'r manylrwydd mwyaf. Yr hyn a dynn sylw yr ymwelydd ar unwaith yw y goflech ar fur mewnol yr eglwys er coffadwriaeth am Iolo, a'i fab Taliesin, yn Gymraeg a Saesneg. Gorffwys gweddillion y bardd a'i fab y tufewn i furiau yr eglwys, yn union islaw y goflech. Ganwyd Iolo yn Pennon, yn ymyl Llancarfan, un o lanerchau enwocaf Bro Morgannwg, ac o fewn ychydig filldiroedd i Drefflemyn; a ffaith hynod yw nad oes yno yr olion lleiaf o'r annedd lle y gwelodd y bardd a'r llenor gyntaf oleu dydd. Felly canfyddir i Iolo dreulio y rhan helaethaf o'i oes faith o fewn cylch cymharol fychan o'r Fro brydferth, a lle y claddwyd ef yn y flwyddyn 1826.

Cafwyd anerchiad rhagorol gan Syr T. Marchant Williams, llywydd Cymdeithas Cymrodorion Caerdydd, yn yr hwn y datganai ei edmygedd dirfawr o gymeriad a llafur ac athrylith Iolo Morgannwg, a'r gwasanaeth gwerthfawr a gyflawnodd dros iaith a llenyddiaeth ei genedl. Gwerthfawrogai ei ymdrechion diflino yn teithio hyd a lled y wlad yn ei ymchwil am hen lawysgrifau Cymreig, a'i fedr dihafal yn nehongliad y cyfryw.

Un o neilldutolion pennaf Iolo oedd y pwys a roddai ar ddefnyddio ei holl amser i'r amcanion uchaf, ac na threuliai hyd yn oed funud byth mewn segurdod.

Pwysleisiai Mr Evan Owen, Y.H., y serch dwfn a ysgogai holl symudiadau bywyd Iolo, nes peri iddo ymgymeryd â phererindodau meithion ar droed er sicrhau y cofnodion amhrisiadwy sydd heddyw ym meddiant y genedl, a'r gwerth a ddylid ei roddi arnynt gennym ni, a chan genedlaethau sydd eto heb eu geni.

Mr David Beynon a sylwai ar bwysigrwydd y dyn hunan wneuthuredig, a'r math arbennig hwnnw o hunan ddiwylliant a arddangosir yn fynych gan gymeriadau o'r nodwedd hwn. Mewn adgof ai yn ol i'r adeg pan oedd yr Ysgolion Nos mewn bri, ac yr adnabu aml i gymeriad cryf a drowyd allan ganddynt o fewn cylch ei adnabyddiaeth ef. Edmygai Iolo fel un o'r cyfryw, ac fel un yn hollol ymwybodol o werth penderfyniad ac ymroddiad i lafur a brofai o fudd anrhaethol i'w wlad a'i genedl.

Pwysai Mr J. Austin Jenkins, B.A., ar y cyferbyniad dirfawr rhwng bywyd a dreulir i ddibenion materol rhagor y bywyd a gyflwynir i'r amcanion uchaf yn feddyliol a moesol. Awgrymai hefyd y fantais amhrisiadwy a ddeilliai i ieuenctid, ac i blant ein hysgolion cyhoeddus, pe deuent ambell dro i lanerchau fel Trefflemyn a mannau ereill lle y gorffwysai rhai o enwogion ein gwlad, lle'r eglurid iddynt hanes ac esiampl y gwroniaid hyn, er symbyliad iddynt hwythau yn eu bywyd personol eu hunain.

Dyma un o amcanion pennaf Cymrodorion Caerdydd yn trefnu ymweliadau achlysurol i'r mannau cysegredig hyn, er trwytho ein pobl ieuainc yn arbennig yn hanes bywyd a llafur gwyr blaenaf a meddyliau cyfoethocaf ein cenedl yn y gorffennol. Hyderwn y rhydd coffhad achlysurol fel hyn o hanes Iolo, yr hwn a ystyriwn yn un o ragorolion pennaf ein cenedl, awydd i ddarllen ei hanes, ac y pery ei esiampl yn hir i ddylanwadu yn ddyrchafol ar feddyliau ieuainc Cymru Sydd, ac y profa Cymru Fydd ei hun yn deilwng o, neu hyd yn oed i ragori ar, yr athrylith fwyaf aruchel â'r hon y breintiwyd Cymru Fu yn nhymhorau gogoneddusaf ei hysblander a'i bri. Teimlai pob Cymrodor ei fod yn gwerthfawrogi bywyd Iolo Morgannwg yn fwy wedi yr ymweliad hwn â gorffwysfan ddistaw un o addurniadau dysgleiriaf cenedl y Cymry.

*The second extract by 'Pilgrim' (Pererin) relates an encounter with an English farm labourer at Flemingston whose derisive comments about Iolo's supposed foolishness and his part in demolishing the cottage where Iolo had lived caused considerable offence to his interlocutor.*

*Pererin, 'Ar Bererindod',* Yr Ymofynydd, *XV, no. 11 (1915), 242–3.*

Hyd hyn, nid oeddwn wedi dod i gyffyrddiad ag un dyn, na benyw, na phlentyn. Braidd na chredwn fod y lle wedi ei lwyr adael. Ar ol myned allan, fodd bynnag, gwelais ddyn yn y pellter yn dod tua'r pentref, a chyfeiriais innau fy nghamrau fel ag i osod fy hun ar ei lwybr. Pan ddaeth ataf, cyferchais ef yn y dull arferol; arhosodd yntau, a chawsom ymddyddan diddorol. Gweithiwr fferm ydoedd, cymharol wybodus. Bob yn dipyn, fel rhagarweiniad i'r hyn yr hoffwn ymddiddan âg ef yn ei gylch, gofynnais iddo, 'Ydych chi wedi byw yn hir yn y gymydogaeth hon?' 'Ydwyf, tua deugain mlynedd.' Yr oedd tua thrigain oed. Dylwn sylwi hefyd mai Sais ydoedd. 'A glywsoch chi am Iolo Morgannwg?' 'Do, yr oedd yn byw yn y pentref hwn. Bum yn cynorthwyo i dynnu lawr y ty yr oedd yn byw ynddo.' 'Ydyw man ei fedd yn wybyddus?' 'Nac ydyw; fe'i claddwyd yn y fynwent hon; ond ym mha fan ni fedraf ddweyd.' 'Oes carreg uwch ei fedd?' 'Nac oes; ond y mae cof-daflen ar y mur tu fewn i'r Eglwys.' 'Ydyw hi yn bosibl imi gael ei gweled?' 'O ydyw; fe gewch yr allwedd yn y Ficerdy.' Yna dywedodd ym mhellach, 'y mae cryn lawer o fobl yn dod yma i helynta yng nghylch Iolo' (*a good many people come here fussing about old Iolo* oedd ei eiriau); 'yr oedd yn ddyn mawr yn ddiameu, ond yr oedd hefyd yn ddyn ffol iawn – *he was a big fool.*' 'O falle wir' – dyna'r unig ateb fedrwn roi ar y pryd, gan fod y modd trwsgl y [illegible word] wedi bron rhoi atalfa ar fy anadl. 'Falle wir,' meddwn yr ail waith, ar ol imi gael hamdden i ddod ataf fy hun, 'dyna rywbeth hollol newydd.' 'Arferai gadw ceffyl,' meddai ym mhellach, 'ond nid oedd byth yn ei farchogaeth, yn hytrach cyd-gerddent i bob man. Dim ond dyn ffol wnelai'r fath beth a hyn. Arferai fyned i'r farchnad ym Mhontfaen bob dydd Mawrth yn rheolaidd, gyda'r hen geffyl yn ei law. Cychwynai am wyth o'r gloch i'r fynyd. Yna ar yr heol anghofiai ei hun yn llwyr, ac efallai mai yn Llanfihangel y delai ato ei hun, amryw filltiroedd o'r ffordd i'r Bontfaen. Cyrhaeddai i'r lle olaf tua hanner dydd, pan oedd y farchnad ym mron bod drosodd. Dywedir iddo wneud ymgais un adeg o'i fywyd i fyw ar borfa. Pwy ond dyn ffol wnelai hyn i gyd, a llawer o bethau eraill ellid enwi?' 'Nid oedd hyn,' meddwn wrtho mewn atebiad, 'ond yr hynodrwydd eithriadol sydd mor fynych yn cydfyned âg athrylith eithriadol.' 'Efallai. Yr oedd yn ddyn mawr yn ddiameu, ond yr oedd yn un hynod er hyny – ie, yr oedd yn ffol mewn llawer o bethau.' Wrth ymadael, ni wyddwn yn iawn ai diolch iddo ynte ei felldithio ddylwn wneud. Diolch iddo, fodd bynnag, wnaethum.

### 4. The Generosity of Iolo Morganwg

*This account reveals that, even fifty years after Iolo's death, his compassion and readiness to intervene during legal proceedings were an integral part of his legend.*

'Parish Sketches of the Vale: At the Tomb of Iolo Morganwg. Flemingstone, III', Glamorgan Gazette, *12 May 1876.*

The Vale at this present day is full of his doings and sayings. I happened to fall into conversation with an old man who is in his eightieth year. He had spent a long time in the same parish with Iolo, and knew his ways and disposition thoroughly. I have no wish at present to give but an instance or two of his everyday life; I hope they will prove acceptable to the readers generally . . . For instance, when he was in the prime and vigour of manhood, a poor little child, under the then existing code of parish relief, was hired from time to time into the families of the neighbourhood. It must have been a hard and cruel life, short commons in bed and board, well this little unfortunate could bear it no longer, and so it decamped. There was a rubbing up of parochial authority to recapture the little runaway, a serious case in those times, amounting almost to sheep stealing or highway robbery. The poor child was caught and taken before the judge at the Cardiff assizes. The bard attended, not out of curiosity, but as a father and friend. The sentence was about to be pronounced on the young incorrigible when Iolo tendered to the judge a note at the point of his memorable staff. The decision was not delayed, when the child and its deliverer were safe without the clutches of their miserable tormentors. It caused a stir at the time, naturally enough, to suppose that Iolo was the judge's judge.

*Some of Iolo's surviving correspondence, in this case a letter to Owen Jones (Owain Myfyr) in 1778, was used to illustrate his generosity towards the penurious clergyman Evan Evans (Ieuan Fardd) and the extent to which his largesse contrasted sharply with the miserliness of hard-hearted rich people.*

Cefni, 'Twysenau oddiar Faes Hynafiaeth', Y Geninen, XI, no. 2 (1893), 136.

... fel y tystia Iolo Morganwg mewn llythyr o'i eiddo at Owain Myfyr, dyddiedig Gorphenaf 10, 1778: – 'Y mae Ieuan Fardd ac Offeiriad yn awr yn weinidog Maesaleg: eithr nid oes yno un Ifor Hael. Y mae y bardd wedi troi yn ddyn sobr a chrefyddol iawn; ond mae y byd yn isel iawn arno. Yr wyf yn meddwl mai yr un tlotaf o'i alwedigaeth yn yr ynys yw. Ni fyddai fawr beth i'r Cymmrodorion ei anrhegu âg wyth neu ddeg punt, yr hyn a fyddai er mawr les a gwasanaeth iddo, ar hyn o dro.' Da iawn, Iolo! Rhoddes lawer pryd o fwyd, llawer noswaith o gysgu, a llawer swllt yn ei law, pan yr ydoedd llawer boneddwr goludog, a llawer crachfardd gwyntog, a'u calonau mor gauedig a chloedig, o ran cydymdeimlad a thosturi tuag atto, â choffr haiarn y cybydd!

## 5. The Discovery of the Samson Cross or Pillar

*The extraordinary manner in which Iolo discovered the Samson Cross or Pillar at Llantwit Major was often seized upon by Victorian antiquaries and helped to celebrate his reputation as an archaeologist and an antiquarian. Here, the artist and lecturer T. H. Thomas was deeply impressed by his discovery.*

T. H. Thomas, 'About Llantwit Major', The Red Dragon, II (1882), 226.

Against the wall of the porch stands the 'Pillar of Samson' (Golofn Samson). This is a huge quadrangular stone, 6ft. 6in. in height, three-quarters of a yard broad at base, and half a yard thick; at the top is a hollow, probably to receive a cross head. An oblong panel nearly occupies the front, and contains the inscription, almost entirely in miniscule letters ... 'In the Name of the High God, here begins the cross of the Saviour which Samson the Abbot prepared for his own soul and the soul of King Ithael and of Artmael the Deacon.' ... This monument is the one so intimately connected with the history of Iolo Morganwg. Iolo had heard a strange story from an old man of a Llantwit youth called 'Will the Giant'. This youth had attained the height of seven feet seven inches. He died at the age of seventeen, and desired to be interred at the foot of this stone. In digging his grave the pillar was rendered insecure, and immediately after the interment fell into the still open grave. It was left therein, and covered with earth. Iolo at last determined to test the truth of this tradition, and one Summer afternoon in 1789 searched for it: it was soon discovered, he obtained assistance, raised it and copied the inscription. It was afterwards lifted to its old position against the wall of the porch, and from Iolo's list of dimensions we must conclude that three feet are now sunk in the ground.

### 6. Iolo Morganwg and the Bishop of St David's

*These accounts demonstrate the process of communication through the pages of the Victorian periodical press. Both authors offer competing versions of a significant episode in Iolo's life. The first is based on oral tradition conveyed in Waring's biography, while the second quotes from a letter, but both reveal the influence of the myth of Iolo Morganwg.*

J. Rowland (Giraldus), 'Iolo Morganwg and the Bardic Chair of Dyfed' in Arthur Mee (ed.), Caermarthenshire Notes and Miscellany for South West Wales (Antiquarian, Topographical, and Curious). *Reprinted with Additions from the 'Welshman' (3 vols., Llanelly, 1889–91), II, p. 33.*

The bardic chair of Dyfed was kept almost a sacred relic at Llangunnor Vicarage by the late Canon Griffiths during his lifetime. He took great pride in the chair with its ancient motto, 'Calon wrth galon.' Every visitor to Llangunnor Vicarage had the honour of sitting in this seat. When Iolo Morganwg visited Carmarthen he always slept in this bardic chair at the old vicarage. He was a martyr to asthma, and for twenty-seven years he never slept in a bed. Iolo was always a welcome guest at Abergwilly Palace, and a great favourite of the Bishop's. He always slept in the library, and in the night he used to get up and examine the books. One night a great noise was heard in the library, and a servant was sent to see what was the cause of the disturbance. He was terrified to see a tall man dressed in a blue coat with bright buttons, wearing a tall night-cap, taking the books down from the shelves. He rang the bells and summoned the inmates together. The Bishop laughed heartily when he heard of the commotion. Iolo was admitted to the palace unknown to the servants, the Bishop being well acquainted with his habits.

Alcwyn C. Evans, 'Iolo and the Bishop of St. David's'
in ibid., *III, pp. 75–6.*

Vol. II., p. 33, contains a paragraph concerning Edward Williams, the Glamorganshire Bard, whom it places in a ridiculous light. The so-called anecdote is transplanted from a book written by Elijah Waring, termed his 'Recollections, &c.' How different is the reality! The following copy of a letter speaks for itself. It was written by a reverend gentleman to his brother:– 'Evesham, November 10, 1818 . . . I should not omit to tell you that the Bp, of

St David's, Lord Dynevor, and others, have lately formed a Society at Caermarthen for ye promotion of Welsh Literature. Iolo was written to by ye Bp, and his Lordship besides sent Archdeacon Beynon a message to him (Iolo) on purpose. Iolo attended with a load of his books and MSS. After ye Meeting at the White Lion, he was invited to the Bp's palace, where he spent from *Wednesday till Saturday. The Bp. sat up with him ye first night till 4 in ye morning, and every night after, after all others went to bed.* Some historical work of Iolo's is to be published first, of about 6 vols. 8vo., Welsh and English on opposite pages; Iolo, of course, to superintend its publication. *I had the honour of his company for several days at Caermarthen, after he had left the Bp . . .* I preached my farewell Sermon (Nov. 1st). In ye evening ye house was crowded. Poor Iolo was present, and was powerfully affected. With tears he came to me after the evening service, and, while standing under the pulpit, audibly bestowed his blessing.' Iolo visited the Bishop's palace only on two occasions, after being repeatedly invited. His spirit was a little too high to be surreptitiously 'admitted, unknown to the servants.' In a quite different style did Southey, the Poet Laureate, speak of

> Iolo, old Iolo, him who knows
> The virtue of all herbs of mount or vale,
> Or greenwood shade, or quiet brooklet's bed,
> Whatever love of science or of song
> Sages and Bards of old have handed down.

## 7. The Rights of Man

*This is the longest version of 'Iolo and the Rights of Man', the most popular anecdote about Iolo Morganwg in Victorian Wales. The fact that it was prefaced by gratuitous remarks by a Calvinistic Methodist accounts for the animus against the French Revolution and its promise of liberty. Having commended Iolo for stocking in his Cowbridge grocery shop East Indian sugar 'uncontaminated with human blood' ([m]elusion yr India heb eu cymysgu â gwaed dynol), Williams then recounts how Iolo sold to two government spies (here named as Rich and Curtis) a bible wrapped in a paper cover on which he had inscribed 'The Rights of Man'. When the two men returned to accuse Iolo of fraud, he retorted that the Bible was the finest collection of the rights of man known to him, and that he was glad to see God's word in their hands for once. The two foxes had met their match.*

*William Williams, 'Iolo Morganwg [Recollections and Anecdotes of Edward Williams, the Bard of Glamorgan; or Iolo Morganwg, B.B.D. By Elijah Waring. London: Charles Gilpin. 1850]', Y Traethodydd, XI (1855), 51.*

Pan dorodd y chwyldröad mawr allan yn Ffrainc, dallwyd llygaid ein bardd, a swynwyd ei serch gan y rhagolygfa o 'ryddid i ddynoliaeth' a ddaliai y chwyldröwyr o flaen y byd. Yr oedd plaid lïosog yn y wlad yma yn cydymdeimlo â hwy, ac ymunodd Iolo â'r blaid hono. Bu hyn yn foddion i beri iddo golli llawer o'i gyfeillion, ac i dynu arno lawer o ddrwgdybiau ac anfoddlonrwydd. Yr oedd yn dra chyfarwydd a chyfeillgar â Paine, awdwr 'Oes Rheswm', a 'Iawnderau Dyn', ac âg amryw o bentewynion eraill y dyddiau hyny. Cydwelai a chydymdeimlai âg egwyddorion gwleidiadol Paine; ond gwrthodai ei ddidduwiaeth gyda'r casineb mwyaf. Darfu y ffaith o'i fod yn cynnal cyfeillach â'r fath bentewyn beri i rai edrych yn fanol ar ei ol, gan geisio achos i'w erbyn. Dywedasom eisoes ei fod wedi bod yn cadw maelfa yn y Bontfaen. Yr oedd hon yn cynnwys darpariadau ar gyfer y ddwy ran sydd mewn dyn: bara a chaws, tê a siwgr, ar gyfer ei gorff; a llyfrau ar gyfer ei feddwl. Gwnaethai Iolo i ffenestr ei *shop* amlygu ei gasineb at gaethwasanaeth, oblegid crogai ynddi bapyr ar ba un yr oedd yn hysbysu fod i'w cael o fewn 'felusion yr India heb eu cymysgu â gwaed dynol.' Siwgr yr India Ddwyreiniol yn unig a werthai. Ni chai yr un Orllewinol, ar gyfrif yn y byd, ddyfod o dan ei gronglwyd ef. Ond aeth y sî ar led ei fod yn dirgel werthu llyfrau Tom Paine. Yr oedd dau ddyn tra theyrngarol yn y Bontfaen, o'r enwau Rich a Curtis. Cymerodd y rhai hyn arnynt wylied syniadau y bardd. Tebyg fod llawn gymaint a fynai hunangarwch â'u gofal a theyrngarwch, oblegid os gallent ei ddal ar ryw fai, buasent yn sicrhâu gwobr iddynt eu hunain oddiwrth y llywodraeth. Daeth Iolo i wybod am eu clefyd, a darparodd feddyginiaeth. Gosododd lyfr yn y ffenestr ar ba un yr oedd yn ysgrifenedig y geiriau ystyrfawr, 'Iawnderau Dyn.' Tynodd hyn sylw un o'r ddau farcut – gwnaeth hwnw y darganfyddiad yn hysbys i'r llall – ac fel yr adar hyny yn arogli ysglyfaeth, prysurasant ynghyd tua maelfa y bardd. Aeth un o honynt i mewn, pwrcasodd y llyfr, a thalodd am dano; ond cyn bod y ddau gyfaill wedi myned nebpell o ddrws y faelfa, aethant i edrych ar gynnwysiad y llyfr gwaharddedig – ac er eu mawr siomedigaeth, pa beth oedd ganddynt hwy ond Y BIBL! Trodd un o honynt yn ei ol, a chyhuddai Iolo o fod yn dwyllwr, am roddi y Bibl iddo o dan yr enw 'Iawnderau Dyn.' 'Na,' meddai'r bardd, 'nid twyllwr wyf fi, ac ni ddarfu i mi eich twyllo chwi chwaith – yn y llyfr yna y deuwch o hyd i wir iawnderau dyn, ac y mae yn dda genyf, gyfaill, fy mod wedi cael cyfle i roddi y Bibl yn eich llaw chwi am unwaith yn eich oes.' Nid oedd help am dani; yr oedd y ddau gadno wedi cyfarfod âg un mwy cadnöaidd na hwy eu hunain.

## 8. *'Strike a Welshman if you dare'*

*The two versions of the anecdote 'Strike a Welshman if you dare' reproduced below demonstrate how oral transmission over a period of time resulted in variations in form and content.*

*In the first published version Iolo is refused entry because the nobleman in question is otherwise engaged, which makes his insistence on entry appear petulant. The nobleman, as yet unnamed, and not on first-name terms with Iolo, was nevertheless aware of his reputation as the 'Welsh bard'.*

William Williams, 'Iolo Morganwg [Recollections and Anecdotes of Edward Williams, the Bard of Glamorgan; or Iolo Morganwg, B.B.D. By Elijah Waring. London: Charles Gilpin. 1850]', Y Traethodydd, XI (1855), 54–5.

Pan unwaith yn y brifddinas, derbyniodd genadwri oddiwrth foneddwr urddasol yn dymuno arno alw gydag ef cyn yr ymadawai. Yr oedd y boneddwr wedi clywed am Iolo, ac yr oedd y sôn am dano wedi creu awydd ynddo am ei weled. Ryw ddiwrnod, aeth y bardd at ei dŷ, curodd, a daeth y trulliad at y drws. Gofynodd i hwnw os oedd ei feistr i mewn. 'Ydyw,' oedd yr ateb, 'ond y mae ganddo gwmni; os ydych am ei weled, rhaid i chwi alw rywbryd arall.' 'Na,' ebe Iolo, 'rhaid i mi ei weled yn awr.' Aeth y gwas â'i neges i'r parlawr; dywedodd fod gŵr o ymddangosiad pur dlawd ac ysgrepan wen ar draws ei ysgwyddau, yn sefyll wrth y drws gan ymofyn ei weled; ac wele orchymyn eto iddo i ymadael, a galw rywbryd arall. Ond ni chymerai Iolo ball; yr oedd yn rhaid iddo ef gael gweled y boneddwr ar hyny o bryd. Y diwedd fu i'r boneddwr lidio, cyfododd ar ei draed, ymaflodd yn y chwip, rhedodd tua'r drws gan fwriadu gwneyd i'r dyeithr eon ddefnyddio ei draed, a chododd ei law – '*Strike a Welshman if you dare*,' ebe Iolo,–

'*Strike a Welshman if you dare,*
*Ancient Britons as we are,*
*We were men of great renown,*
*Ere a Saxon wore a crown.*'

'What!' ebe'r boneddwr, '*are you the Welsh bard?*' 'Ai chwi yw y bardd Cymreig? Deuwch i fewn – deuwch i fewn yn y fynyd.' Ac i mewn yr aeth. Ond ni ddarfu ymgyfeillachu â mawrion droi ei ben na rhwydo ei galon.

*The last published account of 'Strike a Welshman if you dare', which appeared in 1913, was the only version in the corpus to feature the prime minister, William Pitt.*

Marianne Robertson Spencer, Annals of South Glamorgan (Carmarthen, 1913), p. 241.

It appears that Pitt heard of a Welsh bard who was then in London, and expressed a wish to see him. He therefore called one evening, and rang the bell at the Prime Minister's door. The footman told Pitt that there was a poorly dressed man with a wallet over his shoulder who wished to see him. Pitt said he was too busy to see anyone, and on being informed that the poor-looking stranger insisted upon seeing him, he seized a whip, and hurried to the front door. Iolo, noticing the whip in Pitt's hand, broke into impromptu verse: –

> 'Strike a Welshman if you dare,
> Ancient Briton [sic] though we are;
> We were men of great renown
> Ere a Saxon wore a crown!'

Pitt cried, 'Are you the Welsh bard? Come in, come in at once.' Dressed as he was, Iolo joined the party at dinner, and delighted everyone, not only with his conversational abilities, but also with his wide range of knowledge.

## 9. *Gorsedd Beirdd Ynys Humbug*

*This virtually untranslatable Welsh-language satire takes the form of an eisteddfod announcement. It plays on the ritual, symbols and language developed by Myfyr Morganwg for his Rocking-stone Gorsedd. The mystic sign has been turned upside down and the (still recognizable) mottoes have been changed into nonsensical phrases such as 'Humbug Be Humbug' (Humbug bid Humbug) and 'Silliness against the World' (Dwli yn erbyn y Byd). The description of the proceedings highlights the arcane nature of Myfyr Morganwg's Gorsedd rituals and, through references to characters such as Cerberus and Satan, expresses widespread public suspicions that such rituals were pagan. The list of subjects for prize poems and essays betrays similar concerns, but also ridicules fashions such as orientalism, the proliferation of obscure bardic pseudonyms and the increasing importance ascribed to prize moneys at eisteddfodau. For instance, for the best essay on the relationship between the serpent of Eden and the Rocking-stone serpent, the winner is promised 'ten-and-a-half boxes on the ear, and a kick in the crupper' (Deg bonclust a hanner, a chic yn y crwper). This piece of satire reminds us that the follies of the Gorsedd were often held up to ridicule at a time when 'respectability' was thought to serve the public image best.*

'Sect y Maen Chwyf: Gorsedd Beirdd Ynys Humbug', Seren Gomer, XXXVIII, no. 479 (1855), 382–3.

### GORSEDD BEIRDD YNYS HUMBUG

*Yn ngwyneb Ieuan Myfyr, a Llygad Dallhuan Cwmcawlyd.*
*Oes Porchellyn pobi i Iaith y Pendronwyr! Dwli yn erbyn y Byd!*

Bydded hysbys, y cynnelir Eisteddfod Gyfeiliorn, o dan nawdd y Nôd Cyfrin a'i wadnau i fyny, –

\ | /

yn ol Braint a Defod Cyfrinion Annwn, y Sarff Dorchog, y Maen Chwyf, a Belphegor! Gwaedd uwch adwaedd! Hip hwre! teirgwaith tair, a naw gwaith naw, a naw etto!

## OYES!    OYES!!    OYES!!!

Bydd yr Orsedd i'w chynnal yn swyngylch Llys Caccamwcci, a dadblygiad y Llyswen Bendwll, ar lanau Gwyllionwy, yn Mhendefigaeth Cerberus, Satan, a Suddas, pan y bydd hawl i bawb a geisiant fraint a thrwydded i ffolinebu, i bendroni, i rigmarolio sothach, i chwareu ffwl pen ffair, i ddawnsio '*Jim Crow*,' a'r '*Polka*,' i gyrchu i'r lle am naw o'r gloch cyn dydd, a chynnal ger gwawl gwelwlas brwmstan, Jack-y-lantern, ellylldan, a chynffon Beelzebub, gorsedd *Strim Stram Strellach*, *Hit my Legs*, a *Much Ado about Nothing*; lle a phryd y bydd yn arwynebol, Tri Cyntefigion y Sedd, nid amgen,

## PW, POSH, A HUMBUG!

a chyda nhw Myfyr Difyfyr, Coeg-rigymwyr, Clebardorddion, a holl deulu Piserfurum chwydd gyffro, o Bont Abertinllwm, a Mân-seirff, Budr-chwilenod, a Chacwn yr Urdd!

## HUMBUG BID HUMBUG!

Yn enw'r D—l a phob Drygioni, Bidw, Thoth, a Chrisnhw, a'r holl Wallgofion Myfyraidd, gwobrwyir y Buddugoliaethwyr ar y testunau a ganlyn:—

1. Am y Traethawd goreu ar Satan, Tad yr Orsedd: Deg gwydraid a hanner o *bwnch* brwmstan.
2. Am y Traethawd goreu yn dangos y berthynas rhwng Sarff y Maen Chwyf a Sarff Eden: Deg bonclust a hanner, a chic yn y crwper.
3. Am y Traethawd goreu ar y llesiant a wna athrawiaeth y Maen Chwyf, er diddymu y Bibl, Cristionogaeth, a phob ofergoeliaeth cyffelyb, a sefydlu yn eu lle athrawiaeth y Traednoethion, Serddewiniaeth, a Thyphoniaeth: Deg o gilddannedd, ac un o ddannedd blaen *Prajapati*.
4. Am y Traethawd goreu ar Nôd Cyfrin Iolo Morganwg, a llun troed brân Myfyr. Yr unig ffordd i ennill y wobr hon yw diraddio yr hen Iolo, a chodi Myfyr ar *lapstone* Cilfenydd, yn uwch nâ Bidhw, Thoth, a Chrisnhw: Deg Oriawr ledr, a *guards* gwellt.
5. Am y Traethawd goreu ar gyd-darawiad swydd weinidogaethol y Parchedigion W. Roberts, Blaenau; R. Ellis, Syrhowi; a J. Emlyn Jones, â'u cymmeriadau fel dysgyblion Myfyr ab Humbug: Deg o gyfrolau *folio*, a bach i'w hongian, yn cynnwys Gweithiau awdurol M-my-myf-myfyr, sef ei awdlau cadeiriol, traethodau buddugol ar wahanol bynciau, yn nghyd a hanes ei deithiau a'i *hocus pocus* drwy yr Aifft, Buarth Arthur, y deuddeg arwydd, Gardd Eden, &c., yn nghyfeillach Iolyn ab Dadwrth, Hunan ab Cegrwth, a Luciffer.
6. Am y Traethawd goreu ar y lles deilliedig i Genedl y Cymmry drwy ddysgyblaeth Gwylliaid y Maen Chwyf, a'r effaith a gafodd ysgymun-erthyliad Dewi Essyllt drwy gynffon y Sarff, a melldithiad Talhaiarn gan Myfyr Difyfyr, ac Ifor Cwmgwys, a Chilfenydd ab Gwargam ab Tywalltgeg, yn

gymmaint ag nad yw Ifor wedi amryson â'r ceidwaid hely fyth wedi hyny, na Chilfenydd wedi anturio i Nant y Baril ond bob tro y caffai *hen gount*: Deg ŵy derwydd, wedi eu berwi yn mhenboethder arch-hudolwr y gareg siglo, pan syrthiodd ar ei grwper i bair Ceridwen.

7. Am y Traethawd goreu ar ryfyg T. Stephens, o Ferthyr, yr hwn na ennillodd ond cannoedd o bunnau yn wobrau, yn beiddio gwrthebu y cawr a loriodd y 'Quick yn Tân,' ar ddadl y ddiod fain driagl, yr hwn sydd wedi ennill cynnifer o filoedd o binnau a chadeiriau gwellt a botymau: Deg buddau gorddi, ym mha rai y corddwyd y môr, yn nghyd âg ymenydd Myfyr Difyfr hyd nes aeth yn lasdwr.

8. Am y Traethawd goreu ar hanes Mahomed, Johanna Southcott, Joe Smith, Myfyr Difyfyr, a'u hessill, yn nghyd a desgrifiad pa faint o fwnci sydd eisieu bod i gael mwnciod i'w ddilyn: Deg o felldithion Archasyn y Maen Chwyf, yn nghyd â deg rh–ch gan yr asynod bach ar eu gwaith yn codi eu cynffonau, ac yn carlamu ar ol y march asyn tuag annwn, ac yn neidio clwyd Luciffer heb dalu'r doll.

Nid ydys yn cynnyg gwobrau i'r Beirdd, fel y byddo Cilfenydd ab Celgwrnddwyn Ysgwyddgam yn sicr o gael chwareu têg. Attelir y gwobrau, yn ol Braint a Defod, ac os bydd y cyfansoddiadau yn gyfartal, ceir help gan Myfyr Difyfr i ranu y gwobrau, er gwneyd cyfiawnder, pe yn gynnifer o ranau ag sydd o fân gythreuliaid yn curo ei gefn wrth ffurfio yr athrawiaeth Faen Chwyfaidd. Ffurfir gorymdaith anrhydeddus o'r Bont hyd y Maen, pan y bydd Gwilym Gellideg i dywys haid o Wyddonesau poethysgowtffwrch China, a Gomach Grythor yn chwareu 'Hob y deri dando' o'u blaen. Traddodir araeth ar Achau'r Cwrw, gan Cilfenydd ab Gweflboer, ar y Maen, yn nghyd âg annogaeth i bawb draflyncu a allont, er llanw pislathau lliwdy Ieuan ab Iago, Bardd Brwnt y Diafol. Traddodir araeth Dr y Bendro gan Ifor Cwmgwys, ac ar ol rhoi urdd yr orsedd dinglerol i'r ymgeiswyr moelgreichion, Myfyr ab Typhon ab Chrishnw a ddatgan ei gerdd freuddwydiol ar Hud a Lledrith.

Beirniaid y Traethodau – Plenydd Bolrwth, Alawn Gwag ei Boced, a Gwron na châr y Geirwir. Anfoner y cyfansoddiadau i Annwn erbyn Dygwyl Andras. Cynnelir cyfarfod y nos dan arwydd Telyn Cenfigen, i yfed, ffraeo, a blagardio y Beirniaid.

> Ennynwch, feibion annwn, – eich doniau,
>   Crach dynwch i'r lecsiwn;
> Daw wythgant o felldithgwn
> O din y Sarff – dyna swn!

CALLWR CELLWEIRUS, *Ysgrifenydd*.

## 10. The Grand Eisteddfod of Llangollen, 1858

*This report by John Williams Ab Ithel of his 'Grand Eisteddfod of Llangollen, 1858' offers a colourful account of the proceedings of this seminal event and portrays some of the principal (and bizarre) participants. But it also betrays some of the mid-Victorian neuroses which troubled the Welsh – their determination to assert the Christian provenance of the Gorsedd ceremonies and to promote the interests of the Welsh language at a time when Anglicizing trends were threatening its future well-being. Most of the 'historical facts' presented by Ab Ithel were derived from Iolo's writings in the Llanover collection.*

*John Williams, 'Gorsedd of the Bards of the Isle of Britain; the Royal Chair of Powys; and the Grand Eisteddfod held at Llangollen On Alban Elfed, 1858', Cambrian Journal, V (1858), 262, 265–72.*

The National Gorsedd of British Bards, and the Royal Chair of Powys, accompanied by a Grand National Eisteddfod, in accordance with the 'privileges and customs of the Bards of the Isle of Britain,' commenced at Llangollen on Tuesday, 21st September, and extended over the four succeeding days, during which prizes to the amount of £400 or £500 were awarded to successful candidates in the various departments of poetry and general literature, oratory, music, heraldry, arts, manufactures, &c.

The Eisteddfod was appointed to take place on Alban Elfed, which, Anglicised, is the autumnal equinox, and the province selected was that of Powys, in which Llangollen is situate, and which claims the privilege of a 'Royal Chair,' according to the usages of bardism.

The preparations were in every respect on a scale worthy of a national event, the successful issue of which must, however, be attributed to the zealous and energetic exertions of the Revd John Williams Ab Ithel, MA, rector of Llanymowddwy, and the Revd J. Hughes (Carn Ingli), Meltham Parsonage, Huddersfield, the joint secretaries of the Eisteddfod, whose efforts were also most efficiently seconded by the local secretaries, Messrs Humphreys and Hughes, of Llangollen, and the Revd T. R. Lloyd (Estyn), Llanfynydd. The Llangollen people, too, one and all, appear to have come out with spirit on the occasion. A main object with the promoters has been to adhere as closely as possible to the orthodox rules and customs of bardism, which, with respect to the Gorsedd and the national congress always accompanying it, are defined and established, and the principal aim of which is the elevation of the social, moral, and religious status of the people of Wales, the encouragement of nationality, the perpetuation of the Cymraeg, and the cultivation of Welsh literature, Welsh music, &c . . .

### THE PAVILION

The spot selected for the Eisteddfod was the Bowling Green, adjoining the *Ponsonby Arms Hotel*, &c., so close to the river Dee as to be within hearing of the sound of the impetuous torrent as it sweeps over the picturesque falls near this point. Here a spacious pavilion was erected, and fitted up with every convenience for carrying on the proceedings, and for the accomodation of no fewer than 5000 people. It measured about 180 feet long, by 144 feet broad, forming a parallelogram, roofed in three spans, the three front gables being decorated by three flags respectively of the bardic colours, blue, green, and white, and bearing the inscriptions 'Heddwch', 'Gwybodaeth', 'Sancteiddrwydd', the attributes of the three orders. The interior was formed in three compartments, in the middle one of which, at the north end, was a raised dais or platform (constructed for 120 persons), for the use of the president and others taking part in the business of the congress. Over the president's seat was the red dragon of Wales, with the motto, 'Y ddraig goch a ddyry gychwyn', painted on canvas, by Mr Thomas Jones (Taliesin o Eifion), Llangollen. The figure of the dragon was no less than five or six feet long. On the other side of the pavilion, immediately opposite, was an elegant blue banner, bearing the sacred emblem, with the mottoes of the British Gorsedd and Powysian Chair, wrought in gold letters, very prominently set forth, 'Y gwir yn erbyn y byd', 'A laddo a leddir'. The walls were hung around with the armorial bearings of the fifteen royal tribes of Wales, together with the five royal arms, properly so called, being those of the reigning princes, all of which were kindly lent to the committee by T. L. D. Jones Parry, Esq., Madryn, and amongst the other mottoes displayed, were the following: – 'Lle taw Duw, nid doeth yngan', 'Nid gwiw gwir heb ei ganlyn', 'Cas gwr na charo y wlad a'i macco', 'Nid da lle gellir gwell', 'Calon wrth galon', 'Duw a phob daioni', 'Heb ddechreu ni cheir terfyn', 'Oes y byd i'r iaith Gymraeg', 'Myn y gwir ei le', 'Nid da lle gellir gwell', &c. The roof timbers were festooned with evergreens, the entire decorations being in keeping with the object in view, and in good taste. Adjoining the pavilion was a committee room, communicating with the platform, and large enough to accommodate 100 people, and close by, on the same ground, Mr Allen, the landlord of the hotel, had erected three spacious first and second class refreshment tents, capable of dining from 300 to 400 persons. The tent was erected by Mr Henry Hughes, Broughton, the amount of the contract being £200, the materials to be returned. The canvas was supplied by Mr Oakes, Chester.

### PRELIMINARY MEETING

At seven o'clock on Monday, a miscellaneous meeting was held in the pavilion, the object being more especially to test the capability of the structure acoustically as regards the human voice, and also to hear the effect of the harp. The chair was taken by Ab Ithel, who was supported by a number of bards and others.

Mr Jerome Pym ap Ednyfed gave a brief sketch of Taliesin and Cattwg Ddoeth. G. H. Whalley, Esq., Plas Madoc, addressed the meeting on the objects of a bardic congress, after which the Welsh air of 'Hob y deri dando' was sung by Miss Roberts, accompanied on the harp. The Revd Mr Morgan, PC, Tregynon, next spoke, and specimens of pennillion singing were given by Llew Llwyfo and others.

Carnfaldwyn, a young man from Montgomeryshire, next gave some curious illustrations of the Welsh *cynghanedd*, or consonancy, to show the peculiarities of the twenty-four confined metres, &c. This was followed by the favourite air 'Clychau Aberdovey', played on the harp by Mr Ellis Roberts, and sung by Miss Roberts, after which Llew Llwyfo delivered a Welsh address, and Ab Ithel having announced the programme for the morrow, the meeting dispersed. The attendance, although numbering some hundreds, appeared scanty.

Before the termination of the proceedings, the Revd Mr Morgan announced that if any person had any subject affecting the national interests of Wales, or touching the Welsh language, which should be brought before the Gorsedd, due notice of the same should be given to the committee, in order that it might be brought before that convention.

The tent, which was lit up with gas, looked remarkably well, and it was stated that the speeches could be distinctly heard from all parts of it, but with respect to the harp, the sound of the instrument was necessarily weak in such an extensive place.

Tuesday, 21st September.<br>
THE GORSEDD.

At 10 a.m. the bards, druids, ovates, and others, assembled in the pavilion, and were marshalled in order of procession. The scene now presented was to most, if not all present, novel. Those who were members of the three privileged orders were attired in their appropriate habiliments, the bard in a loose habit of blue, the druid in snowy white, and the ovate in a green vestment. One of the ovates bore a *peithynen*, or *coelbren y beirdd*, the means by which poetic effusions were recorded in the earliest times. It consists of slender pieces of wood, fitted into an oblong frame, each piece having four lines of poetry cut thereon, in old British characters. The *coelbren* in question contained Gwallter Mechain's *cywydd*, 'Cofiant Iolo Morganwg', and comprised twenty-three staves, on which were inscribed ninety-two lines of poetry. They were ingeniously executed by Mr Edward Lloyd, Cefn y bedd. Bard, druid, and ovate, also displayed on his breast three ears of ripe wheat, symbolical of Alban Elfed, the season of harvest. The procession marched through the town, and thence to the spot known as the Green, in the following manner; –

Standard bearer, carrying the banner of the Red Dragon of Wales.<br>
Brass band.<br>
Blue flag of the bards.<br>
White flag of the druids.<br>
Bards, druids, and ovates, bare-headed, and in costume.<br>
Green flag of the ovates.<br>
People four abreast.

As the procession wended its way over the bridge (considered at one time one of the wonders of the Principality), through Chapel Street, Collen Terrace, and back through High Street, the number of people welled immensely, until the line of march became densely crowded. Many of the houses were decorated with flags. On arriving at the Green, we found that a large body of people had already posted themselves near the bardic circle, intent upon witnessing the ceremonial about to take place. There were several carriages also on the ground. The band played 'The March of the Men of Harlech', and other appropriate Welsh airs. After coming to a halt, the pressure towards the centre of attraction, where the bardic officials were congregated, was very great, and it required the unceasing efforts of Mr Denman, the chief constable, and his men, to keep a clear space; but never have we seen the duty more good-naturedly, and at the same time effectively, discharged, than on this occasion, by Mr Denman.

The Gorsedd consisted of the *maen arch*, or *maen llog*, the chief stone placed in the centre, round which, in a circle of 30 feet diameter, are the '*meini gwyngil*,' being twelve stones set on end, to represent the signs of the zodiac. The sun was considered as a type of God – the Sun of Righteousness; hence the construction of the druidical places of worship in a circular shape. Towards the east, on the outside of the circle, were three other stones, at a distance of nine fathoms from the centre piece, and placed in such positions with respect to the latter, that lines drawn from it, through the three, would indicate the points in the heavens at which the sun rises on the solstices and equinoxes of the year respectively. These lines or pencils of light, as they are termed, form the mystic symbol known amongst the Bards and druids as the Name of God – the 'Word' or attribute of creation – it being held by the Bards that God created the universe by showing and pronouncing His own name. It was, we understand, the original intention of the committee to have the stones of such magnitude, and so placed, as to be a permanent memento of the Eisteddfod, but the ground being a charitable bequest to the inhabitants for the purposes of recreation, of which the Board of Health are trustees, this intention could not conveniently be carried into effect.

During the procession, Glas Ynys, a bard according to the privilege and usage of the Isle of Britain, carried a sheathed sword, taking hold of it by the point. On entering within the precincts of the circle the sword was slowly pushed backward out of its scabbard, and placed, being laid hold of by the naked point, on the Gorsedd or central stone.

Before the formal opening of the Gorsedd, Ab Ithel, who, as the presiding bard, stood on the central stone, whilst the others were ranged in position near the stones which formed the circle, delivered an address in Welsh on the aspects of bardism in the Isle of Britain. In outward appearance it might be likened to a tree exhibiting two branches. The branches were the Eisteddfod and the Chair, the trunk from which they sprang being the Gorsedd. The Eisteddfod originated in the time of Owain ap Maxen Wledig, on the departure of the Romans, after exercising their rule here for more than 400 years. Its object was to encourage bardism, music, and the general literature of the Cymry, maintain the Welsh language and customs of the country, and cultivate a patriotic spirit amongst the people. The 'chairs' were established, or rather, perhaps, resuscitated, about the sixth century. The chair was a kind of provincial or local convention, where disciples were trained, and bardic matters discussed, preparatory to the great or national Gorsedd. There were at present four chairs in Wales, viz., the Chair of Gwent and Morganwg, Chair of Dyfed, Powys Chair, and the Gwynedd Chair. That of Powys was termed 'royal,' because it had been established by three royal bards, Llywarch Hen, Brochwel Ysgythrog, and Gwron ab Cynfarch. The chairs had their distinctive mottoes. That of Gwent and Morganwg was, – 'Duw a phob daioni'. Dyfed, – 'Calon wrth galon'. Powys, – 'A laddo a leddir'. Gwynedd, – 'Yr Iesu'. The motto of the Gorsedd of the Bards of the Isle of Britain was that which embraced all the others, – 'Y gwir yn erbyn y byd'. Other 'chairs' have been in existence which are no longer in an active state, such as Arthur's Chair, or the Round Table, with its motto at first, – 'Da yw'r maen gyda'r efengyl'; and then, – 'Nid da lle gellir gwell'. The chair of Bryngwyddon, – 'Coel clywed, gwir gweled'. Beiscawen yn Nyfnaint, – 'Nid byth, ond bythoedd'. Urien Rheged (of which Taliesin was principal bard), – 'Myn y gwir ei le'. Raglan, – 'Deffro mae'n ddydd'. The Gorsedd, in its present form, is as old as the period of Prydain ab Aedd Mawr, who lived about a thousand years before the Christian era. There were bards and bardism prior to that date, but they had no organized system, nor any means save song whereby to perpetuate their traditions, nor any established law to preserve their privileges. Lest the old traditions should be lost, Prydain caused a Gorsedd, or national meeting, to be convened, for the purpose of eliciting all that had been retained in the memory of the people respecting the occurrences of ancient times; and it was found that three of the old bards, or, as they were then called, the 'Gwyddoniaid,' i.e., men of knowledge, viz., Plenydd, Alawn, and Gwron, remembered and knew more than all the rest. These three classified the old traditions, and they divided the old order into three sections – bards, druids, and ovates; and this arrangement, having undergone the examination of succeeding Gorseddau for three years, received national warranty. Such was the origin and commencement of the Gorsedd in its outward aspect, as it now appeared. But as regarded its essential requisites, it might be said that bardism was as old as Noah, or even Adam himself, the father of all mankind. The Almighty was pleased to grant to Adam, when created, a revelation of Himself, and of the unseen world. This revelation was a second time given to Noah, unless, indeed, we are to suppose that the first revelation had been sustained in memory. He again taught the whole to his children and posterity, and whilst he and they lived together in the East, it was not possible to fall deeply into religious error. When the general dispersion took place, the heads of families carried along with them that which they knew of the primary religion into their new abodes; and, in the course of time, from the natural corruption of the human heart, the weakness of memory, and from opposing circumstances from without, the patriarchal religion suffered deterioration more or less. God chose one nation out of the whole to maintain the true religion, by means of continued revelations, leaving the rest by natural means to support that which had once been given to them. Of the nations left to themselves, the Cymry succeeded, beyond all others, in keeping the old religion uncorrupted; and thus, when the Messiah came, they saw that He completely answered to the types they had of Him, and they received the Gospel as the superstructure or completion of Druidism. Their ancient system was clothed with Christianity. But this, rejoins some one, is all gone by; what benefit can result from keeping up these old customs any longer? He answered – much in every respect; but, as time was short, he would mention only one. Their act in holding the Gorsedd of the Bards was a public witness that the Cymry at all times considered and believed the unison and agreement that existed between the two dispensations – that the one answered to, and was as the fulfilment of, the other – that God was the same in all ages, and that He carried on His works gradually towards perfection. Alluding to the degenerate condition of the rest of the Gentile world, the reverend gentleman proceeded to explain the ceremonies observed at the Gorsedd. Having glanced at the symbols of the sacred circle, he explained the dresses of the three orders, and their emblems; that of the bard having reference to the blue vault of heaven, indicating peace and tranquillity; that of the druid indicating purity, by its snowy whiteness, intended to resemble light; and that of the ovate, borrowed from the grass of the field, a state of growth and progression. Another ceremony was that of bearing the sword; taking it by the point, instead of the hilt, and in that manner replacing it in the scabbard, intended to show the peaceful occupation of the bard, and that no arms could be borne in the Gorsedd, the mode of sheathing being designed to illustrate the fact that, by his office, the bard should turn the sword against himself before he did so against any other man. (His address was received with frequent marks of applause.)

The Revd M. Morgan (Mor Meirion) then advanced into the circle, and repeated the 'Gorsedd Prayer' composed by Talhaiarn, a bard of the fifth century, as follows: –

> Dyro, Dduw, dy nawdd;
> Ac yn nawdd, nerth;
> Ac yn nerth, deall;
> Ac yn neall, gwybod;
> Ac yngwybod, gwybod y cyfiawn;
> Ac yngwybod y cyfiawn, ei garu;
> Ac o garu, caru pob hanfod;
> Ac yn caru pob hanfod, garu Duw.

After this the presiding bard recited the 'Gwaedd uwch adwaedd', or proclamation, introducing it with the national motto, – 'Y gwir yn erbyn y Byd'; and concluding with the provincial motto, – 'A laddo a leddir'. In this proclamation all candidates for bardic honours were invited to the Gorsedd, 'where there was no naked weapon against them', and seek them at the hands of the graduated bards present. Whilst Ab Ithel pronounced the words just quoted, all the bards approached the central stone, and assisted in sheathing the sword.

The following appeared as candidates for the honour and degree of Bard:– Ceiriog, Pererin, Carnfaldwyn, and Llew Hiraethog, who had previously sent in testimonials of their qualifications. As each presented himself, the presiding bard published the 'Gosteg Cadair' three times, thus, –

> 'A. B. – Bardd yn hawl ac arddelw ger bron y gadair, ac os oes neb a wyr ac a ddengys achaws cyfiawn a phaham nas gellir, ac nas dylid Bardd o hono, o gradd herwydd a welir yn gyfiawn wrth fraint a defawd Beirdd Ynys Prydain, dangosed.
> 'Llafar bid lafar.'

And as no one proferred any objection, he took each by the hand, and, looking eastward, addressed him solemnly, –

> 'Goleuni Duw rhag dy lygaid,
> Goleuni Duw yn dy gydwybod,
> Gwirionedd Duw ar dy dafawd.

'A ymgeisi di yn dy swydd fel Bardd wellhau moes a defod, cynnal heddwch, a moli pob daionus a rhagor?'

And on receiving the answer, –

> 'Gwnaf ar air a chydwybod,'

he made the declaration, –

'Bardd ydwyt, gair dy air ar bob un na fo bardd, ac nid un gair o neb un nad bardd arnat ti.'

Whereupon Mor Meirion tied a blue ribbon round his right arm, and he was presented with a *brysyll* or wand of the same colour, emblematical of 'privilege.' Next, the following appeared as candidates for the degree of Ovate: – Morddal, Madoc, Glyn Afon, Dinmael, Elfynydd, Ap Ednyfed, Peblig, Gwilym Tawe, Eos Llechid, Gwilym o Fôn, Ivan Avan, Euronwy, Eiluned, and Meillionen Meirion. These were respectively presented by graduated bards, who declared 'on their word and conscience' that they were worthy. On which the presiding bard proclaimed, –

> 'A. B. – Dywed yr hwn a'i cyflwyna ar air a chydwybod y gellir Bardd o hono (neu honi); ac yna barna y Beirdd yng ngorsedd y dylir Bardd o hono (neu honi) yngradd Ofydd ym mraint Beirdd a Chadair Powys.
> 'A laddo a leddir.'

And each was invested with a ribbon and a wand of a green colour. The ceremony of graduating Druids was similar, *mutatis mutandis*, but instead of these being admitted 'on the word and conscience' of a privileged bard, they were elected by a majority of votes. The following were received into the order of Druids: – Ivan Avan and Pererin.

Glas Ynys then delivered the *Traethawd*, or charge, to those who had been initiated, exhorting them to be true to their order by the maintenance of peace and good will amongst themselves, and by the cultivation of poetry and other branches of literature in the Welsh language.

Mathonwy then recited a Welsh poem, and, it having been announced that the Gorsedd would be open on each of the succeeding days, the proceedings for the present terminated with the singing of the Doxology, which was done with grand effect. The procession afterwards returned to the tent in the same order as before.

## THE EISTEDDFOD

was arranged to commence at half past one, in the pavilion, but it was considerably later before the ceremonies commenced. Upon the platform the bards, druids, ovates, and others were congregated, the first-named wearing light blue dresses, the druids were habilitated wholly in white, while the ovates wore green. Those just graduated wore merely a ribbon tied round the arm, of either blue, white, or green, according to their degrees. There were several others, ladies and gentlemen, on the platform, some of whom were in full costume, as Dr Price, who wore a truly patriarchal beard, and was attired in a green jacket suit trimmed with scarlet, and a primitive fox-skin cap. Miss Price, daughter of Dr Price, also wore a fox-skin head-dress, and a scarlet habit. There could not have been less than 5000 people in the pavilion, and the scene altogether was a most interesting one.

The Eisteddfod opened with a sound of trumpet, when Ab Ithel proposed, and Carn Ingli seconded, that T. Oldfield, Esq., (Eryr Moelfre) of Bettws, near Abergele, should preside. This was carried by acclamation, and the President made a few observations to the effect that he should always be happy to support Welsh nationality, and would do his utmost to fulfil his duties on the present occasion.

A concert of harps then struck up with the 'Rising of the Lark', which was admirably played by Messrs Ellis Roberts (harpist to the Prince of Wales), Thomas Griffiths (harpist to Lady Hall, of Llanover), John Roberts, and Richard Pugh. Some Welsh *englynion* were next recited by, among others, the Revd D. Jones, Revd R. Ellis, (Cynddelw), Thomas Edwards, of Corwen, Alaw Goch, and Idris Vychan. These productions were generally well received, and afforded much amusement.

Mr Owain (Owain Alaw), professor of music, Chester, then called upon the company to join in the chorus of the next song, which was a truly national one. Mr Lewis (Llew Llwyfo), of the Liverpool Philharmonic Concerts, hereupon sang, in capital style, 'O, let the kind Minstrel', in the chorus of which the audience heartily joined.

## 11. A Monumental Sculpture in Merthyr Tydfil

*In 1860 the accomplished Merthyr sculptor Joseph Edwards, who had been educated at Taliesin ab Iolo's school, used the mystic sign and the* englyn *'T'r meirwon mae Duw'r mawredd – yn addaw' to adorn a striking monument to a local inhabitant who had been killed in an accident. The anonymous writer of the newspaper article who reported the event seized the opportunity to explain – in the most florid terms – to his English-speaking audience the meaning of Iolo's poem and the mystic sign.*

'Monumental Sculpture', Merthyr Telegraph, *9 June 1860.*

An exceedingly beautiful monument has just been erected in Graig Chapel, Troedyrhiw, to commemorate the late Mr Lewis Morgan, of Graig Cottage, whose distressing death in September, 1856, while crossing the railway on horseback near Merthyr, caused deep sympathy in the public mind, and a heartfelt sorrow to his relatives and friends, by whom he was greatly and deservedly esteemed. The impersonation of this mournful feeling, at the sad accident, in a *relievo* figure of Grief, bowed down in subdued anguish at the tomb of the lamented gentleman commemorated, is the principal object in the monument; and most feelingly and ably has this figure been treated by the sculptor. The attitude and expression, the extremities, general form and drapery are all admirable. The accessories also in the design have a consoling and deep significance; such as the star of hope seen above the end of the tomb indicated on the monument, accompanied by the monogram of the Redeemer between the letters Alpha and Omega, and by the *nôd kyvrin* – the triadic sign of the inexpressible Name of the Deity as creator, preserver, and ruler of all things who 'turneth the shadow of death into morning, and maketh the day dark with night'. Below these and on the indicated tomb is inscribed the following brief but sublime quotation from Isaiah:– 'The morning cometh and also night'; to which is added the accompanying grand text from 1 Chron. 29th chapter 15th verse, 'Our days upon the earth are as a shadow, and there is no abiding.' Both quotations are in the Welsh language and are followed by a charming couplet by Gwilym Hiraethog expressive of the keen sorrow produced by the deceased having been so suddenly consigned to the darkness of the grave: –

> 'Gwaew enaid i'n gwânu
> Ei roi tan y gwer[y]d du.'

Immediately under this couplet the figure of Grief is bowed down as if 'pierced by the agony of the soul'. The subjoined inscription and *englyn* are on the tablet under the figure: –

> In sacred remembrance of
> LEWIS MORGAN, ESQ.,
> Who died on the 5th of September, 1856,

> In the 56th year of his age.
> He lived at the Graig Cottage, near this Chapel, and
> was sincerely respected in life,
> and deeply lamented in death,
> by his bereaved relations, friends, and acquaintances.
> 'I'r meirwon mae Duw'r mawredd – yn addaw
> Newyddoes di ddiwedd;
> Cyfodant, cuaf adwedd,
> I dir y byw o dy'r bedd.'

This *englyn* is by *Iolo Morganwg*, and is beautifully descriptive of the revealed assurance that there is another and a better land whereto the dead shall be raised with a new and most dear existence which shall have no end. On the upper part of the background of the monument, forming the culminating object in the design, and adding to its high and solemn tone, there is an emblem of the Holy Spirit, as a dove . . . Beaming, too, immediately above this symbol, and as if ever attending it, the *nôd kyvrin* is again introduced, – here as the sign of the Eternal's Name, which, though unutterable by the human voice, is, however, in successive myriads of ages, according to a poetic fancy, sounded forth by the Almighty himself, when, in an instant, out of the circumambient realm of nothingness and night, the countless hosts of astral systems in space, with all their respective immutable laws, bound into existence with a shout of ecstatic joy! After millions upon millions of years have passed in succeeding progressive or retrogressive conditions, they, with, of course, our solar orb and its attendant planetary troop, again instantly, and by a similar utterance of God's most holy name, rebound out of existence with the like joyful ecstasy; and thus, in the stillness of eternity, they alternately appear and disappear for ever and for ever. These accessories, though suggestive of poetic ideas so vast and appropriate, are yet so unobtrusive that they would not be even noticed by many. The extreme size of the monument is only 4 feet 9 inches high by 2 feet 11 inches wide, and the light and shade upon it, as seen in the chapel, are unfortunately far from being good for such a work, which is carried out in the finest Italian marble. It has been designed and executed for Mr Morgan, of Abercwmboy, and Mrs Williams, of Penyradw – brother and sister of the deceased, by Mr J. Edwards, of Robert-street, Hampstead road, London, who is, we are glad to say, a native of Merthyr.

## 12. *The Druids of Dresden*

*By the 1880s the influence of Iolo's bardism had penetrated Continental Europe, where members of druidical orders feverishly sought to affiliate themselves to Welsh Gorseddau and their contemporary representatives. This entailed applications for druidic licences.*

'Literature, Art, and Archæology of the Month',
The Red Dragon, VIII (1885), 498.

The Druidic scholar, 'Myfyr Morganwg,' Pontypridd, has received an application from Dresden for his sanction as Druid of the Bardic Gorsedd of Wales to open a Gorsedd in Germany, affiliated to the school of Morganwg, named also 'Beirdd Tir y Iarll'. The application is signed by Professor Lloyd Wollen, who is MA, PhD, and LLD of two British Universities; Paul Georg Benner, AM; Otto Crienitz, LitD; Adolph Foerster, LitD; Richard Grundmann, PhD; Major Kahl, LLD; Hugo Carl Georg Rosen Kranz, LLD; and Alexander Schuricht, all of Dresden, Saxony. Professor Lloyd Wollen is described as 'scrutiniser and translator to the German Imperial Government.' It appears that the applicants regard the Eisteddfod Gorsedd as the primitive religious centre of the ancient world; that its palmiest days were those preceding the Roman invasion of Britain; that it was carried into the mountains of Wales with the retreating Cambro-Britons, and preserved there, through all national misfortunes, by the heroic Silurians, or the people of South Wales; that it went also under the name of the Round Table of Arthur, and that Pontypridd Common is the only place in the wide world where its ancient philosophy is still taught in its pristine purity.

## 13. Authenticating Druidism

*This letter from Thomas Price (Carnhuanawc) to Jane Williams (Ysgafell) highlights the way in which Taliesin ab Iolo (probably unwittingly) authenticated his father's inventions. Quoted here from Carnhuanawc's* 'Literary Remains', *it was considered significant enough to be reprinted in* 'A Few Observations on Certain Very Ancient Traditions Among Certain Primitive Nations', Cambrian Journal, *II (1855), 227–8. Such passages served to attest and perpetuate Iolo's spurious material. It is worth noting that Carnhuanawc believed that Taliesin was 'as secret and mysterious as Abaris himself'.*

Jane Williams (ed.), The Literary Remains of the Rev. Thomas Price,
Carnhuanawc, Vicar of Cwmdû, Breconshire; and Rural Dean *(2 vols.,
Llandovery, 1854), II, pp. 264–6.*

Mr Price wrote the following admirable letter in answer to one which had been addressed to him by the hand now engaged in tracing his Biography.

'Crickhowel, May 13, 1840
When I had the pleasure of receiving your very interesting letter some weeks ago, I was on the point of seting off from home for a few days; and as I had then no time to notice your inquiries in the way I wished, I laid the letter by until my return. And I must confess to you that when I took it up after-

wards, I found so many difficulties in the subject you refer to, that I have from time to time deferred attempting an answer. And now I write to acknowledge the receipt of your communication, rather than to give any explanation of those subjects.

With reference to Druidism, I fear we are to remain for ever in the same state of ignorance as our predecessors; for I cannot find that the present age has thrown any light upon the tenets of that order. One thing only appears certain respecting the Druids – they knew how to keep their own secrets. As to the classics, I am satisfied they contain but very little information. The late Archdeacon Payne, of this town, made for his own use a collection of all that he could find in the classics relative to Druidism; and it forms a thick quarto, closely written, being extracts regularly brought down. And I believe that even he himself, after all his labour, was obliged to confine himself to a few very remote conjectures as to the tenets of Druidism; at least, I have never heard him give an opinion otherwise than in a very undecided manner. Then as to the Bardic remains, I must acknowledge that I myself cannot see my way at all through them. Davies is very amusing; but he does not convince me. Amongst the works you name as having read, there are two which I do not see in your list, 'Britannia after the Romans, 1836', and 'An Essay on the Neo-Druidic Heresy in Britannia, 1838', both thin quartos. They will amuse you a good deal, and leave you in the same state of mystery as ever; the author is not known, but I have heard that his name is Herbert. If I had any means of conveying them to you, and were sure of receiving them back in a stated time, I should have much pleasure in sending them to you. The price is 30s. and 14s. London, Bohn; but I think the 1st volume is out of print, there were but a few copies printed.

I ought to inform you there is one person living who professes to be a Druid, and to have received the secrets of the order from his father and others, i.e. Mr Taliesin Williams, of Merthyr Tydfil, son of Iolo Morganwg; and he is the only one of the order now surviving. He is as secret and mysterious as Abaris himself could have been, if Abaris was a Druid. All that he will say is, that Davies and all the rest knew nothing about the matter; and he says that he himself was for twenty years under a sort of Druidical training with his father, and that the system is of so sublime and intellectual a nature, that unless he can find some one qualified in such a way as to be a worthy member of the order, the secret shall die with himself. Of course, in such a case it is impossible to form an opinion; sometimes I have been able to discover in conversation a tendency to approve of the doctrine of the metempsychosis. But, as far as my own observation goes, I assure you I have not been able to form the most distant idea of ancient Druidism from anything that he may have said. I will confess that he has now and then staggered me a good deal by referring to some ancient Bardic lines, when I have doubted the antiquity of his system. For instance, the Bardic symbol at the head of their written composition is this / | \

which they say contains the elements of the bardic Alphabet, as there is no letter in that alphabet that is not formed of one or more of those lines; and also that all the ancient European alphabets may be resolved into these elements, the round strokes being later additions for the facility of writing with a pen, &c.; whereas the Coelbren letters were cut on sticks, and therefore the horizontal and round lines would not do, as the grain of the wood did not admit of it. / | \ would do very well, but − O ( ) would splinter; and in accordance with this elementary system of three lines / | \ they have a story about its being revealed to some one in a vision of three rays of light, and announced by three shouts of voices, &c. Now all this I thought to be the mere production of the leisure hours of old Iolo Morganwg, or some other person in modern times; but one day, by accident, I happened to open upon an ancient *englyn* in the *Myf. Arch.*, attributed to Gwenddydd, the sister of Merlin Silvestris, in which it is said, that on some future time when some events shall take place (which I cannot understand), then 'happy the mouth that shall utter three words of the old original language'. 'Gwyn ei fyd y genau yn frwydd gyfeistrin, A lefaro trigeir o'r heniaith gysefin.' 'There,' said Ab Iolo, 'that's Druidism'; and he directed my attention to so many expressions bearing upon the same subject, that I was completely mystified, and was obliged to acknowledge there appeared to be something handed down in these poems in concealed meanings, and which could not be made out by ordinary readers.'

## 14. The Llanover Collection

*This introduction to one of the last volumes largely based on Ioloic material describes the contents of the Llanover collection and demonstrates that the ready access granted to researchers meant that a considerable amount of material entered the public domain without necessarily being associated with Iolo's name.*

'Hopcyn', 'Introduction' to 'Cadrawd' and idem, Hen Gwndidau, Carolau, a Chywyddau being Sermons in Song in the Gwentian Dialect by Forty-Two Bards of Tir Iarll of the Tudor Period *(Bangor, 1910), pp. ix–xi.*

Courteous Reader,

In my researches for materials wherewith to illustrate the life and surroundings of the Elizabethan bard, Hopkin Thomas Philip of Gellifyd, in the parish of Llandyfodwg and County of Glamorgan, I naturally found in the manuscripts which I consulted much of the deeds and works of his contemporaries, which led me to study not only the works of that bard himself, but those of his companions and neighbours who formed the poetical fraternity known as the bards of Tir Iarll in the reign of good Queen Bess.

There are at Llanover, in the County of Monmouth, in the possession of the Hon. Mrs Herbert, a large number of manuscripts, in the Welsh language chiefly, which were written or collected by Iolo Morganwg; who was probably the most industrious scribe and antiquarian which Wales produced in the eighteenth century. Besides the old manuscripts collected by Iolo, some of them written by Llewelyn Sion of Llangewydd, in the reign of Queen Elizabeth; others by Thomas ab Ievan of Tre Bryn, in the parish of Coychurch, a little later, there are a number written in older hands. The bulk of the collection, however, was written by Iolo Morganwg himself on all sorts of paper, some on pages of old diaries, some on prospectuses and account books, others on advertisement sheets of various kinds. All these were collected together, sorted out apparently according to their sizes and bound so as to form volumes of different sizes, from a hundred pages to more than six times that number, from duodecimo to folio. There are altogether 75 of these volumes in the Llanover collection, some in the British Museum, and others in the possession of the descendants of the industrious scribe; the last, so the papers at Llanover say, numbering about half of what are now in the careful custody of the Hon. Mrs Herbert.

From the collection of Llanover, Welsh writers have been in the habit of contributing to magazines and periodicals, time after time, without acknowledging the source from which they gained their information. This remark is as true in the compilation of glossaries and dictionaries as in contributions to periodicals. Old Iolo carefully wrote down every rare word he heard or came across and put it in its setting. The results of his researches in various ways have been made use of by men who have had a reputation for scholarship and carefulness, while Iolo himself who provided them with the information, has sometimes been looked upon as a man who was careless in his transcripts and unscholarly in his methods. A comparison of Dr Gwenogvryn Evans's edition of the Black Book of Carmarthen with Iolo's transcripts may do somewhat to remove the erroneous opinion as to the one; and the assertion as to the other has in most cases been made by those who have never seen a Iolo MS so jealously are they guarded by their present custodian.

In the pages which follow, I have for convenience sake called every manuscript at Llanover from which I have quoted, or to which reference is made, which is not in the hand of Iolo Morganwg, – *Llanover MS*, while every MS in Iolo's handwriting has been called *Iolo MS*. They both form part of the same collection but it is necessary that such a distinction should be made.

There is nothing at Llanover which can justify the name of 'Catalogue' with regard to the collection. Ab Ithel who had the MSS. in his possession for some time drew up some sort of list of the volumes, but it is so meagre that if the student wishes to verify any particular passage or find out the source of information published in Welsh magazines in days gone by, he has to wade through MS after MS till he reaches what he desires to obtain. For instance, when the present writer tried to trace the source of a statement recorded in a valuable parish history that Lewis Hopkin the Bard, Wil Hopkin of Llangynwyd, the

Hopkiniaid of Coychurch, and Iolo Morganwg were descended from the same stock, he traced it to the magazine *Taliesin* published in 1859, where it appeared as information in a letter signed in Welsh 'Hynafieithydd,' with no indication that it was taken from the Iolo MSS. Thinking, however, that this was the case, I had to peruse 63 MSS. at Llanover before the information was found in the hand of Iolo Morganwg himself, almost word for word as it appeared in *Taliesin*, for the catalogue gave me no help at all in the matter, and there is no sort of index to what the Iolo MSS contain. Yet these volumes form the primary authority for the history of Glamorgan in whatever manner it may be treated and contain all sorts of information from the best way of planting a hedge to a Latin Calendar.

Iolo was the link between the Glamorgan bards of his day and that school of London Welshmen which did so much to enrich our national literature. He was, if I may so put it, their 'eye' in Glamorgan, and from an examination of the MSS of the (London) Welsh School in the British Museum and those at Llanover we know what a large portion of the *Myvyrian Archaiology* was due to his labours as collector and scribe.

## 15. 'The Summer'

*Many of the poems which Iolo had authored but had attributed to the medieval Welsh poet Dafydd ap Gwilym became favourites with scholars, translators and lay audiences. The poem 'The Summer' in particular was treasured as a work which not only demonstrated the supposed poetic gifts of Dafydd ap Gwilym, but also served to bind the 'Welsh Petrarch' closer to Iolo's Glamorgan.*

'The Summer' in Arthur James Johnes (Maelog), Translations into English Verse from the Poems of Davyth ap Gwilym, a Welsh Bard of the Fourteenth Century *(London, 1834), pp. 96–100.*

### THE SUMMER

The bard petitions the Summer to visit Glamorganshire with its choicest blessings. This fine poem was evidently composed after the death of his early patron, Ivor. The melancholy and affecting allusion to the lost friend of his youth, with which the poet concludes his gorgeous description of the summer landscape of South Wales, forms a transition of great beauty and pathos.

> THOU Summer! Father of delight,
> With thy dense spray and thickets deep;
> Gemmed monarch, with thy rapt'rous light,
> Rousing thy subject glens from sleep!
> Proud has thy march of triumph been,
> Thou prophet, prince of forest green!

Artificer of wood and tree,
Thou painter of unrivalled skill,
Who ever scattered gems like thee,
And gorgeous webs on park and hill?
'Till vale and hill with radiant dies,
Became another Paradise!
And thou hast sprinkled leaves and flow'rs,
And goodly chains of leafy bow'rs;
And bid thy youthful warblers sing
On oak and knoll the song of spring.
And blackbird's note of ecstacy
Burst loudly from the woodbine tree,
Till all the world is thronged with gladness –
Her multitudes have done with sadness!
Oh, Summer! Do I ask in vain?
Thus in thy glory wilt thou deign
My messenger to be?
Hence from the bowels of the land
Of wild, wild Gwyneth to the strand
Of fair Glamorgan – ocean's band –
Sweet margin of the sea!
To dear Glamorgan, when we part,
Oh, bear a thousand times my heart!
My blessing give a thousand times,
And crown with joy her glowing climes!
Take on her lovely vales thy stand,
And tread and trample round the land –
The beauteous shore whose harvest lies
All sheltered from inclement skies!
Radiant with corn and vineyards sweet,
And lakes of fish and mansions neat,
With halls of stone where kindness dwells,
And where each hospitable lord
Heaps for the stranger guest his board!
And where the gen'rous wine-cup swells;
With trees that bear the luscious pear
So thickly clust'ring every where,
That the fair country of my love
Looks dense as one continuous grove!
Her lofty woods with warblers teem,
Her fields with flow'rs that love the stream,
Her vallies varied crops display,
Eight kinds of corn, and three of hay;
Bright parlour, with her trefoiled floor!
Sweet garden spread on ocean's shore!
Glamorgan's bounteous knights award
Bright mead and burnished gold to me;

Glamorgan boasts of many a bard,
Well skilled in harp and vocal glee:
The districts round her border spread
From her have drawn their daily bread –
Her milk, her wheat, her varied stores,
Have been the life of distant shores!
And court and hamlet food have found
From the rich soil of Britain's southern bound.
And wilt thou then obey my power,
Thou Summer, in thy brightest hour?
To her thy glorious hues unfold
In one rich embassy of gold!
Her morns with bliss and splendour light,
And fondly kiss her mansions white;
Fling wealth and verdure o'er her bow'rs,
And for her gather all thy flow'rs!
Glance o'er her castles white with lime*
With genial glimmerings sublime;
Plant on the verdant coast thy feet,
Her lofty hills, her woodlands sweet;
Oh! lavish blossoms with thy hand
O'er all the forests of the land,
And let thy gifts like floods descending
O'er every hill and glen be blending;
Let orchard, garden, vine express
Thy fulness and thy fruitfulness –
O'er all the land of beauty fling
The costly traces of thy wing!
And thus mid all thy radiant flowers,
Thy thick'ning leaves and glossy bowers,
The poet's task shall be to glean
Roses and flowers that softly bloom,
(The jewels of the forest's gloom!)
And trefoils wove in pavement green,
With sad humility to grace
His golden Ivor's resting place!

To enable the reader to perceive the full force of many of the allusions contained in the foregoing beautiful poem, it is necessary to give a brief account of the peculiar features of the fine district to which it relates. Glamorganshire, in its northern districts, is occupied by wild and romantic mountains, from the foot of which to the sea extends the rich vale of Glamorgan, proverbially called the garden of Wales. In this latter division, the

---

\* 'Her castles white with lime.' 'It has from very remote antiquity been the custom', says Edward Williams (Iolo Morgamog) [sic], to 'whitewash the houses in Glamorganshire, not only the inside but the outside also.'

climate is so mild that the products of the more southern countries of Europe are found to ripen in the open air; hence there is a peculiar splendour in the opening of this poem, where the bard contrasts the bleak mountains of North Wales, amongst which he is a sojourner, with this delicious region, in favour of which he invokes all the gifts of the summer and the sun.

This country is equally remarkable for the diversified beauty of its landcapes. 'Its scenery', says a tourist, 'is distinguished by unbounded variety; *it is full of pictures* from one end of the district to the other.'* The ruins of its princely castles, in which the bard was entertained, still excite the admiration of the tourist. Edifices 'white with lime' continue a distinguished feature in the landscape. Even the cottages are generally of a dazzling white, and adorned with the woodbine and eglantine – images which so often occur in the productions of the bard.

The last lines of the poem, in which the poet describes himself as gathering flowers to decorate the grave of Ivor, allude to a usage still prevalent in Glamorganshire and other parts of Wales, where it is considered a mark of respect and affection to plant flowers over the remains of the dead. Without adverting to this beautiful custom, the pathetic lines with which the bard concludes would not be fully understood. It will appear from the life of the poet, that the county of Glamorgan was to him – as he represents it in this poem – a land of hospitable patrons and kind protectors, whose mansions were ever open to receive him, and by whose generosity he was released from prison in the extremity of his distress.

## 16. *The Bardic Line of Succession at Tir Iarll*

*This poem, which Cadrawd composed for L. J. Hopkin-James's volume on the poets of the Hopkin family of Glamorgan, condenses the embellished literary history of Glamorgan in content and form. Written in the* triban *metre, of which Cadrawd had collected many examples and copied many others from Iolo, it eulogizes Glamorgan as 'the land of the bards and the harpists' ('gwlad beirdd a thelynorion'). The county's history is recounted through its (invented) line of succession, which stretches from the eponymous founder Morgan to Arthur, Rhys Goch ap Rhicert, Ieuan Fawr, Edeyrn Dafod Aur, the women of Tŷ Talwyn, Wil Hopcyn and Iolo Morganwg.*

---

* Malkin's South Wales.

*Cadrawd, 'Cyfarchiad i'r Awdur. Ar fesur 'Triban Morganwg' in Lemuel James 'Hopcyn',* Hopkiniaid Morganwg Being a Genealogical Biography of the Hopkin Family of Glamorgan with the Works of Hopkin Thomas Philip and Lewis Hopkin *(Bangor, 1909), pp. xiii–xiv.*

### CYFARCHIAD I'R AWDUR
#### Ar fesur 'Triban Morganwg'
#### Gan CADRAWD

'Morganwg Muriau Gwynion,'
Sy' 'rioed uwch ben ei digon;
Toreithiog o bob ffrwythydd pêr,
A syber foneddigion.

Gwlad Beirdd a Thelynorion,
Llyngeswyr, Cadfridogion;
Cenhadon Hedd, na bu eu gwell,
A chawell dysgedigion.

Gwlad Forgan eang enwog,
A'i Bröydd maeth gwerddonog;
A'i Blaenau'n anad unrhyw Sir
Mewn mwnau'n wir gyfoethog.

I hon mae Cadair hynod,
Mor hen ag Arthur fawrglod;
Ag ym Morganwg ym mhob oes
Bu cynal, 'MOES A DEFOD.'

Tir Iarll a wnaed yn Glodgar,
Gan Feirdd fu'n llon eu trydar; –
Wrth gadw'n fyw gofiannau hen,
A choledd awen hygar.

Rhys Goch a'i gerdd fugeiliol,
A Ieuan Fawr synhwyrol;
'Sgrifenodd ini yn ddiflin,
Y Mabinogion gwrol.

Hen Edeyrn a'i Aur Dafod,
A Gwilym Tew fy hyglod;
A Dafydd Ddu, mor llawn o swyn,
A Llawdden fwyn a pharod.

Mhlith rhai o uchel alwad,
Fu'n cadw'r iaith mor decad;
Cawn Lewys o Forganwg lòn
Ag Einion y Pen Lefiad.

Y nesaf dorf sy'n canlyn,
Hil merched y Tytalwyn;
A'r rhai yn meddu'r Awen gûn,
I'r rhai'n bob un yn perthyn.

Yn Nghelli Fid heb eudyb
Bu Hopcin Thomas Phylyb;
Yn flaenaf wr mysg lleyg a llèn,
A'i Awen ddigyffelyb.

Enwocaf o'r Morganiaid,
Yw tylwyth yr Hopciniaid;
Mae'i hanes yma yn ddiwên
Brydyddion hen a thelaid.

Ceir sôn am Lewys ddiwg,
O'r Hendref, Llandyfodwg;
Ac hefyd am Wil Hopcyn ddèl,
Y carwr ffèl, ond di-dwg.

Cawn yn y gyfrol yma
Rhai o'r gwroniaid cynta,
Sefydlodd y Weriniaeth Fawr
Ei gelwir 'nawr Amer'ca.

O Einion Llangyfelach,
Hyd Iolo na bu'i ffelach;
Mae'r edryb yn y gyfrol hon,
Gan Berson Ystrad Mynach.

## 17. 'The Lark'

*Most of the poetry attributed to Iolo was published to illustrate aspects of his character. This* englyn *to the lark was one of the few examples to be published on the strength of its poetic merits.*

W. Rowlands, 'Cadwen o Englynion', Y Traethodydd, XXII (1867), 119.

I'r Ehedydd:
'Hedydd yn brydydd bwriadawl – a gyrch
  A gorchest blygeiniawl,
    I weini'n bur awenawl,
Cynnar ei gerdd, cân i'r gwawl.
                            *Iolo Morganwg*

## 18. In the Service of the Unitarian Faith

*The fourth stanza of psalm no. 21 from the first volume of Iolo's* Salmau yr Eglwys yn yr Anialwch *(1812) provided the basis for the question, 'How does the religious experience of Iolo Morganwg reinforce the moral of these verses?' which was included in a Unitarian catechism for advanced pupils. The verses were designed to encourage pupils to strive to make this world a better place in obedience to God's will.*

Y Gymdeithas Undodaidd Gymreig, Adran yr Ysgol Sul,
Holwyddoreg ar Elfenau Crefydd: Safon II *[gan Rees Jenkin Jones]*
(Treforis a Clydach, n.d. ante 1911), p. 8.

26. G. Sut mae profiad crefyddol Iolo Morganwg yn cadarnhau addysg y gwersi hyn? –

>Dod i mi'r fendith, fy Nuw mawr,
>Fod rhan o'r byd lle'r wyf yn awr,
>Yn nes at ffyrdd dy 'wyllys di,
>Yn well ryw faint o'm achos i:
>Os hyn a gaf o'th nefol ddawn,
>Caf y byd hwn yn hyfryd iawn:
>Tra threiglwyf ei ddiffaethwch ef
>Caf deimlo'm enaid yn y nef.

## 19. Assessing Early Criticism

*This anonymous judgement on the relative merits and demerits of the work and opinions of Iolo and Edward 'Celtic' Davies is reasonably balanced and perceptive.*

Anon., 'A Sketch of the History of the Britons continued', Cambrian Register, III (1819), 8–9.

Of all our modern writers on the subject of druidism none have distinguished themselves so much as Messrs Edward Williams, William Owen, and Edward Davies. They are all very intimately and extensively acquainted with British antiquities and bardic lore, and have thrown considerable light on many of the points they have investigated; but there are some important points on which the latter differs very widely in opinion from the others. This may not be very hard to account for. Messrs Williams and Owen, being of the bardic order, would naturally think favourably of druidism; Mr Davies, on the other hand, being himself of a very different order, would view druidism in a different light, and discover defects in it which the others had overlooked, while he himself, perhaps, would overlook defects equally glaring belonging to his own order or hierarchy ... The former placed too much reliance on the institutes of the chair of Glamorgan, whose legitimacy is doubted, and the latter was, perhaps, equally influenced and misled by the Bryantian System of Mythology ... The former may also be said to have been carried too far by his strong attachment to liberty and the rights of man, and the latter by a dread of innovation, and a wish to perpetuate the present established order of things. Under such circumstances their accounts or disquisitions would necessarily prove defective, and like too many historical productions, afford the authors but a slender claim to the merit or praise of impartiality.

## 20. Thomas Stephens and the Bardic Script

*Thomas Stephens of Merthyr was unquestionably the most important amateur critic of Iolo's work in Victorian times. He was the first Welsh scholar to apply principles of source and textual criticism to Iolo's material in order to establish its authenticity. Although he maintained that 'the character of old Iolo has come out unscathed through this inquiry', Stephens fatally undermined Iolo's reputation for historical accuracy and truthfulness.*

*Thomas Stephens, 'An Essay on the Bardic Alphabet called "Coelbren y Beirdd"', Arch. Camb., fourth series, III, no. 11 (1872), 181–210.*

### AN ESSAY ON THE BARDIC ALPHABET CALLED 'COELBREN Y BEIRDD'

The Chair of Glamorgan, meaning the traditions, speculations, and usages connected therewith, will form a very interesting chapter in the record of Cambrian bardism whenever the literature of Wales shall attain the dignity of having a historian; but hitherto its real origin, true character, actual importance, and correct place in history, have been the subjects of much misapprehension. Originating in the fourteenth century, it claims an antiquity coeval with the world itself; forming the laws of Hywel Dda into triads, it calls and has called them the laws of Dyvynwal Moelmud, who, living in the sixth century of our era, has been thrust back six centuries before Christ; pilfering Arthur from Cornwall, it places him at Caerlleon, and calls him king of Gwent and Morganwg; taking Brân ab Llyr Llediaith *ab Brychwel Powys* from the people of Merioneth, it places him at Dunraven; and antedating him at least six hundred and fifty years (*Brochwael Eschitrauc moritur* A.D. 662, *Annales Cambriae*), it claims for Morganwg the first acquaintance with Christianity; and for its historical triads, many of them the fabulous and fictitious things of yesterday, bearing the unmistakable marks of recentness in their ideas and phraseology, it claims authority to modify and supersede all authentic history.

The Chair of Glamorgan is an instructive illustration of the extravagances of the Silurian imagination, which has vitiated to a greater or less extent all the literary records of this district, and appears to have been so greatly preponderant over the logical faculties as to have rendered the mind of Morganwg incapable of scientific accuracy or of historic truthfulness. The bards of Morganwg have created a system of bardism bearing inherent evidences of recent fabrication; a bardism the exact reverse of that of classic history; a bardism which degrades the Druid from the first place in the trinity of Druids, Ovates, and Bards, and elevates the bard from the lowest rank to the first; a bardism which never could have existed until real Druidism became a thing of tradition; and, in short, a fabrication of the fourteenth and subsequent centuries, of which one fact will reveal both the *animus* and the age. In the Laws of Howel, the clerk of the courts of law is invariably a *priest*; but in the fabricated laws of Dyvynwal Moelmud, things which Mr Aneurin Owen (the best authority upon the subject) has declared to be no older than the sixteenth century (Laws of Howel, preface, xx, vol. i), the place of the *priest* is invariably filled by a *bard*! Here is a key to the age and object of the new hierarchy. *Verbum sapienti satis est.*

To conclude. The Chair of Glamorgan has falsified the history of bardism, corrupted the genealogies of Glamorgan, vitiated the chronicles of Gwent and Morganwg, deluded the weak-minded with specious absurdities, and given such currency to 'a falsehood, a delusion, and a snare,' that the author of the *Celtic Researches* was almost the only Welshman sagacious enough to detect the forgery, strong-minded enough to resist its seductions, and honest enough to expose its real character.

'Coelbren y Beirdd' is the offspring of the same parent. It claims to be an emanation from Heaven. It is an emanation from the Roman alphabet. It professes to have descended to us from the creation of the world. It was the creation of the fifteenth century. It assumes to have been known wherever the Cymric race existed. It was not practically known and used beyond the limits of Gwent and Morganwg. Let us, however, be more minute in our inquiries. Let us examine the proofs adduced in favour of its antiquity, and let us produce proofs to sustain these counter-assertions.

1. First, then, let us examine the evidences adduced by the late Ab Iolo in his essay upon this subject, – an essay which we may praise at once for the fulness of its treatment of the subject, the clearness of the arrangement, and the ability with which the antiquity of the 'Coelbren' is urged and defended.

In the notes to the poems of Lewis Glyn Cothi, edited by Tegid (p. 260), published in 1837, we find the following remarks:

'Dr W. O. Pughe received the 'Coelbren y Beirdd' as genuine from the profound antiquarian and poet, the late Mr Edward Williams of Glamorganshire, well known by the bardic appellation of 'Iolo Morganwg.'

'In the archives of the library of Jesus College, Oxford, there is a mahogany *Peithynen*, on which is inscribed the bardic alphabet, consisting of sixteen primitives and twenty-two derivatives, cut with a knife by Iolo Morganwg, and presented by him to the College. Dr W. O. Pughe, in his Grammar, has, however, arranged the order of the alphabet differently to that on the *Peithynen*, and *has also added five letters to the class of derivatives*, of which additional letters he acknowledged himself to be the author. *But the public has not as yet been informed from what source Mr Edward Williams received the bardic alphabet, of which he has been the promulgator, not to say the inventor.*

...

A prize was offered for an essay upon the subject, at Abergavenny, in the following year (1838). Two competitors appeared, if I recollect rightly, and the prize was awarded to Ab Iolo, of whose essay the Rev. Thomas Price gave the following opinion: 'I must say that this is one of the most extraordinary and important productions that have come under my notice, either as a prize composition or one of any other description, inasmuch as the author, in supporting the theory of the *Coelbren*, does not merely establish the possibility of its genuineness by shewing its consistency with the alphabets of ancient times, but he produces most distinct and decided evidences of its having been in use amongst the Welsh bards as late as the sixteenth century.'

Since that time the antiquity of the *Coelbren* has become an accepted fact, and the only living critic who has refused to accept this conclusion is the author of *The Literature of the Kymry*.

...

Many upholders of the *Coelbren*, having neither the learning nor the candour of Ab Iolo, still affect to believe it to be original, and to have been regularly developed from the straight lines in the 'Nod Cyfrin,' / | \; and as all the letters are made in straight lines, there is a speciousness about this hypothesis which has a great charm for unreflecting people. But may not the / | \ have been the consequence, and not the origin, of the *Coelbren*? It must also be observed that this hypothesis provokes more questions than it answers. If the alphabet is original, how comes it to have such a close resemblance to the Roman as to have the same letters for the same sounds, without a single exception? How comes it to resemble the Roman so closely in form that by changing an angle into a curve, or a curve into an angle, the two alphabets are mutually convertible?

...

How, again, does it come to pass that where the Roman alphabet is defective, then the older forms of the *Coelbren* are defective also? The Welsh is a language full of mutations which the Roman alphabet is incompetent to express; and yet here, where an alphabet professing to be original might be expected to be most complete, the *Coelbren* is just as deficient as the Roman alphabet, for all the derivatives are known and confessed to be of recent introduction; and even Ab Iolo does not claim for them a higher antiquity than the twelfth century. Iolo attributes the revival of the *Coelbren* and invention of some of the derivatives to the fourteenth century. (Waring, p. 189.)

2. *Coelbren y Beirdd* was always cut on wood; and the reason alleged by the old bards of Glamorgan for the use of that material was, that wood was obtainable where paper and parchment were not. (Ab Iolo, 38.) But our modern bards are not quite so candid, and they must needs have a grander reason. It is this. Wood was selected because it was suited to the alphabet, *i.e.*, to the form of the bardic letters. It will at once occur to the reflective mind that the cart is here placed before the horse. But for the present let that pass.

The practice of cutting letters on wood was known ages before *Coelbren y Beirdd* was ever heard of, and probably will be practised when the *Coelbren* is either rightly appreciated or consigned 'to the tomb of all the Capulets.' Thus in the Bible we read, in Ezekiel, 'The word of the Lord came again unto me, saying: Moreover, thou son of man, *take thee one stick*, and *write upon it*, For Judah, and for the children of Israel, his companions: then *take another stick*, and *write upon it*, For Joseph, the stick of Ephraim, and for all the house of Israel, his companions.' (Ezek, xxxvii, 15, 16; see also 17–20.) The same practice is alluded to by Horace in a passage of the *De Arte Poeticâ*, descriptive of the functions and influence of the ancient poets.

In this passage it is probable that Horace has embodied Greek traditions; and for that reason I have inverted the ordinary chronology, and given the Roman lyrist precedence of the Greek philosopher named in the next sentence. Inscriptions on wood were well known to the Greeks, and we have an authentic evidence of the fact in the case of the laws of Solon. 'All his laws,' says Plutarch, 'were to continue in force for a hundred years, and were written upon wooden tables, which might be turned round in the oblong cases that contained them.' Some small remains of them are preserved in the *Prytaneum* to this day. They were called *cyrbes*, as Aristotle tells us; and Callinus, the comic poet (Englished), thus speaks of them:

> By the great names of Solon and of Draco,
> Whose *cyrbes* now but serve to boil our pulse.

(Plutarch, *Life of Solon*.) Here, then, we have cases in point, where the Hebrew, the Greek, and possibly the Roman alphabet, were written on wood; and yet each of those alphabets had angles, as we know, but *also horizontal lines*, which the *Coelbren* has not; and they were, in nearly all respects, essentially different. The argument, therefore, fails most completely. The alphabets of various nations have been and may be cut upon wood without any further deviation from their original form than a tendency to substitute angles for curved lines, where such exist; and a comparison of letters will at once shew that the angles of the *Coelbren* correspond to the curves of *the italic letters, but to those of no other letters whatever*.

. . .

There is no doubt that the Germans and Scandinavians had alphabets of their own anterior to having had any intercourse with the Christian missionaries; but beyond the fact of their being in the habit of writing on planed rods, there is nothing to countenance *Coelbren y Beirdd*; for the Runic alphabet consisting, like the ancient Greek, of sixteen letters, was different in many respects from the bardic and the Roman letters.

...

II. The next subject of inquiry is the antiquity of this alphabet. Very extraordinary assertions are made on this head; and the pretensions of the *Coelbren* to a remote antiquity may be embodied in the following propositions:

1. 'That the ineffable name of the Deity, / | \, was revealed to Menyw ab y Teirgwaedd at the creation (Menyw being the first man, Adam); and that from these elements his son, Einigan Gawr, formed an alphabet of ten letters.'

2. 'That the nation of the Cymry extended the number of characters to sixteen before they left their original country, called *Deffrobani* (Taprobane, *i.e.*, Ceylon); and that since their arrival in Britain they added two other letters, *having eighteen letters prior to the arrival of the Romans.*'

3. 'That the number of primitives was afterwards extended to twenty; that at a subsequent period eighteen derivatives were added; and that some of these compounds appear in old MSS., but that all of them do not.'

4. 'That *Coelbren y Beirdd*, or the bardic alphabet, was anterior to *Coelbren y Myneich*, or the alphabet of the monks, and the latter anterior to the alphabet on the tombstones of Lantwit Major; and that these were respectively modifications of each other.'

5. 'That *Coelbren y Beirdd* was known to the ancient bards and to the bards of the middle ages.'

6. 'That it was used as late as the sixteenth century.'

Let us now examine these statements in detail. The recklessness of assertion which characterises the bards of Glamorgan may be judged of by the positiveness with which they speak of remote periods, when Gildas tells us *that there were no British documents in his day*; when Nennius, professedly recounting the traditions of his ancestors, gives not the slightest sanction to the recent speculations of Glamorgan; and when it is borne in mind that authentic Welsh tradition does not even penetrate the Roman period, nor ascend beyond the sixth century. This is a crucial test: during four hundred years of Roman occupation, Welsh history cannot add a single fact to the scanty statements of the Roman and Byzantine historians; and Gildas, in writing the history of Britain prior to 560 A.D. had to depend wholly and solely upon foreign sources of information. Under such circumstances we have a right to ask for some proof of such positive assertions; but not a scrap of evidence, documentary or monumental, can be produced in support of assertions at variance with all authentic history, and depending only on the statement of men of recent date, whose historical knowledge is extremely incorrect, and whose information was as inaccurate as their assertions were untrue. Thus Llywelyn Sion says that *ten* characters (*i.e.*, a, p, c, e, t, i, l, r, o, s) were brought by the Cymry to Britain; and afterwards six other characters were added, viz., m, n, b, f, g, h; *'and in the time of Dyvynwal Moelmud, about six hundred years, by record and computation, before the birth of Christ,* the sixteen letters were established.' This date is precisely that given by Geoffrey of Monmouth, and *that is false*; for, as I shall presently shew, Dyvynwal lived six hundred years after Christ. But this, with a hundred other instances which I might cite, will serve to shew that the traditions of the Chair of Glamorgan are founded on the lies and misrepresentations of that prince of fabulous historians. How the theory has been constructed is clear. It is not founded on history, but on speculations. The first ten letters are primitives, or represent distinct sounds. The others represent modifications of those primary sounds; and the same rule will apply to all the subsequent additions. Welsh traditions of the sixteenth century cannot be accepted as authorities upon this subject, even if they did not contradict each other, which they frequently do; for while one account states they had eighteen letters before the arrival of the Romans (Waring's *Iolo Morganwg,* 189), a second expressly states that the seventeenth and eighteenth were introduced after the coming of the faith in Christ (*Iolo MSS* 617); and while one says they had sixteen letters on coming to Britain, another says they had only ten (*Iolo MSS* 623). Such is the testimony on which the antiquity of the *Coelbren* depends, and by which it is supposed to be proved, – a testimony, moreover, which bears inherent evidence of recentness; for the idea that all the human race came from Taprobane (Deffrobani Ynys), or the island of Ceylon, belongs to the twelfth and fourteenth centuries, and is of monkish origin. The Glamorgan theory of British colonisation by Hu Gadarn belongs to the same period; and instead of being older than the Trojan theory, is very much later. Aedd is a Gaelic or rather Scottish name; and probably the whole theory, with Hu Gadarn, Aedd, and Prydain, have been borrowed from the traditions of North Britain. It certainly is not one of pure Cambrian growth; and the first notice we have of it occurs in the poem of Rhys Brydydd, at the close of the fourteenth century, when Sion Cent described the bards of Glamorgan as 'the lying bards of Hu.'

We come, in the next place, to notice the *Coelbren* in connexion with Menw ab y Teirgwaedd. According to the speculations of the sixteenth century, Menw was Adam, the first of living men; but according to the more authentic tradition embodied in the Mabinogi of Kilhwch and Olwen, *Menw ab y Teirgwaedd was the contemporary of King Arthur;* and upon such a subject, a document of about the twelfth century is entitled to respect. The force of this objection has been felt; and an attempt has been made to evade it under cover of the assumption that the Arthur of this tale was not the famous hero, but a mythological personage belonging to the dawn of creation. A wild speculation of Mr Owen's in the *Cambrian Biography*, that the Arthur of the tale was Nimrod, gives some support to this assumption; but really it is not too much to expect that our antiquarians should at least read the documents they profess to interpret. Had Mr Owen done this, his speculation would probably never have been formed. The Mabinogi of Kilhwch and Olwen belongs to the first class of the Arthurian romances in which the truth of history had not yet been violated, and the hero had not been transferred from Gelliwig to Caerlleon. It makes frequent allusions to his residence at Gelliwig in Cornwall, and enumerates among his friends, relations, or courtiers, all the great names of that day. Let us select a few: – 1, Cynwyl Sant; 2, Sandde Bryd Angel; 3, Morvran ab Tegid, – the three men who escaped from the battle of Camlan in A.D. 542; 4, '*Teleesin pennbeird*', about 560–600; 5, '*Gilda m. Kaw*', who died in 570 (*Annales Cambriae*); 6, '*Morgant Hael,*' of Glamorgan, *i.e.* Morgan Mwynvawr; 7, Morvudd, daughter of Urien Rheged who fell in 584; 8, Dunawd, son of Pabo, who died in 595; 9, Sawyl Benuchel, his brother; 10, Rhuvawn Bevyr ab Gwyddno, who fell at Cattraeth in 603; 11, Manawyddan ab Llyr (brother of Brân), ditto; 12, Eurneid, daughter of Cynon ab Clydno, ditto; 13, Maelwyr, son of Baeddan, who signalised himself at Cattraeth; 14, Gwrhir Gwalstawd Ieithoedd, circa 612; 15, *Dyvynwal Moel* (*i.e., Dyvynwal Moelmud!*); 16, Menw. m. Teirgwaed; 17, Annyaniawc. m. Menw. m. Teirgwaed.

Here, then, are seventeen names out of about two hundred, selected because their age can be ascertained; and fourteen out of the seventeen were living about the time named in the Mabinogi. Being substantially correct in all the instances in which we can test it, on what ground shall we deny the correctness of that document in the cases of the three persons last named? There is no ground for doubting the correctness of this statement. Menw ab y Teirgwaedd lived in the sixth century of the Christian era, and in the twelfth century he was deemed to have been the contemporary of King Arthur. The account of Menw given in the Triads corresponds with this statement. He is there said to have been the contemporary of Uthr Pendragon, the father of King Arthur, to whom he showed his magical arts; and the coincidence of these authorities is quite conclusive as to the age of Menw, – Menyw Hen, or Menw ab y Teirgwaedd, as he is variously described. He is also called the son of Gwaedd, and said to have been the son of a bard. (*Myv. Arch.*, ii, 71.) Davydd ab Gwilym appears to refer Menw to the same period, for he speaks of him in his military character as one of the knights of King Arthur:

> Tri milwr gynt, trem olud,
> A wyddyn' cyn no hyn hud;
> Cad brofiad, ceidw brif enw,
> Cyntaf, addfwynaf, oedd Fenw,
> Ar ail fydd dydd da deall,
> Eiddilic Cór, Wyddel call;
> Trydydd oedd ger muroedd Mon,
> Maeth, rhwy' arfaeth rhi Arfon.
> (Works, 207.)

And the editors of his works were of the same opinion, for their note on this passage runs thus (p. 540): 'Menw, or Menyw ab Teirgwaedd, famous for being one of the three chief conjurors of Britain, and a disciple of Merddin Emrys', a bard of the latter part of the fifth century. Thus we make 'assurance doubly sure'.

The character attributed to him in these documents deserves more attention. In the Mabinogi above named he is represented to have had the power of transforming himself into any shape he desired, and of casting an illusion over the eyes of others, so as to see all others, but to be himself unseen. The two oldest sets of Triads, placed first in the *Myv. Arch.* (vol. ii), attribute to him the same character. He is termed one of the three 'priv lledrithiawg', or chief enchanters of the island; and also one of the three 'gwyr hud a lledrith,' or men of illusion and phantasy; and the illusion (*i.e.*, the art of Menw) which he taught to Uthr Pendragon, is said to have been one of the three greatest illusions of the isle of Britain. (*Myv. Arch.*, ii, 7, 12.) The third set of Triads is written in the Glamorgan dialect of the sixteenth century, and is fuller than the others; but it is also later than the others, and contains a larger portion of romantic, mythologic, and unhistoric matter. To the magical attributes above named it adds a new character, but whether that was clerical or educational depends upon the interpretation of the word 'mebydd'. The word occurs in a compound form in the following triad: 'Tri chynfebydd ynys Prydain: Tydain Tad Awen; Menyw Hen; a Gwrhir bardd Teilaw yn Llan Daf: a thri meib beirdd oeddynt.' (*Myv. Arch.*, ii, 71; tr. 93.) What is the meaning of 'mebydd' in this compound, 'cynfebydd'? Mr Owen (*sub* 'Menyw') translates it 'instructor', and (*sub* 'Deiniol') 'bachelor'; but both renderings appear to be unsound, else what shall we make of 'Einion, *Mebydd* Clynog Fawr', and of the 'mebyddiaeth' given to Geoffrey in Llandaff? (*Myv. Arch.*, ii, 566.) Williams follows Owen in the former instances; in the latter cases, Owen and Williams read, 'Einion, mebydd, or *archdeacon* of Celynog'; and Williams (*sub* 'Geoffrey') renders 'mebyddiaeth' by an 'archdeaconry'. If this be so, we should read, 'The three primary archdeacons of the isle of Britain: Tydain, the father of poetic genius; Menyw the aged; and Gwrhir, the bard of Teilo, at Llandaff; and they were three sons of bards.' Hence we have another link in the chain of evidence which locates Menw in the sixth century, and makes him to have been a Christian priest.

These two meanings, however, are not irreconcilable: archdeaconries were the rewards of learning, and Geoffrey received his for his learning and knowledge ('am ei ddysg ai wybodau,' – *Myv. Arch.*, ii, 566).

This brings us to the consideration of the relation of Menw to Welsh literature. Is there no foundation for the traditional belief which attributes to him the invention of the *Coelbren*? for it is sometimes attributed to him as well as to his son (?) Einigan. In strict truth I believe there is none. Menw no more invented the *Coelbren*, or any other alphabet, than Orpheus tamed lions or Amphion built the Theban wall. But there may be a sense in which the statement has some truth, and it is this. During the whole period of the Roman occupation of this island we hear or read nothing of the British bards. When the legions had departed, the national spirit revived. A century afterwards, or a little more, we have the poems of Llywarch Hen and Taliesin; and we read of other bards, that they sang sweetly in their day, though their strains have been disjointed in the lapse of time, and have not come down to us. The Welsh language, as it exists in the poems of the bards, exhibits a high degree of cultivation; and during the fifth and sixth centuries there certainly was either a new creation or a revival of Cymric poetry.

In that revival the people of Ireland may have played an important part. Towards the close of the Roman occupation a colony of them settled on the western coast, and though driven from South Wales, retained for centuries the hold they possessed on Mona and Arvon. These were the people whose memory survives in *Cytiau'r Gwyddelod*; and it was from them that there sprang the celebrated magicians, Math ab Mathonwy, Gwydion ab Dôn, 'Eiddilic Cór, Wyddell call', and probably Menyw ab Teirgwaedd. The people of Ireland never were subdued by the Romans; and during the whole period from A.D. 43 to 449, when the legions left, they had preserved their own language and their own literature. The Gwyddelod of Mon and Arvon were celebrated for their knowledge in the sixth century, and I am not without a strong suspicion that they exerted considerable influence in the revival of Cambrian literature at that time.

This is probably the latent truth embodied in the traditions of Glamorgan, and in that literary movement it is possible that Menyw may have been an active agent. There was no need for him to invent an alphabet at a time when the Latin and ecclesiastical historians were read and studied, and when Gildas wrote his *De Excidio Britanniæ*; but there was a necessity for giving a written form to the language of the Cymry, and Menyw may have been the first who did so. The alphabet used in the sixth century, to express the Welsh language, was that of the Romans, as witness the oldest Welsh inscription known to exist, that on the stone of St Cadvan.

The *Coelbren*, therefore, was not known in the sixth century; and it is worthy of remark that no document that can be shewn to be older than the sixteenth century, connects the name of Menw with that alphabet; or, indeed, attributes to him any literary character at all. The Mabinogi, the passage from Davydd ab Gwilym, and the Triads, attribute magical knowledge to that personage; but not one of them makes the least allusion to the invention of the *Coelbren*, or to letters of any kind. The earliest allusion to Menw in that character occurs in 'Englynion of Gorugiau,' printed in the *Iolo MSS* (pp. 262–4), *without a hint as to whence they have been derived*. They profess to be the productions of the tenth century. Their language is as regular as that of the present day, as witness the verse in question:

> Goruc Menw ap y Teirgwaedd
> Gof glud ar y glywai floedd,
> A chyd a chadw cyfarwydd.

Here are three *dd*s; and yet that consonant (*d*) only began to be doubled, to express this sound, after A.D. 1620. (Lhwyd, *Arch. Brit.*, 227.) The internal evidence also is opposed to the idea of the antiquity of these verses; and it is in vain that Iolo attempts to get over this difficulty. Geraint Vardd Glas, the asserted author, is said to have been the same person as *Asserius Menevensis*, who died in A.D. 906 (*Brut y Tywysogion* and *Brut y Saeson*, *Myv. Arch.*, ii, 484 and 485); and yet these verses name the enactment of the Welsh laws as the achievement of Hywel Dda, who framed his laws about 926, and died in 948! These verses contain all the historical mistakes of the old Glamorgan bards, and they are probably of the same age as the prose *Cyfymbwyll*, etc., and other stories of the same kind. They belong to the sixteenth century.

As to Einigan, we may come to the same conclusion. There were two persons, at least, of that name in the sixth century, viz., Enddigant, the bard; and Einygan, the father of Eiddin or Heiddyn ab Einigan, the assassin of Aneurin. The latter personage is sometimes called Einiawn (*Myv. Arch.*, ii, 77) instead of Einigan; and, as we have seen, the Mabinogi gives the name of Annyaniawc to the son of Menw. Are they the same? The rampant bards will have Einigan to have been the Enoch of the antediluvian world, and for my part they are welcome to think so; but I must be permitted to observe that this is only another case of a fallacy very prevalent among us Cambrians. We reasoned in the same way during the reign of Elizabeth, and our logical failing attracted the notice of Shakespeare, who displays the weakness in the character of Fluellen: 'There is a river in Macedon and a river in Monmouth, and there is salmon in both,' *ergo* they are the same. Just so in this case. There was a man named Enoch, and one named Einygan: there was a man in India named Menu, and a Cambrian named Menw. There was a Hu Gadarn; the learned chancellor of Llandaff rejoiced in the name of Hugh: *ergo* they are the same, for let us supply the major premiss. There never was but one Enoch, Menw, or Hugh! This is a fair specimen of the bardic reasoning generally; and but that it afforded an opportunity for making these remarks, the asserted identity of Enoch and Einigan might have been left to die a natural death.

. . .

Ab Iolo asserts that *Coelbren y Myneich* was a variation of *Coelbren y Beirdd*, and the alphabet on the Lantwit stones a variation of *Coelbren y Myneich*. Here, again, we have the old practice of begging the question. The inscriptions at Lantwit speak for themselves. They are in Latin, and belong to the sixth and seventh centuries, *i.e.*, the earliest; and when the upholders of the *Coelbren* produce evidences of an earlier date, it will be soon enough to derive the Lantwit alphabet from that. At present the probabilities are all the other way. There is no historical authority for the antiquity of the *Coelbren* older than Llewelyn Sion, writing in 1613; and the same person is also the sole authority for the existence of such a thing as *Coelbren y Myneich*. The vague assertions of such an authority are valueless; and we cannot accept any man's *ipse dixit* for the establishment of an error, the more especially as this is a matter of history transcending the limit of personal experience. If there be any relation at all between the Lantwit inscriptions and the *Coelbren*, it must be the opposite of that expressed in the proposition, and the *Coelbren* must be the child, and not the parent.

In support of the assertion that the *Coelbren* was known to the older bards, Aneurin and Taliesin, the only semblance of proof is that adduced by Ab Iolo; but unfortunately only two of the first twelve extracts have any claim to be accounted old, and only one of them really is so.

...

The last proposition is the only one that is really true. It is clear, from the language of Llywelyn Sion (and when speaking of his own personal knowledge his testimony is conclusive), that the practice was known in the sixteenth century, though it had nearly died out in his day. His testimony, however, is very instructive, and is here translated: 'When the art of making parchment became known, writing letters on wood ceased; but yet the bards and poets preserved the old art, and until recent times there was not one in a hundred of the regular bards who could not read the *Coelbren*, and cut it with his own hands, as is required by the usage of the bards, viz., three things a bard should make with his own hands, his *Coelbren*, his roll, and his parchment. Many besides the poets knew the *Coelbren*, in the memory of persons now living; and many, not long ago, used to keep their domestic accounts on tallies cut with a knife.' (Ab Iolo, p. 22.) Assuming this to have been written about 1613, it would point out 1550 as about the time when the *Coelbren* was in frequent use. The earliest bardic testimony is that of Davydd ab Gwilym, who died about 1400, and composed the elegy of Gruffydd ab Adda after 1390. The period between the years 1400 and 1550 will, therefore, form the era of the *Coelbren*; and the question now arises, how came it to assume prominence at that time?

It will be observed that the *Coelbren* is first referred to in our poetry soon after the insurrection of Owen Glyndwr. This drew upon the Cymry two hard enactments, dated 1401 and 1403 (the second and fourth of Henry IV), in which it was decreed that no Welshman should hold any office or trust, or keep a castle; that no Welshman should carry arms into a town, nor along any public road; that no Welshman should marry any Englishwoman, nor any Englishman marry a Welshwoman; that no public gatherings should be celebrated without license; and that the minstrels, bards, rhymers, 'westours,' and other vagabond Welshmen, were not to levy *cymhortha* under a penalty of imprisonment for one year. (*Wotton's Leges Walliae.*) Officers were to see that no arms were introduced in the guise of merchandise; and according to the traditions of Glamorgan (*Iolo MSS* 620), *paper*, parchment, and writing materials, were also forbidden to be brought into Wales, or manufactured there. This seems to be the foundation-stone in the history of the *Coelbren*; and when it is borne in mind that paper-making was then unknown in England, and that all the paper used was imported from Venice, France, and Holland, we can easily conceive that the supply could be completely prevented. The excitement of the period quickened the inventive faculties of the people, and accordingly they had recourse to the practice of cutting letters on wood. The attempt to cut the Roman letters on wooden billets led by a natural transition to the invention of the *Coelbren*. Llewelyn Sion states that there was a recollection and *recovery* of the practice at this time; and if we read 'invention' instead of 'recovery' we shall probably be exactly right.

...

The *old Coelbren* of Gwilym Tew was probably the primary and parent form of the *Coelbren*; and as he flourished from 1410 to 1470, and composed a poem which was recited at the Abbey of Pen Rhys before its suppression in 1414, he was at the height of his reputation at the time here indicated as that in which the *Coelbren* first saw the light of day. But little doubt can now exist upon that subject, and accordingly I proceed to another part of my subject, with only this remark, – all the bardic passages cited by Ab Iolo from the bards of the fifteenth and sixteenth centuries are not relevant to the inquiry, but the great majority of them are quite conclusive upon this part of his case.

The *Coelbren* in the fifteenth century appears to have been known to a few of the bards of North Wales as well as to those of Glamorgan; but when Henry VII removed the interdict off paper and parchment, the practice of the *Coelbren* was confined to the latter; and so exclusively had it been forgotten elsewhere, that to Rhys Cain, a native of Merionethshire, and a well known bard, living at Oswestry about 1580, it was wholly unknown; for when a Glamorgan bard shewed his *peithynen* at an Eisteddfod where Rhys Cain was present, the latter sang this *englyn*:

> *An* Englyn *to a Wooden Book*
>
> A skeleton in a bag! It is not a wise lip that praises it,
> The song-book of a purblind bard.
> It is difficult to understand it rightly:
> It will suit one who is blind.

From this notice, and from other incidents already passed in review, it must now be quite clear that Glamorgan was the headquarters of the *Coelbren*. On the first appearance of the curiosity it became known to the bards of other districts; but when the necessity for such shifts had died away, paper and parchment superseded the wooden books; and the knowledge of the *Coelbren* in the latter part of the sixteenth century was confined to the district of Morganwg, to which it before owed its invention, and to which it has since owed the preservation of its history. Many thanks be to Llewelyn Sion for this service! for though I regret his fable, the facts he has placed on record are interesting and instructive. And here, in conclusion, I may now remark that the character of old Iolo has come out unscathed through this inquiry. Ab Iolo has successfully shewn that his father was not the inventor of the *Coelbren*, and that he drew his information from Llywelyn Sion. It is due to the old bard that we thank him for the preservation of the history of the bardic alphabet, though we decline to accept his guidance in the interpretation of the facts.

One word more, and we have done. The Welsh language has sounds which cannot be represented by single Roman letters: the projectors of the *Coelbren* attempted to remedy this defect, and in that respect the project deserves hearty commendation. Letters for those sounds are still desiderated, and it is to be hoped that the idea may yet be carried out.

Here, then, we close our inquiry, and the results are embodied in the following propositions:

I. That *Coelbren y Beirdd* has no pretensions to a high antiquity, and is neither found on sculptured stones nor in old MSS.
II. That it was invented in the beginning of the fifteenth century, when paper and parchment were forbidden to the Cymry, and that the inventor was in all probability the bard Gwilym Tew.
III. That it was not an original alphabet, except in respect of derivatives, but an imitation of the Roman letters.
IV. That it was in common use in the fifteenth century, as is shewn by the poems of the bards, and that by the end of the sixteenth it had all but ceased to be known.

THOMAS STEPHENS

## 21. Edward Owen and the Madogwys

*Since Edward Owen devoted sixty years to undertaking research at the British Museum in London, he deserves to be taken seriously. He proved to be an extremely accurate judge of the authenticity of Iolo's sources. In this series of articles on the legend of the Welsh Madogwys in America he placed Welsh cultural patriotism in its sociocultural context and assessed the contributions made by Welsh scholars from the days of Iolo Morganwg to those of Thomas Stephens.*

Edward Owen, 'The Story of Prince Madoc's Discovery of America', The Red Dragon, IX (1886), II, 172–83; III, 342–53.

It is most interesting to observe that this startling announcement was made to the learned world just at the time when an intelligent interest in Welsh literary and historical remains first began to be displayed. Indeed, if the discussion which arose did not inaugurate that period of Cymric literary activity which is still only in its youth, it imparted into the nascent spirit of inquiry such an amount of interest and vigour as not only to produce a small body of literature within its own province, but drew the attention of Welsh scholars to the wealth of genuine and traditional lore enshrined in the country's story, and gained a hearing for subjects which until then had been considered by Englishmen as unworthy of serious consideration . . .

In close succession came the Revd Edward Davies, one of the most profoundly learned of Celtic scholars of any generation, whose labours were rendered comparatively valueless through the writer's extraordinary ideas . . . And at about the same period did Edward Williams (Iolo Morganwg) and Dr William Owen Pughe (Idrisyn) commence that friendship which, a little later on, by embracing within its bonds Mr Owen Jones (Myfyr), was to produce such honour to their country and delight to scholars throughout the world by the publication of the *Myvyrian Archaiology*. The traditions of this school of writers were continued by Taliesen [*sic*] Williams (Ab Iolo) and John Williams (Ab Ithel), the last of a band whose names deserve to be held in honoured remembrance, and whose failings were those arising from a too enthusiastic contemplation of the literary treasures just disinterred from the dust of centuries.

Viewed by the cold eye of the impartial critic, nothing that is too severe can be said of the methods pursued by this school in their indiscriminate glorification of everything connected with Wales and its history. It is not too much to say that as the influence of the *Historia* of Geoffrey of Monmouth is to be traced in the works of almost every mediæval historian who came in contact with that tissue of fables, so did Edward Williams's influence affect all who came within the range of his magnetic personal power. As Geoffrey had been able by the fascinating form of his legends to lay the clearest intellects of the Middle Ages under his spell, so was Iolo Morganwg through the sheer force of his individuality able to impose his views upon men of much greater learning than himself. Endowed with indefatigable energy, burning with a patriotism that was ever at the white heat of enthusiasm, and possessed with the idea that whatever redounded to the glory of Cambria must be accepted and supported with implicit faith and unswerving devotion, no wonder he exercised such power over his contemporaries as to warp their judgments and take captive their common sense. His influence upon the minds of his countrymen is only now losing its hold through the advances of a more scientific and critical method. One of the greatest debts which Welsh scholarship owes to the memory of Thomas Stephens, of Merthyr, is due to his steadfast opposition through much evil report to the wild speculations and monstrous assumptions of the Morganwg school, and to his firm purpose of proving all things and holding to those alone which he believed to be true.

When, therefore, Edward Williams entered upon his study of early Cymric history, it was but natural that his attention should be arrested by the story of Madoc's disappearance, and equally natural that the discovery by the Revd Morgan Jones of the remnants of the Gwyneddian settlement should receive implicit credence from him and those just banded together as his closest literary friends.

The Welshman loves his native land with an ardour that is imperishable, and with a love that is not proof against excess. Anything that redounds to the honour of his beloved country finds in him an instant supporter, a credulous believer. He does not love too well, but his patriotism is not always tempered with wisdom. The faults of Edward Williams, Owen Pughe, and their followers, upon which we have strongly animadverted, have been readily condoned in view of the spirit which actuated them, and which throughout their lives they so consistently displayed. Their errors were the errors of the Celt in all ages, and it is in the exhibition of a similar spirit by an earlier generation that we find the key to the monstrous growth of the Madoc legend in later days.

## 22. John Morris-Jones and the Gorsedd of the Bards

*The final article in John Morris-Jones's controversial and disquieting series on the Gorsedd of the Bards of the Isle of Britain, published in* Cymru, *recounts the history of the Gorsedd from its inception shortly after the Carmarthen eisteddfod of c.1453 to his own day. While acknowledging the contributions of the likes of William Owen Pughe and Edward 'Celtic' Davies to the development of this pseudo-historical institution, this is a devastating critique of the Gorsedd which Morris-Jones rounds off by calling for its abolition in favour of a 'Court of Poets' and a 'School of Writers'.*

*John Morris Jones, 'Gorsedd Beirdd Ynys Prydain V',*
Cymru, *X, no. 59 (1896), 293–9.*

> Cellwair ffals mal colli'r Ffydd,
> Coelio ystoriâu celwydd;
> Ffei o awen a ffuant –
> Ffagl fawr am ei ffugiol fant.
> — SION BRWYNOG.

BELLACH y mae'r darllennydd yn deall hanes cychwyniad yr Orsedd, a phaham a pha fodd y dygwyd hi i fod. Bu anghydweledigaeth yn Eisteddfod Caerfyrddin, yn 1451, ynghylch dau o'r mesurau cerdd; gwrthryfelodd rhyw dri neu bedwar o feirdd o Forgannwg, a chodasant eisteddfod iddynt eu hunain; galwyd hon ganddynt hwy yn Gadair, a chan eu dilynwyr yn Orsedd. Yr oedd y gwrthgilwyr cyntaf yn honni eu bod yn dilyn yr hen feirdd; aeth eu dilynwyr ymhellach yn ol, a galwasant eu hunain yn 'feirdd wrth fraint a defawd beirdd Ynys Prydain'; ar ol dyfeisio gradd derwydd honasant olyniaeth o'r derwyddon. Yr oedd y gwrthgilwyr cyntaf wedi cofleidio athrawiaethau'r Cabbala a ddygasid i Forgannwg dipyn cyn yr ymrafael; galwyd y ddysgeidiaeth honno'n dderwyddiaeth gan eu dilynwyr, a dyfeisiwyd seremonïau pwrpasol i'r grefydd dderwyddol hon. Na thybied neb fy mod i'n difrio gwlad

Forgannwg wrth ddadlennu gweithrediadau clymblaid fechan y gorseddwyr; oblegid nid oeddynt yn derbyn na chefnogaeth na pharch gan bobl Morgannwg, eithr yn ol tystiolaeth Iolo 'i hunan fe'u llysenwid yn 'Wyr Cwm y Felin,' ac fe edrychid arnynt fel 'anffyddwyr a chonsurwyr, ac nis gwn pa beth.'[*] Dyna ddedfryd pobl eu gwlad a'u hoes hwy eu hunain arnynt; a phwy oedd mewn cystal cyfle i farnu?

Nid yw'n ymddangos fod dim defodau newydd wedi eu dyfeisio yn yr ail ganrif ar bymtheg; ond fe gyfansoddwyd lliaws o engreifftiau o'r hen fesurau, ac y maent yn argraffedig yng Nghyfrinach y Beirdd gydag enwau eu hawduron wrthynt. Yn y flwyddyn 1681 y cynhaliwyd yr Orsedd olaf, ac yn honno y cadarnhawyd yn derfynol ddosparth yr 'hen fesurau'.[**] Yr oedd Dafydd o'r Nant yn un o 'bencerddiaid' yr Orsedd honno; a disgybl iddo ef oedd Dafydd Hopcin o'r Coetty; disgybl i Ddafydd Hopcin oedd Siôn Bradford, a disgybl iddo yntau oedd Iolo Morgannwg, a thrwy'r olyniaeth hon y trosglwyddwyd y traddodiad gorseddol i ddiwedd y ddeunawfed ganrif.

Ychydig iawn o sylw a gafodd yr Orsedd o'i chychwyniad hyd ddyddiau Iolo, y tu allan i Forgannwg. Gelwid ei dosparth yn 'Ddosparth y Cŵn,' a 'Dosparth y Moch,' a 'Dosparth y Dommen';[***] a dywedid mai camenw ar eisteddfodau oedd 'gorseddau';[****] ond gan na wnaethpwyd un proselyt i'r ffydd orseddol allan o Forgannwg, nid aeth neb i drafferth i wrthbrofi ei haeriadau. Yr oedd beirdd yr unfed ganrif ar bymtheg yn byw yn ddigon agos i amser ei genedigaeth i ddeall gwerth yr haeriadau hynny; ac erbyn yr ail ganrif ar bymtheg yr oedd yr Orsedd yn rhy ddi-sylw i ennyn gwrthwynebiad ...

Y mae'n sicr nad oedd Gwilym Ganoldref nac Edmwnd Prys na Siôn Tudur, Dr. John Davies na Charles Edwards yn credu dim yn yr Orsedd, os gwyddent am dani. Yn nechreu'r ddeunawfed ganrif bu Edward Llwyd yn teithio drwy'r holl wledydd Celtaidd i chwilio am hynafiaethau a hen lawysgrifau; fe wnaeth rai darganfyddiadau na ddeallwyd mo honynt y pryd hynny, ac nad ailddarganfyddwyd hyd ganol y ganrif hon. Cyhoeddwyd ei ymchwiliadau mewn llyfr mawr o tua 450 o dudalennau unplyg yn y flwyddyn 1707; cynhwysa'r llyfr gofrestr o hen lawysgrifau Cymreig, ond ni welodd Edward Llwyd ddim sôn am yr Orsedd yn yr un o honynt. Nid yw Theophilus Evans ychwaith, er cymaint a draetha am y derwyddon, yn crybwyll dim am yr Orsedd. Nid yw Lewis Morris, Môn, er mor gydnabyddus oedd â hen ysgrifeniadau'r Cymry, na'i ddisgybl Goronwy Owen ychwaith, yn sôn dim am dani. Y mae Thomas Pennant yn ei *Tours in Wales*, a gyhoeddwyd yn 1779, 1783, yn adrodd cryn lawer am y beirdd a'u heisteddfodau; dyry grynhoad o Ystadud Caerfyrddin hefyd; ond ni chrybwylla air am Orsedd y Beirdd.

---

[*] *Lyric Poems* ii., p. 161.
[**] *Cyfrinach y Beirdd*, tud. 1.
[***] Eto, tud. 4.
[****] *Myv. Arch.*, ail-arg. tud 734. Ni wyddys pwy oedd y Robert Gruffudd a grybwyllir yn y nodyn hwn, na pha bryd yr ysgrifennwyd ef. Olrheinir y copi hynaf i 1651.

Yn 1789, cyhoeddwyd *Barddoniaeth Dafydd ab Gwilym* gan Owen Jones (Myfyr), a William Owen (wedi hynny a gyfenwid Pughe); ac argraffiad rhagorol iawn ydyw. Yr oedd y cywyddau eisoes wedi eu golygu mewn ysgrifen gan y clodfawr Lewis Morris; ond ni ddylid grwgnach rhan dda o'r glod i Owen Jones a William Owen. Yr oedd y ddau wedi chwilio'n fanwl gannoedd o lawysgrifau Cymreig cyn hynny, ond y mae'n amlwg na wyddent ddim am Orsedd y Beirdd. Yn y rhestr enwau ar ddiwedd y llyfr enwir 'Menw ab Teirgwaedd' yn gywir heb yr 'y' o flaen Teirgwaedd, a dywedir mai consurwr oedd, a disgybl i Fyrddin Emrys. Dywedir hefyd yn ddigon cywir mai 'Ovid the poet' oedd Ofydd. Ar ddechreu'r llyfr, y mae gan William Owen draethawd Saesneg ar fywyd Dafydd ap Gwilym yn neilltuol, a barddoniaeth Gymraeg yn gyffredinol. Dywedir yn hwnnw'n ddigon gwir fod y Rhufeiniaid wedi darostwng y derwyddon, ac fod eu barddoniaeth a phob cangen o'u dysg wedi ei lwyr golli; ac ni sonnir cymaint â sillaf am Orsedd y Beirdd.

Yr oedd hynny, fel y sylwyd, yn 1789. Fe wyddai William Owen am Iolo Morganwg yr adeg honno, ond prin iawn yr oedd yn ei adnabod. Eithr cyfarfuont yn fuan wedi hynny; a llyncodd William Owen y chwedl orseddol yn ebrwydd ac yn ddi-halen. Ei lyfr nesaf oedd Gweithiau Llywarch Hên, gyda chyfieithiad Saesneg, a gyhoeddwyd yn 1792. Wrth gwrs nid oes sôn am y fath beth â Gorsedd Beirdd yng nghaniadau Llywarch; y mae holl ysbryd ei farddoniaeth yn hollol groes i ddysgeidiaeth yr Orsedd, a chydnebydd William Owen nad oedd efe'n perthyn i'r urdd. Am hynny, fel eglurhad ar weithiau Llywarch, neu fe allai er dangos gymaint ei golled na buasai'n orseddwr, fe dreulir 60 tudalen allan o'r 76 sydd yn y rhagymadrodd i draethu am Orsedd y Beirdd! Fe goeliodd William Owen lawer gwrachïaidd chwedl ar ol hynny; credodd yn y broffwydes loerig Joanna Southcott, a bu'n archoffeiriad iddi, yn cywiro iaith ei phroffwydoliaethau, oherwydd 'nid oedd yr ysbryd oedd yn ei chynhyrfu,' fel y dywed Cynddelw, 'yn gwybod dim byd am ramadeg.'\* Daeth Iolo hefyd i adnabod yr archoffeiriad yn well; a dywedodd mai efe oedd '*the greatest fool in existence*'. Digon gwir; oblegid, fel y tystia Selyf, 'yr ehud a goelia bob gair'. Eithr petai William Owen yn ddyn call a gredasai efe chwedl orseddol Iolo?

Yn 1809, cyhoeddodd Edward Davies ei *Mythology and Rites of the British Druids*; a phrofodd yn eglur mai ffug diweddar oedd Gorsedd Morgannwg, fel y'i disgrifid yn rhagymadrodd William Owen, a *Lyric Poems* Iolo; ac nid yn unig nad oedd ei hathrawiaethau i'w cael yng ngweithiau'r hen feirdd, ond eu bod yn hollol groes i syniadau'r hen ysgrifenwyr hynny. Eithr yr oedd Edward Davies yn canfod yn yr hen farddoniaeth ryw ddamcaniaeth arall oedd ganddo ef yn ei ben ei hun. Yr oedd Bryant rai blynyddoedd cyn hynny wedi esgor ar ei syniad fod y traddodiad am y diluw wedi aros ymysg yr holl genhedloedd; a'u bod hwythau, yn eu dirywiant, wedi gwneud duwiau o Noah a'r arch; ac

---

\* *Atodiad Blodau Arfon*, tud. 37.

mai llygriadau o'r grefydd honno ydyw holl grefyddau paganaidd y byd.\*
Derbyniodd Edward Davies y ddamcaniaeth hon; ac fe wastraffodd lawer o
ddysg a dawn i geisio olrhain addoliad yr arch yn y gweithiau a briodolir i
Daliesin, ac ereill o'r hen feirdd. Nid oedd Iolo'n credu'r ofergoel hwn mwy
nag y credai Edward Davies chwedlau Iolo; ond fe ddaeth Myfyr Morgannwg
ymhen rhyw ddeugain mlynedd, ac fe gredodd holl ffolbethau'r ddau –
Gorsedd Iolo ac arch Edward Davies; cymysgodd y pethau hyn â thipyn o
Hindŵaeth a pheth aflendid megys ag a hoffai Hargrave Jennings; profodd ei
bynciau i'w foddlonrwydd ei hun drwy gyfrwng ieithyddiaeth gyffelyb i'r un
a darddai *Atlantic Ocean* o 'At y lan Dic! Oh, Siân!' a chymerodd arno ei fod
yn archdderwydd wedi ei urddo gan Daliesin fab Iolo. Y gynysgaeth hon a
etifeddodd Morien; a chaiff fenthyg colofnau'r *Western Mail* i draethu am dani.
Dyry i ni lu o darddiadau at-y-lan-dicyddol sy'n taflu ieithyddiaeth William
Owen a Rowland Jones o'r Weirglodd Fawr i'r cysgod; a sieryd mewn termau
Groeg a Hindŵaidd (a ddysgodd efe gan Myfyr) am bethau na ad gwylder eu
henwi. Y mae gair bach syml fel 'gordd' yn ddieithr iddo; nis gŵyr pa beth yw
ei ystyr, ac nis gwel ynddo ond aflendid. Gofynna Morien i mi paham nad
atebaf ei ysgrifau; ni fuasai waeth gennyf feirniadu gwaith y Bardd Cocos; o'r
ddau y mae ysgrifeniadau'r Bardd yn bereiddiach eu sawyr.

Ni bu'r Eisteddfod farw'n llwyr hyd yn oed yn y ddeunawfed ganrif. Fe
gynhaliwyd cryn lawer o fân eisteddfodau mewn tafarndai a gwestai yma a
thraw yn ystod y ganrif honno; ond Cymdeithas y Gwyneddigion biau'r
anrhydedd o roi ail fywyd yn yr hen sefydliad. Cynhaliwyd y gyntaf o'u
heisteddfodau hwy yng Nghorwen ar y 12fed o Fai, 1789; ac nid oedd
arweinwyr y Gymdeithas, fel y danghoswyd uchod, yn gwybod dim y pryd
hynny am Orsedd Morgannwg. Ond yn ebrwydd wedi clywed am dani, ceisi-
asant ei hadgyfodi hithau. Chwiliasant am feirdd i'w hurddo, a chawsant afael
ar Wallter Mechain; gohebwyd hefyd â Hywel Eryri a Dafydd Ddu. Dywed yr
olaf yn un o'i lythyrau at Sion Lleyn\*\* iddo dderbyn tri llythyr o Lundain,
oddiwrth William Owen, Owen Jones, ac Iolo, yn dweyd am y sefydliad
gorseddol, ac fod 'Iolo mewn meddiant o lyfr a elwir Cyfrinach y Beirdd, yr
hwn sydd mewn bod er amser y Derwyddon; nid oes ond un neu ddau
Ynghymru yn gwybod y gyfrinach, ac nid ellir ei dadguddio heb droseddu y
rheolau mwyaf sanctaidd ... Nid oes neb Yngwynedd yn fardd wrth *fraint* a
*defod*, ac ni chaniattair y fraint ond i myfi yn unig, o herwydd nid oes neb arall
yn feddiannol o'r cynneddfau angenrheidiol (meddynt hwy).' Pa ddrwg oedd
dywedud fod *Cyfrinach y Beirdd* 'mewn bod er amser y derwyddon', gan ei fod
wedi ei ysgrifennu yn yr unfed a'r ail ganrif ar bymtheg gan y 'derwyddon'
Llywelyn Siôn ac Edward Dafydd? Dyma natur haeriadau'r gorseddwyr

---

\* Jacob Bryant's *Analysis of Ancient Mythology*, 3 vols., 1774-76. Dywed yr *Encyclopaedia Britannica*
am y llyfr ei fod yn 'fantastic and now wholly valueless'. Gwrthbrofwyd ei ddamcaniaethau
gan mlynedd yn ol; eto dyfynnir ef fel efengyl gan Morien hyd heddyw.
\*\* *Adgof uwch Anghof*, tud. 14.

newydd; ond tipyn yn wamal y sieryd Dafydd Ddu am danynt, er iddo (mi dybiaf) gymeryd ei urddo yn ol eu trefn. Cynhaliwyd dwy neu dair Gorsedd, mewn lleoedd fel pen Pumlumon, yn ystod 1792–3, ac un yn 1799. Y mae William Owen wedi rhoi ar gof a chadw, yn ei ragymadrodd i weithiau Llywarch, wasanaeth defodol a chyhoeddiad y gorseddau cyntaf hyn; ac y mae ffurfioldeb seremonïol yr ymadroddion yn ddigon plentynaidd i beri i angel wylo.

Aeth yr Eisteddfod ar gynnydd, ond methiant truenus fu'r ymgais i adgyfodi'r Orsedd, hen elynes y sefydliad cenedlaethol. Er hyn yr oedd y blaid orseddol yn ennill gallu; William Owen yn difwyno'r iaith, Iolo'n lledaenu'r adroddiad gorseddol o hanes Cymru, a'r oll yn ymosod ar y mesurau a anrhydeddasid er dyddiau D. ab Edmwnd.

...

Erbyn 1819, yr oedd y blaid yn ddigon cref i fedru pasio penderfyniad fod rhyddid i ganu am y gadair ar holl fesurau Dosparth Morgannwg yn gystal a'r pedwar mesur ar hugain.

Tua'r adeg hon hefyd, wedi methu cadw'r Orsedd yn fyw yn ei grym ei hunan, meddyliodd Iolo am gynllun arall, sef ei himpio ar yr Eisteddfod, er mwyn gallu o honi ffynnu ar draul yr hen sefydliad cenedlaethol yr oedd hi o'i chychwyniad yn ei wrthwynebu a'i ddifrio. Felly, yng Nghaerfyrddin yn 1819, am y tro cyntaf yn hanes yr Eisteddfod, fe gynhaliwyd Gorsedd ynglŷn â hi; gwnaed Iolo'n fardd gweinyddol, rhoddwyd urddau i amryw bersonau, a chwareuwyd defod gweinio'r cledd. Ni lwyddodd y cynllun hwn ychwaith yn oes Iolo, ond fe'i hadnewyddwyd ymhen blynyddoedd gan ei fab Taliesin.

...

Nid oes gennyf ddim yn erbyn cymdeithas o feirdd. Yn yr hen Eisteddfodau, penderfynid y materion barddol drwy bleidlais y beirdd graddedigion. Y mae'r Eisteddfod yn awr wedi eangu ei therfynau; ond fe ddylai'r beirdd eto gael penderfynu llawer o gwestiynau cyffredinol ynglŷn â barddoniaeth yr Eisteddfod, ac nis gellir hynny heddyw heb gymdeithas o feirdd. Ond wrth roddi ar y gymdeithas yr enw 'Gorsedd' teflir sen ar yr Eisteddfod; y mae cysylltu 'Beirdd Ynys Prydain' â'i henw yn sarhâd ar hen feirdd yr Eisteddfod, Dafydd ab Edmwnd, Tudur Aled, ac hyd yn oed ar Wiliam Lleyn ac Edmwnd Prys, Lewis Morris, Goronwy Owen, Dewi Wyn o Eifion, ac ereill y dywedai'r gorseddwyr am danynt, os oeddynt boëtau nad oeddynt *feirdd*; ac yn olaf, y mae cysylltu â'r gymdeithas ddefodau ffôl beirdd Morgannwg yn ddirmyg ar synwyr cyffredin ac ar Gristionogaeth.

Mi ddymunwn ar i bawb y mae anrhydedd llenyddiaeth Cymru yn werthfawr yn ei olwg ystyried y pethau hyn. Fe ddadleuir weithiau fod teimlad gwladgarol, neu *sentiment*, yn ddigon o reswm dros barhau'r Orsedd; ond y mae teimlad dyn yn dibynnu ar ei wybodaeth, ac nis gall neb sy'n gwybod hanes llenyddiaeth Cymru deimlo o blaid yr Orsedd heb fod yn *an*wladgarol. Oblegid fe'i lluniwyd hi, ac fe honnwyd awdurdod Beirdd Ynys Prydain a'r derwyddon i'w mesurau a'i chrefydd trwy dwyll ac anwiredd, er mwyn gwrthwynebu a sarhau rhai o'r beirdd goreu a welodd Cymru, a hynny gan ddyrnaid o rigymwyr na buasai nemor golled i'r wlad pe nad anadlasent erioed. Pwy bynnag a bleidia'r Orsedd efe a bleidia rigymwyr a thwyllwyr Morgannwg, ac a amharcha hen feirdd Cymru. Os mynnech weled barn y gwir Orseddwyr am gymwynaswyr llenyddiaeth Gymraeg, darllennwch eiriau Iolo Morgannwg am Lewis Morris yn y *Brython*, iii., tud. 54. 'Nid oedd ond y celwydd, y twyll, a'r gwagfost yn dal Lewys Morys yng nghyd; fel hanesydd, gwyrdroi pob peth i gydweddu â'i ddychmygion diymbwyll ei hun ydoedd ef yn wastad'; yna geilw ef yn 'd—d *scoundrel*'; a'r cyfan am fod gan Lewis Morris syniad cywirach a mwy rhesymol nag Iolo am hanes a llenyddiaeth Cymru. Y gwir yw, y mae geiriau Iolo am Lewis Morris yn fwy gwir o lawer am Iolo'i hunan; dyfynnaf yr ymadroddion diweddaf yn y darn gan roi Iolo Morgannwg yn lle Lewis Morris ynddynt, gan mor wir ydynt am dano ef. 'Oni bai fod gwybodaeth o'u hiaith eu barddoniaeth eu hynafiaeth, ac o bob peth arall, yn isel dros ben ym mhlith y *gwybodusaf* o'r Cymry, buan, fal us o flaen gwynt yr ai clod Iolo Morgannwg i ddyfnder anghof. Ond nid hawdd dwyn neb oddiar ei eilun; ac eilun crachfeirdd a chrachieithyddion Cymru heddyw yw Iolo Morgannwg. Mawr lles iddynt o hono.' Oni bai fod hyn heddyw'n wir, a geid Syr Lewis Morris tybed, yn codi ei lais o blaid Gorsedd Iolo Morgannwg, a thrwy hynny'n taflu amarch dwfn ar ei hendaid clodforus a ddilornwyd gan yr Iolo hwnnw, ac hefyd ar holl gymwynaswyr goreu llenyddiaeth Gymraeg?

Galwer y beirdd nid yn 'feirdd yr Orsedd,' ond yn 'feirdd yr Eisteddfod.' Llunier cymdeithas newydd, a galwer hi'n 'Llys y Beirdd,' neu 'Ysgol y Beirdd'; neu ryw enw cymwys arall; na dderbynier neb yn aelod o honi na bydd yn drwyadl gyfarwydd â hanes a rheolau barddoniaeth Cymru, ac wedi ei enwogi ei hunan fel prydydd; ynglŷn â'r gymdeithas hon bydded 'Ysgol y Llenorion'; ac na dderbynier i'w chylch neb na bo'n enwog fel llenor neu ysgolhaig Cymraeg; ar wahân i'r ddwy bydded 'Llys y Cerddorion', wedi ei gyfansoddi yn yr un modd o gerddorion gwir deilwng. Y mae Cymdeithas yr Orsedd yn ddifudd, a'i graddau'n ddiwerth, oherwydd y rhwyddineb y gollyngir pob anheilyngdod iddi. Derbynir ymgeiswyr yn aelodau drwy arholiad sydd bum gwaith yn haws nag arholiad isaf Prifysgol Cymru; os bydd dyn wedi ennill rhyw fath o radd mewn prifysgol croesewir ef yn llawen heb arholiad yn y byd; a gwaeth na'r oll, pwy bynnag a fo'n berchen cyfoeth, er bod heb ddeall gair o Gymraeg, ac weithiau heb fedru'n gywir un iaith arall, aiff yr Orsedd o'i ffordd i gyflwyno'i hurddau iddo, a hynny'n aml â gwaseidd-dra a fuasai'n warthrudd ar y gymdeithas fwyaf dirmygedig. Ond pe sefydlid 'Llys y Beirdd' ac 'Ysgol y Llenorion' fel yr awgrymwyd uchod, a phe cyfyngid yr aelodaeth yn ofalus i oreugwyr beirdd a llenorion y wlad, gallai'r cymdeithasau hynny fod o fudd dirfawr, a buasai aelodaeth o honynt yn anrhydedd llawer uwch na graddau cyffredin y prifysgolion.

Wrth gynnal arddanghosfa fwy neu lai digrif ar ddyddiau'r Eisteddfod, nid yw'r beirdd ond yn eu hiselhau eu hunain heb gyrraedd dim amcan da. Rhodder y goreu i'r chware ffol hwn, a'r ymffrostio mawr a'r bloeddio; a gwneler rhyw waith distaw a fo a'i duedd i ddyrchafu iaith a barddoniaeth a llenyddiaeth Cymru. Drwy hynny, fel y dywed Goronwy, yr enilla'r beirdd hefyd barch ac anrhydedd; –

> 'Amlhawn ddawn, ddynion, i'n mad henwlad hon,
>   E ddaw i feirddion ddeufwy urddas.'
>                                                    J. MORRIS JONES.

## 23. John Morris-Jones as Uthr Bendragon

*In this extraordinary attack on one of Wales's principal scholars, the satirist Robert Arthur Griffith (Elphin) depicts John Morris-Jones as the blood-red dragon Uthr Bendragon, who had vowed to destroy every impostor that promoted druidism in those spurious spectacles known as Gorseddau. Spitting fire, the dragon half flies and half strides through north Wales in his attempt to undermine the druidic cause. He confronts the intimidating Archdruid Hwfa Môn (Rowland Williams), swallows him whole, and resumes his depredations until he has devoured every accredited bard. He then establishes a court known as 'Arthur's Court', in which three justices – Uthr Bendragon, the Brass Serpent, and the Oxford Bibliophile – thereafter adjudicate on literary matters.*

*Elphin, 'Enwogion Cymru V. Y Gwladgarwr', Y Geninen,*
*XIV, no. 2 (1896), 119–20.*

### UTHR BEN DRAGON

Yn awr, trown i gyfeiriad arall i ymgydnabyddu â math newydd o wladgarwr. Yn bendifaddeu, y mwyaf ei fri a'i fraint o'r holl wladgarwyr ar hyn o bryd yw UTHR BEN DRAGON. Brodor yw ef o Ynys y Derwyddon; ac, fel y gweddai i'r cyfryw un, mae wedi yfed yn ddwfn o gyfrin-ddysg yr hen oesoedd, yn gyfarwydd âg ieithoedd a llenyddiaeth y cynfyd, ac yn hynod o fedrus mewn pob math o ddewiniaeth. Gyrwyd y gair i gerdded dro yn ol mai UTHR BEN DRAGON ydyw bardd mwyaf Cymru; ac yr oedd rhai yn ddigon parod i gredu hyny: ond aethum i ofyn barn rhyw hen lenor profedig ar y pwnc, ac atebodd yntau gyda winc yn ei lygad: 'Chwedl yw hona i'w hadrodd wrth y *marines*.' Ond faint bynag o fardd yw UTHR BEN DRAGON, mae'n mhell o fod yn hoff o feirdd. Yn wir, gwrthodedig bethau ei enaid ydyw Beirdd Ynys Prydain a'u Gorsedd. Cythruddwyd ei ysbryd i'r fath raddau gan waith y beirdd yn hòni perthynas â'r hen dderwyddon fel y tyngodd y mynai ddifa y giwaid ymhongar a thwyllodrus hyn oddiar wyneb y ddaear. Yn fuan wed'yn, dywedid fod arwyddion dieithr a goruwchnaturiol wedi ymddangos mewn gwahanol fanau, – bolltau tanllyd yn ymsaethu drwy y wybren, twrf mawr yn dygyfor dan y ddaear, a lleisiau ofnadwy yn llefain o'r coed, 'Daw dial, daw!' O'r diwedd, ar ddiwrnod rhynllyd yn Ionawr, tra yr oedd amryw wyr wrthi'n pysgota penwaig oddiallan i Borthdinlleyn, clywsant ysgrêch ferwinol yn treiddio'r nen; a chan edrych oddiamgylch gwelsant ddraig asgellog, gynffonog, yn haner ehedeg, haner carlamu, dros y môr, tuagatynt. Ei lliw oedd goch fel gwaed; allan o'i safn poerai farwor tanllyd; a chan wylltedd ei hymdaith cynhyrfai y môr fel crochan berwedig. Syrthiodd y pysgotwyr druain ar eu gwynebau ar fwrdd y llong, wedi eu llwyr barlysu gan ofn; ac nid oeddynt lai na dysgwyl dyrnod marwolaeth bob eiliad. Ond ni chymerodd y ddraig sylw yn y byd o na llong, na physgotwr, na phenwaig; eithr hi a aeth rhagddi yn syth a ffyrnig, at y lan. Wedi tirio cymerodd wibdaith ar draws Morfa Nefyn tua chwmwd Eifionydd. Pan ddaeth i gŵr y Gaerwen a'r Bettws Fawr, hen ardal fendigaid Rhobert ab Gwilym Ddu a Dewi Wyn, esgynodd yn uchel i'r awyr a rhoddodd oernad o'r fath fwyaf anaearol nes ymwelwi o holl drigolion y fro. Yna ehedodd dros y môr drachefn nes cafodd dir ar dueddau Harlech. Wedi gorphwys enyd ar furiau llwydion yr hen gastell, gwibdeithiodd ymlaen dros fynydd, a dyffryn, ac afon; ac nid arafodd ddim nes cyrhaedd Dinas Mawddwy. Yno, yng nghŵr y fynwent, yr oedd gŵr gwineu, gwledig, yn ceisio darllen rhyw gofnod ar hen feddrod adfeiliedig. Wrth glywed ohono ysgrêch sydyn a threiddlym, trodd y gŵr gwineu ei olwg i fyny; a phan welodd y bwystfil coch yn hofran fel barn uwchben, dechreuodd 'gymeryd y goes,' a cheisiodd ddianc o'i berygl mawr. Ond, megys ar amrantiad, planodd y ddraig un o'i phalfau yn ei wàr, a thaflodd ef ar ei hyd ar lawr. 'Onid tydi yw yr adyn ysgeler fu yn chwedleua fod yr Orsedd Farddol wedi dod i lawr o amser y Derwyddon?' meddai y Ddraig, 'ac oni chefaist ugain punt yn dâl am dy waith?' A'r gŵr gwineu a atebodd, gyda'i ddwylaw ymhleth a'i ddeulin yn crynu, 'Ië, yn wir, myfi yw y pechadur hwnw; a pharod wyf i ymostwng i'r llwch a gwneyd unrhyw benyd am fy nhrosedd. O! Ddraig ardderchog, nid yw y truth hwnw yn cyflëu fy syniadau i o gwbl.' 'Ha!' ebai y Ddraig, 'da y dywedaist. Un peth yn unig a bâr i mi arbed dy fywyd, sef, nad ydwyt na bardd na beirniad; pe amgen, ni chawset fyw yr un pum' munyd yn hwy. Dos, a mynega dy edifeirwch ar goedd y byd.' Wedi gweinyddu y cerydd hwn, ymaith â'r Ddraig drachefn, gan gyfeirio yn syth tua'r gogledd. Cyn hir disgynodd ar lechweddau noethlwm Llanuwchllyn. Yno yr oedd y SARPH BRES – anghenfil mawr melynliw, heb fod yn anhebyg i'r Ddraig ei hun, ond ei fod yn fyr o esgyll – yn aros i groesawu yr ymwelydd. Cofleidiasant eu gilydd yn wresog yn eu dull cynefin; ac yna arweiniodd y SARPH ei gyfaill at agen enfawr yn y creigiau, lle yr oedd saig flasus ac amheuthyn wedi ei harlwyo ar eu cyfer. Gwledd ryfedd oedd hono, – a rhyfedd, rhyfedd oedd yr hyn a ddygwyddodd rhwng y ddau anghenfil. Wedi iddynt ymloddesta eu gwala, dringasant i gopa bryn cyfagos; a dyna lle buont am ysbaid yn cynal cyfrin-gyngor. O'r diwedd, gofynodd y Ddraig i'w chyfaill, 'A ddoi di gyda mi i'r ymgyrch hwn?' a'r SARPH a atebodd, 'Na, nid oes genyf adenydd fel tydi, ac felly nis gallaf mo'th ganlyn: dos dy hunan; cymer di y clod, a chyfranogaf finau yn y llawenydd.' Heb ymddiddan dim yn ychwaneg, cymerodd y Ddraig naid oddiar y bryn a disgynodd yn unionsyth i ganol Llyn Tegid; a chymaint oedd y cynhwrf yn y dwfr nes yr aeth pobl Bala i ofni fod rhyw drychineb ofnadwy ar fin eu goddiweddyd. Yna esgynodd y Ddraig drachefn, ac ehedodd yn chwyrn dros drumau y Berwyn yn nghyfeiriad Llangollen. Yr oedd yr haul yn cilio yn y gorllewin pan ddisgynodd ar lanerch o dir gerllaw Llys Hwfa; ac arosodd yno i wylio ei chyfle. Cyn hir daeth yr ARCHDDERWYDD allan o'i lys, yn ddifeddwl-ddrwg fel arfer, gan gynghaneddu englyn neu doddaid wrtho'i hun; a cherddodd bron yn syth i safn y Ddraig. 'Hylô!' meddai'r hybarch fardd, 'pwy wyt ti, dwad? Dyn byw, o ble y doist ti, y creadur anghynas? Welis i 'rioed fwystfil o dy fath di o'r blaen.' A'r Ddraig a atebodd, gan agor ei safn led y pen, 'Myfi yw UTHR BEN DRAGON, ceidwad pob doethineb, gwybodaeth, a dawn, yn y wlad hon. Gallu sydd genyf i ddeongli pob math o gyfriniaeth, ac awdurdod a roddwyd i mi ar holl diriogaethau iaith, llên, ac awen. Yn y dyddiau hyn mae ffug a gwagogonedd yn ffynu i'r fath raddau nes myned yn orthrwm ar ein pobl a thynu arnom ddirmyg y cenhedloedd. Am hyny, penderfynais y gwnawn ddiwedd ar y genfaint hono a elwir Beirdd Ynys Prydain, a'u Gorsedd, a'u gwag urddau, modd y caffer iawn drefn ar lên a llafar, ac y dyger yr iaith yn ol i'w phurdeb a'i hurddas cysefin. Mynega yn fyr pwy roddodd hawl i ti wisgo yr enw ymffrostfawr o Archdderwydd.' A'r bardd a atebodd, 'Ust! yr ellyll anystyrbwyll, arafa yn dy ryfyg a'th raib. Onid oeddwn fardd cadeiriol cyn dy eni di i'r byd, er mor aruthrol yw dy faintioli? Onid wyf wedi gwneyd fy rhan i gadw i fyny urddas yr Eisteddfod, a hyrwyddo ei llwydd, dros haner canrif o amser? Ac oni urddwyd fi yn Archdderwydd wrth raith a barn Gorsedd, yn ngolwg a chlyw gwlad ac arglwydd, ac yn wyneb haul a llygad goleuni? A phwy wyt ti a feiddi wadu hynafiaeth ac awdurdod Gorsedd Beirdd Ynys Prydain? Mae yr Orsedd hon yn hynach na holl orseddau ac ymherodraethau'r byd, – mae mor gadarn â seiliau'r Gwirionedd ei hun, – ac mi fydd yn blodeuo yn ei gogoniant pan fydd holl filod, a chawrfilod, ac anghenfilod y ddaear wedi diflanu oddiar lwybrau gwareiddiad.' Enynwyd cynddaredd y Ddraig tuhwnt i bob dirnadaeth gan yr araeth hon, – fflachiai mellt o'i llygaid, ymrwyfai ei chorph o'i phen i flaen ei chynffon, a disgynai llysnafedd eiriasboeth o'i safn golynog. Gyda gwaedd ddychrynllyd ymruthrodd ar y bardd, ysgytiodd ef am enyd rhwng ei danedd, ac yna llyncodd y truan yn ei grynswth i'w chrombil. Wed'yn, fel pe wedi ymgynddeirogi wrth flas y wledd, aeth ymaith ar ymgyrch dinystriol drwy y wlad; a lle bynag y canfyddai fardd o unrhyw radd, llarpiai ef yn ddidrugaredd a llyncai ef fel gwybedyn. Ac felly y darfu am Feirdd Ynys Prydain. Mae cof am y gyflafan hon yn creu arswyd hyd y dydd heddyw: nid oedd y difrod a wnaed gan y Brenin Iorwerth ond megys chwareu plant wrth ei gydmaru â'r galanas hwn. Yn fuan wedi hyn, codwyd llys yn y wlad, yn dwyn yr enw *Llys Arthur*; a'i amcan yw gweinyddu barn ar bynciau llên: a thri ynad a eisteddant ar y fainc farnol, nid amgen UTHR BEN DRAGON, y SARPH BRES, a LLYFRBRYF RHYDYCHEN: a chofrestrydd y llys yw y gŵr o Ddinas Mawddwy.

## 24. The Demise of Rhys Goch ap Rhicert

*In this pioneering article Griffith John Williams examines the evidence for and against the existence of the medieval Welsh poet Rhys Goch ap Rhicert, to whom Iolo had attributed twenty poems. He demonstrates that ap Rhicert was unknown to Welsh scholars until he was listed as a poet in the 'Cambrian Biography' published by Iolo's friend William Owen Pughe in 1803. He then discusses the reception afforded to the twenty poems from their first appearance in the* Iolo Manuscripts *in 1848 to the critique applied to five of them by J. H. Davies and Ifor Williams in his own day. On the basis of his researches into the Iolo Morganwg papers at the National Library of Wales, he is in no doubt that the remaining fifteen poems had been composed by the author of the counterfeit Dafydd ap Gwilym poems and the nature and love poems signed 'Iorwerth Gwilym', namely Iolo Morganwg himself. He proves his thesis by making a forensic analysis of the vocabulary, style and grammar of the poems, and by subjecting the provenance of their sources to detailed examination. Thus, by revealing that the historical Rhys Goch ap Rhicert had never composed Welsh poetry, G. J. Williams provides incontrovertible proof of Iolo's creative genius as a forger.*

*Griffith J. Williams, 'Rhys Goch ap Rhiccert',* Y Beirniad, *VIII, no. 4 (1920), 211–60.*

### RHYS GOCH AP RHICCERT

I lenorion Cymru yn y bedwaredd ganrif ar bymtheg nid oedd odid berson mwy diddorol na Rhys Goch ap Rhiccert ap Einion ap Collwyn o Dir Iarll. Iddynt hwy yr oedd y farddoniaeth a ymddangosodd o dan ei enw yn yr *Iolo MSS.* yn 1848 yn profi fod cerddi nwyfus ac ysgeifn i serch ieuenctid ac i natur yn perthyn i gyfnod ymhell y tu hwnt i ddydd Dafydd ap Gwilym, ac felly nid oedd yr olaf ond dynwaredwr bardd a fu byw ym Morgannwg ddwy ganrif o'i flaen. Er i Thomas Stephens geisio dangos mai yn y bedwaredd ganrif ar ddeg y blodeuai Rhys Goch, ac i'r Prifathro J. H. Davies, MA, brofi nad Rhys Goch oedd awdur y caniadau sydd yn yr *Iolo MSS.*, eto fe erys cymaint o ramant o gylch ei enw fel y myn rhai gredu yn wyneb popeth mai ef yw tâd cerddi rhamant a serch, a blaenredegydd Dafydd ap Gwilym.

Yn wir, nid oes dim yn fwy o ddirgelwch yn ein llenyddiaeth nag enw Rhys Goch ap Rhiccert – neu'n hytrach, ei enw fel bardd. Y mae'n sicr na wyddai'r Dr Davies ddim amdano, nac un o'r lleill a fu'n crynhoi rhestri o enwau'r beirdd yn yr ail ganrif ar bymtheg a'r ddeunawfed. Ni cheir ei enw yn rhestr Thomas Richards Llangrallo, yn niwedd ei eiriadur, er ei fod yn byw yng nghanol gwlad lle y gellid meddwl y buasai ei enw yn rhan o draddodiad llenyddol y dalaith. Y tro cyntaf iddo gael ei restru fel bardd oedd yn y *Cambrian Biography* a gyhoeddwyd gan y Dr Pughe yn 1803, lle y dywedir ar dud. 306:

> Rhys Goch ab Rhiccert ab Einion ab Collwyn, an eminent poet of Coetty in Glamorgan, who flourished from about A.D. 1140 to 1170, and of whose compositions there are many preserved. His grandfather was the notable Einion, who brought the Normans into Glamorgan.

Ceir rhywbeth i'r un cyfeiriad gan Robert Williams yn ei *Biographical Sketch* (1836), ac y mae'n ddiameu mai o lyfr Pughe y cafodd Williams ei wybodaeth. Yna cawn gyfeiriad ato yn 'Rhagddarweiniad' Taliesin Williams (Ab Iolo) i *Gyfrinach y Beirdd* (1829), lle y dywed (tud. xi.):–

> Mae son, mewn hen lyfrau casgledig ac ysgrifennedig gann Feirdd a Dysgedigion Cadeiriau Morgannwg a Thir Iarll am ddosparth Rhys Goch ap Rhiccart, dosparth Ieuan Fawr ap y Dewlith, (1170) ...

Yna yn 1848 cyhoeddwyd yr *Iolo MSS.* ac yno y cafodd y Cymry'r olwg gyntaf ar waith Rhys Goch, oherwydd o dud. 228 i 251 fe geir ugain cân â'i enw wrth odre pob un, a dywedir mai Iolo Morganwg a'u cafodd mewn ysgriflyfr oedd ym meddiant Siôn Bradford. Flwyddyn wedi hynny (1849) ymddangosodd *Literature of the Kymry* gan Thomas Stephens, ac ynddo ceir y feirniadaeth gyntaf ar waith tybiedig Rhys Goch. Gwelodd Stephens fod y dyddiad 1140 oedd yn yr *Iolo MSS.* (tud. 229) yn un hollol anghywir, gan ddiweddared diwyg y cerddi. Ceisiodd ef leoli Rhys Goch yn y bedwaredd ganrif ar ddeg. Ni wnaeth Gweirydd ap Rhys yn ei *Hanes Llenyddiaeth Gymreig*, namyn ail-adrodd rhesymau Stephens a cheisio dangos fod rhyw fath ar gynghanedd yng ngherddi Rhys. Yna yn 1902 taflwyd ffrwd o oleuni newydd ar y cwestiwn yn *Hen Ganiadau Serch*, trydedd gyfrol Cymdeithas Llên Cymru, a gynwysai ragymadrodd a ysgrifenasai'r Prifathro J. H. Davies. Dangosodd ef nad oedd enw Rhys Goch fel bardd yn yr un llawysgrif, ac mai camgymryd a wnaeth Stephens wrth wneuthur Rhys Goch yn dad i Rys Lwyd ap Rhys ap Rhiccert, a thybied mai'r un bardd oedd yr olaf â Rhys Brydydd o Lanharan, tad Rhisiart ap Rhys. Yna dywed iddo ddarganfod pump o'r caniadau a briodolid i Rys Goch, mewn diwyg ac orgraff tra gwahanol, mewn llawysgrif o'r unfed ganrif ar bymtheg a'r ail ar bymtheg, ac heb un sôn am Rys Goch nac am yr un bardd arall. Salsbriaid y Rhug oedd perchenogion y llawysgrif ar y cychwyn, ond daeth i feddiant Cymrodorion Llundain, ac yn awr y mae yn yr Amgueddfa Brydeinig lle y gelwir hi *Additional Manuscript* 14,974. Pump o ganiadau Rhys (Rhif 1, 2, 3, 13, a 20) sydd ar gael ynddi, ond y mae'n eglur, o'u cymharu â'r copi sydd yn yr *Iolo MSS.* iddynt gael eu cyfnewid a'u 'diwygio' cyn cael eu hargraffu yno, gan rywun neu'i gilydd. Daw ef i'r casgliad nad Rhys Goch yw awdur y cerddi, a chwalwyd am byth yr ystori amdano fel blaenredegydd Dafydd ap Gwilym. Yn wir, dangoswyd mai Llywelyn ap Hwlcyn (neu Hywel) o Fôn yw awdur un o'r caniadau yn ol llawysgrif Llundain, bod rhai o ganiadau tybiedig Rhys Goch wedi eu hysgrifennu yn yr un llaw, a bod llawer o debygrwydd rhyngddynt. Cryfha Mr Ifor Williams, MA, ddadl y Prifathro Davies trwy awgrymu mai'r un oedd Llywelyn â Llelo Llwyd, awdur dwy arall o'r caneuon yn *Add. MS.* 14,974. Camgymerth rhywun y Llywelyn ap Hwlcyn yma am Lywelyn ap Hywel ap Ieuan ap Gronw, bardd a flagurai ym Morgannwg tua chanol y bymthegfed ganrif, ond ni chydwedda'r caniadau nwyfus hyn â'r ysbryd trist a phruddglwyfus a welir yng nghywyddau'r bardd o Lantrisant. Disgybl i Siôn Cent oedd ef. Tybiais unwaith mai Iolo a gyfnewidiodd Lywelyn ap Hwlcyn yn Llywelyn ap Hywel ap Ieuan ap Gronw, ond, o archwilio *Add. MS.* 14,974, y mae'n eglur fod y camgymeriad yn myned yn ol i ddechreu'r ail ganrif ar bymtheg, oherwydd ysgrifennwyd enw'r olaf gan rywun yn y cyfnod hwnnw wrth odre un o'r caneuon. Beth bynnag am hynny, nid oes amheuaeth nad Llywelyn ap Hwlcyn o Fôn, neu Llelo Llwyd yw awdur amryw o'r caniadau hyn.

Ar ol yr amser hwnnw, y cyfraniad pwysicaf at y ddadl yw erthygl Mr Ifor Williams, MA, yn nhrydedd Gyfrol y BEIRNIAD (1913), tud. 230–244, yn cadarnhau rhesymau'r Prifathro Davies. Dengys yn eglur oddiar brofion ieithyddol na fedrai caniadau tybiedig Rhys Goch fod yn hŷn na chwarter olaf yr unfed ganrif ar bymtheg. Dyry enghreifftiau i ddangos mai dynwared Dafydd ap Gwilym a wnaeth yr awdur trwy gymryd un o gywyddau'r olaf a'i ail-bobi yn y mesur cwndid. Dengys hefyd iddo ddynwared tipyn ar gywyddau Tomas Prys o Blas Iolyn.

Ond fe erys problemau dyrys heb eu datrys. Os pump o'r caniadau sydd yn *Add. MS* 14,974, ymha fodd y mae cyfrif am y pymtheg cerdd arall sydd yn yr *Iolo MSS*? Ym mha fodd y cysylltwyd enw Rhys Goch ap Rhiccert ap Einion ap Collwyn o Dir Iarll â hwynt, a phaham na fuasai sôn amdano fel bardd cyn 1803? Ac ymhellach, paham yr ymddengys y cerddi mewn orgraff a diwyg mor ddiweddar? Ac ym mha le y mae llyfr Siôn Bradford? Hyd yn hyn erys y problemau yma heb eu datrys.

Gan mai o lawysgrifau Iolo Morganwg y codwyd y caniadau gan Ab Iolo, y lle tebycaf i gael esboniad ar y cwestiynau uchod oedd ymhlith y llawysgrifau hynny. O'u harchwilio, cefais yn Llanofer C 40 gasgliad o 'Gwndidau Deheubarth' yn cynnwys gwaith Dafydd o'r Nant, Hopcin y Gweydd o Fargam, Siencyn Lygad Rhawlin ac eraill, a chaniadau tybiedig Rhys Goch ap Rhiccert. O dud. 421–454 ceir yr ugain cân a gododd Ab Iolo i'r *Iolo MSS.*, ac y maent yno bron yn union fel yr argraffwyd hwy, ag eithrio rhyw fân wahaniaethau a ddengys nad oedd Ab Iolo yn gopïwr rhy ofalus. Ar dud. 421, uwchben y gân gyntaf, y mae'r nodiad 'Llyfr John Bradford' wedi ei ysgrifennu mewn amser diweddarach, ond ni ddywed am y lleill o ba lyfr y tynnodd hwy. Mae'n debig mai Llyfr Siôn Bradford oedd yn ei feddwl am y rhai hynny, ond ni cheir ganddo yr un sylw i gadarnhau gosodiad Ab Iolo yn ei nodyn ar odre tud. 228 o'r *Iolo MSS*. Rhaid cofio nad cyfres ar ei phen ei hun mo ganiadau Rhys Goch, namyn rhan o 'Gwndidau Deheubarth.'

Ond ymhellach ymlaen yn Llanofer C 40, deuwn o hyd i ffaith arwyddocaol dros ben sydd yn taflu goleuni newydd ar hanes y caniadau hyn. Ymhlith cyfres o 'Hen Garolau a gasglwyd yng Ngwynedd,' fe gawn y caniadau sydd yn llawysgrif Salsbriaid y Rhug, a gyhoeddwyd yn *Hen Ganiadau Serch*. Cynnwys y rhai hyn wreiddiol y pum cân a briodolid i Rys Goch ar sail dybiedig Llyfr Siôn Bradford. Yn Llanofer C 40 td. 587 ceir gwreiddiol Rhif 2 yr *Iolo MSS* 'Cân i Wallt Merch'. Ar dud. 579 ceir gwreiddiol Rhif 3 'Carol Serch', – 'Claf wyf o serch annerch Anni.' Ar dud. 583 ceir gwreiddiol Rhif 13 'Carol i ddanfon Merch i Rufain', – 'Cyrchu'r Cowrsi mynd i garu'. Ar dud. 585 ceir gwreiddiol Rhif 20 'Carol mawl Merch', – 'Deuliw blodeu Meinion aeleu'. Nid oes gopi o wreiddiol Rhif 1 yn Llanofer C 40, ond ymhlith cyfres gyffelyb o 'Garolau a gasglwyd yng Ngwynedd' yn Llanofer C 73, fe geir Rhif 1 yn ogystal â'r pedair cân arall. Yr unig wahaniaeth rhwng y rhai uchod â'r copi a gafodd y Prifathro J. H. Davies yn *Add. MS* 14,974 ydyw fod y rhain mewn orgraff ddiweddar. Gellir nodi un gwahaniaeth arall rhwng copi Llanofer C 40 ag un Llanofer C 73, sef nad oes teitlau i'r cerddi yn yr ysgriflyfr olaf. Gwelir felly fod Iolo Morganwg yn gwybod am y pum cân a geid mewn ysgriflyfr yn y gogledd, heb enw Rhys Goch na neb arall wrthynt, ac iddo eu copïo pan oedd ar un o'i deithiau trwy Wynedd. Y mae'n amhosibl penderfynu hyd sicrwydd o ba lawysgrif y cododd Iolo hwy, ond, od oedd llawysgrif Llundain ymhlith ysgriflyfrau Dafydd Jones o Drefriw yng Nghaer Rhun yn 1799, y mae'n sicr bron mai'r pryd hynny yr ysgrifennodd hwy yn ei lyfr ei hun.

Gadawn y mater hwn am ychydig yn awr, a chwiliwn y cerddi eu hunain. Wedi eu darllen drosodd lawer gwaith deuthum i deimlo imi weled yr un cyffyrddiadau, yr un hoffymadroddion a'r un grefft lenyddol o'r blaen. Yr oedd y nodau yn ddigamsyniol. A pho fwyaf y darllener hwy, cryfaf y tyf y syniad mai'r un gŵr a'u hysgrifennodd ag a gyfansoddodd y cywyddau a ychwanegwyd at waith Dafydd ap Gwilym yn 1789, ag a ysgrifennodd y 'penillion cynnrych' yng *Nghyfrinach y Beirdd* a'r cerddi rhydd ysgeifn a nwyfus a briodolir i Ddafydd o'r Nant a Dafydd Nicholas o Aberpergwm, ac a gyfansoddodd y cywyddau sydd yn llawysgrifau Llanofer â'r nodyn 'Iorwerth Gwilym a'i cant' o danynt. Wrth gwrs, â pump o'r cerddi yn ôl i'r ail ganrif ar bymtheg (Rhif 1, 2, 3, 13 a 20), ond o gymharu'r cerddi fel yr argraffwyd hwy yn *Hen Ganiadau Serch* â'r copi y dywed Iolo iddo ei dynnu o Lyfr Siôn Bradford, gwelir ar unwaith i'r pump hyn gael eu trwsio a'u 'diwygio' gan rywun. Nid oes eisieu manylu ar y pwynt hwn oherwydd medr yr hwn a fynno gymharu'r gwahanol ddarlleniadau yn *Hen Ganiadau Serch*, ond dylid sylwi fod yr hyn a ychwanegwyd atynt yn arwain yr un nodau â'r pymtheg cân nas ceir yn unman ond yn Llanofer C 40 a'r *Iolo MSS*.

I ddangos hyn, rhaid inni gymryd, yn gyntaf, eiriau a geir yng nghaniadau tybiedig Rhys Goch, nas gwelir yn unman ond yng ngwaith Iolo Morganwg, a geiriau a brawddegau a dull ymadroddion a gafodd yng ngweithiau'r hen feirdd ac a ddefnyddiodd fel ceffylau pren yn ei waith ei hun. Cymerwn yn gyntaf y gair *ernych*. Dangoswyd o'r blaen mai dyma un o hoff-eiriau Iolo. Ceir ef yn nhrydedd gân Rhys Goch (td. 231 o'r *Iolo MSS.*), 'Gaeaf yw arnaf *ernych* Dybryd'. Dyma un o gerddi llawysgrif Llundain, ond nid yw'r llinell hon yn y copi hwnnw. Dyma'n sicr ôl y 'trwsiwr.'

...

Ymadrodd arall yw *o gylchon* a geir yng ngherddi Rhys Goch (td. 244). Ceir yr ymadrodd hwn byth a beunydd yn y caniadau tlysion sydd yn cael eu priodoli i Forgan Pywel, Lewis William, William Llywelyn a Hopcin Twm Philip yn Llanofer C 12 a C 40. Ceir dwy gân gan Rys Brydydd o Dir Iarll yn Llanofer C 18 ac ynddynt hwy hefyd fe geir yr ymadrodd *ogylchon*. Ond y mae profion mewnol yn y caniadau uchod i gyd yn dangos mai gwaith yr un awdur ydynt, ac mai Iolo yw'r awdur hwnnw.

...

Dengys camgymeriadau mewn iaith a chystrawen, a ffurfiau ffug-hynafol hefyd y cysylltiad sydd rhwng caniadau tybiedig Rhys Goch a chywyddau Iolo. Ar dud. 232 o'r *Iolo MSS.*, lle y denfyn Rhys Goch yr adar yn llateion at ferch, ceir y ffurf *saethes* yn y llinell 'E'm *saethes* honn.' Yr oedd *–es* yn hen ddiweddiad i'r trydydd person unigol yn yr amser gorffennol, pan fai'r llafariad yn y sillaf o'r blaen yn -*o*- neu -*oe*-, megis *rhoddes* ac *oeres*. Ni wn a oes un eithriad i'r rheol hon ond *gweles*, a geir mewn rhai hen lawysgrifau yn lle *gwelas*. Ond pan fynnai Iolo ffugio hynafiaeth rhoddai'r hen ddiweddiad yma i bron bob berf, beth bynnag fai'r llafariad flaenorol. Gwelir ef yn *a dawes* (o *tewi*) yn ei farwnad i Lewys Hopcin (*Hopciniaid Morganwg*, td. 362). Yn ei ysgrifeniadau diweddar lle y myn ffugio ysgrifau i gadarnhau dosbarth Morganwg, yr Orsedd a phethau eraill, cawn lu o'r ffurfiau ffug-hynafol yma, sydd yn ein hatgoffau o fref yr asyn yng nghroen y llew. Cymerer *Barddas* (Ab Ithel, Cyf. I.), td. 16, a cheir y ffurfiau *tarddes*, *dealles*, a thud. 20 *clywes*. Yn Rhol Cof a Chyfrif (*Iolo MSS.*, td. 46) ysgrifennwyd ffurf cyn hacred ac mor amhosibl â *cadarnhaes*. Ysgrifennai hefyd y ffurf *eaws* (am *eos*), fel y dengys y llinell hon o'i gywydd i'r bore, 'Eaws yw'r unig awen,' a cheir yr un ffurf ar dud. 245 o'r *Iolo MSS.*, 'Ai goslef maws nawcan eaws.'

...

Wedi ceisio dangos y tebygrwydd mawr sydd rhwng caniadau tybiedig Rhys Goch a chywyddau Iolo Morganwg, casglwn y ffeithiau sydd gennym ynglŷn â'r caniadau hyn ynghyd. Seiliwyd pump ohonynt ar rai a geir mewn llawysgrif a berthyn i'r unfed ganrif ar bymtheg, a dechreu'r ail ar bymtheg. Gwyddai Iolo am y caniadau hyn ac fe'u copïodd. Gwyddai hefyd mai llawysgrif o Wynedd oedd oherwydd mewn casgliad o 'Garolau a gasglwyd yng Ngwynedd' y ceir hwy. Nid oes sôn am y pymtheg cân arall yno. Yna yn Llanofer C 40, td. 421–454 ceir yr ugain cân bron yn union fel yr argraffwyd hwy yn yr *Iolo MSS.* yn 1848. Mewn amser diweddarach ysgrifennodd uwchben y gân gyntaf 'Llyfr John Bradford'. Ond fe welsom wrth ymdrin â Chywyddau'r Ychwanegiad ba faint o goel i roddi ar Iolo pan sonio am lyfrau Siôn Bradford: felly, pan gawn fod y pymtheg cân nas ceir yn llawysgrif Llundain, yn ogystal â'r ychwanegiadau at y pump eraill yn meddu llinellau sydd yn union yr un fath â rhai Iolo, yn meddu geiriau nas ceir ond yng ngwaith Iolo, a'r un camgymeriadau mewn gramadeg, ac yn dangos y bardd yn marchogaeth yr un ceffylau pren, arweinir ein meddwl yn naturiol at yr un casgliad ag y deuthom iddo wrth ymdrin â Chywyddau'r Ychwanegiad, sef mai Iolo ei hun yw'r awdur. Ceisiodd ddynwared Dafydd ap Gwilym, ac yna haeru i'r bardd hwnnw dderbyn ei ysbrydiaeth o ganiadau Rhys Goch yn union fel y gwnaeth â Chyfraith Hywel Dda wrth wneuthur Trioedd Dyfnwal Moelmud.

. . .

Ond, meddir, a chaniatau i Iolo drwsio caniadau a gasglwyd yng Ngwynedd, ac iddo gyfansoddi pymtheg cân arall, a dywedyd mai Rhys Goch ap Rhiccert oedd yr awdur, beth oedd ei amcan? Gwaith anodd iawn ydyw datrys amcanion a bwriadau gŵr fel Iolo, ond nid oes llawer o amheuaeth beth oedd ei amcan wrth briodoli caniadau i Rys Goch ap Rhiccert.

Er mwyn dangos fod traddodiad llenyddol cryf yn Nhir Iarll yn yr oesoedd canol, a bod yr hyn a alwai yn 'Gadair Tir Iarll' yn flodeuog mewn cyfnod mor fore, buddiol fuasai dangos barddoniaeth beirdd y 'Gadair' y pryd hynny. Ofer oedd iddo edrych amdani ymhlith cynyrchion y Gogynfeirdd, oherwydd ychydig iawn ohonynt hwy a hanoedd o'r Deheu. Yn yr argyfwng hwn, haerodd i 'Gadair Tir Iarll' gynyrchu dau fardd o fri yn y cyfnod hwnnw, sef Rhys Goch ap Rhiccert ab Einion ap Collwyn, gŵr y gwelodd ei enw fel ŵyr i'r pennaeth Einion ap Collwyn ac un o hynafiaid teulu athrylithgar Rhys Brydydd o Lanharan, yn y llyfrau achau (gweler y *Report on Welsh MSS*, Cyfr. I, Rhan ii, td. 992), ac Ieuan Fawr ap y Diwlith, gŵr ni welais ei enw yn unman ond yn ysgrifau Iolo. Casglodd oddiwrth y ffaith i Einion ap Collwyn fyw yn yr unfed ganrif ar ddeg mai tua 1140 y blagurai Rhys Goch. Nid yw'n bosibl penderfynu hyd sicrwydd beth a wnaeth iddo ddewis Rhys Goch, oni welodd i lawer o feirdd ddwyn yr enw hwnnw, a'i fod yn un o hynafiaid Rhys Brydydd, Gwilym Tew, Rhisiart ap Rhys, Lewis Morgannwg a Thwm Ifan Prys. Felly dyma ŵr na wyddai neb ddim amdano namyn ei fod yn ŵyr i Einion ap Collwyn yn cael ei anfarwoli fel bardd, trwy ddichell, dros chwe chan mlynedd wedi iddo farw. Ffrwyth dychymyg Iolo, am a wn i, ydyw enw Ieuan Fawr ap y Diwlith, ac amserwyd ef tua 1160–1180, gan i Iolo ei wneuthur yn fab maeth i Rys Goch yn y chwedl farddonol a welir ar dud. 88 o'r *Iolo MSS*.

Ond pa fath ar farddoniaeth y buasai Rhys Goch yn debig o'i chyfansoddi? Tybiai Iolo, fel y dengys ei aml draethodau ar farddoniaeth Cymru mai o Iwerddon a Llychlyn y cafodd y Gogledd ei hysbrydiaeth trwy Ruffydd ap Cynan; a myn i'r Deheu gadw'r hyn a eilw'n *primitive school*, sef ysgol Taliesin a'r Cynfeirdd. Canai'r ysgol hon yn yr hen 'gysefin fesurau', meddai ef, sef mesurau Morgannwg, a dyna ddyry gyfrif am fesurau Rhys Goch. Tybiai i'r Normaniaid wrth sefydlu ym Morgannwg ddyfod â dylanwad y Trwbadwriaid gyda hwy, ac felly i ysgol Rhamant ddechreu yno tua dechreu'r ddeuddegfed ganrif. Dyna a ddyry gyfrif am ddull Rhys Goch o ganu. I ddangos hyn, dyfynnwn rai pethau o blith llawysgrifau Iolo. Dywed yn Llanofer C 21, td. 134:—

About 1130 flourished *Rhŷs Goch ap Riccert ap Einion ap Collwyn*, in Glamorgan. He for the most part, if not wholly, retained the metres and manner of the older schools. But in his poems we find a cast of gallantry which had not before been to any considerable degree admitted into the Welsh Poetry, at least as far as can be judged now from what remains of our old Poetry. In this Poet's Sentiments and manner we find something of the manner of the *Provençal Troubadours*. The *Norman Barons* who had settled in Glamorgan were those who opened the way for this new cast in Poetry. Their Castles or Courts were the Gates thro' which it entered into Wales. *Be this as it may*, we about this period observe a remarkable change (td.135) in the subjects and turns of sentiments in our Poetry. In the works of *Rhŷs Goch ap Riccert* the clear dawn of this new manner appears, which in a century and a half afterwards brightened into the bright summer's noon of *Dafydd ap Gwilym*. Thus founded by *Rhŷs Goch ap Riccert* and beautifully superstructed by *Dafydd ap Gwilym*, we see a new school established in the *Silurian district of Wales*, differing greatly from such as preceded it but much more congenial to human nature in its civilized state. This school must now be considered as distinct from all others, and treated of as such.

A thro arall dywed (Llanofer C 36, td. 246):

I once thought that the antiquity of many pieces of Rhys Goch ap Rhiccert could not be admitted . . . but I think otherwise now especially as . . . we find the same things in Taliesin.

A thro arall (Llanofer C 30, td. 121) dywed:

Rhys Goch was a grandson of Einion and lived at the time when the Provençal literature was in the height of its glory. He was doubtless acquainted with it.

Y mae'n anhygoel bron y medrai dyn ysgrifennu yn y modd yna am bethau o'i waith ei hun, ond fel y dywedwyd o'r blaen, problem mewn eneideg yw Iolo Morganwg. Beth bynnag am hynny, credaf fod yn y dyfyniadau uchod allwedd i esbonio dirgelwch caniadau Rhys Goch. Mynnai Iolo sefydlu ysgol o feirdd ym Morgannwg yn yr oesoedd canol, a gwneuthur Dafydd ap Gwilym yn binacl traddodiad yr ysgol honno. Ac odid nad i ategu hawl Morgannwg i Ddafydd y cyfansoddwyd Cywyddau'r Ychwanegiad.

Credaf felly ei bod yn eglur mai Iolo a wnaeth Rys Goch ap Rhiccert yn fardd, ac mai ef yw awdur pymtheg o'r caniadau a thrwsiwr y gweddill, ac na fu ym meddiant Siôn Bradford erioed y llyfr y sonnir amdano yn yr *Iolo MSS*. Rhaid inni roddi Rhys Goch ap Rhiccert ab Einion ap Collwyn yn ol i'w le cysefin yn y llyfrau achau, o'r lle y cyfodwyd ef gan Iolo, dros gan mlynedd yn ol, i chwarae ei ran yn hanes llenyddol Morgannwg fel y mynnai Iolo i'r hanes hwnnw fod.

GRIFFITH J. WILLIAMS

# Select Bibliography

Anderson, Benedict, *Imagined Communities* (rev. edn., London, 1991).
Anderson, Olive, 'The Political Uses of History', *Past and Present*, 36 (1967), 87–105.
ap Nicholas, Islwyn, *A Welsh Heretic: Dr William Price, Llantrisant* (Llandybïe, 1970).
ap Rhys, Gweirydd, *Hanes y Brytaniaid a'r Cymry* (2 vols., Llundain, 1874).
Ashton, Charles, *Hanes Llenyddiaeth Gymreig o 1651 O.C. hyd 1850* (Liverpool, 1893).
Balcou, Jean, Yves Le Gallo, Louis Le Gouillou (eds.), *Histoire littéraire et culturelle de la Bretagne. Tome III: L'invasion profane, de la Troisième à la Cinquième République* (3 vols., Paris, 1987).
Barrett, Cyril, and Jeanne Sheehy, 'Visual Arts and Society, 1850–1900' in Vaughan (ed.), *A New History of Ireland, VI*, pp. 436–74.
—— 'Visual Arts and Society, 1900–20' in Vaughan (ed.), *A New History of Ireland, VI*, pp. 475–99.
Barthes, Roland, *Mythologies* (London, 1993).
Berthou, Yves (Kaledvoulc'h), *Sous le chêne des druides: Les Triades bardiques avec le texte original gallois; Le Mystère de la vie et du monde, d'après le Barddas; Le druidisme et la destinée de l'homme* (Paris, 1931).
Betts, Clive, *A Oedd Heddwch?* (Caerdydd, 1978).
Bowe, Nicola Gordon, and Elizabeth Cumming (eds.), *The Arts and Crafts Movements in Dublin and Edinburgh* (Dublin, 1998).
Bowen, Geraint, 'Archdderwydd: Y Teitl a'r Swydd', *NLWJ*, XXIV, no. 3 (1986), 358–88.
—— and Zonia Bowen, *Hanes Gorsedd y Beirdd* (Abertawe, 1991).
Bracegirdle, Cyril, *Dr William Price: Saint or Sinner* (Llanrwst, 1997).
Brake, L., A. Jones, L. Madden (eds.), *Investigating Victorian Journalism* (Basingstoke, 1990).
Brierley, George (ed.), *Cymru Fu: Notes and Queries Relating to the Past History of Wales and the Border Counties* (2 vols., Cardiff, 1887–91).
Bromwich, Rachel, *'Trioedd Ynys Prydain'* in *Welsh Literature and Scholarship* (Cardiff, 1969).
—— 'Trioedd Ynys Prydain: The *Myvyrian* "Third Series"', *THSC* (1968), 299–338 (1969), 127–55.
Brown, Terence (ed.), *Celticism* (Amsterdam, 1996).
Carlyle, Thomas, *On Heroes, Hero-worship and the Heroic in History* (London, 1841).
Carr, Glenda, *William Owen Pughe* (Caerdydd, 1983).
—— 'An Uneasy Partnership: Iolo Morganwg and William Owen Pughe' in Jenkins (ed.), *Rattleskull Genius*, pp. 443–60.
Champion, Timothy, 'The Appropriation of the Phoenicians in British Imperial Ideology', *Nations and Nationalism*, VII, no. 4 (2001), 451–65.
Charnell-White, Cathryn A., *Barbarism and Bardism: North Wales versus South Wales in the Bardic Vision of Iolo Morganwg* (Aberystwyth, 2004).

—— *Bardic Circles: National, Regional and Personal Identity in the Bardic Vision of Iolo Morganwg* (Cardiff, 2007).
—— 'Women and Gender in the Private and Social Relationships of Iolo Morganwg' in Jenkins (ed.), *Rattleskull Genius*, pp. 359–81.
Constantine, Mary-Ann, *The Truth against the World: Iolo Morganwg and Romantic Forgery* (Cardiff, 2007).
Cooney, Gabriel, 'Building the Future on the Past: Archaeology and the Construction of National Identity in Ireland' in Díaz-Andreu and Champion (eds.), *Nationalism and Archaeology in Europe*, pp. 146–63.
Cragoe, Matthew, *Culture, Politics, and National Identity in Wales 1832–1886* (Oxford, 2004).
Cullen, Fintan, *Visual Politics: The Representation of Ireland 1750–1930* (Cork, 1997).
Dalsimer, Adele M., *Visualizing Ireland: National Identity and the Pictorial Tradition* (Boston, Mass., 1993).
Davies, Andrew, '"Uncontaminated with Human Gore"? Iolo Morganwg, Slavery and the Jamaican Inheritance' in Jenkins (ed.), *Rattleskull Genius*, pp. 293–313.
Davies, Aneirin Talfan, *Bro Morgannwg* (2 vols., Abertawe, 1976).
Davies, Ann Elsbeth, 'Cerddi Serch a Natur Iolo Morganwg' (unpublished University of Wales M.Phil. thesis, 1999).
Davies, Brian, 'Archaeology and Ideology, or How Wales was Robbed of its Early History', *New Welsh Review*, 37 (1997), 38–51.
—— 'Empire and Identity: The "Case" of Dr William Price' in David B. Smith (ed.), *A People and a Proletariat* (London, 1980), pp. 72–93.
Davies, D. Elwyn J., 'Astudiaeth o Feddwl a Chyfraniad Iolo Morganwg fel Rhesymolwr ac Undodwr' (unpublished University of Wales Ph.D. thesis, 1975).
Davies, Damian Walford, *Presences that Disturb: Models of Romantic Identity in the Literature and Culture of the 1790s* (Cardiff, 2002).
Davies, Edward, *Celtic Researches* (London, 1803).
—— *The Mythology and Rites of the British Druids* (London, 1809).
Davies, Evan, *Gogoniant Hynafol y Cymmry: sef Arddangosiad o Gyfrin-ddysg Hynaf y Byd allan o Gyfrinion Gorsedd Beirdd Cyntefigion Ynys Brydain* (Pontypridd, 1865).
—— *Hynafiaeth Aruthrol y Trwn neu Orsedd Beirdd Ynys Brydain a'i Barddas Gyfrin* (Pontypridd, 1875).
Davies, G. Gerallt, *Gwilym Cowlyd 1828–1904* (Caernarfon, 1976).
Davies, J. Glyn, *Welsh Metrics* (Cardiff, 1911).
Davies, John, *Cardiff and the Marquesses of Bute* (Cardiff, 1981).
Davies, R. Rees, 'Owain Glyn Dŵr a'i Apêl', *Y Traethodydd*, CLV, no. 655 (2000), 198–209.
—— and Geraint H. Jenkins (eds.), *From Medieval to Modern Wales: Historical Essays in Honour of Kenneth O. Morgan and Ralph A. Griffiths* (Cardiff, 2004).
Dearnley, Moira, '"Mad Ned" and the "Smatter-Dasher": Iolo Morganwg and Edward "Celtic" Davies' in Jenkins (ed.), *Rattleskull Genius*, pp. 425–42.
Denning, Roy, 'Druidism at Pontypridd' in Stewart Williams (ed.), *Glamorgan Historian: Volume I* (Cowbridge, 1963), pp. 136–45.
Díaz-Andreu, Margarita, and Timothy Champion (eds.), *Nationalism and Archaeology in Europe* (London, 1896).
Donovan, Patrick J. (ed.), *Cerddi Rhydd Iolo Morganwg* (Caerdydd, 1980).

Dunbabin, J. P. D., 'Oliver Cromwell's Popular Image in Nineteenth-Century England' in J. S. Bromley and E. H. Lossmann (eds.), *Britain and the Netherlands. Volume V: Some Political Mythologies* (The Hague, 1975), pp. 141–63.

Edwards, Huw Meirion, 'The Lyric Poets' in Edwards (ed.), *A Guide to Welsh Literature c.1800–1900*, pp. 97–125.

—— 'A Multitude of Voices: The Free-Metre Poetry of Iolo Morganwg' in Jenkins (ed.), *Rattleskull Genius*, pp. 95–121.

Edwards, Hywel Teifi, *Codi'r Hen Wlad yn ei Hôl, 1850–1914* (Llandysul, 1989).

—— *The Eisteddfod* (Cardiff, 1990).

—— *Gŵyl Gwalia: Yr Eisteddfod yn Oes Aur Victoria 1858–1868* (Llandysul, 1980).

—— 'The Merthyr Tydfil National Eisteddfod, 1881', *Merthyr Historian*, X (1999), 81–100.

—— 'O'r Pentre Gwyn i Llaregyb' in M. Wynn Thomas (ed.), *DiFfinio Dwy Lenyddiaeth Cymru* (Caerdydd, 1995), pp. 7–41.

—— 'The Welsh Language in the Eisteddfod' in Jenkins (ed.), *The Welsh Language and its Social Domains 1801–1911*, pp. 293–316.

—— (ed.), *Cwm Cynon* (Llandysul, 1997).

—— (ed.), *A Guide to Welsh Literature c.1800–1900* (Cardiff, 2000).

—— (ed.), *Merthyr a Thaf* (Llandysul, 2001).

Edwards, Owen M. (ed.), *Gwaith Dafydd ab Gwilym* (Llanuwchllyn, 1901).

Ellis, John S., 'The Prince and the Dragon: Welsh National Identity and the 1911 Investiture of the Prince of Wales', *WHR*, 18, no. 2 (1996), 272–94.

Ellis, Robert (Cynddelw) (ed.), *Barddoniaeth Dafydd ab Gwilym: O Grynhoad Owen Jones (Owain Myfyr), William Owen (Dr W. Owen Pughe), ac Edward Williams (Iolo Morganwg) yn nghydag amryw gyfieithiadau i'r Seisnig* (Liverpool, 1873).

—— *Geiriadur y Bardd: neu yr Odlydd Cyffredinol, at Wasanaeth y Beirdd . . . At yr hyn yr Ychwanegwyd, Cyfrinach Beirdd Ynys Prydain* (Caernarfon, 1874).

Ellis, Tecwyn, 'Ymweliadau Iolo Morganwg â Meirionnydd', *Journal of Merioneth Historical and Record Society*, V, part III (1967), 239–50.

Emrys-Jones, A., *The Life and Works of Edward Williams (Iolo Morganwg), The Bard of Glamorgan (Reprinted from the Manchester Quarterly)* (London, 1889).

Evans, Beriah Gwynfe, *The Bardic Gorsedd: Its History and Symbolism* (Pontypool, 1923).

Evans, D. Delta, *The Ancient Bards of Britain (sometimes called 'Druids'): Being a Critical Inquiry into Traditions concerning their History, Philosophy, Religion, Ethics, and Rites, in the Light of Science and Modern Thought* (Merthyr Tydfil, 1906).

Evans, Frederic, *Tir Iarll: The Earl's Land* (Cardiff, 1912).

Evans, Neil, 'The Welsh Victorian City: The Middle Class and Civic and National Consciousness in Cardiff, 1850–1914', *WHR*, 12, no. 3 (1985), 350–87.

Evans, R. J. W., 'Language and Society in the Nineteenth Century: Some Central-European Comparisons' in Jenkins (ed.), *Language and Community in the Nineteenth Century* , pp. 397–424.

—— '"The Manuscripts": The Culture and Politics of Forgery in Central Europe' in Jenkins (ed.), *Rattleskull Genius*, pp. 51–68.

—— and Hartmut Pogge von Strandmann (eds.), *The Revolutions in Europe 1848–1849: From Reform to Reaction* (Oxford, 2000).

Evans, T. C. (Cadrawd) (ed.), *Gwaith Iolo Morganwg: Y Rhan Fwyaf wedi ei Godi o Lawysgrifau Iolo yn Llanofer* (Llanuwchllyn, 1913).

—— and L. J. Hopkin-James, *Hen Gwndidau, Carolau, a Chywyddau being Sermons in Song in the Gwentian Dialect by Forty-Two Bards of Tir Iarll of the Tudor Period* (Bangor, 1910).

Evans, William, *Diary of a Welsh Swagman 1869–1894* (London, 1975).

Foster, Idris (ed.), *Twf yr Eisteddfod* (Aberystwyth, 1968).

Foulkes, Isaac (Llyfrbryf) (ed.), *Cymru Fu yn cynnwys Hanesion, Traddodiadau, yn nghyda Chwedlau a Dammegion Cymreig (oddiar lafar gwlad a gweithiau y prif awduron)* (Wrexham, 1862).

Fraser, Maxwell, 'Jane Williams (Ysgafell) 1806–1885)', *Brycheiniog*, VII (1961), 95–114.

—— 'Lady Llanover and her Circle', *THSC* (1969), 170–96.

Freeman, Peter, *The Druids and Theosophy* (Glasgow, 1924).

Gaidoz, Henri, 'Extraits des dictons du sage Cadoc, traduits du gallois par M. W. G. Jones', *Revue Celtique*, III (1876), 419–42.

Gaskill, Howard (ed.), *The Reception of Ossian in Europe* (London, 2004).

Gee, Thomas, *Emynau y Cysegr* (Dinbych, 1885).

Gjerset, Knut, *History of the Norwegian People* (New York, 1927).

Griffiths, William Alonzo, *Hanes Emynwyr Cymru* (Caernarfon, 1893).

Gross, Joseph, *A Brief History of Merthyr Tydfil* (Newport, 1980).

Grote, Georg, *Torn between Politics and Culture: The Gaelic League 1893–1993* (Münster, 1994).

Gruffydd, R. Geraint, *Dafydd ap Gwilym* (Caernarfon, 1987).

—— 'Dafydd ap Gwilym: An Outline Biography' in Cyril J. Byrne, Margaret Harry, Pàdraig Ó Siadhail (eds.), *Celtic Languages and Celtic Peoples: Proceedings of the Second North American Congress of Celtic Studies* (Halifax, NS, 1992), pp. 425–42.

Gunn, Simon, *The Public Culture of the Victorian Middle Class: Ritual and Authority in the English Industrial City 1840–1914* (Manchester, 2000).

Hale, Amy, 'Genesis of the Celto-Cornish Revival? L. C. Duncombe-Jewell and the Cowethas Kelto-Kernuak', *Cornish Studies*, 5 (1998), 100–11.

Harvie, Christopher, 'The Folk and the *Gwerin*: The Myth and the Reality of Popular Culture in Nineteenth-Century Scotland and Wales', *Proceedings of the British Academy*, 80 (1991), 19–48.

Hazareesingh, Sudhir, *The Legend of Napoleon* (London, 2005).

Henken, Elissa R., *National Redeemer: Owain Glyndŵr in Welsh Tradition* (Cardiff, 1996).

—— 'The Saint as Folk Hero: Biographical Patterning in Welsh Hagiography' in Patrick K. Ford (ed.), *Celtic Folk Lore and Christianity: Studies in Memory of William W. Heist* (Santa Barbara, Calif., 1983), pp. 58–74.

Herbert, Algernon, *Britannia after the Romans; Being an Attempt to Illustrate the Religious and Political Revolutions of that Province in the Fifth and Succeeding Centuries* (London, 1836).

—— *An Essay on the Neodruidic Heresy in Britannia. Part the First* (London, 1838).

Hess, Scott, *Authoring the Self: Self-Representation, Authorship, and the Print Market in British Poetry from Pope through Wordsworth* (New York, 2005).

Hobsbawm, Eric, *The Age of Capital, 1848–1875* (London, 1995).

Hroch, Miroslav, *Social Preconditions of National Revival in Europe* (New York, 2000).

Hughes, Arthur (ed.), *Cywyddau Cymru* (Bangor, 1908).

Hutchinson, John, 'Archaeology and the Irish Rediscovery of the Celtic Past', *Nations and Nationalism*, VII, no. 4 (2001), 505–19.
Isaac, David Lloyd, *Siluriana: or Contributions towards the History of Gwent and Glamorgan* (Newport, 1859).
James, Allan, *Diwylliant Gwerin Morgannwg* (Llandysul, 2002).
—— *John Morris-Jones* (Cardiff, 1987).
James, Lemuel 'Hopcyn', *Hopkiniaid Morganwg: Being a Genealogical Biography of the Hopkin Family of Glamorgan with the Works of Hopkin Thomas Philip and Lewis Hopkin* (Bangor, 1909).
Jenkins, Dafydd, *Thomas Johnes o'r Hafod* (Caerdydd, 1948).
Jenkins, David, *Thomas Gwynn Jones: Cofiant* (Dinbych, 1973).
Jenkins, Geraint H., *'Perish Kings and Emperors, but Let the Bard of Liberty Live'* (Aberystwyth, 2006).
—— 'The Bard of Liberty during William Pitt's Reign of Terror' in Joseph Falaky Nagy and Leslie Ellen Jones (eds.), *Heroic Poets and Poetic Heroes in Celtic Tradition: A Festschrift for Patrick K. Ford*, CSANA Yearbook 3–4 (Dublin, 2005), pp. 183–206.
—— '"Dyro Dduw dy Nawdd": Iolo Morganwg a'r Mudiad Undodaidd' in idem (ed.), *Cof Cenedl XX: Ysgrifau ar Hanes Cymru* (Llandysul, 2005), pp. 65–100.
—— 'The Unitarian Firebrand, the Cambrian Society and the Eisteddfod' in idem (ed.), *Rattleskull Genius*, pp. 269–92.
—— '"A Very Horrid Affair": Sedition and Unitarianism in the Age of Revolutions' in Davies and Jenkins (eds.), *From Medieval to Modern Wales*, pp. 175–96.
—— (ed.), *Language and Community in the Nineteenth Century* (Cardiff, 1998).
—— (ed.), *A Rattleskull Genius: The Many Faces of Iolo Morganwg* (Cardiff, 2005).
—— (ed.), *The Welsh Language and its Social Domains 1801–1911* (Cardiff, 2000).
Jenkins, R. T., 'Hanes Cymdeithas yr Eisteddfod Genedlaethol', *THSC* (1936), 139–55.
Johnes, Arthur James (Maelog), *Translations into English Verse from the Poems of Davyth ap Gwilym, a Welsh Bard of the Fourteenth Century* (London, 1834).
Johnston, Dafydd, 'Early Translations of Dafydd ap Gwilym' in Alyce von Rothkirch and Daniel Williams (eds.), *Beyond the Difference: Welsh Literature in Comparative Contexts* (Cardiff, 2004), pp. 158–72.
Jones, Aled, *Press, Politics and Society: A History of Journalism in Wales* (Cardiff, 1993).
—— 'Brecknock at the Crossroads: Journalism, History and Cultural Identity in Nineteenth-Century Wales', *Brycheiniog*, XXXV (2003), 103–4.
Jones, Bedwyr Lewis, *Yr Hen Bersoniaid Llengar* (Dinbych, 1963).
Jones, Dot, *The Coming of the Railways and Language Change in North Wales, 1850–1900* (Aberystwyth, 1995).
—— *Statistical Evidence Relating to the Welsh Language 1801–1911* (Cardiff, 1998).
Jones, Edward, *The Bardic Museum: or Primitive British Literature and Rarities* (London, 1802).
Jones, Ieuan Gwynedd, *Explorations and Explanations: Essays in the Social History of Victorian Wales* (Llandysul, 1981).
—— *Mid-Victorian Wales: The Observers and the Observed* (Cardiff, 1992).
—— and David Williams (eds.), *The Religious Census of 1851: A Calendar of the Returns relating to Wales. Volume 1. South Wales* (Cardiff, 1976).

Jones, Ieuan Wyn, *Y Llinyn Arian: Agweddau o Fywyd a Chyfnod Thomas Gee* (Dinbych, 1998).
Jones, John, *On the State of Agriculture and the Progress of Arts and Manufactures in Britain, during the Period, and under the Influence, of the Druidical System* (London, 1851).
Jones, John Bowen, *Hen Emynau* (Merthyr Tydfil, 1877).
Jones, Morgan D., 'Thomas Stephens o Ferthyr Tudful', *Barddas*, no. 163 (1990), 20–3.
Jones, Owen, and William Owen (eds.), *Barddoniaeth Dafydd ab Gwilym* (London, 1789).
——, Iolo Morganwg, and William Owen Pughe, *The Myvyrian Archaiology of Wales* (3 vols., London, 1801–7).
Jones, Philip Henry, 'Printing and Publishing in the Welsh Language 1801–1914' in Jenkins (ed.), *The Welsh Language and its Social Domains 1800–1911*, pp. 317–47.
—— 'Saernïo'r Gofeb: T. Gwynn Jones a *Chofiant Thomas Gee*', *Y Traethodydd*, CXLVII, no. 625 (1992), 183–210.
Jones, Phylip, *Resolfen Reading Room* (Resolfen, 1996).
Jones, R. Emrys, *Rheilffyrdd Cymru / The Railways of Wales* (Penygroes, 1979).
Jones, R. Tudur, *John Elias: Pregethwr a Phendefig* (Bridgend, 1975).
Jones, Rees Jenkin, *Emynau o Fawl a Gweddi* (Aberdar, 1878; 2nd edn., 1883).
Jones, Stephanie, *Charles William Mansel Lewis: Painter, Patron and Promoter of Art in Wales* (Aberystwyth, 1998).
Jones, Thomas Ll. (ed.), *Ceinion Awen y Cymmry* (Dinbych, 1831).
Kedourie, Elie, *Nationalism* (4th edn., Oxford, 1993).
Koch, John T. (ed.), *Celtic Culture: A Historical Encyclopedia* (5 vols., Santa Barbara, Calif., 2006).
La Villemarqué, Hersart de, *La légende celtique et la poésie des cloîtres en Irlande, en Cambrie et en Bretagne* (Paris, 1864).
Ladmirault, Paul, *Abrégé du Barddas ou Livre du Bardisme* (Paris, 1931).
Lambert, Peter, and Phillipp Schofield (eds.), *Making History: An Introduction to the History and Practices of a Discipline* (London, 2004).
Le Stum, Philippe, *Le néo-druidisme en Bretagne: Origine, naissance et développement, 1890–1914* (Rennes, 1998).
Lewes, Evelyn Ann, *Life and Poems of Davydd ab Gwilym* (London, 1914).
Lewis, Ceri W., *Iolo Morganwg* (Caernarfon, 1995).
—— 'Iolo Morganwg' in Branwen Jarvis (ed.), *A Guide to Welsh Literature c.1700–1800* (Cardiff, 2000), pp. 126–67.
—— 'Iolo Morganwg and Strict-metre Welsh Poetry' in Jenkins (ed.), *Rattleskull Genius*, pp. 71–93.
Lewis, Hubert, *The Ancient Laws of Wales: Viewed Especially in regard to the Light They Throw upon the Origin of some English Institutions*, ed. by J. E. Lloyd (London, 1889).
Llobera, Josep R., *The God of Modernity: The Development of Nationalism in Western Europe* (Oxford, 1994).
Lockyer, Norman, *The Antiquity of the Gorsedd: A Lecture delivered to the Royal Institution of South Wales* (Swansea, 1908).
Löffler, Marion, *'A Book of Mad Celts': John Wickens and the Celtic Congress of Caernarfon 1904* (Llandysul, 2000).
—— 'Agweddau ar yr Undeb Pan-Geltaidd, 1898–1914', *Y Traethodydd*, CLV, no. 652 (2000), 44–59.

—— 'Der Pankeltismus vor dem Ersten Weltkrieg im Europäischen Kontext' in Erich Poppe (ed.), *Keltologie heute: Themen und Fragestellungen* (Münster, 2004), pp. 27–89.

—— '"Eu Hiaith a Gadwant": The Work of the National Union of Welsh Societies, 1913–1941', *THSC* (1998), 124–52.

Lord, Peter, *Y Chwaer Dduwies: Celf, Crefft a'r Eisteddfod* (Llandysul, 1992).

—— *The Visual Culture of Wales: Imaging the Nation* (Cardiff, 2000).

—— 'Yr Etifeddiaeth – Delwedd y Werin' in Ivor Davies and Ceridwen Lloyd-Morgan (eds.), *Darganfod Celf Cymru* (Caerdydd, 1999), pp. 82–109.

—— 'The popular iconography of the preacher' in idem, *Gwenllian: Essays on Visual Culture* (Llandysul, 1994), pp. 43–72.

Malkin, Benjamin Heath, *The Scenery, Antiquities, and Biography, of South Wales* (London, 1804).

Martin, Aubrey J., *Hanes Llwynrhydowen* (Llandysul, 1977).

Mee, Arthur (ed.), *Caermarthenshire Notes and Miscellany for South West Wales (Antiquarian, Topographical, and Curious). Reprinted with Additions from the Welshman* (3 vols., Llanelly, 1889–91).

Miles, Dillwyn, *The Secret of the Bards of the Isle of Britain* (Llandybïe, 1992).

Millward, E. G., *Yr Arwrgerdd Gymraeg: Ei Thwf a'i Thranc* (Caerdydd, 1998).

—— 'Merthyr Tudful: Tref y Brodyr Rhagorol' in Edwards (ed.), *Merthyr a Thaf*, pp. 9–56.

—— (ed.) *Blodeugerdd Barddas o Gerddi Rhydd y Ddeunawfed Ganrif* (Llandybïe, 1991).

Moelwyn-Hughes, John Gruffydd, *Die cymrischen Triaden, ihr Ursprung und ihr Verhältnis zu den Mabinogion* (Leipsig, 1903).

Moore-Colyer, R. J., *A Land of Pure Delight: Selections from the Letters of Thomas Johnes of Hafod 1748–1816* (Llandysul, 1992).

—— 'Thomas Johnes of Hafod (1748–1816): Translator and Bibliophile', *WHR*, 15, no. 3 (1991), 399–415.

Morgan, D. Densil, *Christmas Evans a'r Ymneilltuaeth Newydd* (Llandysul, 1991).

Morgan, Owen (Morien), *The History of Pontypridd and Rhondda Valleys* (Pontypridd, 1903).

Morgan, Prys, 'From Long Knives to Blue Books' in R. R. Davies (ed.), *Welsh Society and Nationhood: Historical Essays Presented to Glanmor Williams* (Cardiff, 1984), pp. 199–215.

—— 'Iolo Morganwg and Welsh Historical Traditions' in Jenkins (ed.), *Rattleskull Genius*, pp. 251–68.

—— 'A Private Space: Autobiography and Individuality in Eighteenth- and Early Nineteenth-Century Wales' in Davies and Jenkins (eds.), *From Medieval to Modern Wales*, pp. 160–74.

—— 'Thomas Price "Carnhuanawc" (1787–1848) et les Bretons', *Triade*, 1 (1995), 5–13.

—— (ed.), *Brad y Llyfrau Gleision: Ysgrifau ar Hanes Cymru* (Llandysul, 1991).

Morganwg, Dafydd, *Hanes Morganwg* (Aberdar, 1874).

Morris, Abraham, *Glamorgan: Being an Outline of its Geography, History, and Antiquities with Maps and Illustrations* (Newport, 1907).

Morris-Jones, J., *Cerdd Dafod, sef Celfyddyd Barddoniaeth Gymraeg* (Caerdydd, 1980).

Morus, Ben (Myfyr Teifi), *Enwogion Aber Dâr: Sef Byrr-nodion am rai o Gewri Ymadawedig y Dref a'r Cylch* (Llanbedr Pont Steffan, 1910).

Nicholas, Thomas, *The History and Antiquity of Glamorganshire and its Families* (London, 1874).
Nicholas, W. Rhys, 'Iolo Morganwg a'i Emynau', *Bwletin Cymdeithas Emynau Cymru*, I, no. 2 (1969), 14–25.
Ó Fearaíl, Pádraig, *The Story of Conradh na Gaeilge* (Dublin, 1975).
Ó Murchú, Máirtín, 'Language and Society in Nineteenth-Century Ireland' in Jenkins (ed.), *Language and Community in the Nineteenth Century*, pp. 341–68.
O'Neill, Henry, *The Fine Arts and Civilisation of Ancient Ireland* (London, 1863).
Okey, Robin, *The Habsburg Monarchy, c.1765–1918: From Enlightenment to Eclipse* (New York, 2001).
Owen, Aneurin, *Ancient Laws and Institutes of Wales* (2 vols., Llandovery, 1841).
Owen, Edward, *Catalogue of the MSS. Relating to Wales in the British Museum* (2 vols., 4 parts, London, 1900–22).
Owen, Hugh (Huwco Môn), *Yr Henafiaethydd: Henafiaethau Cemmaes, Llanfechell, Llanbabo, Cemlyn, Llanfairynghornwy, Tregele, Carreglefn, &c.; yn nghyd a Hanes Sefydliad Derwyddiaeth yn Mon* (Amlwch, 1890).
Owen, William, *The Cambrian Biography: or Historical Notices of Celebrated Men among the Ancient Britons* (London, 1803).
—— *A Dictionary of the Welsh Language, Explained in English* (London, 1803).
—— *The Heroic Elegies and other Pieces of Llywarç Hen* (London, 1792).
Parry, John H., *The Cambrian Plutarch: Comprising Memoirs from Some of the Most Eminent Welshmen, From the Earliest Times to the Present* (London, 1834).
Parry, Thomas, 'Barddoniaeth Dafydd ab Gwilym, 1789', *JWBS*, VIII, no. 4 (1957), 189–99.
Peate, Iorwerth C., *Y Traddodiad Heddwch yng Nghymru* (Dinbych, 1941).
Phillips, Bethan, *Rhwng Dau Fyd: Y Swagman o Geredigion* (Aberystwyth, 1998).
Phillips, D. Rhys, *The Romantic History of the Monastic Libraries of Wales from the Fifth to the Sixteenth Centuries (Celtic and Mediaeval Periods)* (Swansea, 1912).
Pictet, Adolphe, *Le mystère des bardes de l'Ile de Bretagne ou la Doctrine des bardes gallois du Moyen Age, sur Dieu, la vie future et la transmigration des ames. Texte original, Traduction et Commentaire* (Genève, 1856).
Price, Thomas (Carnhuanawc), *Hanes Cymru, a Chenedl y Cymry, o'r Cynoesoedd hyd at Farwolaeth Llewelyn ap Gruffydd; ynghyd a rhai Cofiaint Perthynol i'r Amseroedd o'r pryd hynny i Waered* (Crughywel, 1842).
Redwood, Charles, *The Vale of Glamorgan: Scenes and Tales among the Welsh* (London, 1839).
Rees, D. Ben, 'Capeli Cwm Cynon a'r Diwylliant Cymraeg' in Edwards (ed.), *Cwm Cynon*, pp. 71–97.
Rees, Thomas, *A Topographical and Historical Description of South Wales* (London, 1815).
Rees, Thomas, *History of Protestant Nonconformity in Wales* (2nd edn., London, 1883).
Rees, William Jenkins, *Lives of the Cambro-British Saints of the Fifth and Immediate Succeeding Centuries, from Ancient Welsh and Latin MSS., in the British Museum and Elsewhere* (Llandovery, 1853).
Rejhon, A. C., 'Hu Gadarn: Folklore and Fabrication' in Patrick K. Ford (ed.), *Celtic Folklore and Christianity: Studies in Memory of William W. Heist* (Santa Barbara, Calif., 1983), pp. 201–12.

Rembold, Elfie, *Die Festliche Nation: Geschichtsinszenierungen und Regionaler Nationalismus in Grossbritannien vor dem ersten Weltkrieg* (Berlin, 2000).

Rhys, Hywel Gethin, 'Dyfodiad y Rheilffordd i Ganolbarth Cymru, 1845–1870' (unpublished University of Wales Ph.D. thesis, 2004).

—— *'A Wayward Cymric Genius': Celebrating the Centenary of the Death of Iolo Morganwg* (Aberystwyth, 2007).

Richards, William, *Welsh Nonconformist Memorial; or, Cambro-British Biography Containing Sketches of the Founders of the Protestant Dissenting Interest in Wales* (London, 1820).

Roberts, Brynley F., '"The Age of Restitution": Taliesin ab Iolo and the Reception of Iolo Morganwg' in Jenkins (ed.), *Rattleskull Genius*, pp. 461–79.

—— 'Mab ei Dad: Taliesin ab Iolo Morganwg' in Edwards (ed.), *Merthyr a Thaf*, pp. 57–93.

—— '"Yn Wladgarol, Iaithgarol a Chenedlgarol": Cymdeithas Cymrodorion Aberdâr' in Edwards (ed.), *Cwm Cynon*, pp. 261–84.

Roberts, Gwyneth Tyson, *The Language of the Blue Books: The Perfect Instrument of Empire* (Cardiff, 1998).

Roberts, J., *Druidical Remains and Antiquities of the Ancient Britons, Principally in Glamorgan; Containing a General Account of the Same, in England, Wales, Scotland, France, &c.; with Notes and Illustrations on the Learning and Superstitions of the Druids – The Downfall of Druidism as a Religious System – and the Introduction of Christianity into Britain* (Swansea, 1842).

Roberts, J. Iorwerth, 'Eisteddfod Fawr Llangollen, 1858', *Transactions of Denbighshire Historical Society*, VIII (1959), 133–56.

Roberts, T. R., *The Eisteddfod: A Short History of the Gorsedd of the Bards of the Isle of Britain and of the National Eisteddfod of Wales with Notes on the Colwyn Bay Gorsedd Circle* (Chester, 1909).

Røyneland, Unn (ed.), *Language Contact and Language Conflict* (Volda, 1997).

Schulz, Albert (San Marte) (ed.), *Geschichte der wälschen Literatur vom XII. bis zum XIV. Jahrhundert: Gekrönte Preisschrift von Thomas Stephens aus dem Englischen übersetzt und durch Beigabe altwälscher Dichtungen in deutscher Übersetzung ergänzt* (Halle, 1864).

Shankland, Thomas, 'Hanes Dechreuad Gorsedd Beirdd Ynys Prydain', *Y Llenor*, III, no. 2 (1924), 94–102.

Simmons, Jack, 'Wales' in Jack Simmons and Gordon Bridle (eds.), *The Oxford Companion to British Railway History* (Oxford, 1997), pp. 554–5.

Simon, A., *Vercingétorix et l'idéologie nationale* (Paris, 1989).

Smiles, Sam, *The Image of Antiquity: Ancient Britain and the Romantic Imagination* (New Haven, 1994).

—— 'The Image of the Druid in British Art, *c.*1670–1850' in Sabine Rieckhoff (ed.), *Celtes et Gaulois, l'archéologie face à l'histoire: Celtes et Gaulois dans l'histoire, l'historiographie et l'idéologie moderne* (Glux-en-Glenne, 2006), pp. 111–22.

Smith, Anthony D., *Myths and Memories of the Nations* (Oxford, 1999).

—— 'History and Modernity: Reflections on the Theory of Nationalism' in David Boswell and Jessica Evans (eds.), *Representing the Nation: A Reader* (London, 1999), pp. 45–60.

Smith, Robert, 'Elementary Education and the Welsh Language 1870–1902' in Jenkins (ed.), *The Welsh Language and its Social Domains 1801–1911*, pp. 483–504.

Sørensen, Marie Louise Stig, 'The Fall of a Nation, the Birth of a Subject: The National Use of Archaeology in Nineteenth-Century Denmark' in Díaz-Andreu and Champion (eds.), *Nationalism and Archaeology in Europe*, pp. 24–47.

Spencer, Marianne Robertson, *Annals of South Glamorgan, Historical, Legendary, and Descriptive Chapters on some Leading Places of Interest* (Carmarthen, 1913).

Spurrell, William, *Carmarthen and its Neighbourhood: Notes Geographical and Historical* (Carmarthen, 1860).

Stephens, Thomas, *The Literature of the Kymry Being a Critical Essay on the History of the Language and Literature of Wales, during the Twelfth and Two Succeeding Centuries* (Llandovery, 1849).

—— *Madoc: An Essay on the Discovery of America by Madoc ap Owen Gwynedd in the Twelfth Century* (London, 1893).

Stern, Ludwig Christian, 'Davydd ab Gwilym, ein walisischer Minnesänger', *ZcP*, VII (1910), pp. 1–256.

Strong, Roy, *Painting the Past: The Victorian Painter and British History* (London, 2004).

Suggett, Richard, 'Iolo Morganwg: Stonecutter, Builder and Antiquary' in Jenkins (ed.), *Rattleskull Genius*, pp. 197–226.

Taylor, Margaret S., 'Thomas Stephens of Merthyr (1821–1875)', *Merthyr Historian*, II (1978), 135–41.

Teich, Mikuláš, and Roy Porter (eds.), *The National Question in Europe in Historical Context* (Cambridge, 1993).

Thomas, Ben Bowen, 'The Cambrians and the Nineteenth-Century Crisis in Welsh Studies, 1847–1870', *Arch. Camb.*, CXXVII (1978), 1–15.

Thomas, J. L. (Ieuan Ddu), *Cambria upon Two Sticks or, the Eisteddfod and the Penny Readings, to which is added Two Cantos entitled Harry Vaughan, and a Selection of Songs and Poems* (Pontypridd, 1867).

Thomas, T. D., *Bywgraffiad Iolo Morganwg, B.B.D., sef Edward Williams, Diweddar Fardd ac Hynafiaethydd o Forganwg* (Caerfyrddin, 1857).

Thompson, Frank, *History of An Comunn Gaidhealach: The First Hundred (1891–1991)* (Inverness, 1992).

Toelken, Barre, *The Dynamics of Folklore* (Logan, 1996).

Vaughan, W. E. (ed.), *A New History of Ireland, VI: Ireland under the Union II, 1870–1921* (Oxford, 1996).

Vyšný, Paul, *Neo-Slavism and the Czechs, 1898–1914* (Cambridge, 1977).

Walter, Ferdinand, *Das Alte Wales: Ein Beitrag zur Völker-, Rechts- und Kirchengeschichte* (Bonn, 1859).

Walters, Huw, *Cynnwrf Canrif: Agweddau ar Ddiwylliant Gwerin* (Llandybïe, 2004).

—— *John Morris-Jones 1864–1929: Llyfryddiaeth Anodiadol* (Aberystwyth, 1986).

—— 'Beirdd a Phrydyddion Pontypridd a'r Cylch yn y Bedwaredd Ganrif ar Bymtheg: Arolwg' in Edwards (ed.), *Merthyr a Thaf*, p. 252–301.

—— 'Myfyr Morganwg and the Rocking-Stone Gorsedd' in Jenkins (ed.), *Rattleskull Genius*, pp. 481–500.

Waring, Elijah, *Recollections and Anecdotes of Edward Williams* (London, 1850).

Wilkins, Charles, *The History of the Literature of Wales from the Year 1300 to the Year 1650* (Cardiff, 1884).

Williams, Daniel, 'Pan-Celticism and the Limits of Post-Colonialism: W. B. Yeats,

Ernest Rhys and William Sharp in the 1890s' in Tony Brown and Russell Stephens (eds.), *Nations and Relations: Writing across the British Isles* (Cardiff, 2000), pp. 1–29.

Williams, Derek R. (ed.), *Henry and Katharine Jenner: A Celebration of Cornwall's Culture, Language and Identity* (London, 2004).

Williams, Edward, *Poems, Lyric and Pastoral* (2 vols., London, 1794).

—— *Salmau yr Eglwys yn yr Anialwch: Cyfrol 1* (Merthyr Tydfil, 1812).

Williams, G. J., *Iolo Morganwg – Y Gyfrol Gyntaf* (Caerdydd, 1956).

—— *Iolo Morganwg a Chywyddau'r Ychwanegiad* (Llundain, 1926).

—— *Traddodiad Llenyddol Morgannwg* (Caerdydd, 1948).

—— 'Brut Aberpergwm' in Stewart Williams (ed.) *Glamorgan Historian, IV* (Cowbridge, 1967), pp. 205–20.

—— 'Daniel Ddu o Geredigion a'i Gyfnod', *Y Llenor*, V, no. 1 (1926), 48–59.

—— 'Eisteddfod Caerfyrddin', *Y Llenor*, V, no. 2 (1926), 94–102.

—— 'Yr Eisteddfod a'r Orsedd', *Y Llenor*, I, no. 2 (1922), 131–8.

—— 'Eisteddfod Llangollen 1858', *Transactions of Denbighshire Historical Society*, VII (1958), 139–61.

—— 'Gorsedd Beirdd Ynys Prydain', *Y Llenor*, III, no. 3 (1924), 162–71.

—— 'Hanes Cyhoeddi'r "Myvyrian Archaiology"', *JWBS*, X, no. 1 (1966), 2–12.

—— 'Rhys Goch ap Rhiccert', *Y Beirniad*, VIII (1919), 211–26.

—— 'Wil Hopcyn and the Maid of Cefn Ydfa', trans. Mrs E. E. Williams, in Stewart Williams (ed.), *Glamorgan Historian, VI* (Cowbridge, 1969), pp. 228–51.

Williams, Glanmor, 'Local and National History in Wales' in D. Huw Owen (ed.), *Settlement and Society in Wales* (Cardiff, 1989), pp. 7–26.

—— (ed.), *Merthyr Politics: The Making of a Working-Class Tradition* (Cardiff, 1966).

Williams, Gwyn A., *Gweriniaeth y Silwriaid / The Silurian Republic* (Casnewydd, 1988).

—— *Madoc: The Making of a Myth* (London, 1979).

—— *The Merthyr Rising* (Cardiff, 1978).

Williams, Ifor, 'Rhys Goch ap Rhiccert', *Y Beirniad*, III, no. 4 (1913), 230–44.

—— and Thomas Roberts, *Cywyddau Dafydd ap Gwilym a'i Gyfoeswyr wedi eu Golygu o'r Llawysgrifau gyda Rhagymadrodd, Nodiadau a Geirfa* (Bangor, 1914).

Williams, J. Gwynn, *The University Movement in Wales* (Cardiff, 1993).

Williams, Jane (Ysgafell), *A History of Wales, Derived from Authentic Sources* (London, 1869).

—— (ed.), *The Literary Remains of the Rev. Thomas Price, Carnhuanawc, Vicar of Cwmdû, Breconshire; and Rural Dean* (2 vols., Llandovery, 1855).

Williams, John, *Ecclesiastical Antiquities of the Cymry or the Ancient Church: Its History, Doctrine, and Rites* (London, 1844).

Williams, John (Ab Ithel) (ed.), *Barddas* (2 vols., Llandovery, 1862, 1874).

—— *The Barddas of Iolo Morganwg: A Collection of Original Documents, Illustrative of the Theology, Wisdom, and Usages of the Bardo-Druidic System of the Isle of Britain* (Boston, Mass., 2004).

—— *Dosparth Edeyrn Davod Aur, or, The Ancient Welsh Grammar* (London, 1856).

Williams, John, *Digest of Welsh Historical Statistics* (2 vols., Aberystwyth, 1985).

Williams, Jonathan, *Druopaedia; or, A New and Interesting View of the Druidical System of Education; Elucidating the Obscurities in which the Early Parts of British History are Involved* (Leominster, 1823).

Williams, Robert, *A Biographical Sketch of Some of the Most Eminent Individuals which the Principality of Wales has Produced since the Reformation* (London, 1836).
—— *Enwogion Cymru: A Biographical Dictionary* (Llandovery, 1852).
Williams, Taliesin, *Traethawd ar hynafiaeth ac awdurdodaeth coelbren y beirdd yr hwnn a ennillodd ariandlws a gwobr Eisteddfod Y Fenni 1838* (Llanymddyfri, 1840).
—— (ed.), *Cyfrinach Beirdd Ynys Prydain: ys ef Llwybreiddiaeth ag Athrawiaeth ar y Farddoniaeth Gymraeg a'i Pherthynasau, yn ol Trefn a Dosparth y Prif Feirdd gynt ar y Gelfyddyd wrth Gerdd Dafod* (Abertawy, 1829).
—— (ed.), *Iolo Manuscripts: A Selection of Ancient Welsh Manuscripts, in Prose and Verse, from the collection made by the late Edward Williams, Iolo Morganwg; for the Purpose of forming a continuation of the Myfyrian Archaiology; and Subsequently Proposed as Materials for a New History of Wales* (Llandovery, 1848).
Williams, Thomas (ed.), *Awen y Maen Chwyf yn cynnwys Awdlau, Cywyddau, Caniadau ac Englynion* (Merthyr Tydfil, 1890).
Williams, W. Crwys, 'Y Llenor yng Nghymru', *Y Geninen*, XXXI, no. 4 (1913), 244–50.
Williamson, George S., *The Longing for Myth in Germany: Religion and Aesthetic Culture from Romanticism to Nietzsche* (London, 2004).
Worden, Blair, *Roundhead Reputations: The English Civil Wars and the Passions of Posterity* (London, 2002).
Wright, Herbert G., 'The Relations of the Welsh Bard Iolo Morganwg with Dr Johnson, Cowper and Southey', *Review of English Studies*, VIII, no. 30 (1932), 129–38.
Zimmer, Stefan, 'Julius Rodenberg und Ferdinand Walter – deutsche Annäherungen an Wales im 19. Jahrhundert' in Bernhard Maier and Stefan Zimmer (eds.), *150 Jahre 'Mabinogion' – Deutsch-Walisische Kulturbeziehungen* (Tübingen, 2001), pp. 253–64.

# Index

Aasen, Ivar 3
Ab Iolo *see* Williams, Taliesin (Taliesin ab Iolo)
Ab Ithel *see* Williams, John (Ab Ithel)
Aberdare, Unitarianism 127
Abergavenny Cymreigyddion Society (Cymreigyddion y Fenni) 14, 41, 48–9, 68
Abraham, William 128
*Abrégé du Barddas ou Livre du Bardisme*, Paul Ladmirault 92
Alawn 104, 164, 169
Albert Edward, Crown Prince 65
Alexandra of Romania 65
Alfred the Great 88
Alltud Eifion *see* Jones, Robert Isaac (Alltud Eifion)
Alun *see* Blackwell, John (Alun)
American Revolution 129
Amnon II *see* Jenkins, Joseph (Amnon II)
*An Comunn Gaidhealach* (Highland Association) 71
*Ancient Bards of Britain (sometimes called 'Druids'): Being a Critical Inquiry into Traditions concerning their History . . .*, D. Delta Evans 94–5
ancient Britons 36, 37, 38
*Ancient Laws and Institutes of Wales*, Aneurin Owen 89
*Ancient Laws of Wales Viewed especially in regard to the Light They Throw upon the Origin of Some English Institutions*, Hubert Lewis 89
Ancient Order of Druids 74
Aneirin 104, 195, 196
Anglican clergy and eisteddfodau 46
*Annals of South Glamorgan*, Marianne Robertson Spencer 36, 161–2
antiquity, the appeal of 1, 2, 37
Anwyl, Sir Edward 107, 115
Ap Caledfryn *see* Williams, William Morgan (Ap Caledfryn)
ap Ednyfed, Jerome Pym 64
ap Nicholas, Islwyn 40
Appleyard, Ernest Silvanus 100
*Archaeologia Cambrensis* 6, 135, 136

Arlunydd Penygarn *see* Thomas, Thomas Henry (Arlunydd Penygarn)
Arminius 9
Arnold, Matthew 79
Arthur, King 38, 92, 109, 110, 113, 114, 169, 175, 182, 186, 191–2, 206
Ashton, Charles 62, 85, 140
Ashton, Ned 119
*Asiatick Researches*, Sir William Jones 52
Asser 88, 104
astronomy, enlisted to prove the antiquity of the Gorsedd 95
*Athenæum* 83
Austro-Hungarian Empire 2–3
*Awen y Maen Chwyf*, Thomas Williams (Gwilym Morganwg) 69, 99

bard 85, 92, 105–6, 111
  in eisteddfodau and Gorseddau 45, 53, 167–72
  the Welsh bard 15
'Barddas', essay 56
*Barddas: or, A Collection of Original Documents, Illustrative of the Theology, Wisdom, and Usages of the Bardo-Druidic System of the Isle of Britain*, John Williams (Ab Ithel) 82, 92, 94, 95, 99, 213
*Barddoniaeth Dafydd ab Gwilym*, eds. Owen Jones and William Owen 80, 105, 143, 202
bardic alphabet *see Coelbren y Beirdd* (Alphabet of the Bards)
bardic degrees 54
bardic frame *see peithynen* (bardic frame)
bardic metres
  'battle of the metres' ('brwydr y mesurau') 116–17
  *see also* Dafydd ab Edmwnd
*Bardic Museum, The*, Edward Jones 96
bardic session (*seiat y beirdd*) 57–8
bardic tradition 1, 45
  of Glamorgan 108–14, 133
bardism 4, 6, 20, 37, 41–77, 80–1, 84, 91, 96, 132, 138
  association with Christianity 91–2
  Glamorgan tradition of 135, 187

bardo-druidism 8, 82, 89–90, 91, 94, 115, 116, 129, 133, 148
  antiquity of 94–5, 133
  Christian aspects 86, 91–2
  see also bardism; druidism
Bassett, Sir Charles 113
Beaupre Castle
  eisteddfod (1681) 113
  porch 109
Beddgelert, place name 110
Beili Glas see Phillips, D. Rhys (Beili Glas)
Berkerolle, Sir Laurence 109–10
Berthou, Yves (Kaledvoulc'h) 95
Besant, Annie, president of the Theosophical Society 95
Blackwell, John (Alun) 117
Bohemia 3
Bokmål 3
'Boreu Teg o Haf' ('A Fine Summer Morning'), Iolo Morganwg 125
Bradford, Siôn 114, 201, 210, 215
  'Llyfr Sion Bradford' 104, 211, 212, 213
Brawd Estyn see Lloyd, E. (Brawd Estyn)
'Breiniau Dyn' ('Rights of Man'), Iolo Morganwg 119, 129
*Britannia after the Romans . . .*, Algernon Herbert 132
*Britannia Antiqua Illustrata*, Aylett Sammes 90
Brittany 71, 72
'Brut Ieuan Brechfa' (The Chronicle of Ieuan Brechfa) 80
Buffalo, New York 74
'Bugeila'r Gwenith Gwyn' ('Watching the Blooming Wheat'), Wil Hopcyn 114
Bulkeley, Sir Robert 50
Burgess, Thomas, bishop of St David's 27, 43–5
Burns, Robert 31
Bute, Lord 64
*Bye-Gones* 6, 84, 103
Byron, George Gordon, 6th baron 31

Cadair Morganwg see Chair of Glamorgan
Cadair Tir Iarll see Chair of Glamorgan; Tir Iarll
Cadrawd see Evans, T. C. (Cadrawd)
Cadwalader, King 12
Caledfryn see Williams, William (Caledfryn)
'Calon wrth Galon' see 'Heart to Heart'
*Cambria upon Two Sticks*, J. L. Thomas (Ieuan Ddu) 42
*Cambrian, The* 13, 14, 31, 135
*Cambrian Biography*, William Owen Pughe 99, 100, 103, 191, 209
Cambrian Institute 84
*Cambrian Journal* 6, 41, 68, 85, 87, 88, 91, 92, 135, 147
  'Ioloana' 84
*Cambrian Plutarch: Comprising Memoirs from Some of the Most Eminent Welshmen*, John H. Parry 99, 107
*Cambrian Quarterly Magazine and Celtic Repertory* 79, 80, 95, 106
*Cambrian Register, The* 1, 78–9, 80, 96, 101, 106, 132
Cambrian Society 46, 147
*Cambrian Visitor* 26
*Cambro-Briton and General Celtic Repository* 79, 80, 87
Caradog 38
Cardiff, population 4
*Cardiff Times* 113
*Cardiff Weekly Mail* 83
Cardiganshire, gravestones 120
Carlyle, Thomas 14, 98
Carmarthen, railway 7
Carmarthen Literary and Scientific Institution 27
Carnhuanawc see Price, Thomas (Carnhuanawc)
Carw Coch see Williams, William (Carw Coch)
Castletown, Lord, of Upper Ossory, president of the Pan-Celtic Association 74
*Catalogue of the MSS Relating to Wales in the British Museum* (1900–22) 139
Catwg Ddoeth 99, 101–3, 114
  'Dameg y Gwr a Laddwys ei Filgi' ('The Fable of the Man Who Killed his Greyhound') 110
  'The strength of a scholar lies in his resolve' ('Nerth ysgolâig, ei vwriad') 114
  wisdom ascribed to 80, 98, 110, 111
Cawrdaf see Jones, William Ellis (Cawrdaf)
*Ceinion Awen y Cymmry*, ed. Thomas Ll. Jones 106
*Ceinion Llenyddiaeth Gymreig*, Owen Jones 101, 102
Ceiriog see Hughes, John Ceiriog (Ceiriog)
*Celtic Britain*, John Rhŷs 147
Celtic Christianity 2
Celtic Congress
  Caernarfon (1904) 74, 98
  Dublin (1901) 72
  Edinburgh (1907) 73
  St Brieuc (1867) 71
*Celtic Researches on the Origin, Traditions & Language of the Ancient Britons*, Edward 'Celtic' Davies 96, 131–2, 187

Celticism 64, 71
Chair of Glamorgan (*Cadair Morganwg*) 50, 51, 75, 99, 104, 109, 113, 114, 131, 139, 186–7, 191
Chair of Merthyr *see* Chair of Glamorgan (*Cadair Morganwg*)
Chairs of Gwynedd, Powys and Dyfed 114
  their mottoes 169
Chartism in Wales 4, 127–8
Christian credentials of the Welsh nation 5, 90–2
Christian traditions in Wales
  and Druidism 90, 92
  antiquity of 10, 137
'Chronicle of Aberpergwm' ('Brut Aberpergwm') 133, 135
'Chronicle of the Princes' ('Brut y Tywysogyon'), Iolo's version 133
Clwydfardd *see* Griffith, David (Clwydfardd)
*Coelbren y Beirdd* (Alphabet of the Bards)
  contested antiquity of 135–6, 147, 148, 177, 186–98
  proof of superior early Welsh civilization 86, 95–6
  public display of 68–9, 167
  *see also* peithynen (bardic frame)
*Coelbren y Beirdd*, Taliesin Williams 81, 187–98
  translation 98
*Conradh na Gaeilge* (Gaelic League) 71
Cornish language 71–2
Cornwall 71, 72
Creuddynfab *see* Williams, William (Creuddynfab)
Cribyn, worshippers 124
Cromwell, Oliver 9, 12, 14, 99
Cruikshank, Robert 15
cultural heroes 98–108
  *see also* national heroes
*Cyfaill yr Aelwyd* 113
*Cyfraith Hywel Dda see* Laws of Hywel Dda
*Cyfrinach Beirdd Ynys Prydain*, Iolo Morganwg 81, 83, 107, 111, 113, 116–17
  manuscripts of 80, 203
Cymdeithas Cadair Merthyr Tudfyl (Society of the Chair of Merthyr) 50
Cym(m)rodorion societies 10, 79, 102, 118, 127
  Cymrodorion Caerdydd 153–5
  Cymrodorion Llundain 210
  Cymrodorion Society of Aberdare 10
  Powys Cymrodorion Society 47–8
  *see also* Honourable Society of Cymmrodorion
Cymreigyddion society of Taliesin ab Iolo 48, 51
*Cymru*, Owen M. Edwards 6, 7, 70, 84–5, 94, 113, 120, 140
*Cymru Fu: Notes and Queries Relating to the Past History of Wales and the Border Counties*, ed. George Brierley 84
*Cymru Fu: yn cynnwys Hanesion, Traddodiadau, yn nghyda Chwedlau a Dammegion Cymreig*, ed. Isaac Foulkes 18, 85
*Cymru Fydd* 103
Cynddelw *see* Ellis, Robert (Cynddelw)
Cynonfardd *see* Edwards, Thomas (Cynonfardd)
Cynwyl Elfed, plaque 69
'Cywydd y Llafurwr', Iolo Goch 99
*Cywyddau Cymru*, ed. Arthur Hughes 106
*Cywyddau Dafydd ap Gwilym a'i Gyfoeswyr*, ed. Ifor Williams 143
Czech 3

Dafydd ab Edmwnd 204
  twenty-four metres 45, 80, 116
Dafydd ap Gwilym
  authentic canon 105, 107, 143–4
  romantically embellished biography 78, 80, 99, 104–5, 108, 111, 139, 202
Dafydd ap Gwilym, additional poems 80, 106–8, 111, 144, 179–82, 209
  'I Forfudd – Y Bardd Mewn Henaint yn Dwyn i Gof Fal y Bu Gynt' ('To Morfudd – The Bard in Old Age Recalling How It Used to Be') 106
  'I Forfudd Mewn Henaint' ('To Morfudd in Old Age') 107
  'I Yrru yr Haf i Annerch Morganwg' ('To Send the Summer to Greet Glamorgan') 106–7, 111
  'Mawl i Forfudd' ('Praise to Morfudd') 107
  'Mawl i'r Clos' ('Praise to the Grove') 107
  'Mawl i'r Haf – Cwyn o'i Golli' ('Invocation to the Summer') 106
  'Y Breuddwyd' ('The Dream') 106
  'Y Cywydd Diweddaf a Gant y Bardd' ('The Bard's Last Song') 106–7
Dafydd ap Gwilym Society 23
Dafydd Dafis *see* Davis, David (Dafydd Dafis)
Dafydd Ddu Eryri *see* Thomas, David (Dafydd Ddu Eryri)

Daniel Ddu *see* Evans, Daniel (Daniel Ddu)
*Das Alte Wales*, Ferdinand Walter 13, 89
Davies, Edward 'Celtic' 96, 131–2, 133, 141, 185–6, 200
Davies, Evan (Myfyr Morganwg) 41, 51, 52, 55, 62, 64, 70, 94, 127
   controversy surrounding him 53, 58, 93–4, 135
   his Rocking-stone Gorsedd 51–3, 162–4
   his writings 93–4
   international influence 74, 75, 175
   main disciple of Iolo Morganwg 20, 32, 56, 91, 115, 147
Davies, J. Cadvan 63
Davies, J. Glyn 143
Davies, Revd James 74
Davies, John, Neath 134
Davies, Walter (Gwallter Mechain) 44–5, 46, 95, 131
Davis, David (Dafydd Dafis) 32
Deffrobani (summer country) 99, 101, 190, 191
Denmark 2
Dewi Mai (Dafydd Dafydd) 41
Dewi Môn *see* Rowlands, David (Dewi Môn)
Dic Aberdaron *see* Jones, Richard Robert (Dic Aberdaron)
Dic Penderyn 127
*Dictionary of the Welsh Language*, William Owen Pughe 96
Dobrovský, Josef 3
*Dosparth Edeyrn Davod Aur, or, The Ancient Welsh Grammar*, John Williams (Ab Ithel) 82
Dresden 75
*Druid, The* 74
*Druiden-Zeitung* 76
Druidic Order (*Urdd y Derwyddon*) 47
druidism
   criticism of 131, 138
   in Welsh history-writing 82, 90–5, 96, 103, 133, 175–7
   modern, based on Ioloic material 41, 74, 78, 80, 101, 170
   outside Wales 74–5
   *see also* bardism; bardo-druidism
Druids
   as honorary degree 63, 74
   images of 75, 90–1
   in antiquity 91, 92, 94, 100, 101, 133, 187
   in eisteddfod and Gorsedd 44, 48, 50, 55, 60, 167–72
   in Germany 174–5
   in modern times 127, 176, 187, 202

*Druids and Theosophy, The*, Peter Freeman 95
*Druopaedia*, Jonathan Williams 91, 101
Duke of Wellington 17, 31
Dyfnwal Moelmud 87, 88, 89, 99–101, 132, 147, 150
*see also* triads

Eben Fardd *see* Thomas, Ebenezer (Eben Fardd)
*Ecclesiastical Antiquities of the Cymry or the Ancient British Church*, John Williams (Ab Ithel) 92
Education Act (1870) 5, 11
Educational Publishing Company, Merthyr Tydfil 94
Edwards, D. Miall 38
Edwards, Joseph 21, 69, 121, 173
Edwards, Owen M. 6, 28, 88, 113, 125
Edwards, Thomas (Cynonfardd) 77
Edwards, Thomas (Gwynedd) 61
Edwards, Thomas (Twm o'r Nant) 10
Eiddil Ifor *see* Watkins, Thomas Evan (Eiddil Ifor)
eisteddfod 7, 13, 42, 44, 57–8
   pavilion 55, 56, 57, 165–6
   *see also* eisteddfodic symbols and mottoes
eisteddfodau
   Aberdare (1861) 60
   Aberffraw (1849) 49
   Abergavenny (1834, 1835) 50
   Abergavenny (1838) 48, 50, 81, 96, 188
   Abergavenny (1848) 134
   Abergavenny (1853) 135, 148
   Bangor (1902) 75
   Beaupre Castle (1681) 113
   Brecon (1822) 46
   Cardiff (1834) 13, 50–1, 148
   Cardiff (1899) 7, 71
   Carmarthen (*c*.1453) 45, 81, 116, 200
   Carmarthen (1819) 41, 43–6, 49, 114
   Carmarthen (1867) 97, 98
   Conwy (1861) 54
   Denbigh (1860) 54, 57, 59
   Dinas Mawddwy (1855) 55
   Gwernyclepa (1328) 111
   Liverpool (1840) 49
   Llandudno (1896) 72, 141
   Llanelli (1856) 8
   Llangollen (1858) 41, 55–8, 59, 64, 70, 98, 135, 165–72
   London (1909) 65, 74
   Neath (1918) 72
   Newport (1897) 66
   Pontypridd (1814) 42–3
   provincial eisteddfodau (*eisteddfodau taleithiol*) 46–7

Rhyl (1892) 63
Welshpool (1824) 47–8
Wrexham (1876) 59
Wrexham (1888) 37, 62
see also National Eisteddfod
eisteddfodic symbols and mottoes 48, 56, 60, 67–70
  'Y Gwir yn erbyn y Byd' ('The Truth against the World') 67, 68, 70, 97, 166, 169, 170
  'Yn ôl Braint a Defod Beirdd Ynys Prydain' ('According to the Right and Privileges of the Bards of the Isle of Britain') 67
  'Yn wyneb haul a llygad goleuni' ('In the presence of the sun and the eye of light') 67, 68, 208
  see also mystic sign (nod cyfrin)
Elias, John 121
Ellis, Robert (Cynddelw) 18, 20, 23, 53, 81, 172, 202
Ellis, T. E. 28, 82, 128
Elphin see Griffith, R. A. (Elphin)
Emynau o Fawl a Gweddi 123
Emynau y Cysegr, ed. Thomas Gee 125
Emyniadur yr Eglwys yng Nghymru 125
Encyclopaedia Britannica 85, 105
Encyclopaedia Cambrensis: Y Gwyddoniadur Cymreig, Thomas Gee 85, 88, 92
Enwogion Cymru: A Biographical Dictionary, Robert Williams 99, 101
'Er Moliant i Dduw am y Cyfryw Ymweliad Gogoneddus' ('In Praise of God for the Said Glorious Visitation'), Iolo Morganwg 119, 129
Essay on the Neodruidic Heresy in Britannia, An, Algernon Herbert 132
Estlin, J. P. 123
Evan Serfel, carpenter 55
Evans, Alcwyn Caryni 27, 158–9
Evans, Christmas 10, 121
Evans, D. Arthen 22
Evans, D. Emlyn 37
Evans, D. Tudor 147
Evans, Daniel (Daniel Ddu) 13, 32, 50, 119
Evans, Daniel Silvan (Hirlas) 56, 84, 120, 139, 146–7
Evans, David Lewis 39
Evans, Evan (Ieuan Fardd) 24, 32, 157
Evans, Evan (Ieuan Glan Geirionydd) 117
Evans, Frederic 101, 113
Evans, J. J. 129
Evans, John Gwenogvryn 139, 140, 178
Evans, Samuel (Gomerydd) 68
Evans, T. C. (Cadrawd) 2, 83, 84, 94, 101, 112, 113, 118, 120

Evans, Theophilus 137, 201
Evans, Thomas (Tomos Glyn Cothi) 30, 126

*Flamebearers of Welsh History*, Owen Rhoscomyl 94
Flemingston 22
  pilgrimages to 153–6
folklore 1, 34
  of Glamorgan 108, 110, 111, 114
  Welsh 11, 18, 26, 39
*Folklore of Glamorgan*, T. C. Evans (Cadrawd) 111
Foulkes, Isaac (Llyfrbryf) 18
France 9, 131
French Revolution 128, 129, 131, 133
Fricke, Heinrich 75, 76
Friedrich Barbarossa 9
friendly societies 47

Gaidoz, Henri 103
Gee, Thomas 82, 85, 88, 125
*Geiriadur y Bardd: neu yr Odlydd Cyffredinol, at Wasanaeth y Beirdd*, Robert Ellis (Cynddelw) 81
*Gentleman's Magazine* 11
George III 31, 36
George IV 31
Geraint Fardd Glas see Asser
German Order of Druids 75
Germany 2, 9, 74–5, 138, 174–5
Gildas 31, 133, 190, 194
Giraldus see Rowland, John (Giraldus)
Glamorgan
  Anglicization 22
  apple-growing 84, 108, 110
  bardic tradition 108–14, 135, 144
  longevity of its inhabitants 12, 84, 108, 110
  perceived pre-eminence of 78, 108–14, 182–4
  whitewashing houses 108, 110
*Glamorgan: Being an Outline of its Geography, History, and Antiquities*, Abraham Morris 103, 109
Glamorgan classification 45, 116, 117
*Glamorgan Gazette* 31
Glan Alun see Jones, Thomas (Glan Alun)
Glanffrwd see Thomas, William (Glanffrwd)
Glaslyn see Owen, Richard Jones (Glaslyn)
'God Save the King', Iolo Morganwg 128
Goethe 42
*Gogoniant Hynafol y Cymmry*, Evan Davies (Myfyr Morganwg) 93
Gomerydd see Evans, Samuel (Gomerydd)

'Gorau cof cof Llyfr. Nid doeth ni ddarlleno' ('The best memory is the memory of a Book. He will not be wise who does not read') 68, 69
Gorsedd 42–3, 44, 54
  and eisteddfodau 43–4, 47, 48–9, 58–9
  and publicity 7, 53, 55
  and the Pan-Celtic Congress 72–4
  and the Vereinigte Alte Orden der Druiden 74–5
  assumed antiquity 47, 64, 95, 132, 141
  bards 50
  criticism of 57, 62, 70, 139–40, 141–2, 142–3, 144, 200–6
  development into a national institution 55, 58–63, 129, 149
  international influence 71–7, 116
  original radical concept 63, 127, 129
  prayer 57, 64, 92, 170
  ritual 43–4, 52, 54, 56, 64, 92, 93
  robes 56, 57, 64–7
  satire of 64, 70, 162–4
  '*Scrôl cyhoeddi*' (Announcement Scroll) 49–50
  *see also* Gorseddau; processions
Gorsedd Society 62
Gorseddau
  Beaupre Castle (1681) 113
  Glamorgan (1798) 119
  Gorsedd Idris (1824) 49
  Gorsedd of Morganwg (1360) 111
  held by Gwilym Cowlyd at Llyn Geirionydd (1863–1904) 54
  licence to convene in 'New Wales' and in 'Welsh colonies' 74
  Liverpool (1840) 49
  *see also* Rocking-stone
*Gorseth Kernow* (Cornish Gorsedd) 72
'Gorymbil am Heddwch' ('Plea for Peace'), Iolo Morganwg 129
*Goursez Barzhed Gourenez Breizh-Vihan* (The Gorsedd of the Bards of Little Britain) 72
*Grail, The* 31
Griffith, David (Clwydfardd) 60, 66
Griffith, R. A. (Elphin) 54, 206–8
Griffiths, Ann 10
Griffiths, Griffith 'Penar' 20, 23–4
Griffiths, John 128–9
Griffiths, William Alonzo 124
Gruffydd, W. J. 105, 115, 148
*Gwaith Iolo Morganwg*, ed. T. C. Evans (Cadrawd) 118
Gwalchmai *see* Parry, Richard (Gwalchmai)
Gwallter Mechain *see* Davies, Walter (Gwallter Mechain)

Gweirydd ap Rhys *see* Pryse, Robert John (Gweirydd ap Rhys)
Gwenffrwd *see* Jones, Thomas Lloyd (Gwenffrwd)
Gwenynen Gwent *see* Hall, Lady Augusta, of Llanover (Gwenynen Gwent)
Gwenynen Gwent yr Ail *see* Herbert, Lady Augusta, of Llanover (Gwenynen Gwent yr Ail) 71
'Gwerin Cymru', Crwys 28
Gwilym Cowlyd *see* Roberts, William John (Gwilym Cowlyd)
Gwilym Harri *see* Harry, William (Gwilym Harri)
Gwilym Morganwg *see* Williams, Thomas (Gwilym Morganwg)
Gwilym Peris *see* Williams, William (Gwilym Peris)
Gwilym Tawe *see* Morris, William (Gwilym Tawe)
Gwilym Tew 96, 197, 198, 214
'Gwlad y Bryniau', T. Gwynn Jones 74
Gwron 104, 164, 169
Gwyddonwyson *see* Stephen, D. Rhys (Gwyddonwyson)
Gwynedd *see* Edwards, Thomas (Gwynedd)

Hafod Uchtryd 20–1, 27, 32, 152–3
Hafod y Llan, Beddgelert 32
hagiography, Welsh 11
Hall, Lady Augusta, of Llanover (Gwenynen Gwent) 14, 50, 71, 79, 83, 172
Hamburg 75
*Hanes Cymru*, Thomas Price (Carnhuanawc) 115
*Hanes Morganwg*, Dafydd Morganwg 111
*Hanes y Brytaniaid a'r Cymry*, Gweirydd ap Rhys 104
Hanka, Václav 3
harp, the 166, 167, 172
  as a national symbol 58, 67, 75, 97
Harris, James 83, 118–19, 136
Harry, William (Gwilym Harri), of Garw Dyle, Penderyn 68
'Heart to Heart' ('Calon wrth Galon') 73, 97, 158, 166, 169
*Hen Gwndidau, Carolau, a Chywyddau*, T. C. Evans (Cadrawd) 111
'Hen Wlad Fy Nhadau' 72
Herbert, Algernon 132
Herbert, Lady Augusta, of Llanover (Gwenynen Gwent yr Ail) 71
Hermann der Cherusker *see* Arminius
*Heroic Elegies and other Pieces of Llywarç Hen, The*, William Owen Pughe 11, 42, 67, 80, 131, 133

Hirlas *see* Evans, Daniel Silvan (Hirlas)
*Historia Regum Britanniae*, Geoffrey of Monmouth 100
historical narrative 1, 2, 5, 15, 78, 79, 115
*History and Antiquity of Glamorganshire and its Families*, Thomas Nicholas 134
*History of Llangynwyd Parish*, T. C. Evans (Cadrawd) 111
*History of the County of Brecknock*, Theophilus Jones 96
*History of the Literature of Wales from the Year 1300 to the Year 1650*, Charles Wilkins 104–5
*History of Wales, A*, Jane Williams (Ysgafell) 137
*History of Wales, The*, John Jones 132
Honourable Society of Cymmrodorion 118
Hopcyn, Wil 114, 118, 182
*Hopkiniaid Morganwg*, L. J. Hopkin-James (Hopcyn) 113, 114, 182–3
Hopkin-James, L. J. (Hopcyn) 113, 114, 182–3
Howells, John 137
Hu Gadarn (Hu the Mighty) 87, 99–101, 102, 136, 191, 195
Hughes, Hugh (Tegai) 68
Hughes, John Ceiriog (Ceiriog) 53, 54, 60, 70, 118, 171
Hughes, Joshua, bishop of St Asaph 59
Hughes, Thomas, of Neuaddfawr 123
Huwco Môn *see* Owen, Hugh (Huwco Môn)
Hwfa Môn *see* Williams, Rowland (Hwfa Môn)
Hyde, Douglas 71
*Hynafiaeth Aruthrol y Trwn*, Evan Davies (Myfyr Morganwg) 93

Idrison *see* Pughe, William Owen (Idrison)
Ieuan Fardd *see* Evans, Evan (Ieuan Fardd)
Ieuan Glan Geirionydd *see* Evans, Evan (Ieuan Glan Geirionydd)
Ieuan Gryg *see* Meredith, E. P. (Ieuan Gryg)
Ifor Hael 107, 111, 157
Inquiry into the State of Education in Wales (1847) 4, 11, 14, 42, 57, 68, 79
Ioan Ddu *see* Jones, John (Ioan Ddu)
Ioan Mynyw *see* Lewis, John (Ioan Mynyw)
Ioan Pedr *see* Peter, John (Ioan Pedr)
Ioan Triddyd *see* Thomas, John (Ioan Triddyd)
*Iolo Manuscripts, The* 81, 105, 147, 209
    its changing reputation 21–2, 109, 138–9
    its continued use as a source 18, 55, 83, 85, 103, 105, 107, 109, 110, 137

Iolo Morganwg *see* Williams, Edward (Iolo Morganwg)
*Iolo Morganwg a Chywyddau'r Ychwanegiad*, Griffith John Williams 145, 146
Iorwerth Gwilym *see* Williams, Edward (Iolo Morganwg)
'I'r Ehedydd' ('The Lark'), Iolo Morganwg 120, 184
'I'r meirwon mae Duw'r mawredd – yn addaw' ('To the dead the God of the mighty – promises'), Iolo Morganwg 120, 122, 174
Ireland 2, 11, 71, 72, 86
Irish language 2
Irish nation 79, 194
Isaac, David Lloyd (Dafydd Llwyd Isaac) 96, 108, 109, 132
Isle of Man 72

Jaffrennou, François (Taldir) 71
Jenkins, Joseph (Amnon II) 20–1, 152–3
Jenner, Henry 72
John, E. T. 83
John, Sir William Goscombe 64, 66
John, William Richard (Mathonwy) 18, 20, 172
Johnes, Arthur James (Maelog) 105, 107, 111
Johnes, Thomas 20–1, 152–3
Johnson, Samuel 31
Jones, Edward (Bardd y Brenin) 96
Jones, J. Islan 124
Jones, James 'Ifano' 42, 82–3, 118
Jones, John (Ioan Ddu) 94, 107
Jones, John (Talhaiarn) 50, 54, 120
Jones, John Bowen 123
Jones, Josiah Thomas 128
Jones, Michael D. 61
Jones, Owen (Owain Myfyr) 5, 80, 157, 199, 202, 203
Jones, Rees Jenkin (T.C.U.) 28, 123, 124, 185
Jones, Richard Robert (Dic Aberdaron) 32
Jones, Robert Isaac (Alltud Eifion) 58
Jones, T. Gwynn 74, 141
Jones, T. Tudno 61
Jones, Theophilus 131
Jones, Thomas (Glan Alun) 59
Jones, Thomas Lloyd (Gwenffrwd) 117
Jones, Williâm (Myfyr Môn) 59
Jones, William Ellis (Cawrdaf) 48

Kaledvoulc'h *see* Berthou, Yves (Kaledvoulc'h)

*La légende celtique et la poésie des cloîtres en Irlande, en Cambrie et en Bretagne*, Hersart de La Villemarqué 103

La Villemarqué, Theodore Hersart de (Barz Nizon) 48, 103, 148
Landsmaal 3
Laws of Hywel Dda 88, 132, 186, 195, 214
Lewes, Evelyn Anna 105–6, 107
Lewis, Hubert 89
Lewis, John (Ioan Mynyw) 21, 152
Lewys Glyn Cothi 97
Lhuyd, Edward 20, 138
Liberalism 125, 127–8
*Life and Poems of Davydd ab Gwilym*, Evelyn Anna Lewes 105–6
Literary and Scientific Institute(s) 10, 118
literary festivals (*cylchwyliau*) 4, 47, 48, 50
literary meetings (*cyrddau llenyddol*) 47
*Literature of the Kymry*, Thomas Stephens 134, 147, 188, 210
Liverpool 56
*Lives of the Cambro-British Saints, of the Fifth and Immediate Succeeding Centuries . . .*, William Jenkins Rees 82, 103
Llannarth cemetery 122
Llanover 7, 14, 55, 71, 82, 83–4, 114, 126, 142
  collection 84, 88, 92, 95, 113, 144, 165, 177–9
Llanover, Lady *see* Hall, Lady Augusta, of Llanover (Gwenynen Gwent)
Llantwit Major 32
  *see also* Pillar of Samson
Lleurwg 58
Lloyd, E. (Brawd Estyn) 98
Lloyd, J. E. 39–40, 89, 130
Lloyd, John Ambrose 59
Lloyd George, David 128
Llyfrbryf *see* Foulkes, Isaac (Llyfrbryf)
Llywarch Hen 104, 169, 194, 202, 204
Llywelyn ein Llyw Olaf (Llywelyn our Last Leader) 18, 38
Llywelyn Fawr (Llywelyn the Great) 38
Lockyer, Sir Norman 95
Logan Stone *see* Rocking-stone
London 24, 31, 35, 65, 127
Lovell, T. (Tudur Taf) 26, 153–5

Macaulay, Thomas Babington 31
Macpherson, James 78, 148
Madoc 57, 135, 137, 139, 198–200
*Madoc: An Essay on the Discovery of America by Madoc ap Owen Gwynedd in the Twelfth Century*, Thomas Stephens 135
Maelog *see* Johnes, Arthur James (Maelog)
Maen Chwŷf *see* Rocking-stone
Malkin, Benjamin Heath 12–13, 32, 108
manuscripts
  professional study of manuscripts in Wales 139

use of manuscripts for nation-building 1, 10, 79
Marx, Karl 79
Mathonwy *see* John, William Richard (Mathonwy)
Mee, Arthur 83
Meirionwyson 134
Meredith, E. P. (Ieuan Gryg) 98, 148
*Merthyr Guardian* 49
Merthyr Tydfil 4, 36, 60, 127
  Merthyr Rising 127
  monumental sculpture 173–4
Meyer, Kuno 143
*Môd* 71
Moelwyn-Hughes, John Gruffydd 89
Morgan Mwynfawr 109
Morgan, Sir Charles 28, 79
Morgan, Lewis 69, 121, 173–4
Morgan, Owen (Morien) 20, 22, 32, 37, 69, 84, 94, 115, 127, 141, 203
Morien *see* Morgan, Owen (Morien)
Morris, Abraham 103, 109
Morris, M. T. 98
Morris, William (Gwilym Tawe) 59
Morris-Jones, Sir John
  criticism of him 141–2, 148
  founder of *Y Beirniad* 6–7, 142
  his criticism of Ioloic material 74, 130, 139, 140–2, 144, 146, 149, 200–6
  his use of Ioloic material 85, 105, 115
Morus, E. Ben (Myfyr Teifi) 128
Mostyn, Lord 50, 64
Myfyr Môn *see* Jones, William (Myfyr Môn)
Myfyr Morganwg *see* Davies, Evan (Myfyr Morganwg)
Myfyr Teifi *see* Morus, E. Ben (Myfyr Teifi)
mystic sign (*nod cyfrin*) 60, 66, 81, 147, 188
  public use 67, 69, 70, 85
  use by followers of Iolo Morganwg 19, 52, 56, 68, 121, 173
  use in satire 70, 162
myth 5, 9, 10, 130
  of Iolo Morganwg 10–11, 14, 16, 23–40, 117, 128–9
mythologization, process of 10
*Mythology and Rites of the British Druids, The*, Edward 'Celtic' Davies 131, 202
*Myvyrian Archaiology of Wales, The* 11, 80, 81, 82–3, 85, 99, 115, 133–4, 137, 138
  Iolo Morganwg's contributions 28, 80, 82, 86–7, 103, 108, 179, 199

Napoleon Bonaparte 9, 17
Napoleonic Wars 42

Nathan Dyfed *see* Reynolds, Jonathan Owen (Nathan Dyfed)
National Eisteddfod 8, 47, 54, 57–8, 58–9, 60, 61–2, 64, 71–2, 74
   annual *Transactions* 60, 67, 70
   General Eisteddfod Council 59–60
   place of the Gorsedd 63, 149
National Eisteddfod Association 60–1, 63, 70
   Annual Report (1888) 37
national heroes 9, 15, 38, 78, 98–108
national history 5, 15, 58, 63, 108, 130, 135, 138
national identity 2–3, 67
National Library of Wales, The 14, 21, 98, 126, 144, 152, 209
National Union of Welsh Societies 22, 39
nationalism 38, 39
   and history 1–2, 5, 9, 10, 15, 16, 63, 78, 79, 85, 86, 115, 130, 135, 137, 138
   and language 2–3
*Nationalist, The* 130
nationhood 1, 2, 8, 15, 37–8, 39, 59, 79, 83
Nest, elegy 107
'new poet', the rise of 81
'Newgate Stanzas', Iolo Morganwg 29, 30, 129
Nicholas, T. E. (Niclas y Glais) 40
Nicholas, Thomas 134, 146
*nod cyfrin see* mystic sign
Nonconformists 10, 13, 15, 16, 48, 77, 93
   growth of Nonconformist denominations 121, 125
north Wales 3, 4, 7, 111, 182
   eisteddfodau 54, 55, 56, 60, 113
Norway 2–3
Norwegian language 3

O'Curry, Eugene 86
*Oireachtas* (1898) 71
Old Norse 3
*Oliver Cromwell's Letters and Speeches,* Thomas Carlyle 14
oral traditions 1, 4
Ossian epic 78
Ovate(s) 44, 50, 55, 58, 60, 63, 167–72, 187
Owain Glyndŵr 10, 18, 38–9, 99, 108, 109
Owain Myfyr *see* Jones, Owen (Owain Myfyr)
Owen, Aneurin 46
Owen, Edward 137, 139, 198
Owen, Elias 37
Owen, Sir Hugh 58, 60
Owen, Hugh (Huwco Môn) 101
Owen, Richard Jones (Glaslyn) 19, 20, 23

Paine, Tom 30, 31, 160
Palacký, František 3
Pan-Celtic Association 72–4
Parry, Richard (Gwalchmai) 54
Patagonia 74
Peate, Iorwerth C. 40
*peithynen* (bardic frame) 96–8, 112, 167, 187–8
Pentre-bach, parish of Eglwysilan 52
periodical literature 5–7, 9, 10, 16, 34, 84, 110
*Perlau Moliant* 123
Peter, John (Ioan Pedr) 138
Petrie, George 86
Phillips, D. Rhys (Beili Glas) 36, 72, 84, 103
Phillips, Sir John, of Middle Hill 27
Phoenicians, use of in nineteenth-century English politics 86
Pictet, Adolphe 91
Pillar of Samson 26, 109, 157–8
Pitt, William (Pitt the Younger) 17, 29, 30, 31, 36, 161–2
Plennydd 104, 164, 169
*Poems, Lyric and Pastoral*, Iolo Morganwg 13, 80, 83, 86, 118, 119, 132
   preface 11–12
   subscription list 31
Pontypridd 42–3, 52, 55, 77, 175
   section of the Chartist movement 127
Price, Thomas (Carnhuanawc) 71, 96, 136
   his use of Ioloic sources 81, 82, 85, 100, 115, 133–4, 175–7
Price, William 64, 127
Prichard, J. W. 33
Primrose Hill, Gorsedd 42, 54
processions 4, 47–50, 56, 65, 66
provincial (Cambrian) societies 46
Prydain ab Aedd Mawr 169
*pryddestau* 117
Pryse, Robert John (Gweirydd ap Rhys) 104, 107, 210
Pughe, William Owen (Idrison) 5, 32, 46, 132, 137, 148, 187, 188, 199
   dissemination of Ioloic material 80, 200, 202, 209–10
   ridiculed by Iolo Morganwg 34

radicalism 1, 29, 40, 116, 126–7, 129
railway system 5, 7, 8
Raimbach, Abraham 102
*Recollections and Anecdotes of Edward Williams*, Elijah Waring 14, 125–6, 158
*Red Dragon, The* 6, 36, 83, 119
Redwood, Charles 13, 32
Rees, J. Machreth 107
Rees, Thomas 109

Reform and Redistribution Acts (1884–5) 4
Religious Census (1851) 121
revolutions, European (1848) 5, 15
*Revue Celtique* 103
Reynolds, Jonathan Owen (Nathan Dyfed) 22
Rhys Goch ap Rhicert 99, 104, 105, 108, 118, 144, 149–50, 182, 209–15
Rhŷs, Sir John 61, 98, 130, 139, 147
Richard, Henry 128
*Rights of Man*, popular anecdote 17, 29, 30, 119, 159–60
Roberts, Robert, of Holyhead 33
Roberts, William John (Gwilym Cowlyd) 54, 55, 62, 70, 74
 'Arwest Farddonol Glan Geirionydd' ('Poetic Picnic on the Shores of Geirionydd') 54–5
Rocking-stone, the 42–3, 50, 51–3, 162–4
*Romantic History of the Monastic Libraries of Wales*, D. Rhys Phillips (Beili Glas) 103
Romantic nationalism 5, 86
Romanticism 1, 39–40, 79
Rowland, John (Giraldus) 27, 137, 158
Rowlands, David (Dewi Môn) 61
Royal Albert Hall 65
Royal Commission for Ancient and Historical Monuments of Wales 139
Royal Institution of South Wales 95

St Cadog of Llancarfan 101, 103, 108
 *see also* Catwg Ddoeth
St David 18
*Salmau yr Eglwys yn yr Anialwch*, Iolo Morganwg 81, 120, 122, 185
Sammes, Aylett 90, 96
Samson Cross *see* Pillar of Samson
Saxon(s) 36–8, 87, 100
*Scenery, Antiquities, and Biography of South Wales, The*, Benjamin Heath Malkin 12
Schleswig-Holstein 2
Scotland 11, 72
Scott, Sir Walter 31
*Seren Gomer* 6, 16–17, 41, 48, 52–3, 67, 68, 93, 96, 119, 135
Shakespeare, William 22, 31, 37, 195
Shamby, John, of Carmarthen 36
Siancyn ap Tomos ap Gruffudd ap Niclas 97
*Siluriana: or Contributions towards the History of Gwent and Glamorgan*, David Lloyd Isaac 85, 109, 132
Slavonic nationalities 2
Slovac 3
Society for Psychical Research 25
'Solitude', Iolo Morganwg 119
'Song Written for the Cowbridge Volunteers, A', Iolo Morganwg 128
south Wales 3–6, 13–14, 36, 39, 41, 79
 eisteddfodau 60
 poets 53, 59
*South Wales Daily News* 113
South Wales Unitarian Society, the
 formation of 126
Southey, Robert, stanza dedicated to Iolo Morganwg 27, 159
Spencer, Marianne Robertson 36, 108, 137, 161–2
Statute of Gruffudd ap Cynan 54, 80
Stephen, D. Rhys (Gwyddonwyson) 16–17
Stephens, Thomas 4, 20, 32–3, 56–7, 85, 93, 100, 104, 115, 126, 131, 134–7, 140, 147, 186–98, 209, 210
Stern, Ludwig Christian 107
'Strike a Welshman if you dare', anecdote 35–8, 160–2
Sunday schools 10
Swansea 95

Taldir *see* Jaffrennou, François (Taldir)
Talhaiarn *see* Jones, John (Talhaiarn)
Taliesin 54, 104, 113, 166, 169, 194, 196, 214, 215
Taliesin ab Iolo *see* Williams, Taliesin (Taliesin ab Iolo)
Tara brooch 86
Tegai *see* Hughes, Hugh (Tegai)
'theoretical history' 8, 78, 81, 88, 98, 114, 149
Theosophical Society 95
Thomas, Ann (the Maid of Cefn Ydfa) 114
Thomas, David (Dafydd Ddu Eryri) 32, 131
Thomas, Ebenezer (Eben Fardd) 18, 20, 50, 117, 151–2
Thomas, John (Ioan Triddyd) 32
Thomas, Thomas D. 25, 32, 36
Thomas, Thomas Henry (Arlunydd Penygarn) 64, 66, 69
Thomas, William (Glanffrwd) 20, 84, 94, 124
Thurneysen, Rudolf 89
Tir Iarll 111–14
 bardic line of succession 182–4
*Tir Iarll: The Earl's Land*, Frederic Evans 113
Tomos Glyn Cothi *see* Evans, Thomas (Tomos Glyn Cothi)
*Topographical and Historical Description of South Wales*, Thomas Rees 109

*Translations into English Verse from the Poems of Davyth ap Gwilym, a Welsh Bard of the Fourteenth Century*, Arthur James Johnes (Maelog) 105, 106–7, 179–82
'Treachery of the Blue Books' *see* Inquiry into the State of Education in Wales (1847)
'Treachery of the Long Knives' ('Brad y Cyllyll Hirion') 136
Trebor Mai *see* Williams, Robert (Trebor Mai)
Trecefel farm, near Tregaron
  Iolo Morganwg's chair 20–1, 152–3
Tredegar, Lord 66
triads 78
  authentic triads 80, 86–7
  triads composed by Iolo 80, 84, 85, 86–92, 95, 98–9, 100, 115, 131–5, 138, 139, 146, 148, 192, 193, 194
  'Triodd Dyfnwal Moelmud' (triads of Dyfnwal Moelmud) 87, 88, 89, 99, 100, 132, 133, 135, 186, 214
  'Triodd Llelo Llawdrwm' (triads of Llelo Llawdrwm) 87
  'Triodd y Cymro' (Welshman's triads) 87
  'Triodd y Gwragedd' (triads of the women) 87
  'Triodd y Sais' (Englishman's triads) 87
  'Trioedd Barddas' (bardic triads) 83
  'Trioedd Braint a Defod' ('Institutional Triads') 83
  'Trioedd Ynys Prydain' ('Triads of the Isle of Britain') 86–7, 135
*tribannau* (triplets) 114, 182, 183–4
True Ivorites (*Y Gwir Iforiaid*) 47
Tudur Taf *see* Lovell, T. (Tudur Taf)
Twm o'r Nant *see* Edwards, Thomas (Twm o'r Nant)

*Udgorn Cymru* 127
'Un a fo'n iawn ei fywyd – a gedwir' ('One who was righteous in his life – is saved'), Iolo Morganwg 120–1
Unitarian denomination 28, 121, 123–4, 125–6, 126–7, 129, 134, 136
  'Black Spot' (Y Smotyn Du) 121
  gravestones 120–1
United Order of Druids 75
Urien Rheged 169, 192

Vale of Glamorgan 13, 22, 36, 42
*Vale of Glamorgan: Scenes and Tales among the Welsh, The*, Charles Redwood 13, 85
Vallée, François (Abherve) 71
Vercingetorix 9
Vereinigte Alte Orden der Druiden 74–5, 76

Vivian, John Henry 98
von Herkomer, Sir Hubert 57, 64, 66, 72, 75

*Wales*, Owen M. Edwards 6, 7, 141
Walter, Ferdinand 13, 82, 89
Waring, Elijah 11, 13–17, 23, 25, 27, 31–2, 125–6, 151–2, 158
Warner, Anna 69
Watkins, Thomas Evan (Eiddil Ifor) 48
Welsh Americans 30
Welsh history-writing
  amateur 114–15, 133
  change in paradigm of 130, 137–8
  function in nation-building process 1, 5, 10, 15, 16, 18, 38–9, 58–9, 78, 79, 86, 132, 137
  professionalization of 115, 130
  Romantic 78–9, 85, 88–108, 114–15, 137–8
  scientific 134, 135, 138
  visualization of 63–4
Welsh Indians in America *see* Madoc
Welsh language 1, 6, 60, 67, 83, 130, 165
  in eisteddfodau and Gorseddau 54, 60, 63
  rights and promotion of 39, 78, 115, 128
  threat to 5, 115, 128, 149
Welsh Manuscripts Society 81, 82, 89
*Welsh Metrics*, J. Glyn Davies 143
Welsh nation 1, 5, 8, 16, 18, 31, 38, 58, 83, 100–1, 116, 129, 137, 141, 146, 149
Welsh nationality, expressions of 58, 61, 77
*Welsh Nonconformist Memorial; or, Cambro-British Biography . . .*, William Richards 90
Welsh publishing 5, 10
*Western Mail* 94, 141, 145, 203
Whalley, George H. 88
Wilkins, Charles 85, 104, 115, 137, 147
Williams, David E. 97–8
Williams, Edward (Iolo Morganwg) 1–2, 8, 28–9
  as bard of Glamorgan 44, 45, 131, 147
  as 'Bard of Liberty' 16, 17, 29, 30, 129
  as folk hero 29, 30, 39, 129
  as humanitarian 29–30
  as last bard 92, 99, 182–4
  as mythical figure 8, 10, 11–16, 24, 34–8
  as revered antiquary 15, 16, 25–9, 31, 32, 116, 128–9, 147, 148, 157–8
  as saintly sage 16–20, 148
  criticism of 8, 32–4, 115, 130–46, 146–9, 185–6, 186–98
  dissemination of his sources 79–85
  forgotten political radical 126–8

his anti-slavery stance 30–1
his generosity 23–5, 156–7
his hymns 39, 121–5
his manuscripts 13–14, 21, 64, 81–4, 93, 108, 110–14, 138, 177–9
his poetry 40, 116–21, 144, 174, 184
influence of his forgeries 78–115
influence of symbolism created by him 67–70
pilgrimages to his grave 22, 153–6
poems about him 13, 18, 22, 26–7, 151–2, 159, 167
relics connected with him 20–1, 152–3
the Unitarian 1–2, 121–6, 185
Williams, Griffith John 40, 121, 130, 139, 144, 148, 149, 209–15
Williams, Hugh 127
Williams, Sir Ifor 130, 139, 143, 209, 211
Williams, Jane (Ysgafell) 82, 85, 91, 115, 133, 137, 175–7
Williams, John (Ab Ithel) 4, 20, 22, 81–3, 84, 88, 91–4, 100, 115, 127, 147, 199
and Llangollen Eisteddfod 55–8, 64, 165–72
and the *Cambrian Journal* 6, 84
and the Llanover collection 84, 178
Williams, Morgan, the Chartist 20, 23, 27–8, 116, 127
Williams, Robert (Trebor Mai) 54
Williams, Rowland (Hwfa Môn) 60, 66, 71, 72, 75, 90, 141, 206–8
Williams, T. Marchant (the Acid Drop) 36–7, 130, 142, 148, 153–4
Williams, Taliesin (Taliesin ab Iolo) 4, 14, 23, 31, 46, 48–51, 81–2, 98, 126–7, 133–6, 148, 153, 175
Williams, Thomas, hymnologist 124

Williams, Thomas (Gwilym Morganwg) 43, 46, 99
Williams, W. Llewelyn 128, 149
Williams, William, historian of Calvinistic Methodism 20, 25, 35, 117
Williams, William, Pantycelyn 124, 125
Williams, William (Caledfryn) 117
Williams, William (Carw Coch) 128
Williams, William (Creuddynfab) 59, 60
Williams, William (Gwilym Peris) 131
Williams, William Morgan (Ap Caledfryn) 69
Williams Wynn, Sir Watkin 64
Wordsworth, William 42

*Y Beirniad* (1859–79) 91, 135
*Y Beirniad* (1911–20) 6–7, 142
*Y Brython* 41, 58, 68, 70, 84, 87, 110, 135, 151–2
*Y Cymro* 18
*Y Dysgedydd* 91
*Y Geninen* 6, 84, 87, 107, 120
*Y Greal* 80
*Y Gwladgarwr* 13, 48–9, 68, 87, 103
*Y Punch Cymraeg* 41
*Y Traethodydd* 33, 35, 61, 91, 117, 135, 138
*Y Vord Gron* (The Round Table) 60
*y werin Gymreig* (the peasantry) 6, 28, 118, 128, 149, 150
*Young Wales* 45, 61
*Yr Athraw* 138
*Yr Haul* 27, 67
*Yr Ymofynydd* 6, 32, 33, 93, 123, 126, 129, 135
Ysgafell *see* Williams, Jane (Ysgafell)
Ysgolan the bookburner 136